The Principal's Quick-Reference Guide to School Law

Fourth Edition

I dedicate this fourth edition to my family—my wife, Kari, who has always supported my professional career, and to our sons Jack and Evan, who have never really figured out what it is that I do for a living. Once I figure that out myself, they will be the first to know. A final dedication to our sons Chase and Samuel, whose lives were cut short, leaving only to the imagination what could have been, yet have always been in our heart.

The Principal's Quick-Reference Guide to School Law

Reducing Liability, Litigation, and Other Potential Legal Tangles

Fourth Edition

Robert F. Hachiya

FOR INFORMATION:

Corwin
A SAGE Company
2455 Teller Road
Thousand Oaks, California 91320
(800) 233-9936
www.corwin.com

SAGE Publications Ltd.
1 Oliver's Yard
55 City Road
London EC1Y 1SP
United Kingdom

SAGE Publications India Pvt. Ltd.
B 1/I 1 Mohan Cooperative Industrial Area
Mathura Road, New Delhi 110 044
India

SAGE Publications Asia-Pacific Pte. Ltd.
18 Cross Street #10-10/11/12
China Square Central
Singapore 048423

President: Mike Soules
Associate Vice President and Editorial
    Director: Monica Eckman
Senior Acquisitions Editors: Ariel Curry
    and Tanya Ghans
Content Development Manager:
    Desirée A. Bartlett
Editorial Assistants: Caroline Timmings
    and Nyle De Leon
Production Editor: Melanie Birdsall
Copy Editor: Exeter Premedia Services
Typesetter: Exeter Premedia Services
Proofreader: Barbara Coster
Cover Designer: Scott Van Atta
Marketing Manager: Sharon Pendergast

Printed in Canada

Library of Congress Cataloging-in-Publication Data

Names: Hachiya, Robert (Robert F.) author
Title: The principal's quick-reference guide to school law: reducing liability, litigation, and other potential legal tangles / Robert F. Hachiya.
Description: Fourth edition. | Thousand Oaks, California: Corwin Press, a SAGE Company, [2022] | Includes bibliographical references and index.
Identifiers: LCCN 2021048707 (print) | LCCN 2021048708 (ebook) | ISBN 9781071827772 (paperback) | ISBN 9781071871706 (ebook)
Subjects: LCSH: Educational law and legislation—United States. | School management and organization—Law and legislation—United States. | School administrators—United States—Handbooks, manuals, etc.
Classification: LCC KF4119.85 .H33 2022 (print) | LCC KF4119.85 (ebook) | DDC 344.73/07—dc23/eng/20211220
LC record available at https://lccn.loc.gov/2021048707
LC ebook record available at https://lccn.loc.gov/2021048708

This book is printed on acid-free paper.

22 23 24 25 26 10 9 8 7 6 5 4 3 2 1

Contents

Visit the companion website at
resources.corwin.com/principalsquickreferenceguide4e
for downloadable resources.

Preface and Advisement

In previous editions of this book, we stated,

> *Once upon a time there was order in our schools and change occurred so benevolently that it was called "progress." There was a place and a time for everything. There were authorities, too. The principal spoke without hesitation about what was appropriate behavior. Dad and Mom told their children to go to school and "mind the teacher," and students listened and learned and behaved themselves. Teachers and school administrators worked in harmony with each other. Parents left educational decisions up to the schools. The courts rarely got involved with schools and, when they were asked to make a decision, they tended to side with schools.*
>
> *Then something happened. Some say parents failed in their responsibility. Some say schools lost their direction and control. Some say society became too permissive. Some say the courts started to get involved where they did not belong. (p. xiii)*

We could not say then, and we still cannot say definitively what happened (societal changes, court rulings, etc.), but we know that much that was nailed down suddenly came loose. We know that the job of school principal is vastly different today from what it was twenty years ago, ten years ago—or even yesterday. Today's principals grapple with a sea of conflicting demands from their school boards, central office administrators, students, teachers, parents, community pressure groups, and various political agendas. Principals' jobs are further complicated by the seemingly endless and often contradictory statutes, court decisions, and attorneys' general opinions that directly affect the operation of their schools. As a result of these pressures, principals often feel insecure and, at times, powerless when it comes to balancing the pressure to do something, on the one hand, and legal restraints, on the other. Today's principals face an additional dilemma as they address the task of balancing the need for order with the need to respect the legal rights of students, teachers, and parents.

Principals in practice today who see their colleagues retire from the profession understand that school and societal events and changes date their service, because in many ways those events changed practice within the schools. The role and duties of daily practice changed for principals after tragedies, inventions, innovations, and a pandemic. There was the daily life of principals before and after the Columbine tragedy; the 9/11 attacks; the invention of the cell phone; the invention of vaping; and the start of a devastating worldwide pandemic.

All of the above still applies in 2022, but the timing of this text also had to consider the challenges of the COVID-19 global pandemic and the anticipated changes of federal education policy after the 2020 presidential election. Both the pandemic and election result dramatically affect the practice of principals and other educators, and at the time of the publication of this book, how those changes play out as education law issues remains unknown.

Revising a text that includes continually changing statutes, policy implementation, and case law always presents a challenge and the potential to be out of date after any new law is passed or court decision is rendered. The impact of the pandemic on schools and what the future holds is unknown and presents a unique challenge given the purpose of this text and the audience who reads it.

Although a number of good books are available on education law, few focus directly on the specific needs of the principal. Previous editions of *The Principal's Quick-Reference Guide* have been written exclusively for preservice and in-service principals, vice principals, and other building-level administrators, to provide basic information on the current status of law and site-based risk management as it relates to the legal rights and responsibilities inherent in managing and leading schools. The book is also widely adopted in principal preparation programs, which is a major reason why foundational content, perhaps less important to a practicing administrator, remains in the book. Because this book is used as an introductory text for future principals, the book intentionally includes narratives that may not necessarily be of significant benefit to principals in the field, but are very important for those who are aspiring to become principals. Such narratives and in-depth discussion should be valuable to establish the foundational knowledge for those who wish to become principals.

Even with the usual challenges presented in revising an education law text and especially doing so in 2021, there were new considerations that went into the fourth edition. When the book was first published, the wide availability of instant information from the internet was not available, and a book written in this format was indeed a quick reference. As changes in education law took place between each edition, the book added new sections, some of which would have been unheard of in previous editions (such as searching the contents of a cell phone). As a result, the book became lengthy and no longer resembled the "quick reference" as intended in its original form.

WHAT'S NEW IN THE FOURTH EDITION?

Similar to previous revisions of the book, this edition embeds areas of risk management that educators need to know, understand, and address in everyday practice. Each chapter has been updated, as appropriate, with current case law and court rulings to provide educators with the legal knowledge they need for exemplary practice. The cases chosen for the text include landmark decisions that influence education practice, and also have been chosen to be of interest to principals because they relate to the issues that might commonly occur in their daily practice.

In the effort to return to its original intention as a quick reference, the book has been reorganized, with some previous chapters merged in order to provide a more meaningful flow. Some chapters also include suggested practice related to COVID-19 responses, especially as they relate to risk management. New to the fourth edition, the book concludes with topics principals may find valuable as they conduct professional development for teachers with some of the most common education law concepts and circumstances they face each day.

Nearly all school administrators have had a course in school law. They know that the law affects almost every facet of education. However, most school law courses end without helping the principal translate school law and policy into education procedures and practice. This book helps close that gap and places principals in a better position to maintain a safe school and to be proactive in litigation avoidance and conflict resolution.

Most legal actions brought against school principals are not based on areas of education leadership or knowledge of curriculum. Principals who find themselves defendants in court often got there because they did not know the relevant law or did not practice sound management based on an understanding of existing court decisions. This fourth edition continues to help principals understand and provide a stronger foundation for their day-to-day management of risk.

As with previous editions, this book is designed to be a desk reference in which school administrators can quickly find and identify important legal points to consider during decision-making processes when such decisions may have legal consequences. To further assist in that process, we continue to use straightforward, nontechnical language and follow a standard format in presenting pertinent information.

Learned Hand noted in an address to the Association of the Bar of the City of New York in 1921 that "[a]fter now some dozen years of experience [as a judge] I must say that as a litigant I should dread a lawsuit beyond almost anything else short of sickness and death" (Association of the Bar, 1926, p. 87). The operative word in 1921 was *dread*. The operative word in this current edition of *The Principal's Quick-Reference Guide* is *prevention*, and, as was true in previous editions, this practitioner's guide is designed to reduce *ex post facto* decision making (applying law or making rules after the fact) in real-life, school-based risk management and incident resolution. If Latin were a living language, perhaps we could coin a new phrase, *pre facto* decision making, to describe this book's proactive approach to avoiding litigation and managing risk. We hope that by continuing to equip principals and other school leaders to act with both knowledge and understanding of education law, we will help make wise, safe, and legally defensible decisions in the best interests of students, teachers, and parents. We intend this book to make the daunting job of being an effective school leader a bit easier.

Please be advised that this book represents an effort to respond to the professional needs of the reader. The case law interpretation and the presentation of scenarios are not designed as statements of final authority. Only a court of law, guided by individual case facts, can be considered as an authority on a specific issue. That issue may be treated differently from court to court, state to state. This book serves a purpose for the education profession and provides only suggested guidelines for the avoidance of litigation. This book should not be considered a forecaster of impending or future litigation. It should also be noted that any guidelines suggested should be treated with caution in light of the specific subject matter examined and the expected level of personal involvement. There are those administrative and teaching responsibilities that transcend the norm, requiring a higher degree of duty and care, supervision, instruction, and maintenance. This book is designed to provide accurate and authoritative information in regard to the subject matter covered.

In publishing this book, neither the author nor the publisher is engaged in rendering legal service. If legal advice or assistance is required, the services of a competent attorney should be sought.

Acknowledgments

As the sole author of this fourth edition, I would like to acknowledge both Dr. Robert Shoop and Dr. Dennis Dunklee for providing me this opportunity to join their team when I was in my first year as an assistant professor. Their willingness to place trust in my work helped propel me into a new career after a lengthy tenure as a public school teacher and administrator. I also wish to acknowledge Dr. David Thompson, who was the chairperson of the Educational Leadership Department at Kansas State University when I was hired. His guidance and mentorship has been outstanding and greatly appreciated.

Equally important are my colleagues in our department, and I could not have completed this work without their encouragement and continual professional collaboration, especially during the unsettling times of the pandemic. So thank you, Dr(s). Mary Devin; Donna Augustine-Shaw; Jia Liang; Alex Red Corn; Richard Doll; and our chairperson, Jerry Johnson.

Finally, I wish to acknowledge the Education Law Association, which has been a tremendous professional resource for me since I joined in 2012. It has been my great privilege to have met and worked alongside some of the greatest leaders in the field of education law, and I appreciate not only the opportunities ELA has presented, but the relationships that have grown over the years.

PUBLISHER'S ACKNOWLEDGMENTS

Corwin gratefully acknowledges the contributions of the following reviewers:

Debi Gartland, Professor of Special Education
Towson University
Towson, MD

Laura Schaffer Metcalfe, Education Faculty
Grand Canyon University Online
Mesa, AZ

About the Author

Dr. Robert F. Hachiya is an associate professor in the education leadership department at Kansas State University. With twenty-seven years' experience as a teacher, coach, assistant principal, and principal, Dr. Hachiya now teaches courses and advises graduate students at Kansas State University. Among the classes he teaches are Education Law, as well as Ethical Dimensions for Leadership; Principalship; Leadership for Diverse Populations; and History and Philosophy of Educational Administration. He joined the team of Robert J. Shoop and Dennis R. Dunklee for the third edition of this book and is now the sole author of the fourth edition.

Dr. Hachiya has presented across the country at several national conferences, including the National Association of Secondary School Principals (NASSP) National Convention in Philadelphia, Pennsylvania, regarding conducting sexting investigations, and in Boston, Massachusetts, on school violence prevention. In 2021, he presented at the Education Law Association Conference on the practical applications for principals regarding the *Mahanoy Area School District v. B.L.* decision of the United States Supreme Court. He has also presented papers or led discussions at conferences for the Education Law Association (ELA), the University Council for Educational Administration (UCEA), the International Council of Professors of Educational Leadership (ICPEL), and the Kansas United School Administrator (K-USA).

Dr. Hachiya received his BS degree from the University of Nebraska-Lincoln and his master's and EdD degrees from the University of Kansas. He also did post-doctoral work at the School Law Institute at Teachers College, Columbia University.

Introduction

Laws reflect the society that develops them. Similarly, judges and juries operate within a social context that influences the outcome of litigation concerning particular issues. Consequently, laws and judicial decisions reflect the political trends, philosophical attitudes, ethical viewpoints, and even the tendency toward compassion that prevails when legislatures enact them and courts interpret them. Beyond constitutional law, which is more focused because of the actions of the Supreme Court, school principals have to deal with an expanse of law that includes contracts, property, torts, general administrative law, legal relationships, civil rights, risk management, and so forth—all affecting the operation and administration of schools. Because education in the United States is controlled by each of the fifty states, it is sometimes difficult to identify or summarize any single interpretation of law that prevails in all states, much less all school districts.

So what is a principal to do when trying to become knowledgeable about school law to be effective in leading and managing a school? With differing statutory bases from state to state, with widely varying perspectives and philosophies influencing how judges and juries decide school litigation cases, and with schools often being the frontline arenas for conflicting social and political agendas, where can a principal obtain helpful and reliable guidance concerning decision making within the confines of the law? Consulting the school district's general counsel attorney is certainly necessary and appropriate at times, but *not* regarding *every, single* day-to-day decision that has legal ramifications. School principals need to understand the legal concepts and framework on which pertinent education law rests, so they can act decisively—and legally—to manage effective schools.

We believe that the avoidance of education litigation requires *more* than just knowledge of the law. The determination to prevent disputes, avoid litigation, and manage risk is an effective administrative mindset—a mindset referred to as *preventive law,* which increases the prospect of a "safe school" as well as the prospects for court rulings that are favorable to school districts and to the education enterprise in total.

> School principals need to understand the legal concepts and framework on which pertinent education law rests, so they can act decisively—and legally—to manage effective schools.

In addition, certain legal concepts affecting school law remain unchanged regardless of state legislative actions or court decisions. In this new edition, principals will continue to find clear and simple explanations of these concepts. The most critical and knotty legal issues facing schools are highlighted, and points for school administrators to consider in making decisions regarding those issues will be suggested. This book, then, offers principals easy-to-understand guidelines for making decisions that minimize risk and avoid litigation.

However, readers should keep in mind that the precedents we've identified may not neatly fit the numerous peculiarities and conditions of any single incident. We present concepts of law so that school administrators can apply such concepts to real-life school-based situations as they arise and can use this book in decision-making processes before final decisions are made. It is important to understand that the facts of an individual situation are of utmost importance and that small variations in facts often result in large differences in appropriate decision making and, ultimately, in how a court might view the situation under the law.

This book represents an effort to respond to the professional needs of school principals regarding school law. This book should not be considered as a statement of final authority but, rather, as a resource providing suggested guidelines for the avoidance of litigation. As stated in the Preface, only a court of law guided by individual case facts can be considered as an authority on a specific issue—and remember, that issue may be treated differently from court to court, state to state. Also note that any risk management guidelines suggested should be viewed in light of the specific subject matter taught and the expected level of duty and standard of care.

School administrators are expected to know the law. The courts will not accept ignorance of the law as a defense. The majority of legal actions brought against school districts and school administrators are not based on their education leadership or knowledge of curriculum but, rather, on their failure to know the relevant law and to practice sound management based on an understanding of existing court decisions. *Effective school administrators do not want to win lawsuits; they want to avoid them altogether.* Understanding the basic concepts of law adds significant strength to the effective principal's decision-making abilities and catalog of information.

> Effective administrators do not want to win lawsuits; they want to avoid them altogether.

The chapters in this book contain basic principles and guidelines for numerous legal issues. After an explanatory introduction, each chapter and section is presented in a template format. *The use of a template makes the following possible:*

- We have condensed a significant amount of information, resulting in a comprehensive yet compact desk reference.

- The reader can find answers quickly and easily to questions that arise in a particular situation.

The template includes an explanation of relevant law, suggested guidelines for practice and risk management, and considerations related to COVID-19.

- Cases cited to support relevant legal principles in each chapter have been selected on a precedent-setting or best-example basis regardless of jurisdiction or date of adjudication. They provide a baseline for decision making. Choosing this approach ensures that the book is not out of precedent today or even tomorrow.

- Some chapters include considerations for practice related to COVID-19 issues. Although COVID-19 guidance continues to evolve, areas of focus for administrators remain the same.

- The chapters also include suggestions for risk management as well as suggested guidelines for practice for principals and other school officials.

In selecting material to be covered in this book from the vast quantity of existing legal precedents and law, as well as in choosing the legal concepts to discuss, the focus is centered on the daily activities of a typical school principal—specifically, an attempt to answer the question, "What does a school principal need to know about the laws affecting schools to make wise decisions?" This book, therefore, does not claim to explore or even touch on all areas of school law but, rather, concentrates on those areas that are consistently troublesome for school administrative personnel and, as a result, often end in litigation.

The function of law is to regulate human conduct to ensure a harmonious and safe society. School administrators are constantly challenged to achieve a balance that allows students, teachers, other school employees, and parents as much freedom as possible and, at the same time, allows the school to function effectively without unreasonable interference from the conduct of any individuals. This book is designed to assist school administrators in maintaining such a balance.

UNDERSTANDING JUDICIAL DECISIONS

This book does not require students or practitioners to analyze "case law." When possible, the text addresses this for the reader and presents a general overview of the outcomes of cases that directly impact the everyday professional responsibilities of school leaders.

When researching referenced cases to read or analyze, in order to determine why a case is decided in the way it was, it is necessary to find the *ratio decidendi* ("reason for deciding")—the point on which the judgment balances. This is accomplished, for the most part, by carefully analyzing the "facts of the case" that were treated as "material" by the judge. In other words, "material facts" are the *ratio decidendi*. Conclusions or statements by a judge that depart from the *ratio decidendi* are not binding as precedent and are referred to as *obiter dicta* ("other statements of the court that are not necessary for its decision"). This type of *dicta* is evident when

- A statement of law is based on "immaterial" facts.

- A statement of law, although based on established facts in the case, *does not* shape the rationale for the decision in the case. For example, when a judge makes a statement leading to one conclusion but makes a contrary decision on the facts for a different reason.

Llewellyn et al. (1988) explain what to look for when reading and interpreting case law. They noted that "for all our cases are decided, all our opinions are written, all our predictions, all our arguments are made, on certain four assumptions:

1. The court must decide the dispute that is before it.

2. The court can decide only the particular dispute which is before it.

3. The court can decide the particular dispute only according to a general rule that covers a whole class of like disputes.

4. Everything, everything, everything, big or small, a judge may say in an opinion, is to be read with primary reference to the particular dispute, the particular question before him."

THE ETHIC OF JUSTICE

Although not directly addressed in this book, ethics and the ethic of justice cannot be overlooked in at least one instance. That is, although school law coursework remains indispensable in most education leadership programs, school law, when examined in isolation, often creates an ethics tension for practitioners between the legal and moral aspects of commonsense decision making. I have experienced this tension firsthand in many years of managing and leading schools as well as observing it in teaching, advising, and consulting.

Reasoning and rationality occasionally come in conflict with school policy and procedures, for example, what is best for the child (e.g., fairness, equity, and justice in matters concerning access to education); zero tolerance; the realization that children do not start out on an equal footing; and, of course, that some need more or different attention than others in acquiring an education. In addition, school district policies and the inherent disconnects of individually held mores often create an ethic-based tension between the issue at hand and the decision making necessary to resolve the issue "by the book." Challenged with difficult decisions, school leaders commonly rely on the rule of law and/or school policy and procedures to guide their work. This is good and expected, of course. But consider the ethic of justice, or potential lack thereof, of the following.

A second-grader from Anne Arundel County, Virginia, was suspended from his school for chewing a Pop-Tart-like pastry into the shape of a gun. The suspension came at a time of heightened sensitivities about guns in the aftermath of the mass shooting in December 2012 in Newtown, Connecticut. About the same time, children elsewhere were suspended for pointing fingers like guns and, in one case, talking about shooting a Hello Kitty "gun" that blows bubbles. In many disciplinary incidents like these, appeals were granted by school officials, but in many others they were not.

These situations demonstrate the tension caused by (a) the inherent limitations of the law and policy in solving everyday difficulties, (b) the broad discretion provided to school authorities by the judiciary, (c) the often narrowness of school district policy, and (d) the importance of self-reflection and inquiry in making ethically just decisions that may have a profound influence on children and parents—not to mention, a school district's public relations.

Principals must make decisions each day within the context of multiple shades of gray—where rights and rules may clash, where demands and culture may collide, or where degrees of grace or punishment must be determined. Principals must also understand that they yield great power, and the successful ones understand when and how to use that power, and when restraint may be the best tool they have.

 ONLINE RESOURCES FOR PRINCIPALS

I recognize that a reference guide that will be useful to principals across the nation must by nature cover certain topics only in general terms and that in certain areas (such as special education) ongoing legislation and litigation continue to supersede and outdate established precedent as soon as it can be written down. Principals need to access their own specific state's laws and regulations to act in compliance with such legal directives. There are a number of law-based websites available for practitioners to access.

Because case law is extremely fluid, I recommend seeking current updates/court rulings on specific subjects by utilizing the availability and services of the internet. You can find the links to these resources on the companion website: resources.corwin.com/principalsquickreferenceguide4e. The content of these sites changes daily, and while this list is by no means all-inclusive, it is organized to help principals to quickly find school law resources and materials.

CHAPTER 1

The School and the Legal Environment

The U.S. Constitution provides particular protections of individual rights. Various state and federal statutes protect the general welfare of society and implement the constitutional rights of individuals. School districts develop policies, procedures, and regulations that ensure that necessary steps are taken to provide a safe place for employees to work, students to learn, parents to interact, and visitors to feel welcome. With such district policies, procedures, and regulations in place, principals should ask three questions:

- *Am I implementing the regulations?*
- *Am I monitoring the regulations?*
- *Am I assessing foreseeability when it comes to preventing the violation of regulations?*

Although it is next to impossible to keep up with the day-to-day changes in the laws, it is important to remember the foundations on which laws are made and how such laws affect the decision-making processes of the courts and school district counsel.

For those who teach education law classes for aspiring principals, an unfortunate truth often comes to the forefront: there are many students who are in need of a "civics" refresher class, oftentimes because several years have passed since they took high school government class. But such a foundation is important to help understand the basic concepts of education law. This text does not serve as a "civics 101" book, but this chapter helps to provide some of that essential information.

CONSIDERATIONS RELATED TO COVID-19

The text will include in the following chapters considerations related to COVID-19 and significant implications for school leaders conducting school during the pandemic. Such issues will include effects on human resources, adapting to a virtual environment, and the challenges of reducing and avoiding liability as schools attempt to teach school and keep everyone safe.

This chapter provides the foundation for the guidance that principals should follow in their practice. A key that will be emphasized throughout the text is that the state where a principal is employed must always be considered because under the U.S. Constitution, the Tenth Amendment reserves for the states the right to legislate and regulate public education. Public educators' contract law, for example, is different from state to state. Graduation requirements are different not just between the states, but even between different school districts within a given state.

As an additional example, although federal laws such as the Individuals with Disabilities Act (IDEA) cannot be contradicted by the states, frequently there are guidelines that allow states to interpret how they will implement such laws.

Therefore, principals must always be aware of not only federal laws, but laws within their own state as well as their own district master contract, school board policies, and school district-level policies.

SECTION A. THE SCHOOL'S RELATIONSHIP TO THE LEGAL ENVIRONMENT

This section reviews several sources of law and their relationship to the structure and operation of schools and school districts. This review of the structure of law and operation of the state and federal courts provides the foundation for understanding the manner in which our legal system monitors the education enterprise.

Compulsory education laws in the United States have origins from the *parens patriae* doctrine, where the education of citizens is viewed as in the best interest of the public and democratic institutions. In part because of compulsory school laws, it also follows that if students are required to attend school, such school employees and school boards have great responsibility to follow all respective laws governing the education system and to fulfill their mission to educate and protect students. In other words, if students are required to be at school, those working in the school have requirements as well. Those requirements are accompanied by responsibility and accountability.

When school districts and schools did not provide a safe place—a place that not only observes the rights of individuals but also protects those rights—the courts will intervene. Our nation's court system provides the structure that determines the exact relationship between the individual and the law in question. In other words, if schools do not do it, the courts will.

Hierarchy of Laws That Influence Public Education

Public schools in the United States are guided by a hierarchy of laws that affect all educators (Schneider, 2014). Policy and practices are derived from these sources, with each source possessing some type of authority and precedent over lower authorities. This hierarchy includes

- The U.S. Constitution
- Federal statutes
- Federal regulations
- State constitutions
- State statutes
- State regulations
- Collective bargaining agreements
- School board policies
- District administrative policies and directives
- School-level rules
- Department-level rules
- Classroom-level rules

At each level, from the text of the U.S. Constitution or a law passed by Congress, down to a school-level parent/student handbook, different people with potentially conflicting interests frequently disagree with the interpretation of a law or policy.

In theory, a lower authority cannot conflict with a higher authority, and should a conflict exist, there are administrative and legal processes which settle the dispute. On a basic level, this means the classroom policies of a teacher cannot conflict with school policies, school board policies, or the collective bargaining agreement. On a grander scale, a classroom policy or practice cannot conflict with state or federal law or violate the constitutional rights of individuals.

Public education is a mirror of society at large, and disputes and disagreements about policy interpretation and implementation occur on a daily basis. The vast majority of such disputes are resolved without involvement of the judicial system, but avoidance of such involvement isn't always possible, no matter the level of care taken to prevent that from happening.

A point of emphasis is also on order as a reminder for principals and other educators. While the majority of potential legal disputes are settled outside of the judicial system, hundreds, if not thousands, of such disputes do end up involving the judicial system in some way. Not only does this fact have potential negative financial and time outcomes for everyone involved, there is always the possibility of reputational and career damage that could follow any litigation.

Additionally, while only a minuscule number of legal disputes result in precedential court decisions at any level, the potential for that to occur is always present. Your actions or inactions as a principal in response to some event that has occurred in your school could be a determining factor whether a lengthy and potentially highly publicized legal proceeding takes place. One purpose of this book is to provide educational advice to minimize that potential.

Our system of government provides a structure of laws that protects individual rights and guarantees freedom of religion, speech, press, assembly, and the right of each individual to call on the courts or government to correct injustices.

A law is a rule of civil conduct prescribed by local, state, or federal mandates commanding what is right and prohibiting what is wrong. Laws, then, are simply collections of those rules and principles of conduct that the federal, state, and local communities recognize and enforce.

There are separate legal systems for each of the fifty states, the District of Columbia, and the federal government. For the most part, each of these systems applies its own body of law.

All laws are based on the assumption that for each action, there is an expected consequence. Laws are society's attempts to ensure that there are consequences that ought to result if certain prohibited acts are committed. Our system of laws is based on the assumptions that all citizens should be judged by the same standards of behavior, and for every wrong, an inescapable penalty follows.

In our legal system, the principle of due process of law allows people who have been accused of breaking a law, been harmed by other individuals, or been accused of harming another person to bring their side of the issue before a court for a decision as to whether they must submit to the force of government or will be protected by it.

Our government is based on the consent of the governed, and the Bill of Rights denies those in power any legal opportunity to coerce that consent. Authority is to be controlled by public opinion, not public opinion by authority. This is the social contract theory of government; consequently, law is not a static set of printed documents but is, rather, a living and changing set of precepts that depend on the courts for interpretation.

Constitutional Law, Common Law, Statutory Law, and Administrative Law

Constitutional Law

Whether at the federal or state level, a constitution is the basic source of law for the jurisdiction. A constitution specifies the structure of the government and outlines the powers and duties of its principal officers and subdivisions. It also designates the allocation of power between levels of government—between the federal government and the states in the U.S. Constitution and between state and local government bodies in state constitutions. In addition, constitutions spell out the exact limitations of government power. In both the U.S. Constitution and state constitutions, these proscriptions are contained in a bill of rights.

Constitutions are broad philosophical statements of general beliefs. The U.S. Constitution is written in such broad and general language that it has been amended only twenty-six times in more than 200 years. State constitutions are more detailed and specific, with the result that most are frequently amended. Just as the U.S. Constitution is the supreme law in the United States, state constitutions are the supreme law within each state. State constitutions may not contain provisions, however, that conflict with the U.S. Constitution.

Because the U.S. Constitution contains no mention of education, Congress is not authorized to provide a system of education. The Tenth Amendment to the U.S. Constitution stipulates that "the powers not delegated to the United States by the

Constitution, nor prohibited by it to the states, are reserved to the states respectively, or to the people." The U.S. Supreme Court has repeatedly and consistently confirmed the authority of states to provide for the general welfare of their residents, including the establishment and control of their public schools. However, the U.S. Supreme Court has applied various provisions of the U.S. Constitution to jurisdictions to ensure compliance.

Common Law

Many legal experts believe statutes are not law until they are actually tested and adjudicated in a court of law. A court, when confronted with a problem that cannot be solved by reference to pertinent legislation (statutory law), decides that case according to common law. The English common law is defined as those principles, procedures, and rules of action enforced by courts that are based on history or custom, with modifications as required by circumstances and conditions over time. Common law is not automatic but must be applied by a court. Courts decide specific disputes by examining constitutional, statutory, or administrative law. The court determines the facts of the case and then examines prior judicial decisions to identify legal precedents (if any). The tradition of abiding by legal precedent is known as the principle of *stare decisis* (Latin: "Let the decision stand").

Statutory and Administrative Laws

Statutory laws are laws passed by a legislative body. These laws may alter the common law by adding to, deleting from, or eliminating the law. The courts under our system of government are the final interpreters of legislative provisions. Administrative laws are regulations promulgated by administrative agencies. An administrative agency is a government authority, other than a court or legislative body, that affects the rights of private parties through adjudication or rule making. In many cases, the operations of schools are affected more by the administrative process than by the judicial process. It is not uncommon for a state to have several hundred agencies with powers of adjudication, rule making, or both.

How Laws Are Made and Enforced

It is the American ideal that the power to control the conduct of people by the use of public will is inherent in the people. By adopting a constitution, the people delegate certain power to the state. Constitutions divide this power and assign it to three branches of government. Although no one branch performs only one function, each has a generally defined area of influence. The responsibilities belong to three separate but equal branches of government. The legislative branch makes the laws. The judicial branch interprets the law. The executive branch enforces the law.

The Legislative Branch

The primary function of the legislative branch is making laws. It is limited in its function only by the state and federal constitutions. Each state legislature has the absolute power to make laws governing education. It is important to understand that this state-held power makes education a state function, makes school funds state funds, and makes school buildings state property. Although it is an accepted principle of law that the state legislature cannot delegate its law-making powers, it can delegate to subordinate agencies the authority to make the rules and regulations necessary to implement those laws. One such subordinate agency is the state board of education. State boards of education are the policy-making and planning bodies for the public school systems in most states. They have specific responsibility for adopting policies, enacting regulations, and establishing general rules for carrying out the duties placed on them by state legislatures. Local school districts and local boards are created by the state legislature and have only those powers that are specifically delegated by the legislature or that can be reasonably implied.

The power of individual states to legislate their public education systems is an important concept to remember. Such state autonomy is what accounts for the differences in teacher licensure requirements, teacher contract laws, curriculum and graduation requirements, and all other aspects related to the function of public education.

The Executive Branch

Although each state has a unique government structure, the typical executive branch includes a governor, a lieutenant governor, a secretary of state, a treasurer, and an attorney general. The governor is the chief executive officer of the state and is responsible for the enforcement of the laws of the state. The attorney general is a member of the executive branch of government who often has significant impact on the operation of schools in the state. This person represents the state in all suits and pleas to which the state is a party, gives legal advice to the governor and other executive officers on request, and performs such other duties as required by law.

The Judicial Branch

Courts interpret law and settle disputes by applying the law. However, a court can decide a controversy only when it has authority to hear and adjudicate the case. The appropriate jurisdiction emanates directly from the law. Court names vary from state to state. For example, trial courts are called "supreme courts" in New York, "circuit courts" in Missouri, and "district courts" in Kansas. The principal function of the courts is to decide specific cases in light of the constitution and the laws.

In each state, two judicial systems operate simultaneously: the federal court system and the state courts. Courts in both systems are classified as having either original or appellate jurisdiction. Original jurisdiction refers to the right of a court to hear a case for the first time. A trial on the facts occurs in a court of original jurisdiction. Once the initial trial is over and a judgment rendered, the appellate process may begin. Appellate jurisdiction refers to the right of a court to hear cases on appeal from courts of original jurisdiction. In appellate courts, matters of fact are no longer in dispute; instead, questions of law or proceedings from the lower courts serve as the basis for review. The appellate process can proceed to the state's highest court and, under certain circumstances, to the U.S. Supreme Court.

The federal court system of the United States includes district courts, special federal courts, courts of appeals, and the U.S. Supreme Court.

The Supreme Court of the United States The U.S. Supreme Court consists of the chief justice of the United States and eight associate justices. At its discretion, and within certain guidelines established by Congress, the Supreme Court hears only a limited number of the cases. Those cases usually begin in the federal or state courts, and they most likely involve questions about the Constitution or federal law.

U.S. Courts of Appeals The ninety-four U.S. judicial districts are organized into twelve regional circuits, each individually served by a U.S. court of appeals. A court of appeals hears appeals from the district courts located within its circuit, as well as appeals from decisions of federal administrative agencies. In addition, the Court of Appeals for the Federal Circuit has jurisdiction to hear appeals in specialized nationwide disputes, such as those involving patent laws and cases decided by the Court of International Trade and the Court of Federal Claims.

U.S. District Courts The U.S. district courts are the trial courts of the federal court system. Within limits set by Congress and the Constitution, district courts have jurisdiction to hear most categories of federal cases, including both civil and criminal matters.

As previously noted, there are ninety-four federal judicial districts, including at least one district in each state, the District of Columbia, and Puerto Rico. Three territories of the United States—the Virgin Islands, Guam, and the Northern Mariana Islands—have district courts that hear federal cases, including bankruptcy cases.

Each district court has a chief judge and other federal judges appointed by the president. These courts have original jurisdiction in cases between citizens of different states in which an amount of money over $10,000 is in dispute and in cases involving litigation under federal statutes or the U.S. Constitution. The district courts have no appellate function. Appeals from the district courts are made to the courts of appeals in the respective circuits.

The first level of appeal in the federal court system is in the courts of appeals. These courts provide an intermediate level of appeal between the district courts and the Supreme Court. These courts have only appellate jurisdiction and review the record of the trial court for violations of legal proceedings or questions of law rather than questions of fact. The courts of appeals operate with several judges. There is no jury; a panel of three or more judges decides the cases before them. In some cases, the judges may sit *en banc* (together) to decide the case. As noted previously, there are twelve federal circuits in the United States, each with a court of appeals. A thirteenth federal circuit exists to hear appeals regarding certain types of cases (those regarding copyrights, customs, and other matters mostly pertaining to commerce).

The U.S. Supreme Court, alone among the federal courts, was created directly by the Constitution rather than by congressional legislation. This court consists of the chief justice and eight associate justices. Six justices constitute a quorum. The

Supreme Court meets for an annual term beginning the first Monday in October. It has limited original jurisdiction and exercises appellate jurisdiction to review cases by appeal of right and writ of certiorari (an appellate proceeding directing that the record from an inferior court be moved to a superior court for review) over federal district courts, federal courts of appeals, and the state supreme courts. The Supreme Court is the nation's highest court. It is often referred to as "the court of last resort" because there are no appeals to its decisions. A constitutional amendment ultimately could be used to reverse this court's decision; however, this has occurred in only four instances. Typically up to 8,000 cases are appealed to the Supreme Court each year, yet the Court accepts fewer than 100 cases and will deny certiorari in the others, refusing to review the decisions of the lower courts. The denial of certiorari has the effect of sustaining the decisions of the lower courts.

Court Functions

A court is an organizational structure that assembles at an appointed time and place to administer law judicially. The primary purpose of courts is to ensure that every person has a fair and unbiased trial before an impartial arbiter. It is assumed that there are always conflicting interests and that the courts must weigh one against the other. Often, the decision is not between good and bad but between the greater good and the lesser evil. The courts seek to determine legal liability. For a liability to exist, there must be a law and a set of facts that the law defines as illegal. Courts have three general functions: deciding controversies, interpreting enacted law, and performing judicial review.

- *Deciding controversies* consists of determining the facts of the dispute and the applicable law. One or more statutes or regulations may apply. If none do, the court must decide the controversy based on previous decisions of the appellate courts of the state in similar situations. If the case presents a new situation, the court's job is more difficult. When a court does not wait for legislative action and makes a decision, it has, in fact, made a new law. In this process, *stare decisis,* or the adherence to precedent, creates a new foundational common law.

- *Interpretation of enacted law* occurs when a statute does not provide a clear answer to the question before the court. Because it is not always possible to draft legislation that is unambiguous when applied to specific controversies, the court may be forced to strike down a statute that it feels is vague, ambiguous, or contradictory. The courts tend to use the following four approaches, or a combination of these approaches, in interpreting legislation and making their decisions:
  - *Literal:* The courts look to the ordinary interpretation of words to determine their meaning.
  - *Purposive:* The courts attempt to ascertain what the legislature intended the law to mean.
  - *Precedent based:* The courts look to past, similar cases and laws to find support for one interpretation of the law.
  - *Policy based:* The courts interpret the law in relationship to the courts' own views of what is best for society.

- *Judicial review* is a supreme court's power to declare that a statute is unconstitutional. However, this power is not without its limits. Judges at all levels are expected to base their decisions on precedents under the legal doctrine of *stare decisis*. In other words, the court must look to other decisions in similar cases to find direction in dealing with new cases.

SECTION B. CONSTITUTION CLAUSES AND AMENDMENTS THAT AFFECT EDUCATION PRACTICE

Certain clauses and amendments to the U.S. Constitution repeatedly appear as the basis for court decisions regarding specific education issues. Any examination of school law needs to begin, at a minimum, with a solid grounding in these constitutional elements that form the legal environment in which schools operate. Although we can find issues that relate to the education enterprise throughout the U.S. Constitution, the following are the most commonly cited.

Article 1 Section 8

Under Article 1 Section 8 of the Constitution, Congress has the power to "lay and collect taxes, duties, imports and excises, to pay the debts and provide for the common defense and general welfare of the United States." Congress has often used the general welfare clause as the rationale for the enactment of legislation that directly affects the operation of public schools. Article 1 Section 8 also includes the Commerce Clause, which forms the basis of many decisions affecting the states.

First Amendment

The First Amendment states,

> Congress shall make no law respecting an establishment of religion, or prohibiting the free exercise thereof, or abridging the freedom of speech, or of the press; or the right of the people peaceably to assemble, and to petition the Government for a redress of grievances.

This amendment affords pervasive personal freedom to the citizens of this country. It has been used as the basis for litigation involving the use of public funds to aid nonpublic school students, separation of church and state in curriculum matters, students' and teachers' freedom of speech, press censorship, and academic freedom issues. It is from this amendment come the concepts of the Free Exercise Clause and the Establishment Clause with respect to the separation of church and state. It is also where the foundation of "freedom of speech," "freedom of the press," and "freedom of assembly" originates.

Fourth Amendment

The Fourth Amendment protects the rights of citizens "to be secure in their persons, houses, papers and effects against unreasonable search or seizure." This amendment emerged in the late 1960s as the basis for litigation concerning the search of students' lockers and personal belongings. This Amendment has been interpreted differently for searches conducted by law enforcement and those conducted by school officials.

Fifth Amendment

The Fifth Amendment protects citizens from being compelled in any criminal case to be a witness against themselves. Although most due process litigation concerns the Fourteenth Amendment, several self-incrimination issues have been raised in cases concerning teachers being questioned by superiors regarding their activities outside the classroom. Due process for students and teachers originates from the Fifth Amendment.

Fourteenth Amendment

The Fourteenth Amendment provides that no state shall "deny to any person within its jurisdiction the equal protection of the laws." This amendment is frequently cited in education cases that deal with race, gender, or ethnic background issues.

Cases regarding individuals with disabilities, school finance, gender equity, and other civil rights issues also have been based on this amendment. As a corollary, this amendment guarantees the right of citizens to due process under the law and thus has been used to support school employees' claims of wrongful discharge and parents' claims of unfair treatment of their children by school officials. From the Fourteenth Amendment comes the concept of the Equal Protection Clause.

Other Provisions of the U.S. Constitution of Interest to Educators

Amendment VI

"In all criminal prosecutions, the accused shall enjoy the right to a speedy and public trial, by an impartial jury of the State and district wherein the crime shall have been committed, which district shall have been previously ascertained by law, and to be informed of the nature and cause of the accusation; to be confronted with the witnesses against him; to have compulsory process for obtaining witnesses in his favor, and to have the Assistance of Counsel for his defence [sic]." This amendment forms a part of the basis for the due process required in cases of student discipline.

Amendment VIII

"Excessive bail shall not be required, nor excessive fines imposed, nor cruel and unusual punishments inflicted."

Corporal punishment in schools, while prohibited in many states, has been ruled as constitutional.

"The enumeration in the Constitution, of certain rights, shall not be construed to deny or disparage others retained by the people."

Amendment X

"The powers not delegated to the United States by the Constitution, nor prohibited by it to the States, are reserved to the States respectively, or to the people." This amendment forms the basis of what are known as "reserved powers" for the states, such as the responsibility of public education reserved for the states.

SECTION C. SELECTED FEDERAL STATUTES THAT AFFECT EDUCATION PRACTICE

State legislatures have plenary power to make laws that direct how education shall be provided within their states. However, Congress also enacts statutes that guarantee certain rights and protections to students, parents, and school personnel. This section highlights some of the federal legislation that dictates certain practices and protections in the education enterprise. Further details of specific statutes are also included in subsequent chapters.

The Federal Role in Education

The purpose of this text is not to serve as a history of public education; however, the history of federal legislation directly relates to education law. Although the Constitution reserves the power of the states to establish and implement public education and school districts are governed locally by school boards, the federal government has extensive influence and roles in public education in all states.

Such roles can be traced through a history of legislation, including the creation of the Office of Education in 1867, designed to assist states in establishing school systems. Legislation in the mid-1900s helped to ease burdens placed on communities affected by the presence of military bases. In 1944, the GI Bill provided education assistance to veterans returning from military service. In response to the Soviet Union launch of the Sputnik satellite, in 1958, Congress passed the National Defense Education Act with the goal to improve the teaching of science, mathematics, and foreign language.

Changes in societal attitudes brought a wave of sweeping legislation in the 1960s and 1970s that is still in place today. School reform efforts in the 1980s and 1990s have been extended or revised throughout the 2000s. What should be kept in mind is that federal statutes are merely the framework of the intent of the law; the regulations that result from those statutes by federal and state governments determine how those laws are implemented in schools. When keeping in mind the hierarchy of laws that influence education, it is often not only a misapplication or misinterpretation of a law that can end up in litigation, but the regulations and how they are implemented may be challenged as well.

The following includes some of the most significant federal legislation that impacts public schools. Some of the laws were specially written to address schools, while others are broader laws affecting the nation that schools must follow. The intent of many of these laws was to increase educational opportunity, removing barriers based on race, gender, disability, and age. Note also that the intent of some legislation is to improve teaching and learning, with others more directly related to improving the conditions for those who work in education.

The Civil Rights Act of 1871

The Civil Rights Act of 1871 is a law passed by Congress designed to provide protections for former slaves under the Fourteenth Amendment. The act was also known as the Third Enforcement Act or the Second Ku Klux Klan Act. What makes this act important today is that the law was made part of the U.S. Code as 42 U.S.C. § 1983 and more commonly referred to as "Section 1983" and used as a legal tool to seek relief by those who believe state actors have discriminated against them in violation of their constitutional rights.

Those who work in public education are considered state actors, and although the use of Section 1983 is also used in suits against law enforcement and municipalities, Section 1983 lawsuits are very prevalent in the field of public education. Section 1983 will be further discussed in Chapter 3.

The Civil Rights Act of 1964

Title IV of the Civil Rights Act of 1964 had a profound effect on schools. Although segregated schools were outlawed in *Brown v. Board of Education of Topeka* in 1954, the act required schools to take measures to end segregation. The act outlawed discrimination in public schools because of race, color, religion, sex, or national origin. This landmark law also formed the basis of the 2020 U.S. Supreme Court decision that prohibited discrimination of gay, lesbian, and transgender employees in *Bostock v. Clayton County, Georgia* 590 U.S. 207 (2020).

Elementary and Secondary Education Act of 1965

The Elementary and Secondary Education Act of 1965 (ESEA) P.L. 89-10, 79 Stat. 27 (1965) was signed into law by President Lyndon Johnson and was part of the overall sweeping legislation passed in the 1960s.

From its inception, the ESEA was designed as a civil rights law providing grants to school districts serving low-income students, and other funding to educational agencies in order to improve elementary and secondary education. The ESEA established a system of federal support for school districts based on the congressionally established proportion of school-age children of families living below the poverty line. Since first enacted, programs included under the umbrella of the ESEA multiplied, and as a result, Congress used its power under Article 1, Section 8, of the U.S. Constitution (i.e., the spending clause that requires recipients of federal funds to comply with certain obligations) to increase the scope and amount of state and local accountability for federal funds.

Title 1 funding for schools originated in the ESEA and is still the largest federally funded educational program. States determine eligibility for funding using varying measures, including student demographics of homelessness, limited English proficiency, and other at-risk categories.

Every Student Succeeds Act

The Every Student Succeeds Act (ESSA) 20 U.S.C. § 6301 (2015) was the eighth reauthorization of the ESEA of 1965. The ESSA is the primary federal law governing K-12 general public education. The ESSA replaced the controversial No Child Left Behind Act (NCLB), Pub. L. No. 107-110, H.R. No. 108–446, 118 Stat. 265, signed into law in 2002.

The NCLB Act extended federal expectations of schools by requiring each state to implement plans to raise student achievement in general, close achievement gaps, raise the standards of teacher quality, and set adequate yearly progress (AYP) targets that, if not met, would allow parents to transfer their students to other schools. With the passage of NCLB, the involvement of the federal government in local school improvement efforts reached a new level and altered accountability in schools by changing its focus from equal opportunity to learn to the expectation of equal outcomes, primarily as measured on standardized tests.

The ESSA was designed in part to remedy the difficulties school districts encountered to meet the prescriptive requirements of NCLB, which in many states were being administratively waived during the time NCLB was in effect. The ESSA provides more flexibility for states to set their own goals for student achievement. And whereas NCLB focused solely on test scores to measure and evaluate student success, the ESSA allows for additional factors to measure school quality, including academic factors such as graduation rates, or school quality factors such as kindergarten readiness and school climate and safety.

The ESSA also has its share of controversy, with the potential use of the Common Core State Standards. Although a majority of states use the Common Core Standards in some form, the standards became a political hot button issue that remains today.

With the change in presidential administrations in 2021, there will no doubt be changes in how President Biden's administration will revise the administrative regulations based on the ESSA.

Americans with Disabilities Act of 1990

The Americans with Disabilities Act (ADA), Pub. L. No. 101-336, 42 U.S.C. §§ 12101–12213 requires educational institutions to make every reasonable accommodation to ensure access to all facilities, programs, and activities by students and employees, without regard to disability. The ADA is a civil rights law intended to prohibit discrimination based solely on a disability in all areas of public life, including schooling. These requirements apply to private schools and institutions that do not receive federal aid as well as to schools and institutions that are recipients of federal funds. The purpose of the ADA is to ensure that people with disabilities have the same rights and opportunities as those without disabilities.

Individuals with Disabilities Education Act

The Individuals with Disabilities Education Act (IDEA) was amended in 2004 as Pub. L. No. 108-446 and reauthorized as part of the ESSA in 2015. The original law was signed in 1975 as the Education for All Handicapped Children Act. The law guarantees that all children with disabilities receive a free, appropriate, public education consisting of special education and related services designed to meet their individual needs. The IDEA is an education act that provides assistance to state and local education agencies to guarantee special services to eligible students. In addition, IDEA ensures that the rights of children with disabilities and their parents or guardians are protected and directs states and localities to provide for the education of all children with disabilities. The IDEA and issues related to students with disabilities will be discussed in Chapter 8.

Rehabilitation Act of 1973

Section 504 of the Rehabilitation Act of 1973 (Rehab Act), 29 U.S.C. § 794 (§ 504) is of particular importance for students and educators. The act prohibits discrimination on the basis of disability in programs including those receiving federal assistance. An individual with a disability is a person who has a physical or mental impairment that substantially limits one or more major life activities. Students may qualify for accommodations and services under Section 504 who do not qualify for or receive services under the IDEA.

Section 504 of the Rehabilitation Act is a civil rights law that is enforced by the Office for Civil Rights (OCR) in the U.S. Department of Education. A significant difference between the IDEA and Section 504 is that IDEA provides protections and services up to age 21, while Section 504 covers an individual throughout the individual's life.

Equal Educational Opportunities Act

The Equal Educational Opportunities Act (EEOA) Section 1703, 20 U.S.C. § 1703, passed in 1974, was another in a series of civil rights legislation designed to prohibit discrimination against students and those who work in public education. The EEOA requires school districts to provide that no state shall deny equal educational opportunity to an individual on account of race, color, sex, or national origin by the deliberate segregation of students on the basis of race, color, or national origin within schools, or assignment of students to a school other than the one closest to their place of residence if the assignment results in a greater degree of segregation. Among the most important provisions of the law are the requirement to provide classes for those students who are not proficient in the English language and the requirement to communicate in a language understood by the parents. Bilingual education has been interpreted by Congress to be a requirement of school districts.

The Equal Access Act

The Equal Access Act, P.L. 98-377 § 802 (1984), forbids school districts that receive federal funding from denying students to conduct meetings based on "religious, political, philosophical, or other content of the speech at such meetings." The act only applies to schools that allow students to form groups not specifically linked to the curriculum. The act also applies only to groups that meet during noninstructional times, and specifies that such meetings must be voluntary and initiated by students. School employees serving as advisors may attend but not participate in religious content. Such meetings cannot interfere with the educational purpose of the school, and public funding is limited to the cost of providing space for the meetings.

The McKinney-Vento Homeless Assistance Act

The McKinney-Vento Homeless Assistance Act, P.L. 100-77, 101 Stat. 482 (1987) covers education and youth programs for homeless children. The act was reauthorized as part of the ESSA in 2015, and requires public school districts to identify and provide support and appropriate services to homeless children. School districts must ensure such students are provided services through outreach and coordination with appropriate entities and agencies.

Title IX of the Education Amendments of 1972 and the Title IX Regulations

Title IX of the Education Amendments of 1972, 34 C.F.R. § 106–1 *et seq.* is a federal civil rights law which prohibits discrimination on the basis of sex in all federally funded educational institutions and applies to all K-12 and postsecondary institutions that receive any kind of federal financial assistance. The protections of Title IX exist for all students in those educational institutions as well as all employees of the institutions. In 2020, new Title IX regulations were updated, and the new regulations explicitly state that all individuals, including those who identify as LGBTQ+, are protected. Title IX requirements will be outlined in Chapter 7.

Family Educational Rights and Privacy Act of 1974

The Family Educational Rights and Privacy Act of 1974, 20 U.S.C. § 1232G (FERPA) is also referred to as the Buckley Amendment and requires educational agencies and institutions to provide parents of students attending a school of the agency or institution the right to inspect and review the education records of their children. Each educational agency or institution may establish its own procedures for granting parents' requests for access to the education records of their children but must make the records available within a maximum of forty-five days after the parent's request is made. Agencies and institutions that did not provide parental access to records will lose federal funding for their programs. The law further provides that educational agencies or institutions must provide the parents with an opportunity for a hearing to challenge the content of a student's education records, and the law prohibits the release of education records (or personally identifiable information contained therein other than directory information) of students without the written consent of their parents. FERPA will be further discussed in Chapter 9.

Age Discrimination in Employment Act of 1967

The Age Discrimination in Employment Act of 1967 (ADEA), 29 U.S.C. § 621 (§ 623) prohibits employers from failing or refusing to hire, discharging, or otherwise discriminating against any individual with respect to compensation, terms, conditions, or privileges of employment because of the individual's age. The law covers all employees who are forty or older. Passed over fifty years ago, this law has been subject to different interpretations by the courts, including the U.S. Supreme Court. The topic of age discrimination and the ADEA is further discussed in Chapter 11.

The Family and Medical Leave Act of 1993

The Family and Medical Leave Act of 1993 (FMLA), Pub. L. No. 103-3, 29 CFR § 825 is designed to help employees balance their work and family life, with the underlying philosophy that promoting the economic security of families served the national interest including the overall economy. FMLA is administered by the U.S. Department of Labor through a complex set of regulations that integrate its provisions with those of the Americans with Disabilities Act of 1990 (Pub. L. No. 101-336, 29 CFR Part 1630) and state workers' compensation laws. An additional description of FMLA is included in Chapter 11.

SECTION D. SUPREME COURT RULINGS THAT AFFECT EDUCATION PRACTICE

In the third edition of this text we stated: *Desegregation, school finance, student and teacher rights, special education, and the separation of church and state emerged as the notable issues defining elementary and secondary education for the current and previous centuries.* While still true, social and political changes as well as new legislation, regulations, and court decisions have altered the landscape and raised new issues, many of which are unresolved or ongoing.

This section has been revised from previous editions by moving narratives regarding key decisions into other chapters. What follows are selected U.S. Supreme Court decisions affecting major themes in education. Keeping in mind the hierarchy of laws that are interpreted and enforced by the judicial branch, recognize that although Supreme Court cases set the precedents for the entire nation, state courts will resolve the majority of disputes in their state related to education, with most federal issues determined within the U.S. federal circuits. This means that such decisions at the state and federal circuit level are no less important and take precedence unless overturned by higher courts or relevant laws are changed by legislatures.

Major Themes of Court Rulings

The major legislation prescribed in the previous section and the interpretation of the language of the Constitution become subject to significant legal challenges. Many of what are considered landmark U.S. Supreme Court (SCOTUS) decisions that are noteworthy for school principals can be grouped into a few categories, and several such decisions are discussed throughout the text. Longstanding societal issues not only directly affect the operation of public schools but also become reflected in what occurs on a daily basis within the schools.

Such issues start with "who goes to school" and "what schools can students attend" and these questions are reflected in school desegregation, school choice, and charter school cases. School finance cases attempt to answer questions of "who pays for schools" and "how do we pay for schools," which are also based on fundamental questions based on the right to an education. School finance cases at times also combine with issues related to the separation of church and state—how school vouchers using public tax dollars are used in private religious schools or what special services are required to be provided by public school districts for students with special needs who choose to attend private schools.

Cases involving students with special needs are a major area of caselaw and strongly related to the "who goes to school" question as well as "what services must be provided and what do those services look like" for those students. Students with special needs are not the only students who face access and equality issues. Although the SCOTUS has not ruled on a transgender student case, it has as recently as December 2020 declined to hear an appeal of a case that was decided in favor of a transgender student. Other students with access needs include undocumented students, non-native English-speaking students, and those with economic or other challenges.

The COVID-19 pandemic has significantly added additional burdens to students regarding access issues as well as "what school looks like" for all students. Although SCOTUS has not ruled directly on an educational case due to COVID at the time of this publication, the probability that they may eventually have a related case they accept is not out of the question.

Additional categories related to student and teacher rights have significant impact on the daily operation of public schools. Students and teachers retain constitutional rights at school, with certain limitations. What has changed and continues to evolve are how social media and actions committed off school grounds are impacted by those rights. In the case of teachers and other employees, as public employees they retain certain rights that may not be afforded to those who work in the private sector; but at the same time, as public employees they also have different expectations placed on them.

Finally, please note that the cases are referenced here from a historical perspective, *not from a current legal perspective*. In fact, many of the cases listed have by 2022 been modified or even overruled by later decisions. However, think of the impact on education these cases had or continue to have in terms of the context of their time and how each may have impacted future decisions.

There is a wealth of education law resources available for principals in print form and online. On our companion website are selected resources that range from no-cost web resources to education law-related organizations. These can be useful not only for up-to-date information, but for creating your own library of resources to direct teachers to in order to broaden education law-related knowledge in your building and district. These resources can be found at resources .corwin.com/principalsquickreferenceguide4e.

How Cases Are Cited

All of the federal cases below are cited from one of two sources. Those published by the government are cited as U.S. and those published by West in the Supreme Court Reporter are cited as S. Ct. Also included are the names of the parties, the volume and page number of the case decision, and the year of the decision. For example, *Tinker v. Des Moines Independent Community School District* is cited as the following:

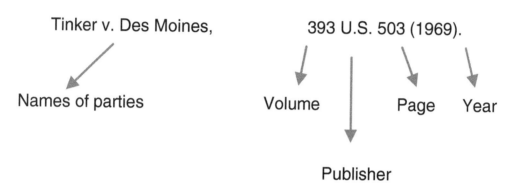

ADDITIONAL CASES OF INTEREST TO EDUCATORS

EQUALITY OF EDUCATIONAL OPPORTUNITY

Racial Inequality

Although the desegregation of public schools in the United States may not be within the daily job description of a principal, without question there are multiple issues centered around race that are part of the daily practice of principals, including what is taught in the curriculum, how students are disciplined, and the racial composition of the staff and faculty. Racial inequality in society has also been reflected in the history of public schools and inescapably linked to the history of public education. Despite the fact that some progress was made in the judicial system to address racial inequality in schools, many scholars now note that racial segregation is still the norm in public and private schools, a condition that is also reflected in the composition of teachers and staff in most school districts.

Plessy v. Ferguson, 163 U.S. 537 (1896). A law requiring the segregation of races in railway cars was upheld as constitutional. The Court held that the Thirteenth Amendment banned slavery but not other burdens based on race. They also held that although the Fourteenth Amendment required equality under the law, it did not ban segregation and commingling of races or abolishing social distinctions based on skin color.

Gong Lum v. Rice, 275 U.S. 78 (1927). The Court upheld a state law that classified a Chinese student as a Black student for the purposes of education; therefore, it was legal to deny admission to a school reserved for the white race.

Brown v. Board of Education, 347 U.S. 483 (1954). Students cannot be denied admission to public schools on the basis of race. The policy requiring separate schools violates the Fourteenth Amendment guarantee of equal protection under the law. Schools that are separated are inherently unequal.

Bolling v. Sharp, 347 U.S. 497 (1954). The Court ruled that the federal government could not deny admission to public schools on the basis of race. The Court stated that there was no essential government purpose served by separating races and that, because the Fourteenth Amendment applies to the states, it would be unthinkable that it would not also apply to the federal government.

Cooper v. Aaron, 358 U.S. 1 (1958). Citing intense public opposition to desegregating schools under *Brown* and with the support of the governor and legislature who wished to maintain law and order, Arkansas school board members filed suit to delay the implementation of a desegregation plan. The Court stated that officials were bound by the decision in *Brown,* and because the Supremacy Clause of Article VI made the Constitution the supreme law of the land, and *Marbury v. Madison* made the Supreme Court the final interpreter of the Constitution, the decision in *Brown* was the supreme law of the land. The decision in *Brown* was binding in all states, regardless of any state laws that attempted to contradict it.

Griffin v. County School Board of Prince Edward County, 377 U.S. 218 (1964). Although the decision in *Brown* mandated school district desegregation with "all deliberate speed," many school districts ignored the mandate. In this case, the school board refused to provide funding for public schools but allowed for tax credits for white students to attend private schools. This policy was unconstitutional under the Equal Protection Clause of the Fourteenth Amendment.

Green v. County School Board of New Kent Cnty., 391 U.S. 430 (1968). In a town that was not geographically segregated, the school district still operated two schools: one for Black students and the other for white students. The district adopted a "freedom-of-choice" plan, yet no white students chose to attend the Black school, and only 15% of the minority group attended the white school. The Court ruled that states must discontinue plans that are shown to be ineffective and adopt plans that are effective. Green established what became known as the "Green factors" as criteria courts would use to evaluate the progress of desegregation efforts. Those factors were related to faculty, staff, transportation, extracurricular activities, and facilities.

Swann v. Charlotte-Mecklenburg, 402 U.S. 1 (1971). A desegregation plan implemented in 1965 that did not achieve racial balance by 1969 prompted a federal court to impose a plan. The Court held that when school districts did not provide remedies to segregation, federal courts have broad discretion to implement a plan.

Keyes v. Sch. Dist. No. 1 of Denver, 413 U.S. 189 (1973). The Court ruled that for actions taken by a school board that result in a significant portion of the district to be segregated, the entire district can be determined as segregated. The lower court may order an entire district desegregation plan when segregation in one part of the district results in segregation of another part of the district.

Milliken v. Bradley (Milliken I), 418 U.S. 717 (1974). This case came about after a desegregation plan was implemented. Although the city did not have a history of *de jure* segregation, discrimination of both public and private created residential segregation, and the school board plan to create attendance zones created a dual school system based on race. The Court held that absent showing that outlying school districts had policies that fostered discrimination in other school districts, a court-ordered desegregation plan cannot cross school district lines to implement their plan.

Milliken v. Bradley (Milliken II), 433 U.S. 267 (1977). After *Milliken I,* a court ordered a new city only plan that shared the cost of the plan between the school district and the state. The state challenged the authority of the court to impose a financial burden on the state. The Court held that a court can order remedial and supportive programs for children who have been subjected to past segregation, especially when local school boards propose such plans, and those plans can be ordered funded by the state.

Missouri v. Jenkins (Missouri I and II), 495 U.S. 33 (1990). The Court held that a federal court must allow the local school district the opportunity to devise its own remedy before it imposed a local tax to pay for the desegregation plan.

BOE of OKC v. Dowell, 498 U.S. 237 (1991). A federal court ordered the Board of Education of Oklahoma City to implement a school busing desegregation plan. Five years later, the court withdrew the enforcement of the plan, and seven years later the board lessened the amount of school busing. The original plaintiffs sought to reinstitute the original court order. The Supreme Court held that such court injunctions were always intended to be temporary and that a court could remove the injunction when it determined the school district was in compliance and "unlikely to return to its former ways."

Freeman v. Pitts, 503 U.S. 467 (1992). When federal courts are supervising desegregation plans, the court has the authority to relinquish such supervision in incremental stages before the school district has reached compliance in every area of the operation of the district. The Court acknowledged the *Green* factors in the decision.

Missouri v. Jenkins, 515 U.S. 70 (1995). The Court held that a federal court order to approve salary increases to improve "desegregation attractiveness" to mitigate white flight exceeded their authority. The Court also noted that the order requiring funding by the state could not be sustained and the focus should be on the *Freeman* factors, outlined in *Freeman v. Pitts.*

Gratz v. Bollinger, 539 U.S. 244 (2003). The use of racial preferences in admission is impermissible if there is a less restrictive measure that could be used to achieve the compelling interest of a diverse student body.

Grutter v. Bollinger, 539 U.S. 306 (2003). The use of race in an applicant's file does not violate the Fourteenth Amendment if the process is "narrowly tailored" to achieve a compelling state interest. Diversity in the student body in public higher education settings can be a compelling interest.

Parents Involved in Community Schools v. Seattle School District No. 1, 127 S. Ct. 2738 (2007). Although diversity can be a compelling state interest in K-12 student assignment plans, two school districts' use of race in public school assignment violated the Equal Protection Clause because the policies were not narrowly tailored. The use of race had a minimal effect on student assignments and the districts did not consider other race-neutral methods instead.

Meredith v. Jefferson County, 551 U.S. 701 (2007). In a 5–4 decision, under a "strict scrutiny" framework, the Court held that a plan to achieve racial diversity in a school district violated the Equal Protection Clause of the Fourteenth Amendment. The plan allowed students to choose schools but not all schools could accept all applicants. Chief Justice John Roberts noted in the opinion, "The way to stop discrimination on the basis of race is to stop discriminating on the basis of race."

Compulsory School Attendance

Meyer v. Nebraska, 262 U.S. 390 (1923). The Court held that a statute prohibiting teaching in a language other than English was not constitutional. The state has the power to prescribe a curriculum, but this law was arbitrary and "without reasonable relation to any end within the competency of the state."

Pierce v. Society of Sisters of the Holy Names of Jesus and Mary, 268 U.S. 510 (1925). Parents cannot be required to have students attend public schools rather than private schools, and such a statute unreasonably interferes with the liberty of parents to direct the upbringing and education of their children.

Plyler v. Doe, 457 U.S. 202 (1982). A Texas law was passed to deny funding for the education of students who were "illegal aliens." School districts were also authorized to deny enrollment to such children. The Court held that denying funding and admission to children deprived them of their rights under the Fourteenth Amendment. The Court reasoned that although the children were not citizens, they nevertheless were people who should be afforded protections.

Bilingual Education

Lau v. Nichols, 414 U.S. 563 (1974). The Court held that any school district receiving federal funds must provide special instruction for non-English-speaking students when the language barrier hampers the education of students. Title VI requires that students are provided a meaningful opportunity to participate in public education.

Students With Disabilities

BOE v. Rowley, 458 U.S. 176 (1982). This case concerned what is considered "appropriate" in FAPE. The Court concluded that the purpose of the Education for All Handicapped Children Act (now IDEA) was to open the door for students rather than provide a floor for qualifying students. The Court held that an individualized education plan (IEP) should be reasonably calculated for the student to achieve passing grades and advance from grade to grade. An "appropriate" education was to provide instruction and support services sufficient enough to permit the child to benefit educationally from the instruction.

Irving ISD v. Tatro, 468 U.S. 883 (1984). The Court held that a student who required clean intermittent catheterization (CIC) during the school day was entitled to have the service provided by the school district. The CIC qualifies as a "related service" required under IDEA. Without such service the child would not be able to attend school and receive FAPE.

Burlington School Community v. Department of Education, 471 U.S. 359 (1985). Parents who enrolled their child in a private school during legal proceedings regarding the child's IEP and services are entitled to reimbursement of tuition if it is determined that the placement of the child is appropriate and the placement by the district was inappropriate. The school asserted that the "stay put" provision called for the child to remain in place during the proceedings but the Court held that cutting off the reimbursement would defeat the principal purpose of the Education for All Handicapped Children Act.

Honig v. Doe, 484 U.S. 305 (1988). School authorities may not exclude disabled students for longer than ten school days without following the due process procedures under the Education for All Handicapped Children Act (now IDEA). The language of the "stay put" provisions are unequivocal. The Court also determined that the act allows for procedures and remedies regarding "dangerous" disabled students.

Cedar Rapids Com. Sch. Dist. v. Garrett F., 526 U.S. 66 (1999). The Court held that school districts that receive funding under IDEA must fund one-to-one nursing assistance for qualifying students if the services are "related services" necessary to enable the child to access educational services. Nursing is considered a "related service" while "medical services" are those that require a physician.

Winkelman v. Parma City, 550 U.S. 516 (2007). In an IDEA case, after exhausting administrative remedies, parents sought action in federal court acting as their own counsel. IDEA provides rights to not only children with disabilities but also to parents. The Court ruled that parents are entitled to proceed *pro se* in federal court to enforce at least the rights they hold as parents under IDEA.

Forrest Grove v. T.A., 129 S. Ct. 2484 (2009). The Court held that the lack of previous enrollment in a special education program does not bar tuition reimbursement under IDEA. A court or hearing officer may require reimbursement of tuition to parents for private school enrollment if it is found that previously the student was not provided FAPE or had previously received special education and related services.

Fry v. Napoleon Cmty. Schools, 137 S. Ct. 743 (2017). The Court ruled that the IDEA's requirement that plaintiffs exhaust administrative remedies before suing under the ADA and the Rehabilitation Act is not required if the plaintiff's claims are not based in the denial of FAPE. If a lawsuit is not seeking relief for denial of FAPE, then it is not seeking an available remedy under the IDEA, and the exhaustion requirement does not apply. The case involved a student who was not allowed to bring her service dog to school, and they sued for damages under the ADA. Lower courts held that the IDEA did not provide for relief they sought, and that the parents had not exhausted remedies under the IDEA.

Endrew F. v. Douglas County School District, 580 U.S. ___ (2017); 137 S. Ct. 988 (2017). The Court ruled that in order to provide children an appropriate public education guaranteed under IDEA, school districts must provide an IEP that is reasonably calculated to enable each child to make progress appropriate to the child's circumstances. This requirement is substantially more than a "de minimus" benefit.

Gender Equality

Gloucester County School Board v. G.G. (no citation). This case centered around the issue of transgender student rights. The Supreme Court remanded the case to the Fourth Circuit due to a change in guidance from the Department of Education in 2017. In 2021, the Supreme Court declined to hear the appeal of the state, signifying the end of the litigation in favor of the student.

SCHOOL FINANCE

Educational Finance of Public Schools

San Antonio v. Rodriguez, 411 U.S. 1 (1973). The Court ruled that a state funding system based on local property taxes that provided a minimum educational service to all students was constitutional. Despite the large disparities in per-pupil funding between districts, the Court held that there was no violation of the Fourteenth Amendment because all students of all incomes and races suffer alike. The case is significant because the Court ruled that the Constitution does not protect education as a right, and a minimum education guaranteed to every student was sufficient. The Court left it to the states to determine more strict standards.

Mueller v. Allen, 463 U.S. 388 (1983). A state statute allowing income tax deductions for expenses related to tuition, textbooks, and transportation to attend elementary or secondary schools does not violate the Establishment Clause.

Aguilar v. Felton, 473 U.S. 402 (1985). Using Title I funds to pay the salaries of teachers working in public and parochial schools was ruled unconstitutional. Public school employees worked in parochial schools to provide remedial instruction and other services in a clearly sectarian environment.

Edwards v. Aguillard, 482 U.S. 578 (1987). The Court held that it was a violation of the Establishment Clause to prohibit the teaching of the theory of evolution in public schools unless accompanied by instruction of creation-science.

Agostini v. Felton, 521 U.S. 203 (1997). A publicly funded program that provided supplemental instruction and materials on the premises of a parochial school with proper safeguards for neutrality is constitutional. The ruling reversed the decision in *Aguilar v. Felton.*

Mitchell v. Helms, 530 U.S. 793 (2000). The loaning of public school educational materials and equipment to parochial schools as part of a neutral program for all K-12 schools was not in violation of the Establishment Clause. The decision reopened the debate surrounding vouchers. The ruling of the Court that some federal aid for private and parochial is permissible opened the question of how broadly the decision can be applied.

Zelman v. Simmons-Harris, 536 U.S. 639 (2002). A school voucher program that allowed parents a choice between private, religious, and public schools was constitutional because the primary effect of the program was secular and was neutral with respect to religion.

STUDENT RIGHTS

Student Speech Rights

West Virginia State Board of Education v. Barnette, 319 U.S. 624 (1943). A statute requiring students to salute the flag of the United States was ruled unconstitutional. The case was decided on free speech even though the refusal to salute the flag by the plaintiffs was for religious reasons. The case reversed *Minersville School District v. Gobitis*, 310 U.S. 586 (1940) from just three years earlier.

Tinker v. Des Moines Independent Community School District, 393 U.S. 503 (1969). This is a landmark freedom of speech case that famously states students do not "shed their constitutional rights at the schoolhouse gate." Schools may not restrict student private speech absent imminent or material substantial disruption or infringes on the rights of others.

Bethel School District No. 403 v. Fraser, 478 U.S. 675 (1986). The case modified *Tinker* stating that schools can regulate speech that is "lewd or vulgar" and the Constitution does not prevent school officials from determining if the speech would "undermine the school's basic educational mission."

Hazelwood School District v. Kuhlmeier, 484 U.S. 260 (1988). The case modified *Tinker* again by ruling that school officials do not violate constitutional rights of students when they regulate the style and content of school-sponsored student publications or other speech that is reasonably related to pedagogical concerns or connected in some way to the school.

Morse v. Frederick, 127 S. Ct. 2618 (2007). An additional modification of *Tinker* was created when the Court held that schools' educational need to prevent illegal drug usage permits them to restrict student speech at school that might be protected outside of the school setting.

Mahanoy Area School District v. B.L., (594 U.S. ____ 2021). The Supreme Court held that students retain First Amendment protections for speech that is initiated off-campus, although the school retains an interest in regulating such speech that may be bullying or threatening to staff or students. The case centered around an angry and profane rant posted on the social media platform Snapchat by a student who was upset after not making the varsity cheerleading team.

Student Due Process

Goss v. Lopez, 419 U.S. 565 (1975). This is the landmark case relating to due process rights for students. The right to attend school is protected by the Due Process Clause, and exclusion from school requires some kind of notice and an opportunity to refute the allegations. This decision provides guidance surrounding short-term suspensions of fewer than ten days as well as longer suspensions and expulsions.

Wood v. Strickland, 420 U.S. 308 (1975). A school board member or other education employee is immune from liability for damages under Section 1983 unless they knew or reasonably should have known the action would violate the constitutional rights of the affected student.

Ingraham v. Wright, 430 U.S. 651 (1977). The Cruel and Unusual Punishment Clause of the Eighth Amendment does not apply to disciplinary corporal punishment in public schools. Students do have a liberty interest for the purpose of due process when they are subjected to corporal punishment.

J.D.B. v. North Carolina, 131 S. Ct. 2394 (2011). The age of a child can be a relevant factor when determining whether a juvenile suspect merits a *Miranda* warning. The age of a child will not be a significant or determinative factor in every case, but the reality of the age of the suspect can't be ignored.

Student Search and Seizure

New Jersey v. T.L.O., 469 U.S. 325 (1985). The Fourth Amendment applies to searches of students but school officials need to only meet a "reasonable suspicion" standard rather than the higher "probable cause" standard required of police. A search of a student is legal if it is (1) reasonable at its inception and (2) permissible in scope.

Vernonia School District 47J v. Acton, 515 U.S. 646 (1995). The Court held that drug testing by random urinalysis of student athletes does not violate the Fourth Amendment.

United States v. Lopez, 514 U.S. 549 (1995). A high school student was caught carrying a concealed weapon into his school and was charged with violating the Gun Free Zones Act of 1990. The Court invalidated the act, ruling that it exceeded the authority of Congress.

Board of Education of Independent School District No. 92 v. Earls, 536 U.S. 822 (2002). A district policy requiring the drug testing of all students who participate in competitive extracurricular activities does not violate the Fourth Amendment.

Safford Unified School District No. 1 v. Redding, 129 S. Ct. 2633 (2009). Public school officials' strip search of a student violates the Fourth Amendment where they do not have reasonable suspicion that items being sought posed a danger to the student or others. The content of the reasonable suspicion needs to match the degree of intrusion, and to make the "quantum leap" requires the support of danger.

Riley v. California, 573 U.S. 373 (2014). Although not a school case, because of the force of the rare 9–0 decision, it may be instructive for school officials. The Court ruled that, in general, absent a warrant, law enforcement cannot search the digital contents of a cell phone confiscated upon arrest. The Court noted that modern cell phones are not just for technology convenience but hold the "privacies of life" and the fact that technology allows a person to carry such information in their hand does not make the information less worthy of Fourth Amendment protections.

Title IX

Franklin v. Gwinnett County Public Schools, 503 U.S. 60 (1992). The Court held a private damages remedy under Title IX permissible. The case stemmed from the sexual harassment and abuse by a male teacher toward a female student.

Gebser v. Lago Vista Independent School District, 524 U.S. 274 (1998). Damages for teacher-on-student sexual harassment under Title IX are available only when a school official had actual notice of the harassment or was deliberately indifferent to the conduct. The notice must be to a school official who has the authority to take corrective action.

Davis v. Monroe County Board of Education, 526 U.S. 629 (1999). A school district may be liable for damages under Title IX for student-to-student sexual harassment only where the district is deliberately indifferent and has actual knowledge of harassment that is so severe, pervasive, and objectively offensive that it deprives the victim of educational benefits or opportunities provided by the school.

Jackson v. Birmingham Board of Education, 544 U.S. 167 (2005). The Court ruled that retaliating against a person who complained about gender discrimination against others creates a private right of action and is intentional discrimination on the basis of sex under Title IX.

TEACHER RIGHTS

Teacher Speech and Other Rights

Pickering v. Board of Education, 391 U.S. 563 (1968). A teacher's First Amendment right to speak out is balanced against the school's interest for efficient operation of the school. If the comments by the teacher in the public interest do not impair the daily operation of the school, the teacher should enjoy the same protection as any other member of the public. The case stemmed from a letter to the editor of a newspaper written by the teacher that was critical of the school board.

Board of Regents of State Colleges v. Roth, 408 U.S. 564 (1972). In the area of procedural due process, the Court determined that a school system is not required to establish cause for the nonrenewal of a probationary teacher's contract.

Perry v. Sinderman, 408 U.S. 593 (1972). A governmental benefit may not be denied because of the exercise of protected rights. Public criticism of supervisors on a matter of public concern is protected speech and cannot be the basis for termination regardless of tenure status.

Cleveland Board of Education v. LaFleur, 414 U.S. 632 (1974). Public school teachers challenged the constitutionality of mandatory maternity leave that required them to leave work before they desired. The Court held that mandatory maternity leave that has an absolute, early exit date and an absolute belated return date is unconstitutional because it violates the Fourteenth Amendment. The Court held that freedom of personal choice in matters of family is a liberty protected by the amendment.

Mt. Healthy City School District v. Doyle, 429 U.S. 274 (1977). The Court determined that even if a teacher's expression is constitutionally protected, school officials are not precluded from disciplining or discharging the employee if sufficient cause exists independent of the protected speech. This decision modified the finding in *Pickering*.

Givhan v. Western Line Consolidated School District, 439 U.S. 410 (1979). Two years after *Mt. Healthy,* the Court concluded that as long as a teacher's expression pertains to matters of public concern, in contrast to personal grievances, statements made in private or through a public medium are constitutionally protected.

North Haven Board of Education v. Bell, 456 U.S. 512 (1982). The Court held that employment was within the scope of intent of Title IX, concluding that Title IX prevented discriminatory employment practices.

Connick v. Myers, 461 U.S. 183 (1983). The Court held that when a public employee speaks as an employee on matters of only personal interest and not as a citizen of matters of public concern, there is no First Amendment protection. If the employee does speak as a matter of public concern, the government interest in efficiency can still outweigh the challenge. The content, form, and manner of speech help determine if such speech is a matter of public concern.

Cleveland Board of Education v. Loudermill, 470 U.S. 532 (1985). The Court held that public employees dismissed only for cause are entitled to oral and written notice of the charges against them, an explanation of the evidence, and an opportunity to present their side of the story prior to termination.

Ansonia v. Philbrook, 479 U.S. 60 (1986). A teacher required six days of leave per year to observe religious holidays but the collective bargaining agreement permitted only three days per year for religious holidays but not sick or personal leave. The Court held that Title VII must provide religious accommodations that do not provide undue hardship to the school district. If there is more than one reasonable accommodation possible, the district does not have to provide the preferred alternative of the employee. The alternative of unpaid leave is a permissible option as long as other leave is available without discrimination based on religion.

Garcetti v. Ceballos, 547 U.S. 410 (2006). In a case with significant implications for educators, the Court held that when public employees make statements pursuant to their official duties, they are not speaking as citizens for First Amendment purposes, meaning in such circumstances the Constitution does not prevent discipline by their employer. The employer can restrict speech if such speech has some potential to affect the employer's operations. The decision was concerning for educators regarding academic freedom because teachers are nearly always speaking and writing pursuant to their official duties. The concern still exists in spite of the fact that the majority opinion noted, "We need not, and for that reason do not, decide whether the analysis we conduct today would apply in the same manner to a case involving speech related to scholarship or teaching."

Janus v. American Fed. of St, Cnty, and Muni. Employees Council 31, 138 S. Ct. 2448 (2018). The Court overturned a 1997 decision in *Abood v. Detroit Board of Education* that allowed a public employer whose employees were represented by a union but did not join the union to nevertheless be required to pay union fees because they benefited from the collective bargaining agreement. This decision held that withholding such fees from nonconsenting employees was a violation of their First Amendment protections.

Bostock v. Clayton County, 590 U.S. ___ (2020). In a landmark decision that did not involve education but is far reaching, the Court held in favor of a gay man who was terminated from his public employment after he participated in a gay recreational softball league. Although he had received positive evaluations over a period of ten years, he was fired for "conduct unbecoming of its employees." The Court ruled that an employer violates Title VII of the Civil Rights Act of 1964 when they fire an employee for merely being gay or transgender. The Court reasoned that the act prohibited discrimination because of an individual's "race, color, religion, sex, or national origin." Critics of the decision argued that when the law was written in 1964, the definition of "sex" would not have applied to gay or transgender people, but the majority held that discrimination on the basis of their sexual identity requires an employer to intentionally treat employees differently because of their sex, which is the very practice Title VII prohibits.

CHURCH AND STATE

Establishment Clause and Free Exercise Clause

Engel v. Vitale, 370 U.S. 421 (1962). A local school district under order of state law violated the First Amendment prohibiting the establishment of religion when they required a daily recitation of a nondenominational prayer in the presence of their teacher at the beginning of each school day.

Abington v. Schempp, 374 U.S. 203 (1963). The Court struck down a law that promoted the reading of Bible verses and the recitation of prayer on school grounds under the supervision of school employees during school hours, even if such practice was voluntary.

Epperson v. Arkansas, 393 U.S. 97 (1968). A state law prohibiting the teaching of the theory of evolution was found unconstitutional because the purpose of the law was not to prevent the teaching of evolution in the curriculum but instead to proscribe a discussion of a subject that was found objectionable by a religious group.

Lemon v. Kurtzman, 403 U.S. 602 (1971). Laws providing public funding for salaries of teachers in nonpublic schools even when the teachers only taught secular subjects violate the Establishment Clause. Additionally, a law providing reimbursement to nonpublic schools for expenses incurred when teaching secular subjects was also in violation. The Court created what became known as the *Lemon test*, which was a three-part test. A statute or policy (1) must have a secular purpose; (2) must have a principal effect that neither advances nor inhibits religion; and (3) must not foster an "excessive government entanglement with religion."

Wisconsin v. Yoder, 406 U.S. 205 (1972). A law requiring compulsory attendance infringed on the free exercise of religion for an Amish community who refused to send their children to any school past the eighth grade because they believed such schooling impeded preparation for adult life and for the religious practice within their community. The basis of the ruling was that the law violated the Free Exercise Clause.

Widmar v. Vincent, 454 U.S. 263 (1981). Colleges that maintain "limited open forums" for student groups cannot violate the speech rights of a religious club by refusing to allow them to meet. An equal access policy would not have a "primary effect" that violates the Establishment Clause.

Sch. Dist. of the City of Grand Rapids et al. v. Ball, 473 U.S. 373 (1985). Programs for students enrolled in primarily parochial private schools funded by public finances in classes taught by public school teachers were ruled as unconstitutional.

Wallace v. Jaffree, 472 U.S. 38 (1985). A statute allowing a moment of meditation or voluntary prayer that does not have a clearly secular purpose violates the Establishment Clause.

Board of Education of Westside Community Schools v. Mergens, 496 U.S. 226 (1990). The Court held that the Equal Access Act does not violate the Free Speech Clause of the First Amendment's proscription against the establishment of religion. A "non-curriculum related student group" means one that is not directly related to the curriculum. Several student clubs and groups met after hours and the school denied the request of a Christian club solely on the basis of religion.

Lee v. Wiseman, 505 U.S. 577 (1992). Invocations and benedictions led by clergy at public graduation ceremonies violate the Establishment Clause of the First Amendment. Prayer exercise in public school carry the risk of coercion, and graduation ceremonies can be coercive even though attendance is technically voluntary.

Santa Fe Independent School District v. Doe, 530 U.S. 290 (2000). The Court held that a policy permitting student-led and student-initiated prayer before football games was a violation of the Establishment Clause. The decision was made against the district even though they had not yet implemented the policy.

Elk Grove Unified School District v. Newdow, 542 U.S. 1 (2004). A case that centered on parental rights and standing to challenge in federal court involved a noncustodial parent who objected to his child having to recite the Pledge of Allegiance and including the words "under God." The Court ruled that the parent had no standing to make a federal claim because the state law did not give him the right to sue on the child's behalf.

Trinity Lutheran Church v. Comer, 137 S. Ct. 2012 (2017). The Court held that a state policy denying religious organizations from using a playground scrap tire material violated the Free Exercise Clause because the decision was based solely on religious character. The law did not need to impede the practice of religion but it was sufficient that the law denied the religious organization from the same benefit otherwise available to all secular organizations. It was also noted that other government benefits such as fire and police services are not prohibited, and a safety benefit of children should be similarly treated.

Espinoza v. Montana, 591 U.S. ___ (2020). In a 5–4 decision that included several written opinions (concurring and dissenting), the Court held that a state cannot exclude religious schools from receiving tax credit-funded scholarships. The state discriminated against parents who wished to send their children to religious schools and did not meet the narrowly tailored standard that the policy achieved a government interest "of the highest order." The decision has been interpreted to set a precedent that state voucher and other school choice programs cannot exclude religious schools and institutions.

School Program

Board of Education, Island Trees Union School District No. 26 v. Pico, 457 U.S. 853 (1982). Local school boards may not remove books and materials from libraries merely because they do not like the ideas presented. The board objected to materials and ignored their own review board recommendation and removed the books.

Owasso Independent School District No. 1-011 v. Falvo, 534 U.S. 426 (2002). FERPA does not cover grades on students' papers before the teacher records the grades as an education record. The case centered around students grading the work of other students. The Court held that FERPA requirements relate to "maintained" records, and students do not maintain records when they score papers of other students.

CHAPTER 2

Preventive Law
Developing Risk and Crisis Management Programs

Accidents, incidents, or transgressions are organizational and managerial problems and not always, as we tend to think, people problems. Regardless of the cause of problems that may lead to litigation, such events are too often dealt with ex post facto *rather than by means of a well-planned, proactive program of risk anticipation and litigation prevention. Risk factors diminish with a well-defined, proactive program of preventive law. The function of preventive law is to regulate human conduct to ensure a harmonious society by attempting to strike a balance between allowing individuals as much freedom as possible and enabling society to function without unreasonable interference from the conduct of individuals.*

School districts should make preventing liability a high priority in daily operations. In many school districts, responsibility for preventing litigious actions or inaction and loss is relegated to middle- and low-level staff members. The longstanding misperception is that safety and loss programs involve minor personnel matters and relatively insignificant details. Yet when a major incident, accident, or loss occurs, it requires significant top-level time and energy. A senior manager should be assigned the responsibility for a district's risk management prerogatives. In the development and implementation of policies and procedures, school districts, in cooperation with their legal counsel, should include the concepts and practice of preventive law as a major component of their overall risk management program. A tendency in many school districts is to temporize and downplay the significance of legal problems, seeking answers to such problems at the operational level rather than at the organizational level, and school districts often rely on legal counsel only after they are in trouble. That said, despite district initiatives, principals can significantly reduce their exposure to liability by incorporating and practicing preventive law as outlined here.

CONSIDERATIONS RELATED TO COVID-19

Minimizing the likelihood of students and staff from contracting the virus is clearly the most important priority for school districts and principals. There are other risks that are associated with school operations affected by the pandemic that have also become apparent, some of which previously existed but have become magnified due to COVID-19.

Achievement deficits and opportunity gaps have worsened. This is especially true for those students with special needs and those who may not qualify for services but still are in need of in-person, consistent classroom attention. Future planning and resources must be directed at these deficits.

Similarly, virtual learning has further exposed the gaps between those who have access to devices and internet services and those that do not. Forced to move toward virtual learning required the immediate addressing of equity issues that have always existed but in many cases were still allowed to continue. Even though this has created additional budgetary and implementation pressure, being forced into action toward greater equity has produced many positive results, including partnerships with businesses, internet service providers, and other agencies that will hopefully continue in the future.

Rising rates of youth suicides in 2020 have been linked to the impacts of COVID-19. School districts and educators have not only a moral obligation to do all they can to prevent youth suicide through conscientious suicide prevention programs, but a legal obligation as well. The social–emotional effects are also present as they relate to overall student and staff trauma, and as will be noted in further chapters, there is now litigation related to trauma as a disability.

SUGGESTED GUIDELINES FOR PRACTICE

Somewhat arguably, there are three major daily functions and responsibilities of educators each day school is in session—teaching; keeping everyone safe; and dealing with the social, emotional, and physical needs of students. Hopefully inarguably, the number one concern each day is that no one is injured in any way or that no acts of violence are committed on the campus.

Minimizing risk is not only a legal obligation but a moral one as well. This chapter deals with ways to minimize risks, with the following chapter describing remedies in place when incidents occur through either negligence or willfulness of some kind.

Principals and other educators are not expected to prevent all possible accidents, injuries, or other potential injurious events, but they are expected to take every precaution to prevent them from occurring as much as a possible.

Principals are reminded of the idiom "nothing is an emergency except an emergency." Successful principals have a sense of what requires immediate action and response and what does not. The reason this is important is that placing too much focus on what isn't truly an immediate "crisis" can prevent you from seeing far more serious problems that jeopardize health and safety. For example, the presence of gum left in a drinking fountain is a nuisance but not worthy of being distracted from a bubbling issue of social media bullying of a student who may be reaching the breaking point.

SECTION A. PREVENTION AND RISK MANAGEMENT

Tenets of Preventive Law and Risk Management

The concepts of preventive law and the management of risk, which are interwoven throughout this book, are illustrated by six general beliefs or tenets:

1. *An understanding of the substance of law limits an education organization's culpability and exposure.* Effective principals base their day-to-day decision making on substantive law, which consists of both an understanding of the basic tenets of law and knowledge of current education litigation decisions.

2. *The proper application of procedures, informed decision making, and foreseeability reduces liability and environmental and organizational loss.* Effective principals adhere to procedures and precedents established by law, exercise reasonable and prudent judgment in situations not directly addressed by the law, and integrate foreseeability when practicing preventive law, thus minimizing exposure to liability and loss.

3. *Working with counsel reduces budget loss.* When they have questions about legal issues that are not directly addressed in established laws and procedures, effective principals consult legal counsel.

4. *Flexibility endangers system stability but enhances conflict resolution.* Although principals must strictly adhere to, enforce, and monitor all policies and procedures, effective principals demonstrate flexibility and reduce conflict (and avoid litigation) by fostering a school climate in which divergent ideas may be presented, respected, permitted to flourish, and channeled into productive results for the school.

5. *Knowledge of precedent, constitutional compliance, and public information needs enhances crisis and motivational management and monitoring.* Effective principals understand the legal ramifications of precedent-setting cases and consider the significant protections provided to students, teachers, and others under various interpretations of the Constitution when making decisions. They also know that it is often up to them to educate parents and others about how court actions influence the daily operations of the school.

6. *Leadership in the education enterprise must be coupled with leadership in preventive law.* Effective education leadership sometimes involves taking calculated risks when complicated situations warrant decisive action; however, such risks must be legal and must demonstrate a commonsense commitment to preventive law.

What Is Preventive Law?

Preventive law is generally defined as a program, supported by policies, procedures, and regulations, that endeavors to minimize the risk of litigation or to secure, with more certainty, legal rights and duties. Preventive law emphasizes the importance of *pre facto* planning to avoid legal problems and their consequences should litigation ensue. There are four components of preventive law, all of which should be put into everyday practice at the building level by principals:

1. The *anticipation* of legal challenges (foreseeability);

2. The *evaluation* of the legal merits of potential challenges;

3. A *consideration* of the policies (in effect or proposed) affected by potential challenges;

4. *Implementation or modification,* where appropriate, in response to the first three steps.

Identifying Potential Risks

To the extent that human behavior and the law are reasonably foreseeable, informed school principals practicing preventive law and common risk management methods can predict certain legal risks and reduce their scope through policy, procedure, and practice. In those areas in which the law is less certain, principals can at least *identify* and *analyze* risk and choose courses of action that are less precarious than others. *Risk identification* focuses on the question, "What losses can happen?" whereas *risk analysis* goes further, asking, "How likely is it that the loss will happen, and, if the loss happens, how serious will it be, and how often might it occur?" Thus consideration is given to both frequency and severity probabilities. Figure 2.1 provides a simple tool to analyze foreseeable risks. The figure presents a formula that integrates three key factors of preventive law: (1) how *likely* an event is to occur, (2) the *frequency* with which the opportunity exists for such an occurrence, and (3) the *potential consequences* of such an event. The formula provides numerical ratings for each factor that, when multiplied together, produce a risk score. In other words, *likelihood* times *exposure* times *potential consequences* equals the level of *potential risk* ($L \times E \times PC = R$).

The following example shows how the formula can be used to support districtwide or site-based risk management. Examples that principals can apply to their own buildings and operations follow.

A newspaper reports the explosion of a water heater in a local office building. There are several fatalities, severe injuries, and significant structural damage to the building. Your school district records indicate that the water heaters in most of your buildings are more than ten years old and have not been inspected for seven years. Should your district allocate resources for a full inspection of its facilities' water heaters? If yes, when should this be done? First, the *likelihood* of an explosion needs to be identified. Most people would probably rate the likelihood as 5 (unusual but possible). The *exposure* rating usually depends on how frequently the piece of equipment is in use.

In the case of a water heater, that rating would normally be a 10 (continuous). However, school officials might be concerned with how frequently people are in the vicinity of the operating water heater and might rate the exposure as 8 (frequent, daily). In this example, a school official might use a composite rating of 9. The third factor is an estimate of the *potential consequences* of an explosion. The potential consequence scale suggests three interrelated types of consequences: physical injury, financial loss, and public relations problems. In this example, the school official assumed that the potential consequences ranged between 7 (very serious) and 8 (disaster), for a composite rating of 7.5. To estimate the risk, the school official multiplied 5 times 9 times 7.5, which produced a risk score of 337.5. This score indicates that a *substantial risk* exists and *timely correction* (inspection) is advised.

FIGURE 2.1 Risk Analysis Model

Likelihood Scale		Exposure Scale		Potential Consequences Scale	
Probable	10	Continuous	10	Catastrophe (many fatalities, critical financial loss, critical public relations problem)	10
Might well be expected	9		9		9
Quite possible, could happen	8	Frequent (daily)	8	Disaster (multiple fatalities, critical financial loss, critical public relations problem)	8
	7		7	Very serious (fatality, significant financial loss, significant public relations problem)	7
	6		6		6
Unusual, but possible	5	Regular (once a week)	5	Serious (disability results, serious financial loss, serious public relations problem)	5
	4	Occasional (monthly)	4		4
Remotely possible	3		3	Important (serious injury, serious financial loss, serious public relations problem)	3
Conceivable, but unlikely	2	Minimal (a few times a year)	2		2
Practically impossible	1	Rare (once a year or less)	1	Noticeable (minor injury, potential financial loss, minimal public relations problem)	1
Likelihood	x	Exposure	x	Potential Consequences	

=

Risk Scale	
1000	Very high risk; consider discontinuing operation
750	High risk; immediate correction required
500	
450	Substantial risk; timely correction required
250	Possible risk; non-routine attention required
200	
100	Known risk; routine attention recommended
Risk	

Although the risk analysis model presented here is clearly subjective, it provides at least a consistent way of thinking about risk and preventive law, as well as a simplified way of reporting. Most importantly, the model aids in the process of forecasting, an important concept in the law, commonly called *foreseeability*.

When applying the model to the COVID-19 pandemic, the polarization of attitudes about the pandemic can be illustrated. Those who view the virus as something not to be taken seriously and as of little consequence would take far fewer precautions than those who would be on the opposite side of the scales. School districts and educators do not have any leeway to casually dismiss the guidance of world health experts and local health authorities no matter what their own personal viewpoint may be surrounding COVID-19 and schools. Unfortunately, school boards and educators are caught in between the different viewpoints in the public on the pandemic, and while being caught in the middle of a social or public health debate may seem like familiar territory to veteran educators, clearly COVID-19 has been perhaps the worst crisis most educators have faced in their careers.

The usefulness of the model in both scope and diversity is further demonstrated in the following selected examples derived during field testing.

Example 1: A school principal calculated the school's risk regarding injuries related to slippery entry areas during inclement weather as follows:

- *Likelihood* = 10 (Probable)

- *Exposure* = 3 (Occasional)

- *Potential consequences* = 1 (Noticeable). The resultant risk score of 30 indicates *a known risk* with routine attention recommended.

Example 2: A school principal calculated the school's risk regarding injuries related to children falling over the sides of a playground slide as follows:

- *Likelihood* = 3 (Remotely possible)

- *Exposure* = 10 (Continuous)

- *Potential consequences* = 4 (Serious). The resultant risk score of 120 indicates *a possible risk* with nonroutine or focused attention advised.

Example 3: A school principal calculated the school's risk regarding injuries related to students traveling on field trips in school-owned vehicles as follows:

- *Likelihood* = 6.75 (average of 3–8, from Remotely possible to Quite possible, could happen)

- *Exposure* = 5 (Regular)

- *Potential consequences* = 6 (average of 4–7, from Serious to Very serious). The resultant risk score of 202 indicates *a possible risk* with nonroutine or focused attention advised.

Example 4: A high school principal in a mid-Atlantic state calculated the school's risk regarding injuries related to a disturbance resulting from a group of students displaying a Confederate flag as follows:

- *Likelihood* = 6 (average of 5–7, from Unusual but possible to Quite possible, could happen)

- *Exposure* = 8 (Frequent)

- *Potential consequences* = 1 (Noticeable). The resultant risk score of 48 indicates a *known risk* with routine or focused attention advised.

Example 5: A school principal has become concerned about social media being used by students from off-campus who may be bullying, sexting, or making derogatory or threatening statements to students and staff. The principal has rated this risk as follows:

- *Likelihood* = 10 (Probable)

- *Exposure* = 10 (Continuous)

- *Potential consequences* = 7 (average of 4–7, from Important to Very serious). The resultant risk score of 700 indicates immediate *high risk* with timely correction required.

During the preceding century, changes in American culture created numerous conflicts in society. These conflicts led to new issues. New issues required new laws. Needless to say, for effective principals to practice preventive law and risk management, it is imperative that they seek out current updates on laws, policies, and procedures that affect education. All too often, unfortunately, the need to know is considered *ex post facto*. Effective principals do not wait for legal counsel to provide preservice—they take the time to read, listen, and actively apply what they know to their schools to prevent harm to students and others and to short-circuit incidents that might lead to litigation. Although it is not suggested that principals walk around with Figure 2.1 in their hands, the model presented here gives principals a framework for a mindset in practicing preventive law—an effective way for principals to think about risk and liability prevention as they go about business as usual.

Identifying Risk Is Only the First Step

In the past few years, an unprecedented number of crisis situations have been reported in our nation's schools. Some of these emergencies were caused by natural disasters, others were the result of accidents, and still others the result of violence and malicious or suicidal acts. School districts and individual school administrators are accountable and can be held legally liable for the safety and well-being of students, district employees, and visitors to the district's facilities. The direct and indirect costs when losses occur can be great. Creating and maintaining a safe environment require both an active risk management program—to prevent foreseeable dangers—and an effective crisis management program—to manage the emergency and limit the damage once crisis occurs.

A key element in crisis management is preparedness. Effective response in emergency situations requires structure, order, discipline, and linear thinking and action on the part of crisis managers.

When a crisis appears or is impending, a school district's response is critical. To safeguard resources, certain actions must be preplanned so that responses to crises are prompt and effective. Effective crisis management protects the integrity of the *in loco parentis* responsibilities to students that are inherent in the education enterprise. Effective crisis planning integrates and coordinates school procedures with similar crisis plans at the district, municipal, county, and state levels.

Nearly every industry has career specialists who focus solely on risk analysis and all aspects of prevention, including, among other areas, product liability; cybersecurity; workplace safety; and physical, social, and psychological risks. Some risk is not controllable but measures can be taken to mitigate possible loss when such uncontrollable events occur. Schools located where the possibility of tornados is high would fall into such a category. Educators cannot prevent a tornado from hitting their school, but they can take steps to keep everyone as safe as possible should they find themselves in the path of a tornado.

Schools benefit from the guidance of professionals to minimize serious risks to students and staff. But ultimately it is the responsibility of those working in schools to not only adhere to such professional advice, but acknowledge that their own behaviors and decisions are critical and could become the weakest link in prevention efforts should they fail to properly perform their duties. The point being made is that there are multiple layers of safety and prevention that are in place every day, some layers of which are in place because of well-researched best practices and other layers because everyone is attuned to doing their job. Educators should view safety and prevention as part of an entire system.

James Reason (1990) and his associates devised the "Swiss Cheese Model" used in risk analysis applied to multiple fields, including engineering, business, and health care. The idea of the model is simple—individual slices of Swiss cheese have holes of various sizes, but when multiple layers of the cheese are stacked together, the holes tend to be covered by different slices. When viewing the model in terms of school safety and prevention, we can see that just one strategy of prevention is insufficient, but when multiple strategies are put in place, the systemic effect increases prevention and minimizes risk. If one layer of prevention fails to work, the hope is that a different layer of protection will work, even if it is the final layer.

The Prevention of School Violence

This model applies very well to help conceptualize the efforts to prevent school violence. In the wake of the tragedy of the Columbine school shooting in 1999, twenty years of school violence prevention efforts have been undertaken at the federal law and policy level, state legislative level, and with school-level policies and actions. Many times the public becomes aware of times when potential acts of violence have been prevented, and there are no doubt other acts of violence that have been prevented by some action that school authorities, parents, or the public are unaware of. Unfortunately, despite the two plus decades of such efforts, school shootings did not completely disappear, to the point where one student interviewed on national media after a shooting at her school said she wasn't surprised it happened and knew it was a matter of time (Eltagouri, 2018).

Litigation against school and law enforcement officials is not uncommon in the wake of school shooting incidents, and although costly for such entities, most cases have not resulted in legal liability. Often it is the shooter or the families of the shooter who face legal liability. However, obviously the moral obligation to prevent school violence is paramount for educators.

What we have learned since Columbine are multiple layers of prevention that work and unfortunately also layers that either don't work or are clearly not effective on their own without sufficient other protections in place. Kenneth Trump, a school violence prevention expert, has noted that after Columbine the nation had to play catch-up after years of neglecting school security concerns. He advises that we must be careful not to have knee-jerk reactions or overreactions, because such efforts tend to merely create the perception of increased security instead of an actual increase in security.

School districts at times are caught between the public justifiably wanting the school to do all they can to prevent violence and needing to determine which prevention efforts are effective, practical, cost effective, and least restrictive to students' rights and a positive school culture. Kenneth Trump notes that historically such efforts have a skewed focus on security hardware and products and an understandable desire to "do something; do anything; do it differently; and do it fast (Trump, 2018).

Given this background, and returning to Reason's model, there are prevention strategies that are known to work, especially when layered with a variety of strategies designed to work when another may fail. The overreliance on a single prevention measure is doomed to fail, at times tragically. Prevention measures that rely on human factors, such as antibullying programs and positive school climate initiatives, depend on training, skills in relationship building and sustaining those relationships, a commitment to continual diligence, and a willingness to evaluate and revise as needed. Measures that rely on technical and hardware efforts to prevent violence also require training and people to understand how to use the technology. Such measures can lead to a false sense of security, and it must always be kept in mind that should a technology measure fail, there needs to be some other type of backup plan in place. For example, if a system designed to automatically lock all doors fails, there needs to be a plan to alert all staff in the event they may need to lock their own doors.

> The overreliance on a single prevention measure is doomed to fail, at times tragically.

It is imperative that school districts train school administrators, teachers, and support staff (i.e., secretaries, custodians, and bus drivers) regarding school violence prevention and school security and actively include the community in school emergency planning. Any plan needs to include a working partnership with public safety officials. Working with these groups is paramount, even if at times such groups may appear to have conflicting roles and goals. It has been said that it is much more preferable to be *partners* who work together than to later be *co-defendants* because you didn't.

School crisis plans must be continually revised, accessible, and reviewed thoroughly during professional development. Throwing the crisis plan in a drawer and attempting to thumb through it once a crisis occurs is professional malpractice.

Following are a few important "musts" for school leaders to consider:

- The first and best line of defense is a well-trained, highly alert school staff and student body.

- Prevention efforts should focus on the goal to disrupt the path to violence. Research has shown that over 80% of all school shooting incidents involved the shooter telling someone ahead of time in some manner. Almost no incidents included someone who "snapped," indicating opportunities existed to stop the path to violence.

- School police and resource officers can become a positive culture within the school, but the creation of that positive culture is not created without effort on the part of school officials and law enforcement.

- School administrators should be aware of their own roles to prevent an overreliance on law enforcement to perform functions that fall within the job description of administrators and not police officers.

- Do not overrely on any single threat assessment or profiles because they are not predictive and can be seriously misused.

- Keep in mind that *prevention efforts* are still in effect and in place even during an incident.

- Security is often associated with equipment such as metal detectors, surveillance cameras, and other physical, tangible methods. Although these measures are necessary and play an important part, *such equipment is only as good as the human element supporting or operating it*. When security equipment is used in schools, it must be viewed as a supplement to, but not a substitute for, a more comprehensive school safety program.

- Research has shown the single most effective safety measure for schools is the capability to lock building and classroom doors.

- Gaps in previous emergency plans may include problematic outdated content in the original plans, a lack of training of school staff on emergency plans, and a lack of exercising plans in cooperation with public safety officials. For example, school safety or emergency plans should address preparedness procedures such as lockdowns, evacuations, parent–student reunification procedures, mobilizing school transportation during the school day, emergency communications protocols with parents and the media, and mobilizing mental health services.

- Schools should determine ways to incorporate social media into safety plans, especially since, during a crisis, students (and their parents) will be using social media.

- Schools should work with public safety officials to identify potential staging areas for media, parents, medical personnel, and others who are expected to respond in an emergency.

- School officials should meet annually with public safety officials—police, fire, emergency medical services, and emergency management agencies—to discuss safety, security, and emergency planning strategies.

- Most states mandate practice lockdown drills over the course of a school year in the same manner they practice fire drills, tornado drills, and so on. Keep in mind the traumatic nature such drills may have on students, especially very young children.

- Schools should number each entrance/exit door so first responders can easily identify specific entrances/exits when called to respond to an incident and/or to manage a tactical response. In addition, schools should provide police and fire departments with updated floor plans and blueprints for their reference for tactical responses.

Suggested Risk Management Guidelines

As stated previously, all schools should have a written crisis management plan that includes the specific procedures to be followed in emergencies. The following information is often included in crisis management procedure manuals:

- The purpose, scope, and organization of the manual
- The structure of the crisis management organization, including key contact personnel (most important: who's in charge!)
- Evacuation instructions, including explanations of alarm signals and diagrams of exit routes
- Communication procedures to be followed during and after the emergency
- Potential sites of emergencies
- Appropriate responses to emergencies
- Arrangements for obtaining assistance from emergency service organizations and local government agencies
- Procedures for coordinating use of district resources and personnel during emergencies
- Available district resources
- A system for informing the district of the emergency and for notifying parents or guardians
- Plans for taking the following actions, if appropriate:
  - School cancellation
  - Early dismissal
  - Evacuation
  - Sheltering

In addition,

- Develop, disseminate, and implement a comprehensive crisis management plan that clearly identifies and communicates the procedures to be followed in the event of emergencies.
- Provide training to appropriate personnel to ensure that they will be able to respond promptly and effectively in a crisis.
- Coordinate crisis planning with appropriate district, municipal, and county agencies.

SECTION B. DUTY AND RISK MANAGEMENT

Affirmative Duty of School-Based Personnel in Risk Management and Prevention

A. Duty of Building Administrator (Principal, Head Teacher) to Students and Parents (at a Minimum)

1. Ensure compliance with applicable federal, state, and local laws and regulations; enforce established school policies, procedures, and rules; and establish additional rules, as necessary and appropriate in the particular education environment, to ensure the safety and well-being of students while under the care of the school.

2. Provide effective supervision of the education program (including the development, oversight, and evaluation of appropriate curricular, intracurricular, and extracurricular activities).

3. Promote the hiring of competent administrative, teaching, and support staff appropriately trained in specific disciplines.

4. Provide effective supervision of staff (including the appropriate delegation of authority, formalization and assignment of specific responsibilities, direction of daily work activities, and observation and evaluation of performance).

5. Manage the school's physical facilities and material and financial resources to ensure the maintenance of a safe and productive learning environment.

6. Develop and maintain communication channels and media that promote effective two-way communication about school-related issues (including student progress) between administrators and parents, administrators and teachers, administrators and students, teachers and parents, and teachers and students.

B. Duty of Education Administrator (Associate or Assistant Principal, Dean, Supervisor, Department Chair, et al.) to Students and Parents (at a Minimum)

1. Adhere to applicable federal, state, and local laws and regulations; adhere to and enforce established school policies, procedures, and rules in the performance of assigned duties and responsibilities; and recommend additional policies, procedures, and rules, as appropriate, within the scope of delegated authority.

2. Provide effective supervision of the instructional activities presented by staff members of programs within the scope of delegated authority.

3. Provide effective supervision of all staff members assigned to, or working with, programs within the scope of delegated authority.

4. Facilitate effective two-way communication about school-related issues (including student progress) in programs within the scope of delegated authority, between administrators and parents, administrators and teachers, administrators and students, teachers and parents, and teachers and students.

C. Duty of Teacher to Students and Parents (at a Minimum)

1. Adhere to applicable federal, state, and local laws and regulations; adhere to and enforce established school policies, procedures, and rules in the performance of assigned duties and responsibilities.

2. Develop and present instructional activities that are appropriate to and consistent with the approved education program and specifically designed to increase students' knowledge; facilitate the development of learning skills, life skills, and appropriate social behavior; and prepare students to interact effectively in general society.

3. Provide effective supervision of students participating in instructional activities that are within the scope of assigned responsibility to ensure students' safety and general well-being.

4. Facilitate effective two-way communication about school-related issues (including student progress) in programs within the scope of assigned responsibility, between administrators and parents, administrators and teachers, administrators and students, teachers and parents, and teachers and students.

SECTION C. WORKING WITH THE MEDIA

During and after a crisis, schools need effective communications with the media, employees, students, parents, and the community at large. Postcrisis communications should inform employees and patrons as soon as possible of the extent of the losses caused by the crisis and describe the school district's or school site's short- and long-term recovery plans.

Suggested Risk Management Guidelines

(*Note*: Should be tailored to meet school district policies or procedures)

- Although schools are public buildings, administrators do not have to allow the media on campus.

- Permission must be granted by the administration for members of the press to be on campus.

- Police answer questions regarding criminal investigations. Administrators should focus on what the school is doing to secure student safety and maintain student welfare.

- Identify one school spokesperson.

- Identify and maintain a media staging area. (This should be coordinated with police.)

- Do not let reporters wander.

- Direct all media to the school spokesperson to maintain consistency.

- Prepare factual written statements for the press in cooperation with the police and your school district's community relations personnel. Provide updates, when appropriate.

- Be certain that every media member receives the same information.

- Be accurate. If uncertain, do not speculate. When appropriate, refer media to other agencies, such as the police or the health department.

- Set limits for time and location.

- When giving an interview,

  - Ask in advance what specific questions will be asked.
  - Do not say, "No comment." If an answer is not known, offer to get information and to get back to the reporter. Do not speak "off the record."
  - Keep answers brief and to the point.
  - Emphasize positive action being taken. Turn negative questions into simple positive statements.

- Ensure that the sensitivities of those who are touched by the crisis are respected by the reporters.

- Before agreeing to let staff members be interviewed, obtain their consent.

- Students under the age of eighteen may not be interviewed on campus without parental permission.

- Yearbook and school newspaper photographs are public documents. Access to them must be provided.

ADDITIONAL CASES OF INTEREST TO EDUCATORS

Ratner v. Loudoun County Public Schools, 16 Fed.Appx. 140 (4th Cir. 2001). Courts have upheld zero tolerance policies even when they may disagree with the wisdom of the decisions of the school. In this case, a 13-year-old was expelled after school officials learned the girl had a knife and was contemplating suicide. The court held that federal courts were not "properly called upon to judge the wisdom of a zero tolerance policy" used in the case.

Porter v. Ascension Parish School Board, 393 F.3d 608 (5th Cir. 2004). A student drew a sketch depicting violence toward his school, including a missile launcher and a brick directed at the principal. The sketch never made it to school as it was thrown in a closet at home. Two years later, his younger brother found the sketch pad and took it to school. The original artist was detained by law enforcement and disciplined by the school. The court held that the two-year delay and distance from the school were factors overturning the discipline but granted qualified immunity to the principal.

S.G. v. Sayreville Board of Education, 333 F.3d 417 (3rd Cir. 2003). A young elementary student was suspended for telling a student on the playground "I will shoot you." Because of previous threats at the school and the principal discussing with all students such behavior would not be tolerated, the court upheld the suspension. The court noted that the prohibition of threats by school officials was a legitimate concern of principals and therefore not a violation of First Amendment free speech rights.

Wisniewski v. Board of Education of the Weedsport Central School District, 494 F.3d 34 (2nd Cir. 2007) *cert denied.* The court upheld the suspension of a student, under the *Tinker* standard, who displayed an AOL message depicting a pistol firing at the head of the principal.

Parmertor v. Chardon Local School District, 47 N.E.3d 942 (Ohio 2016). The court noted that the bar for proving gross negligence or willful disregard for student safety in a school violence act is very high and difficult to meet.

DeShaney v. Winnebago County Department of Social Services, 489 U.S. 189 (1989). The U.S. Supreme Court held that generally the Fourteenth Amendment does not impose a duty on the state to protect individuals from acts of private violence.

Castalado v. Stone, 192 F.Supp.2d 1124 (D. Colo. 2001). The state case related to *Columbine* noted that compulsory attendance laws do not create the necessary special relationship to be held in violation of the Fourteenth Amendment. The case also discussed foreseeability and the state created danger theory.

At press time, nearly twenty-five lawsuits had been filed related to the February 14, 2018, school shooting at Marjory Stoneman Douglas High School in Parkland, Florida. For example, see:

L.S. by Hernandez v. Peterson, 982 F.3d 1323 (11th Cir. 2020)

Pollack v. Cruz et al., N. CACE-18-009607-(26) (Fla. Cir. Ct. 2018)

Guttenberg et al. v. The Broward County School Board, 303 So.3d 518 (S. Ct. Fla 2020)

Guttenberg v. FBI and *Schentrup v. FBI*

Israel v. DeSantis, No. 4:19cv576-MW/MAF (N.D. Fla. May 5, 2020)

The following case from the *Sandy Hook Elementary School* tragedy resulted in a finding for the defendants based on governmental qualified immunity:

Lewis v. Town of Newtown, 214 A.3d 405 (Conn. App. Ct. 2019)

CHAPTER 3

Tort Liability

The obligation of the school to provide a safe space can hardly be overemphasized. It is a legal principle with strong and widely spread roots in the ethics of our society. Adults are responsible for the care and protection of children; teachers and administrators are responsible for the care and protection of students. The courts demand a high standard of performance from educators in the area of student welfare. They also expect educators to possess a high standard of reasonable-person traits.

Changes in certain legal doctrines have modified the special status accorded to schools. For example, the doctrine of governmental immunity—protecting the public school from legal liability—has been judicially or legislatively abrogated in many states. Educators' duty has been reduced by statutes that provide qualified immunity for employees or denote liability only for injuries resulting from willful or wanton misconduct; however, schools are still frequently given the same status and held, by the courts, to the same duty as any individual or corporation providing goods or services. The problem facing school districts and, ultimately, teachers and principals is not whether they are immune from lawsuits but whether they can develop solutions to minimize their legal liability.

Tort liability laws are the primary source for the definition of the educator's basic responsibilities for duty and standard of care. Without an adequate knowledge of liability, educators cannot have a clear understanding of their status under the law. Although the major emphasis is on *student* welfare in this chapter, a principal's responsibility *not* to be negligent also pertains to the welfare of faculty, staff, parents, and visitors. The basic concepts are the same. The sections in this chapter are restricted to the tort liability of educators for negligence, that is, the personal liability for injury to students or others for which school personnel may be held accountable under the law.

CONSIDERATIONS RELATED TO COVID-19

COVID-19 has and will influence how school districts approach the issue of standard of care as they take measures to protect students and staff from contracting the virus. Although it may be difficult

(Continued)

to prove how someone has contracted the virus, defending allegations of possible negligence would be expensive. The key will be the definitions of what is considered reasonable efforts to prevent the spread of the virus.

School districts must strictly adhere to HIPAA privacy guidelines but are also tasked with keeping the public informed about the spread of the virus among staff as well as students. Principals should follow local policy but also be very mindful of potential privacy law violations.

In some school districts, the use of facial recognition technology to be used for contact tracing has been considered. Facial recognition technology will bring emerging issues into the school environment and will be unsettled law as the technology grows.

Most states provide qualified immunity to some health-related areas, but it may be unclear how COVID-19 might apply in all circumstances. In addition, insurance policies may not cover liability related to communicable diseases, and it's possible that those that do will be cost prohibitive at renewal due to COVID-19.

It is not known at the time of this publication what the Biden administration will propose in terms of COVID-19 assistance and guidance. There is disagreement regarding liability waivers with some asserting that the waivers will lead school districts to neglect key safety measures and unsafely cut costs, while others say that without such waivers, school districts cannot operate efficiently.

There is no question that COVID-19 has increased costs and changed operating procedures, many of which will remain in place even as the pandemic subsides. Schools will increase costs of cleaning, transportation, insurance, and other expenses while at the same time face the prospect of losing students and funding due to decreased enrollments.

There is also a likelihood that even when conditions return to a more familiar normal, virtual learning will remain and be used in greater numbers than before, as more choose to take advantage of distance learning. What this means in terms of liabilities remains to be seen; however, whether students are learning face to face or virtually, schools will still be expected to achieve student learning outcomes. And the effects of COVID-19 on student achievement and future success are still a great unknown. There will likely be some litigation related to the closure of schools should there ultimately be significant achievement deficits blamed on such closures.

SUGGESTED GUIDELINES FOR PRACTICE

Principals are reminded that even though fault may rest on individual faculty or staff for their actions, depending on the response you take to such actions, the accountability could rest with you. Principals must not increase their own liability through improper action or lack of action in response to incidents that occur on their campus. In addition, often it is not the incident that occurs that becomes the story in the eyes of the public, but instead it is the response by the administration that becomes the focus. It is one thing to be part of a story, it's quite another to actually *be* the story.

Ensure that a higher standard of care and supervision is evident in laboratories, in physical education classes, in contact sports, on field trips, and in areas of student congestion in the hallways.

Ensure that there is a proper supervision plan before the school day begins or after the school day ends and continually evaluate the plan, revising as needed.

Ensure that teachers understand that foreseeability of harm is a critical element in determining negligence in a given situation.

Ensure that personnel take into consideration a student's special needs or limitations, abilities, age,

and pre-existing medical conditions when making supervisory decisions and planning classroom activities.

The purpose of this chapter is to help understand how to minimize risks for others as well as reduce the risks inherent with the job responsibilities of principals.

SECTION A. THE LAW OF TORTS AND THE CONCEPT OF NEGLIGENCE

The law of torts is difficult to define and difficult to understand. Because tort law is essentially the result of judicial decisions—case or common law rather than statutory or legislative law—the study of torts can be inconclusive in answering specific inquiries. Court decisions are primarily of two sorts: (1) interpretation of constitutional and statutory law and (2) application of common law principles. These principles are applied when a particular set of circumstances has not been legislated on and the rights of the parties must be decided by the court on general principles handed down over the years.

The Law of Torts

A *tort* is defined as an actionable wrong against the person, property, or reputation of another, exclusive of a breach of contract, which the law will recognize and set right. Torts are historically classified into three categories:

1. The direct invasion of someone's legal right (e.g., invasion of privacy)

2. The breach of some public duty that causes some damage to an individual (e.g., denial of constitutional rights)

3. The violation of some private obligation that causes some damage to an individual (e.g., negligence)

The underlying concept of torts involves the relationship between individuals. Under our system of law, *individuals have the right to be free from bodily injury whether intentionally or carelessly caused by others*. However, societal changes have caused the courts to define new legal responsibilities between individuals with each litigated verdict. Negligence is the main cause of tort liability suits filed against educators, and due to their more direct contact with students, teachers and principals comprise the class of school employees most likely to have suit brought against them. Judgments in negligence suits can be financially and emotionally crippling.

Tortious actions speak directly to the professional educator through the principle of *in loco parentis*. Although the *in loco parentis* doctrine is continuously challenged, the current interpretation assigns definite responsibility to the school for the welfare of each student it serves in the absence of the student's parent or guardian. With this assignment, society legally assumes that, during the time the student is away from home, the student's interests, welfare, and safety are directed by responsible adults trained as teachers and administrators. Because elementary and most secondary students are legally required by law to attend school, courts usually review very carefully any alleged breach of normally expected *duty and standard of care* by educators. Failure to meet such duty and standard of care is negligent, and the courts may find the educator guilty of a tort.

Within the framework of the tort of negligence, this chapter examines the standards and relationships inherent in the following areas: duty and standard of care, proper instruction, proper supervision, proper maintenance, field trips, postinjury treatment, athletic liability, and spectator safety. Both the framework of negligence and the standards and relationships inherent within this framework are examined under the following concepts, described and defined as follows:

The Concept of the Reasonable and Prudent Person

A reasonable and prudent person, in the eye of the court, is a person who

- Has physical capabilities comparable to the defendant's
- Is of normal intelligence, perception, and memory
- Has a minimal level of experience
- Possesses any superior skills that the defendant possesses or presents as possessing

School administrators and teachers hold college degrees that denote possession of specialized skills and superior knowledge of the teaching and learning process, methods of instruction, and the education environment, and they present themselves to the community as possessing such superior knowledge and skills. School administrators and teachers are, therefore, held to a higher standard of care when fulfilling their professional roles than the average citizen would be in a similar circumstance.

To resolve the question of reasonable standard of care, courts use the model of a reasonable and prudent person. This hypothetical ideal of human behavior embodies the community's ideals and possesses all the special skills and abilities of the defendant. Court dicta provide this generic description:

> The defendant is not to be identified with any ordinary individual who might occasionally do unreasonable things; he or she is a prudent and careful person who is always up to standard. It is not proper to identify him or her with any member of the jury who is to apply the standard; he or she is rather a personification of a community ideal of reasonable behavior, determined by the jury's social judgment.

This abstract being, conceived in the law's imagination, performs under the question of foreseeability.

The Concept of Foreseeability

This concept addresses the "degree to which the defendant could have or should have reasonably been able to anticipate the risk of injury or harm to the plaintiff that might result from the action or inaction" (Alexander & Alexander, 1998, p. 329). Foreseeability regarding the risks inherent in an education setting is greater for educators, because of their superior knowledge, special skills, and professional experience in working in an education environment, than it would be for the average citizen, who is not professionally trained and experienced as an educator. *If the educator could have or should have foreseen or anticipated an accident, the failure to do so may be ruled as negligence.*

The concept of foreseeability expects the educator to perform as a reasonably prudent person of similar training and circumstances should perform. This degree of care is based on the standard equivalent of the age, training, maturity, and experience, as well as any other related characteristics of the educator. The law does not require the educator to be able to see everything that might appear in the immediate future, and the courts do not require the educator to completely ensure the safety of students. Courts do, however, expect educators to act in a reasonable and prudent manner. If the ordinary exercise of prudence and foresight could have prevented an accident, courts have ruled educators to be negligent when they have not avoided a foreseeable danger to students, personnel, and patrons.

The Concept of Standard of Care

The standard of care is the degree of care necessary to protect students from *foreseeable* risk of injury or harm, based on the particular circumstances and the age and mental and physical capabilities of the students. The standard of care required is higher when the students are young and immature. The standard of care required is also higher when the students have diminished mental, learning, or physical abilities. The illustration in Figure 3.1 demonstrates the inverse relationship between duty and standard of care and the age of the student.

COVID-19 has dramatically influenced thinking regarding the standard of care required to prevent the spread of the virus within a school. Clearly, if school districts completely ignored the pandemic and carried on all school operations as they did before the rise of the pandemic, there would be reason to conclude there was an insufficient standard of care being provided for both students and faculty. It's a dilemma, however, to try to understand what needs to be done on the opposite end of this problem, because schools also face criticism from the public for "going too far" with their prevention measures.

Evolving Issues

COVID-19 raises foreseeability issues because the likelihood of students and staff contracting the virus absent precautionary measures is clearly a foreseeable outcome. Courts have been cognizant of burdens placed on educators when determining liability, but such burdens do not relieve educators of the responsibility for their actions or inactions. Educators are responsible for any harmful consequences of their conduct.

Principals and all educators must recognize that over time new areas of focus are created or arise from increased knowledge and awareness. For example, today more attention is given to head injuries and concussions related not only to athletics, but to concussions from all causes. The potentially fatal consequence of food allergies is a growing issue. New antibullying laws mandate the protection of all students. Additionally, the rapid changes in technology availability and usage create situations for principals that were nonexistent only a decade ago.

The Concept of Intentional Torts

An intentional tort is committed if a person, with or without malice, *intentionally* proceeds to act in a manner that impairs the rights of others. Intentional tort actions in the education setting generally involve charges of assault and battery. Assault, simply defined, consists of an overt attempt to place another in fear

FIGURE 3.1 The School's Duty and Standard of Care as Related to Student Age*

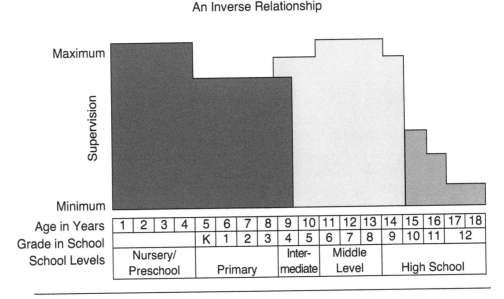

*Students with disabilities require a higher degree of duty and standard of care at all ages and school levels.

The courts routinely differentiate the required degree of duty and standard of care at only two age levels—ages 1 to 14 and ages 15 to 18.

The authors believe that the required degrees of duty and standard of care decrease during the elementary school years, that the onset of puberty and adolescence may require a return to maximum levels of duty and standard of care during the middle school years, and that the required level decreases progressively for senior high school students.

Note: The courts, to date, have held that children under the age of 7 may not be held responsible for their own negligence.

Source: Shoop, R. J., & Dunklee, D. R. (1992). *School Law for the Principal: A Handbook for Practitioners,* p. 157. Allyn & Bacon.

of bodily harm; no actual physical contact need take place. However, when an assault results in physical injury to a person, then battery has been committed.

The Concept of the Age of Plaintiffs

This concept, based on the *Rule of Seven,* is often used to determine the liability for negligence. This legal doctrine requires the court to examine a student's age in determining negligence. Children are expected to exercise a degree of care for their own safety in proportion to their age, capacity, experience, and intelligence. Historically, courts have held that children from birth to age seven cannot be considered negligent under the law. Such children do not realize or understand the degree of care that must be exercised to prevent injury to themselves. Teenagers, on the other hand, are expected to have developed a general understanding of the care required for their own safety.

Common Defenses in Tort Cases

In tort cases that involve accusations of negligence, the first defense would be whether the incident was an unavoidable accident. Additionally, questions would surround the duty owed to the parties involved; whether the action or inaction of the defendant was the proximate cause of the injury; and whether or not there were actual injuries.

Most states have statutes that specify timelines and notice requirements that must be met in order to proceed with a claim, and if those requirements are not met, the claim will not be allowed to move forward in court. Typically states will have statutes of limitations for filing claims, and when the clock starts between an alleged injury and the filing of a claim can be an element of dispute. An example of this requirement is seen in a case where a bricklayer was injured on a construction site but did not realize the extent of his injuries until a required second surgery a year later. A court dismissed his case based on failure to file a timely notice of claim. Although he filed for workers' compensation when the accident occurred, he did not file a court case until the time to do so expired, and the court noted that he understood the extent of his injuries when he filed the workers' compensation claim (*Grajko v. City of N.Y.,* 57 N.Y.S. 3d 11 (N.Y. App. Div. 2017)).

Notice of claim requirements frequently become involved in cases of sexual abuse of minors, raising the issue of when accrual begins—when such abuse occurs or when perhaps years later a victim recalls abuse in counseling or for other reasons. Many states have changed the statute of limitations in such cases to a greater number of years or to even an unlimited number of years.

In most states, claims against school boards must be filed within what could be a short amount of time in order to meet a timely notice of claims. School boards are given time to conduct investigations, collect evidence, and perhaps settle a claim before it reaches a courtroom.

Finally, regardless of the merits and strong evidence in a claim, missing a statutory deadline may be grounds for dismissal of the case. The bottom line is that following the statutory requirements is essential for all parties involved.

Other common defenses are included in the following descriptions:

The Concept of Unavoidable Accident

An unavoidable accident is an event that occurs without fault, carelessness, or omission on the part of the individual involved. While expecting educators to display a high level of care in the performance of their duties, the courts recognize that accidents happen when no negligence has occurred.

The Concept of Assumption of Risk

This common legal defense against negligence is based on the general legal theory that no harm is done to one who consents. Although the consent may be expressed or implied, the legal theory is based on one's ability to understand and appreciate the dangers inherent in the activity. Even though the student voluntarily placed themselves in a position of danger, the defense must show that the student understood the danger, had foresight in regard to the consequences, and accepted the danger. Assumption of risk varies by the activity involved, with high-contact sports being an example where there are elements of known risk involved.

The Concepts of Contributory Negligence, Causal Relationship, and Comparative Negligence

When an injury to a student is sustained as a result of the injured student's own negligence, and this negligence is proved, then the student has contributed to their own injury. Of course, the age and ability of the students involved is a factor to consider regarding the degree to which they contributed to their own injury. In addition, when a student disregards the instruction, warning, or advice of an educator, the student can be held liable for their own injury. To counter a charge of contributory negligence, the student must establish a causal relationship between the negligence of the educator and the injury.

The majority of states permit some recovery under the concept of comparative negligence, in part because many hold the view that it is rather drastic that there would be no damages awarded at all if there is any degree of contributory negligence involved. This legal doctrine prorates the damages to the degree of negligence determined by the court for each party found liable for negligence.

Qualified Immunity

In most states, government entities are provided qualified immunity by statute. The concept is derived from sovereign immunity, and although the United States was not founded on the principle of the divine right of kings, sovereign immunity provides government agencies from liability protections in the performance of their duties. The purpose of immunity is to provide some level of protection for educators to make decisions without being questioned or worried about every possible choice they make while they perform their job duties. Such immunity has a long history, but is also controversial, and more states have moved away from longstanding immunity protections. Similar controversy surrounds immunity afforded to law enforcement practices.

Immunity is not unlimited, and most states distinguish between what are known as discretionary acts and ministerial acts. Discretionary acts are those that require judgment and may afford a degree of qualified immunity. Ministerial acts are those that are required by law or by policy, and failure to perform ministerial acts is not afforded qualified immunity. Frequently in litigation, whether a party was performing a discretionary or ministerial act is a matter of dispute.

As an example, imagine a scenario where a track coach preparing for practice determines that written policy requires athletes to remain indoors if a thunderstorm is approaching. If the coach ignores the policy, the coach might be in violation of a ministerial duty written in the guidelines. Should a student get hit by lightning, it would be likely that the coach would not be afforded qualified immunity because of ignoring ministerial duties.

However, if the athletes remain indoors until the storm passes and the coach then uses his judgment that the danger has passed, the coach was likely performing a discretionary duty. If an athlete were to then go outside but slip on the wet track, it is likely that (absent other factors) the coach would be afforded a level of immunity because in his judgment it was safe to go outside and he was not in violation of any policy when the decision was made.

SECTION B. THE CONCEPT OF NEGLIGENCE AND ITS APPLICATION TO DUTY AND STANDARDS OF CARE

Negligence is a word used commonly to cover a variety of behaviors, actions, and inactions. However, in the legal world, the term is more narrowly defined as follows: The failure to take reasonable care to avoid commissions (actions) or omissions (inactions) that one can reasonably foresee would be likely to injure another. Stated a bit differently, negligence is the failure to exercise the degree or standard of care for the safety or well-being of others that a reasonable and prudent person would exercise under similar circumstances.

The Concept of Negligence

Negligence has been defined as conduct that falls below the standard established by law for the protection of others against unreasonable risk or harm. Four elements must exist to sustain a valid claim of negligence:

1. *There must have been a duty to protect.* Duty is an obligation that derives from a special relationship between the parties involved (teacher and student, principal and teacher, principal and student, and other parties such as parents and visitors). It is the special relationship that creates the duty. While there may be a moral obligation to assist someone who trips and falls in a store

parking lot, a person who just walks by and witnesses the fall does not have a duty owed to the person because they don't have a special relationship. Some states have "good Samaritan" laws that shield from liability those who render aid to those with whom they have no established duty.

2. *A failure to exercise a standard of care must have occurred.* A failure to exercise a standard of care is determined by measuring the actual conduct against the conduct of a reasonable person. The standard of care is relative to the need and to the occasion. What is proper under one circumstance may be negligent under another.

3. *The conduct must have been the proximate cause of the damage.*

4. *An actual loss (injury of some kind) must result.*

The law recognizes the duty of due care that one person owes to another. It requires a certain standard of conduct for the protection of others against unreasonable risks. One has a legal duty to act as an ordinary, prudent, reasonable person in the circumstances. Such duty can be specified by statute or as a matter of common law. The duty and standard of care imposed on school districts demand that the responsibility for protecting the safety of students and employees be accepted and fulfilled. In our litigious society, principals need to recognize their potential liability for negligence.

Suggested Risk Management Guidelines

Ask the following questions in any situation in which a person claims to have suffered an injury (see also Figure 3.2):

1. *Did the defendant have a duty to the plaintiff?* The defendant must have a duty to the plaintiff. Plaintiffs, in actions addressing the school setting, usually have little difficulty in proving that the defendant teacher or principal owes the student a duty.

2. *Did the defendant exercise a reasonable standard of care in their actions?* The defendant must have failed to exercise a reasonable standard of care in their actions. This area is usually the major point of contention, that is, whether or not the educator involved exercised a reasonable standard of care. What makes a reasonable standard varies from person to person and from their own areas of expertise, training, job description, and the circumstances of the situation.

3. *Were the defendant's actions or inactions the proximate cause of injury to plaintiff?* The defendant's actions must be the proximate (direct) cause of the injury to the plaintiff. Even in situations in which a recognized duty is breached by the failure to exercise a proper standard of care, liability will not normally be assessed if there is no causal connection between the actions of school personnel and the injury. Actions that may initially appear to be the proximate cause of the injury may in fact not be supported upon investigation. The action must be a substantial cause of harm and absent any intervening act that may have occurred.

4. *Did the plaintiff suffer an actual injury?* The plaintiff must prove that they suffered an actual injury. Actual injury and proximate cause are usually a matter of fact. For liability to be assessed under proximate cause, negligent conduct of school personnel must be the proximate or legal cause of the injury.

FIGURE 3.2 Risk of Negligence

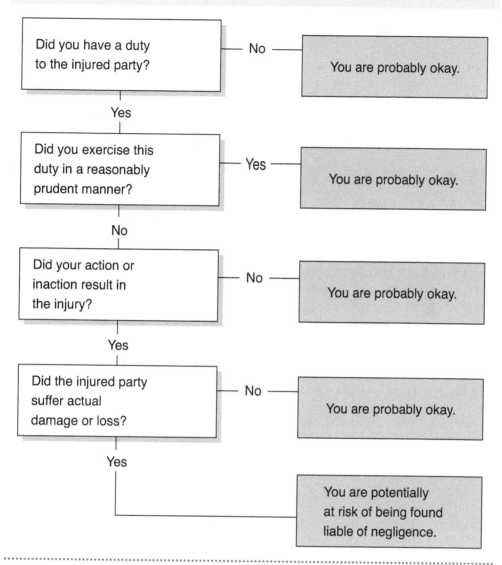

Source: Shoop, R. J., & Dunklee, D. R. (1992). *School Law for the Principal: A Handbook for Practitioners,* p. 270. Allyn & Bacon.

Negligence may occur in one of three ways: nonfeasance, misfeasance, or malfeasance.

1. *Nonfeasance* is the failure to act when there is a *duty* to act. Nonfeasance is an act of *omission,* such as passive inaction, by which an injury occurs due to the lack of protection the law expects of a reasonable individual. In order for nonfeasance to result in liability for negligence, a duty to take positive action or to perform a specific act must be established. This duty may be established by a legal statute or by the relationship (e.g., principal, teacher, and student) between the parties involved.

2. *Misfeasance* is acting in an improper manner. Misfeasance is taking an improper action when there is a *duty* to act and may be either an act of *omission* or an act of *commission.*

3. *Malfeasance* is acting, but guided by a bad motive. Malfeasance is an illegal act that should not be performed at all. It occurs when the individual acts *beyond the scope of duty*. A hypothetical case may illustrate the salient points best. Assume that a teacher administers corporal punishment to a student even though school district policy prohibits a teacher from administering such punishment. The student is injured as a result of the punishment and brings charges against the teacher and others. The court would likely rule for the student because the act was illegal under school district policy.

Examples of Management Cues

Imagine the following scenario during outdoor recess at an elementary school. A group of teachers tasked with supervising recess are standing together talking in a location where they can see the entire playground. Standing from about twenty-five yards away, a teacher sees one of his fifth-grade students climbing the six-foot chain link fence that surrounds the playground. Without question, the teacher has a duty owed to the student who may be injured by climbing the fence. The questions will surround the standard of care exhibited in the following scenarios; if any action by the teacher was the proximate cause of any injury; and if there was an actual injury.

Scenario 1: The teacher observes the student climbing the fence and yells out to him to get off the fence. The student complies.

Scenario 2: After the student gets off the fence, a few minutes pass by and the student climbs the fence again. This time the teacher observes the student but does not yell at him to stop and ignores the behavior. The student gets to the top of the fence, attempts to walk across the top, and falls, breaking his arm.

Scenario 3: When the teacher first notices the student climbing the fence, he yells at the student to stop, and when the student ignores his request, he walks over to the student and tells him directly to get off the fence, and the student complies.

Scenario 4: When the teacher first notices the student climbing the fence, he yells at the student to stop and he does not comply; the teacher then yells at another student who is closer to the fence to tell the student to get down. However, instead, that student pushes the first student off the fence and the climber is injured when he hits the ground.

Scenario 5: The teacher becomes annoyed with the student ignoring his commands to get off the fence and goes over to the fence. When the student still does not comply, the teacher shakes the fence, causing the student to fall and injure himself.

In each of these scenarios, there is no question that the teacher owed a duty to the student because he was required to supervise the playground. It was also foreseeable that the student could be injured climbing the fence. The question surrounds what a reasonably prudent and similarly situated adult (a teacher) would do in each of the scenarios. What actions would likely *not* be what a similarly situated teacher does? Does the fact that in Scenario 4 it was a student who pushed the climbing student off the fence make any difference regarding the potential misfeasance of the teacher? Was it malfeasance in Scenario 5 when the teacher shook the fence since it should have been foreseeable that shaking the fence might cause the student to fall? In fact, what are the implications if the teacher actually wanted the student to fall when the teacher shook the fence?

The above scenarios are not at all out of the ordinary of what happens or could happen in any school on any given day. Should something like this occur, principals would be tasked with investigating the incident and taking any appropriate action if the teacher was responsible in any way for the incident.

As a simple example to understand the concept of duty, imagine the entrance to the school having pools of water from melted snow that has been tracked into the building. A parent enters and nearly falls. She notices a bucket and mop that have been placed by the door, but proceeds to the office. Later a school custodian enters the building and he too nearly falls, but he walks past the bucket and enters his office because it was his morning break time. Minutes later, a student enters the building, slips, and breaks an arm.

In this scenario, the parent owed no duty and had no obligation to use the mop to remove the water. However, the custodian would have a duty based on his job description to attempt to remedy the slick floor. (*Note*: this example is not intended to imply a possible determination of any outcome regarding the custodian, but is merely to show how duty applies differently in the same situation to different people.)

The Concept of Duty and Standard of Care

There are two basic types of duty. The first type exists when the duty is inherent in the situation. *This includes nearly every situation in which an educator has the responsibility to supervise a student.* The second type of duty exists when a person voluntarily assumes or creates a relationship in which no previous relationship existed. An assumed duty exists when an educator acts in a way that leads parents or students to reasonably assume that a supervisory relationship exists.

The school district and the personnel it employs owe a legal *duty* to protect students, employees, and visitors from unreasonable risks of injury. The duty to meet a particular standard of care stems from two primary sources:

The duty may be inherent in the situation or required by statute. Nearly every situation in which an educator engages has an inherent standard of care arising from it. These duties derive from the educator acting *in loco parentis,* acting as a professional, or acting as the administrator. Generally speaking, the school will owe a duty of ordinary care to all personnel, children, and adults involved in educational pursuits, academic or otherwise, if sponsored under the school's authority. This standard is based on an objective test consisting of the standard of conduct demanded under the circumstances, that is, "the reasonably prudent person." The ordinary care standard takes into consideration the risk factor that may be apparent and the circumstances of the situation. The defendant's capacity—based on age, intelligence, knowledge, skill, and so forth—to handle those circumstances is also considered in certain cases.

An educator may voluntarily assume a duty. A person who does not have a legal duty to meet a particular standard of care may incur one by voluntarily creating a relationship with someone else. Assuming a duty commonly occurs in a situation that many schools face: students arriving well before the start of school and staying well after the end of school. Although the principal disapproves of this practice, the principal ignores it, and although aware of the need for supervision, does not provide any. The principal continues to remind parents of the fact that no one is available at the school to provide supervision and that their practice of dropping children off so early in the morning is dangerous. Such a warning appears in the school's back-to-school summer letter as well as in other principal–parent newsletters throughout the school year. But when schools take no action when students arrive thirty to forty minutes prior to the stated arrival time, they may have voluntarily assumed a duty to those students. The "official" arrival time in such instances may not be what is posted, but instead what the school has allowed it to be.

The assumption of duty also plays a role when arming teachers or other staff with weapons. As schools adopt this practice, questions are raised concerning whether school districts have assumed an increased duty to protect students by having nonlaw enforcement personnel armed with weapons. Other questions regarding their training and a protocol for the use of those weapons undoubtedly arise. For example, would a person educated and certified to perform the duties of a teacher, including protecting and nurturing students, be expected to have the same duty and standard of care if, at a second's notice, that same person is expected to perhaps shoot one of their students?

Liability results most often when school personnel fail to meet that reasonable standard of care (breach of duty) while instructing, supplying equipment to, and supervising students. Breach of duty is determined, in part, based on the nature of the activity for which the educator is held responsible. Various school activities require different levels (standards) of care and duty. Questions normally posed by courts regarding an alleged breach of duty and standard of care are

- Whether the conduct of school personnel met the *reasonable person* standard required in a given situation
- Whether school personnel should have *foreseen* possible injury

The fact that a student is injured in a particular situation does not necessarily imply that a breach of duty has occurred. School personnel are not insurers against all possible harm. They are, however, expected to take reasonable steps, based on inherent duty to students, to prevent harm that is reasonably foreseeable. Failure to act in this instance would constitute a breach of duty.

In summary, principals should become aware that educators have been found financially responsible for their professional actions when it has been proven that their actions or inactions led to injury of students or adults. They are responsible for any harmful consequences of their conduct.

Foreseeability and proper instruction that takes into consideration the age, abilities, and needs of students is also a critical factor and is often cited in cases where students are unsupervised in nearly any type of situation. The reasonable person standard is always measured against the actions taken, or not taken, in a given situation.

Finally, keep in mind that educators have been found liable when they use excessive force against a student, especially when such force goes beyond what is allowed by district policy. Educators have also been found liable in bullying and harassment cases where it can be demonstrated they did not protect students or they demonstrated deliberate indifference to the bullying and harassment.

Establishing Guidelines

Establish professional standards that take the *very basic meaning of duty and standards of care* (i.e., application to all citizens) and apply it specifically to the education arena. Simply stated, many problems would be avoided and possible tragedies averted if educators were steadfastly mindful of the following:

- Do not leave students unattended.

- Provide age- and ability-appropriate instruction/supervision.

- Do not put students in privately owned vehicles.

- Know and comply with policies, including school board policies, faculty and student handbooks, crisis management plans, and all other district documents.

Provide guidelines that can be used both in *establishing* sound practices in the area of duty and standard of care and as definitive standards in *measuring* duty and standard of care of educators in a school setting. Such guidelines should be foundational but considered critically important, enforced, taught during professional development, and monitored for compliance and should serve as the *underlying structure* for any other suggested guidelines.

SECTION C. NEGLIGENCE, DUTY, AND STANDARDS OF CARE IN SCHOOL ACTIVITIES

The wide range of activities in which educators are regularly engaged with students and the public creates multiple areas of duty and standard of care. This section looks at the principal's duty and standard of care with regard to proper instruction—ensuring that students are adequately warned of dangers inherent in an activity.

- *Proper supervision—ensuring that an appropriate number of capable adults are providing an adequate level of oversight to protect students and others from foreseeable danger*

- *Proper maintenance—ensuring that equipment, facilities, and grounds are kept in proper repair and pose no foreseeable safety hazards to students and others*

(Continued)

- Field trips—*maintaining the same duty and standard of care that would exist if students were on the school premises*

- Postinjury treatment—*taking appropriate care of a student or other person who is injured on school grounds or while engaged in a school-sponsored event*

- School athletics and spectator safety—*ensuring that participants are properly selected, instructed, and supervised; that equipment and facilities are maintained and safe; and that proper medical attention is available in the event of injury to participants or spectators*

The following addresses each of these areas of potential liability.

The Application of Negligence Law to Proper Instruction

Cases involving various aspects of instruction frequently come before the courts. The most common complaint is that the student did not receive adequate instruction (how to or how not to do something), and as a result of inadequate instruction, the activity caused physical harm to someone. The courts tend to favor those educators who have provided adequate instruction in the proper use of equipment and methods of safety and who have warned students of the dangerous nature of any activity in which injury might occur. Failure to do either—instruct or warn—could be cause for establishing liability for negligence. Though not nearly as common, there have also been cases in which plaintiffs have claimed harm to the intellect—commonly referred to as *education malpractice*—as a result of negligence due to improper instruction.

Authorities agree that instruction involves the teaching of a particular skill as well as instilling in the student the proper behavior for individual and class safety. In *Laveck v. City of Janesville* (1973), the court stated,

> The teacher occupies a position in relation to his pupils comparable to that of a parent to children. He [*sic*] has a duty to instruct and warn pupils in his custody of any danger which he knows or in the exercise of ordinary care ought to know . . . and to instruct them in the methods which will protect them from these dangers. A failure to warn students of such danger or to instruct them in the means of avoiding such danger is negligence.

Educators are expected to select activities appropriate to students' ability to perform and understand and to take into consideration the students' sizes, ages, skills, conditions, or special needs. When an activity entails risks to students, it is not sufficient merely to inform or warn of risks; students must also understand and appreciate the risks. Appreciation is influenced by factors such as experience, mental ability, and the obviousness of the danger.

A lack of ability was alleged, in *Govel v. Board of Education in the City of Albany* (1962), when a junior high school girl was injured during a soccer game. The teacher stated she believed that children were "naturally skilled in running and kicking and did not need an extended session on such skills." The court ruled against the teacher, asserting that "the preparation of students to participate in such an activity required more than a superficial assessment of skill in running or kicking." In similar litigation involving the case of *Ehlinger v. Board of Education of New Hartford Center School District* (1983), negligent instruction was ruled when a teacher failed to follow *state guidelines* for instructing students to take necessary precautions during a physical fitness speed test, and a student was injured.

Age and Condition of Participants

Educators have a responsibility to tailor required activities to the age and condition of students. In *Luce v. Board of Education* (1956), a teacher was found negligent for failing to consider the history of a student's physical condition. The teacher had required an eleven-year-old student who had previously suffered two broken arms to participate in a "rough" activity. The student fell and broke her arm again. The teacher knew of the student's history and had been asked to excuse her from "rough" activities.

Educators must be aware of health issues of students that may impact how they provide instruction and supervision. Food allergies are not merely inconveniences that students must accept, but instead potentially life-threatening situations. Since food products are brought to school each day and shared between students, policies should be put in place to know and identify students with food allergies and to monitor and control items that are brought to school.

Equipment and Materials

Activities that require the use of equipment often give rise to allegations of improper instruction. Although school personnel have a duty to provide appropriate instruction to protect students from unreasonable hazards, students must also act in a reasonable manner. School personnel will generally not be found negligent if students completely disregard the instructions and warning provided as long as they were also properly supervised.

A thirteen-year-old student built a model volcano at his home, then took it to school for a demonstration in the classroom as a science project. He was injured during an encore performance for his schoolmates at the bus stop on the periphery of the school grounds. Although the boy's father had helped him build his volcano, the student claimed that the school was "negligent in supervision, instruction, and warning, since the project constituted academic homework." The court, in *Simmons v. Beauregard Parish School Board* (1975), agreed and held for the student, citing improper instruction as well as improper supervision.

In *Roberts v. Robertson County Board of Education* (1985), a student's misuse of a drill press resulted in a serious head injury to a classmate. The teacher had *not* instructed the students on the use of a specific drill bit, had *not* warned of dangers associated with its improper use, and *was absent* from the shop during the use of the drill. The court found the teacher negligent.

Age, Mental Abilities, and Appreciation of Risk

When a participant is inexperienced, the teacher is required to make a greater effort to communicate any risk. Educators have been found negligent for improper instruction when the student was shown to have had inadequate knowledge to complete the task assigned.

In *Brevard County v. Jacks* (1970), a student with an intellectual disability drowned in a swimming area that had a sudden drop off. Although the area was normally marked by a rope-and-buoy line, the line was not in position on the day of the accident. Instead, there was a sign warning, "Swim at Own Risk." The court ruled that the student was unable to appreciate the dangers of deep water in a swimming area.

Education Malpractice

In the past, almost all cases filed against educators for inappropriate instruction that reached the appellate court level involved *physical harm to the person rather than harm to the intellect*. However, in recent years, plaintiffs have initiated litigation that tests intellectual harm, which can also be related to educational opportunity. So although this chapter limits its discussion to physical harm, it is advisable for the prudent educator to be aware it is likely that when a strong case appears in a more receptive judicial climate, the results may be different from those of past cases in which the courts have generally held to the dicta of the California Court of Appeals in *Peter W. v. San Francisco Unified School District* (1976), which stated,

> Unlike the activity of the highway or marketplace, classroom methodology affords no readily acceptable standards of care, of cause, or injury. The science of pedagogy itself is fraught with different and conflicting theories of how or what a child should be taught. . . . Substantial professional authority attests that the achievement of literacy in the schools, or its failure, is influenced by a host of factors which affect the student subjectively, from outside the formal teaching process, and beyond the control of its ministers. They may be physical, neurological, emotional, cultural, environmental; they may be present but not perceived, recognized, but not identified. [Holding schools accountable] would expose them to the tort claims—real or imagined—of disaffected students and parents in countless numbers. They are already beset by social and financial problems which have gone to major litigation, but for which no permanent solution has yet appeared. The ultimate consequences, in terms of public time and money, would burden them—and society— beyond calculation.

Although related more to alleged lack of resources and not negligent instruction, two recent cases illustrate emerging areas that relate to students receiving appropriate education. In *Gary B. v. Snyder*, 329 F. Supp.3d 344 (Dist. Court. E.D. Mich. 2018), the U.S. Court of Appeals for the Sixth Circuit ruled that children have a constitutional right to a minimum basic education. The suit alleged that the conditions of public schools in Detroit lacked enough resources and opportunities that the schools were "functionally incapable of delivering access to literacy" compared to other school districts in the state. The basis of the case was the right to literacy and could form the basis of other such challenges in the nation. After the ruling of the Sixth Circuit, a settlement agreement was reached that included proposed legislation to provide for literacy-related programs in the Detroit Public School Community District.

In a case that overlaps *Gary B.*, a case from Rhode Island is on appeal at press time for this book. In *Cook v. Raimondo*, Case 1:18-cv-00645-WES-PAS (Dist. Ct. RI 2020), the argument presented by the plaintiffs revisited those presented in *San Antonio v. Rodriguez* in 1973. The plaintiffs assert that there is a Fifteenth Amendment guarantee that all citizens have a right to vote, and under the First Amendment a right to the exercise of free speech, and as Justice Thurgood Marshall noted in 1973, a person cannot exercise those rights without some level of basic education. The central theme of education being necessary for citizenship and democracy is weaved into the argument. An interesting note is that one of the plaintiffs in the case is a child who at the time was in prekindergarten, providing potentially lengthy standing in the case as well as hoping for future benefits should the case be found in their favor.

The following guidelines relate specifically to avoiding the risk of exposure to liability for education malpractice:

- Develop exemplary standards of practice to guide the instructional program.

- Ensure that teachers and other instructional personnel are well prepared and focused on instructional duties.

- Ensure that all required competencies and skills are taught and that curriculum objectives are translated into subject matter actually taught in the classroom.

- Provide remediation programs for students who fail to master required skills and competencies or who have difficulty learning.

- Make informed decisions regarding the appropriateness of curriculum, textbooks, and instructional policies.

- Develop flexible and varied instructional strategies and techniques to meet the individual needs of students.

- Use well-prepared promotion and retention standards as guides to decisions affecting student progress.

- Avoid inappropriate testing procedures that could result in misclassification or inappropriate placement of students.

- Develop appropriate methods to monitor instructional practices.

The Application of Negligence Law to Proper Supervision

One of the most common allegations of negligence directed toward educators is that of *negligent supervision*. It is estimated that nearly one-fourth of negligence cases identify improper supervision as the primary or secondary cause of an injury. Courts recognize that it is impossible for educators to personally supervise every movement of every student every day and that accidents will occur; no amount of supervision can completely prevent such occurrences. Schools are not insurers of student safety but owe a duty to adequately supervise students in their care and can be held liable for foreseeable injuries proximately related to an absence of adequate supervision.

Educators, however, are expected to exercise a reasonable degree and quality of supervision and to be physically in the general vicinity, fulfilling the responsibilities associated with the supervision assignment. In the absence of board of education policy, principals have a duty to promulgate rules for their schools, and with teachers and other employees, they have the duty to enforce reasonable and lawful rules established for the safety of students and others.

Schools must provide competent supervision in sufficient quantity to cover the supervisory needs of the situation. Liability arising from supervisory activities is not limited to the failure to provide competent supervision. Situations occur when competent supervision has been provided but, for various reasons, the supervisor is absent when an accident occurs. Liability in such cases usually depends on the foreseeability of an accident. If the supervisor's presence at the time of the injury would not have prevented the injury, there is likely to be no liability. However, if the accident was foreseeable and the supervisor's presence would have prevented the injury, the principal, teacher, or other school employee may be subject to litigation.

Activities and School Areas That Increase Risks

Student participation in school-related hazardous activities requires a great deal of careful supervision by school personnel; similarly, some areas in the educational setting have a greater risk of student injury associated with them than do others. Educator negligence in supervising such activities is generally predicated on a failure to instruct the student properly in the correct use of a dangerous instrument or to warn of the inherent dangers associated with an activity or experiment. The most prevalent forms of hazardous activities involve vocational training, science experiments, cooking classes, physical education, playground activities, and athletic or intramural activities.

Teachers and principals need to maintain a special awareness of the risks associated with high-risk areas in and around the school and provide such supervision as would be reasonable and prudent under the circumstances.

Principals should also be mindful that risk areas continually change. For example, students may change the popular areas of school that they congregate at various times. Special activities may bring groups of students to campus from other schools that require some type of supervision. Construction, renovations, or other physical plant concerns are reasons to take appropriate additional measures to ensure the safety of students and staff.

Specific Supervision and General Supervision

Establishing the standard of supervision is difficult. What may be adequate in one situation may not be so in another. Specific supervision is required when students are unfamiliar with an activity or when an activity is unusually dangerous. The need for specific supervision is frequently related to the age of the student. General supervision is all that is required under normal situations. During playground time, general, rather than specific, supervision is usually adequate.

In *District of Columbia v. Royal* (1983), a six-year-old student was injured at a construction site next to the elementary school in which remodeling was being done. School officials knew of the potential dangers at the site, and although they

THE PRINCIPAL'S QUICK-REFERENCE GUIDE TO SCHOOL LAW

reminded students daily to stay away from the area, they took no other precautions to protect students. The court found against the school, citing negligent supervision.

Unattended Classroom or School Area

A difficult determination of proper or improper supervision occurs when teachers leave the classrooms for which they are responsible. A primary responsibility of a teacher is to provide supervision for the classroom. After a teacher's classes have been accounted for, secondary duties, such as hall, cafeteria, or playground assignments, may be assumed. Court dicta concerning this area of supervision demonstrate the importance of classroom supervision but at the same time are somewhat ambiguous. One element that is important is related to the ministerial or discretionary duties that are assigned to a particular situation.

The Application of Negligence Law to Proper Maintenance

Like other entities, school districts have an obligation and a common law duty to keep school premises, including grounds, facilities, and equipment, reasonably safe and in good repair. Courts have awarded damages to students, parents, school employees, and visitors who have been injured as a result of defective conditions on school-owned property when school employees were aware of, or should have been aware of, hazardous conditions and did not take the necessary steps to repair or correct such conditions.

Proper and Preventive Maintenance

The courts hold school district personnel liable for injury when they "knowingly" leave or provide a dangerous instrument exposed in a place likely to be frequented by children who, because of their age or other special condition, cannot realize or appreciate the danger. The age of the child and the child's ability to comprehend danger are always debatable issues in court, and there are a number of interpretations of age and ability when proper maintenance is litigated. Schools owe a duty to the public to take all necessary positive steps to ensure that buildings and grounds are free of any potentially hazardous conditions.

A school district has the affirmative duty to exercise reasonable care not to provide equipment that it knows or has a reason to know is dangerous for its intended use. Some jurisdictions have rephrased this standard of care, requiring an affirmative duty to supply effective equipment. Although most defective equipment suits involve playground equipment, schools have been sued, for example, for supplying defective blankets, gymnastic apparatus, football equipment, playground toys, and hockey helmets.

Occasionally, the nature of the subject matter being taught by the teacher requires students to use special apparatus. Such devices may present a hazard to student safety, especially if improper equipment is used or if the equipment is not maintained in proper working order. Teachers and others have been held responsible not only for the activities associated with a program but also for not preventing accidents caused by the unsafe condition of equipment and facilities.

The increased use of and the intricacy of equipment in today's education programs require more care on the part of educators to avoid possible injury. As a result, courts view such care as a primary responsibility of schools and generally rule that schools have a duty to provide safe equipment and comprehensive instruction to ensure its proper use. Furthermore, as the age of the school site or the size of the student population and number of activities increase, the possibility is greater that defective equipment and unsafe conditions exist. Courts tend to favor the injured student or adult in cases in which school officials know that dangerous equipment or unsafe facilities exist and fail to remedy them.

The courts define inspection of equipment and facilities as a general *daily* responsibility. Inspections must include the building and grounds, fixed and movable equipment, floors, lighting fixtures, and seats. It is teachers' and principals' responsibility to report any dangerous condition that needs to be corrected and to modify programs to isolate hazards until proper corrections have been made.

In *Ardoin v. Evangeline Parish School Board* (1979), a Louisiana appellate court found a school district negligent in the case of a student who fell and injured his knee while running bases in a physical education class. The student claimed that the school was negligent because school personnel knew of a concrete slab that protruded about an inch above the surface of the ground on the path between two bases. The slab, the student claimed, constituted such a hazardous condition that it was a breach of the standard of care required of the school to allow it to exist on the playground. The court ruled in favor of the student.

Nuisance

Under common law, people cannot press for an action in tort for a nuisance unless the plaintiffs can show that they were injured due to negligence. One example is litigation concerning school roofs, which have frequently been an attraction for children to climb. In *Barnhizer v. Paradise Valley Unified School District No. 69* (1979), the case involved a thirteen-year-old student who died from injuries after falling from the school roof. The court ruled against the district for negligence, for maintaining an attractive nuisance, and for not preventing students from climbing to the roof.

The legal status of one who is injured is also important in deciding claims of nuisance. The general rule is nonliability for injuries suffered by an adult trespasser. Liability has been found, however, when the trespasser is a youth who, because of their age, cannot perceive the danger of an attraction.

An *attractive nuisance* is seen by the courts as an unprotected, unguarded, unsafe condition that may attract a child to play. Schools can be held liable for allowing a nuisance to exist. For example, a first-grade student arrived in the school yard before school and began swinging on the monkey bars. Located adjacent to the bars was a tetherball pole about ten feet in height. When the student reached the top of the bars, she grabbed the pole and attempted to slide to the ground. Attached to the center of the pole was a screw that protruded approximately one-and-a-half inches and lacerated the inside of the child's thigh when she slid over it. In *Givens v. Orleans Parish School Board* (1980), the plaintiff alleged that the location of the tetherball pole in such close proximity to the monkey bars provided an "attractive nuisance" for the student. The court agreed and ruled in favor of the child and her parents.

The Application of Negligence Law to Field Trips

Field trips are school-related activities that take place away from school grounds. The legal obligation of educators to exercise reasonable care and supervision of students so that they will not be at risk on such trips is the same as in any other site-based supervisory situation. Field trips, including athletic events, are considered extensions of the school. Just as in the classroom and in the school, negligence on a field trip leaves the educator open to court action. Schools owe the same duty of care and supervision to take reasonable precautions to avoid foreseeable injuries to students who participate in mandatory field trips and excursions as would be owed to the students during the normal school day.

Control of Students

The assessment of liability on field trips, during which students are taken into unfamiliar situations, often turns on whether the students are on the premises solely for their own benefit or the host organization derives some benefit from the visit. In general, three legal statuses of students are recognized by law:

- *Invitees,* when the host organization has invited the group. Invitees are due a higher standard of care from the host organization than licensees.

- *Licensees,* when permission has been granted, on request from the educator, to visit or perform. Licensees visit the premises at their own peril, because the permission to visit does not carry with it the same standard of care as in the case of invitees.

- *Trespassers,* when no permission has been granted to students to visit the premises. An example would be if, during a field trip, students decided on their own to visit a site without the permission or knowledge of the supervisor. Trespassers have little, if any, protection when on property without permission, unless it can be proved that the site was an attractive nuisance to the students due to their age and inexperience.

Foreseeability and Warning

School personnel have a duty to protect the health and safety of students while they are in their charge. Consequently, when students are injured, it is common to inquire whether the injury is due to a breach of this duty by a school employee. If a student is injured while on a field trip, educators may be able to prove that they took reasonable care if they can demonstrate that they visited the site prior to the trip to determine, in advance, that dangers might be involved (foreseeability) and that students were warned (proper instruction) beforehand.

In cases pertaining to breach of duty in field trips, lack of supervision is commonly demonstrated. In one case, a mentally challenged student member of a Special Olympics team was killed while walking with a group three blocks to a gymnasium. The student was accompanied by one teacher while another teacher followed in a car. The student ran into the street at a busy intersection and was struck by a car. The parents of the student claimed that the teachers were negligent by exposing the student with a disability to unreasonable and foreseeable risk of injury. The parents further claimed that the school failed to provide an adequate number of supervisory personnel and to select the safest route. The court found in favor of the parents in *Foster v. Houston General Insurance Co.* (1981).

Waiver of Liability (Permission Slips)

Although requiring permission slips may provide certain public information or psychological advantages, permission slips or other forms of releases should *not* be considered a waiver of liability. Parents cannot waive liability for damages which they are not aware of. Although in some instances the parent may waive liability, there is some disagreement whether the parent can waive the rights of the child to recover damages for an injury. Therefore, even with a release, students may still sue for injuries they sustain.

School districts cannot be absolved of their obligation toward students by a parental waiver or release. It may be that the waiver of the parent may affect only the liability arising from the act of taking the students on the trip itself. However, the above facts of law do not mean that some form of permission slip should not be used. To a certain degree, the liability may be diminished with a signed document from a legal guardian granting permission to participate in the activity. Such releases have been seen by some courts as evidence of acknowledgment of some level of assumption of risk for the activity.

A high school band member drowned in a hotel pool while on a trip with the band. The student dove into the water and minutes later was found at the bottom of the pool. Two chaperones who were supervising the pool activity gave immediate mouth-to-mouth resuscitation until an ambulance arrived. The parents of the student claimed negligence in failure to provide adequate supervision for their son, who did not know how to swim. The father, however, had given written permission to use the pool and did not inform anyone that his son could not swim. The court in *Powell v. Orleans Parish School Board* (1978) ruled in favor of the school, citing the age of the student, proper supervision on the part of the field trip sponsors, and negligence on the part of the father.

Errands

Although it is common practice for educators and other school employees to send students on errands for them, there is no legal authority for educators to use students in this manner. When a student is sent on a personal or school-related errand for a school employee, and the student suffers an injury while on the errand, the legal question that arises is whether the school acted reasonably in sending the student on the errand. What constitutes reasonable action depends on the circumstances of each case. Also important is the fact that, while on an errand for the school employee, the student may be classified as an agent of the school and the liability for any damage done to, or caused by, the student may fall on the school. Such actions may fall under the doctrine of state-created danger, which is discussed later in the chapter.

Transportation

The most common area of field trip litigation relates to transportation—both that which is provided by teachers or principals and that which is contracted for, such as public or private bus service. When schools undertake to provide transportation service for students to or from any school activity, the school's duty of care regarding that transportation is at least equal to that owed on the school premises. When transportation is provided by independent contractors, duty and liability rest with them rather than with the school, except when it comes to proper supervision of students, which is still the duty of the educators present.

The issues of duty and proximate cause are not quite so clear when schools play an intermediary role in organizing, arranging, or sanctioning the transportation of students by private vehicle. The issue of parental responsibility when driving on school-sponsored field trips was addressed in *Sharp v. Fairbanks North Star Borough* (1977), in which the court stated that "the duty of care, and the liability for negligence which proximately causes injury to a student, shifts from the school to a parent who undertakes to provide transportation for school children other than his own." Schools do not so easily avoid liability when supplementary transportation to school activities is provided in vehicles operated by school personnel or by students themselves and is arranged or sanctioned by school officials. Schools may be bound under the doctrine of *respondeat superior* with regard to their employees or by their duty to exercise reasonable care in the selection, approval, and supervision of student cars and drivers.

The Application of Negligence Law to Postinjury Treatment, Athletic Liability, and Spectator Safety

The common use of the term *first aid* refers to the immediate and temporary care given to the victim of an accident or sudden illness in order either to sustain the life of the injured person or to prevent further injury. Educators have a duty to provide the degree of assistance to injured students under their supervision commensurate with their training and experience. *Although courts do not expect educators to be physicians, they do expect people who work with children to be able to administer life-saving first aid whenever needed, as long as the emergency care is rendered in a proper and prudent manner.*

School officials have the duty to render first aid and the duty not to render anything more than first aid. Although educators are not authorized to provide general medical treatment to students, they have a duty to administer emergency aid. Either lack of action or unwise action may lead to an allegation of negligence against the educator. In some states, Good Samaritan laws shield individuals providing treatment in emergency situations from liability. Because of the special duty of care required in the student–educator relationship, such laws often do not indemnify school personnel from liability for unreasonable action. Courts have recognized that public policy considerations dictate an obligation to ensure that medical treatment given by a school is competently rendered.

Although educators have the responsibility to implement acceptable and careful procedures, they cannot diagnose or treat injuries past the emergency state. When an emergency is indicated, educators are obligated to do the best they can relative to the amount of training and experience they possess. The range of postinjury treatment may be summed up with the generalization that educators are required to take appropriate steps in the case of an injury to a student or visitor but may be held liable if an attempt is made to help too much—or if they fail to do enough.

Millions of students engage in some type of interscholastic sport each year. Although educators may be somewhat comforted by the available defense of assumption of risk if a participant is injured, an athletic participant may generally assume the risks inherent in a particular sport but not the risks resulting from educator negligence. In applying the concept of negligence specifically to school athletics, a major consideration is the duty educators owe to the participant to

- Provide proper and adequate instruction and supervision
- Provide and maintain safe facilities and equipment
- Provide proper medical attention
- Reasonably select and match participants

When an athletic injury occurs, educators often turn to the defenses of contributory negligence and assumption of risk for protection from liability. Of the two defenses, assumption of risk appears to be the most successful. However, assumption of risk does not have universal acceptance in the courts. In some states, it has been expressly abolished on the basis that reasonableness of conduct should be the basic consideration in all negligence cases. Nevertheless, if a school district or school employee has been negligent in duty and standard of care, neither defense would probably be upheld by a court. Students assume only the *known* risks inherent in a particular athletic activity.

Increased awareness and medical knowledge about the dangers of concussions require school principals and policy makers to respond accordingly. Since 2009, forty-nine states have passed laws on concussions in sports, often called Return to Play Laws. Most of these laws include requirements to educate coaches, parents, and athletes regarding concussions; removing the athlete who is believed to have a concussion; and requiring permission from a medical professional in order to return to play.

Awareness of the seriousness of head injuries and concussions related to football was raised significantly by a settlement agreement in 2015 between the National Football League and the NFL Players Association to diagnose and compensate former players who may develop brain disorders related to playing the sport. The settlement does not directly impact school-age students playing football or other sports; however, there are lessons to be learned for school districts as they care for their student athletes, and the awareness of the seriousness of the issue brought major changes in rules and school athletic governing associations.

Proper instruction is especially important in high-contact sports, as improper technique can be a significant cause of increased risk. Note that intentionally teaching improper technique would bring additional liabilities, possibly including criminal charges.

Express assumption of risk, in which students and their guardians sign waivers of liability for claims against the school district and school personnel for their negligence, is generally useless. Although these waiver forms are contracts, minors can disavow most contracts at will. Waivers signed by parents, guardians, and adult students also are generally unenforceable because they are usually contrary to public policy.

Courts have also recognized that education institutions have a duty toward spectators. Even in states that provide government immunity, dangerous facilities fall outside of most immunity provisions. Spectators must be able to have confidence that physical structures, walkways, and other facilities are safe and well maintained. In addition, crowd control procedures must be apparent, and appropriate first aid must be available.

Courts have also recognized that schools have similar duties toward spectators, in terms of supervising events, providing and maintaining safe facilities and equipment, and providing first-aid assistance when needed.

Two areas of concern that can be somewhat perplexing to an educator can be seen in the following questions:

1. When an athletic injury occurs, are the defenses of contributory negligence and assumption of risk adequate for protection from liability?

2. What responsibilities, if any, does the school have in providing a safe place for spectators?

Postinjury Treatment: Failure to Act Versus Proper Action

As long as educators administer emergency care in a proper and prudent manner, the courts appear to favor the educator. In such circumstances, both duty and the reasonable person standard are important. While all educators owe a duty to protect all students, what may be a reasonable action by a licensed school nurse may be viewed differently from reasonable actions by a staff member not generally expected to know how to treat a student injury.

Administering Medication and Medical Marijuana

Educators and school personnel regularly find themselves being asked to give medication to students during school hours. School personnel are not medical professionals and need to restrict their administration of medication and any medical procedures to those that they are trained and authorized to conduct, in accordance with school district policies and procedures. To ensure the safety of school children and minimize the administration of medications to children during the school day, each school district should develop guidelines.

An emerging issue for educators is policy related to medical marijuana in schools (Weiler & Westbrook, 2020). A majority of states in 2021 allow for not only recreational marijuana but prescription medical marijuana, including prescriptions for minors. The dilemma for schools rests on the policies and protocols for students who may have a prescribed marijuana dose during the school day. School nurses may be in a position to choose between following one set of state laws that go against federal laws that are still in existence that prohibit all forms of marijuana.

Schools must develop their own policies related to their state statutes, and most states have guidelines that either have a parent come to administer the prescription or that the medical marijuana must come in a nonsmoking form. Marijuana use, both medical and recreational, in the educational space, will continue to be an evolving issue for many years, especially as more states relax their prohibitions on such use.

General Guidelines for Administering Medication

These are general guidelines—more specific guidelines may be available from the state department of health in particular states.

- Require that written requests from the parent or guardian and from the physician or dentist accompany any medication to be administered, including over-the-counter drugs such as aspirin, ibuprofen, and cough medicine. Make these forms available for convenient access for parents on school and district websites.

- Require the physician request form to be dated and to identify the time of day medication is to be given and the anticipated number of days.

- Require that any changes in the type of drug, dosage, or time of administration also be accompanied by new physician and parent permission signatures.

- Require that the medication be provided to the school in the original prescription container.

- Require that registered nurses, physicians, or dentists be responsible for overall administration of medication in the schools. Delegate administration to a licensed practical nurse or unlicensed staff member only after an initial assessment by the school nurse.

- Limit medications to be administered by school personnel, if possible, to oral or topical medications, except in emergency situations. Exceptions might include the administration of eye drops, ear drops, and rectal suppositories.

- Prohibit school personnel from maintaining supplies of over-the-counter medications on school premises including athletic areas, unless a prescription is provided along with written parent permission to administer.

- Keep an individual and comprehensive record of any medication administered to students and keep all medication in a locked container.

- Require that all medications be inventoried at least once a semester by a licensed health care professional.

- Have parents pick up out-of-date medications or destroy them. Seal needles and syringes in a puncture-proof container and dispose of properly.

- Provide all local physicians and dentists with the school board-approved policy regarding administration of medication and conduct of medical procedures at school. Make the school district's request for administration of medication forms readily available to local health care professionals.

Athletics and Spectator Safety

- Provide adequate instruction and warning to students and parents.

- Provide adequate supervision of athletic participants and all other sports-related student organizations (e.g., cheerleaders).

- Ensure that only proper equipment is used and that proper maintenance of equipment takes place.

- Practice only reasonable matching of participants.

- Hire and retain only qualified athletic personnel and trained coaches. Even if allowed by state athletic associations, state law, or regulations, be especially cautious allowing "volunteer coaches" in any capacity.

- Ensure that there is proper supervision, including formal evaluation, of adult personnel by administration.

- Restrict activities to proper facilities and playing fields.

- Ensure that proper health care is available to participants and that participant fitness and health are monitored. Require medical examinations prior to allowing students to participate in athletic activities.

- Ensure that all school athletics and activities are conducted in compliance with statutory guidelines, regulations, safety rules, and eligibility requirements.

- Provide proper and safe transportation to athletic and other extracurricular school activities.

SECTION D. STATE-CREATED DANGER AND DELIBERATE INDIFFERENCE

School District Liability at the Federal Civil Level
Based on the Fourteenth Amendment's Due Process
Clause and Section 1983 of Chapter 42 of the U.S. Code

Procedural due process generally specifies how government actions are to be applied and requires that specific safeguards be satisfied before a government action affecting life, liberty, or property can take place. In contrast, *substantive due process*, generally defined, is a protection requiring such government actions to be fair and reasonable in content as well as application. When a government action is both unfair or unreasonable and damaging to life, liberty, or property, it is said to violate substantive due process.

In school-based cases, plaintiffs' claims typically center on school districts' failure to take steps that would have prevented dangerous situations that, as a result, had adverse impacts on people's Fourteenth Amendment rights. Plaintiffs typically claim that they have an affirmative right to government protection from danger under the Due Process Clause. Courts have recognized such an affirmative right when a "special relationship" exists between a state and the individual or when a "state-created danger" exists (*Deshaney v. Winnebago County Department of Social Services*, 1989).

As an example, the Eighth Circuit Court recognized two distinct situations in which they believe the state owes an affirmative obligation to protect its citizens. They noted that the Due Process Clause imposes a duty on "state actors" to protect and care for citizens (1) "in custodial and other settings in which the state has limited the individuals' ability to care for themselves" and (2) "when the state affirmatively places a particular individual in a position of danger the individual otherwise would not have faced." As early as 1988, they stated in *Wells v. Walker* that "state actors have an affirmative duty to protect citizens in situations of danger creation." In 1996, in *Doe v. Wright,* they reaffirmed their 1988 statement, noting that "[t]his court has held that the Due Process Clause imposes a duty on state actors to protect citizens . . . when the state actor creates the danger."

Plaintiffs seeking to file their complaints in a federal, rather than a state, court often allege, in addition to their claim of a violation under the Fourteenth Amendment, that the school district violated their rights under Section 1983 of Chapter 42 of the U.S. Code, which states,

> Every person who, under the color of any statute, ordinance, regulation, custom, or usage, of any State . . . subjects, or cause to be subjected, any citizen of the United States or other person within the jurisdiction thereof to the deprivation of any right, privileges, or immunities secured by the Constitution and laws, shall be liable to the party injured in an action at law, suit in equity, or other proper proceeding for redress.

This clause, commonly referred to as Section 1983, has had a huge impact on the federal court system. Included in that impact are cases that have a direct bearing on public education. Vodak (1999) noted, for example, "mistreatment of school-children, deliberate indifference to medical needs, and the seizure of property without advance notice or sufficient opportunity to be heard." Courts have held school employees to be proper "persons" subject to suit under Section 1983 (*B.M.H. v. School Board of the City of Chesapeake,* 1993). The Supreme Court stated that "acting under the color of state law" traditionally requires that a defendant "exercised power possessed by virtue of state law and made possible only because the wrongdoer is clothed with the authority of state law" (*West v. Atkins,* 1998).

Although litigation based on federal violations under Section 1983 is not new, in 1989, the U.S. Supreme Court issued a decision in *Deshaney v. Winnebago County Department of Social Services,* and in one sentence of the language (dicta) of its overall opinion, generated the theory of state-created danger:

> While the state may have been aware of the dangers that Joshua faced in the free world, it played no part in their creation, nor did it do anything to render him any more vulnerable to them.

Although the Court in the *Deshaney* case found no liability, other courts have taken this language and "turned it on its head to create a new theory of liability" (Levin, 2000). Since the *Deshaney* case, many federal courts have grappled with this new theory of liability, its application, and the consequences of using the Due Process Clause of the Constitution as a conduit for state liability.

In 1995, the Third Circuit Court, in *Mark v. Borough of Hatboro,* adopted the theory of state-created danger and developed a four-part test to determine whether a claim under this theory has validity. Plaintiffs alleging state-created danger must demonstrate that the following four elements exist within a cause of action:

1. The harm to the plaintiff was ultimately foreseeable and fairly direct.
2. The state acted in willful disregard for the safety of the plaintiff.
3. There existed some relationship between the state and the plaintiff.
4. The state used its authority to create an opportunity that otherwise would not have existed for the third party's crime to occur.

Other courts have summarily added to this list of elements by including dicta that incorporate such fundamentals as a showing by the defendants of deliberate indifference to the rights of the plaintiff(s) by the conscious or reckless disregard of the consequences of their acts or omissions. For example, in *Huffman v. County of Los Angeles* (1998), the Ninth Circuit Court noted, "[T]he danger-creation plaintiff must demonstrate, at the very least, that the state acted affirmatively and with deliberate indifference in creating a foreseeable danger to the plaintiff, leading to the deprivation of the plaintiff's constitutional rights [under the Fourteenth Amendment]."

The key to state-created danger cases lies in the defendants' culpable knowledge and conduct in affirmatively placing the plaintiffs in a position of danger, effectively stripping the plaintiffs of their ability to defend themselves or cutting off potential sources of aid. In other words, to be held liable, the environment created by the defendants must be dangerous; they must know that it is dangerous; and they must have used their authority to create an opportunity that would not otherwise have existed in which the plaintiff suffered harm. Beyond this prevailing concern, the elements, as more simply described in *Johnson v. Dallas Ind. School District* (1994) and again in *Armijo v. Wagon Mound Public Schools* (1998), are as follows:

- Plaintiff was a member of a limited and specifically definable group.
- The defendant's conduct put the plaintiff at substantial risk of serious, immediate, and proximate harm.
- The risk was obvious or known.
- The defendant acted recklessly in conscious disregard of that risk.
- Such conduct when viewed in total is "conscience shocking." In *Hayes v. Faulkner County, Arkansas* (2004), for example, the Eighth Circuit Court noted, in a prison-related case, that "[d]eliberate indifference to prisoner welfare [or a student's welfare] may sufficiently shock the conscience to amount to a substantive due process violation."

Although the theory of state-created danger is unresolved and still being contested in federal courts across the country, it is wise for educators to be aware of this particular premise of negligence and add this knowledge to their practice of risk management. Some examples provide a better idea of how all of the above might fit into a school environment.

In *Armijo v. Wagon Mound Public Schools*, a special education student with known suicidal tendencies was suspended from school and driven home, without parental permission or notification, to an empty house with accessible guns. He fatally shot himself. In this case, the Tenth Circuit Court found that the school's conduct in suspending the student, taking him home, and leaving him alone with their knowledge of his fragile mental state had increased the risk of harm to the student. In taking such actions, the school officials acted in conscious disregard for the student's safety, and their conduct could be viewed as conscience shocking.

In a particularly egregious case, school authorities devised a plan with a fourteen-year-old girl to be used as "bait" to catch a student who was a known sexual harasser and was known to have victimized the girl in the past (*Hill v. Madison County School Board,* No. 14-12481 (11th Cir. N.D. Al. 2015)). Under school policy, a student could not be disciplined for sexual harassment unless "caught in the act." The plan was to have the girl lure the boy into a restroom and school officials would follow and intervene. Unfortunately, although the girl did what was requested of her, the school authorities did not, and she was raped in a school bathroom. The student was disciplined multiple times for different sexual harassment incidents, and there were rumors that the student had been soliciting girls to meet him to have sex during school hours. After the girl told a teacher aide that she was approached to have sex, the aide told her that she should agree to meet him in order to catch him in the act. Initially the girl said she didn't want to do that, but a few minutes later said she would.

The aide and the girl went to an administrator's office and told her of the plan. Although the administrator seemed disinterested, she did not stop them or inform them not to proceed. When the girl went into the bathroom with the student, the teacher aide could not find which bathroom they were in, and it took several minutes and other staff members to find the students.

The case took a lengthy legal course through the courts. The plaintiff student lost her lawsuit against the school board and administrators at the district court level, but that decision was reversed on appeal. The appellate court held that a female student sexually assaulted by another student could proceed to trial on her Title IX claim against the school board. The court reasoned that Title IX applied because there was evidence presented that a jury could reasonably conclude that the school knew that the harassment by the student was sufficiently severe, pervasive, and objectively offensive to deprive the victim of educational opportunities.

Although this case was not decided on the doctrine of state-created danger, it is illustrative for school principals in educational terms. Had actions taken, and not taken, by school officials never occurred, the rape of the student, at least in this instance, would not have happened.

ADDITIONAL CASES OF INTEREST TO EDUCATORS

Hutchison v. Toews, 4 Or.App. 19, 476 P.2d 811 (1970). An injured student with knowledge of risk involved is contributorily negligent. The case involved two students who removed chemicals stored in a locked cabinet that they knew would cause an explosion.

Richard v. St. Landry Parish School Board, 344 So.2d 1116 (La. App. 1977). A teacher went home and left students unsupervised after school in her classroom.

One student found a knife in an unlocked drawer and cut himself. A court determined that leaving students in the classroom was not the proximate cause of the injury to the student.

Hunter v. Board of Education, Montgomery County, 439 A.2d 582, 292 Md. 481, 292 Maryland 481 (1982). An educational malpractice case where parents claimed that their child was negligently tested and misdiagnosed which resulted in misplacement in school that caused embarrassment and declining school performance.

Simonetti v. School District of Philadelphia, 308 Pa.Super. 555, 454 A.2d 1038 (1982). A momentary absence from classroom by a teacher does not constitute negligence. Upon returning from recess, the teacher was standing at the classroom door and inside the room a student was injured by a pencil that propelled from the hand of a student who tripped and fell.

Fallon v. Indiana Trail School, 148 Ill.App.3d 931, 102 Ill.Dec. 479, 500 (N.E.2d 101 1986). A trampoline is not abnormally dangerous for the purpose of imposing strict liability. The court affirmed a lower court ruling against the plaintiff, noting that a trampoline itself was not dangerous but injuries occur due to the manner of its use.

Wagonblast v. Odessa School District, 110 Wash.2d 845, 758, P.2d 968 (1988). A court affirmed that releases or waivers that parents are required to sign as a condition of a student engaging in school activities and that absolve school districts from liability for negligence are invalid. In particular, the waivers specified that parents were releasing the school district from liability for all potential future negligence, which the court found to be in violation of public policy.

Stevens v. Chesteen, Ala. Sup. Ct. 561 S0.2d 1100 (1990). A brief absence from class by a teacher does not constitute a breach of duty of reasonable supervision. A student who had previous knee surgery was excused from participating in physical education class but was standing too close to an area where students were conducting an activity. He did not see students coming in his direction and was hit, causing a re-injury to his knee. The plaintiff claimed he was forced to stand in a hazardous area and the teacher did not supervise him. The court noted that it was not possible to personally supervise every student all the time.

Brown v. Tesack, 566 So.2d 955 (La. Sup. Ct. 1990). A breach of duty of reasonable care imposes liability on a school board. The case centered around how highly flammable duplicating fluid was discarded on school property that was eventually taken by youths. The youths later ignited a fireball resulting in severe burns.

Rich v. Kentucky Country Day, Inc., 793 S.W.2d 832 (Ky. Ct. App. 1990). Parents sued the school district claiming that it was malfeasant in its contractual duty to provide educational expertise by failing to recognize a learning disability. A court concluded that they did not present sufficient facts to support their claim.

Eisel v. Board of Education of Montgomery County, 597 A.2d 447 (Md. 1991). In a reversal of a lower court, an appellate court held that school counselors have a duty to use reasonable means to prevent a suicide when they have notice of suicidal intent by a student. Friends of the victim told school counselors of the victim's intent to commit suicide but they took no action and did not inform her parent about the information.

Brownell v. Los Angeles Unified School District, 4 Cal.App. 4th 787, 5 Cal. Rptr. 2d 756 (1992). An appellate court reversed a lower court decision against the school district. The school district did not have reason to foresee the gang-related shooting of a student that occurred adjacent to the school after school was dismissed.

Hammond v. Board of Education of Carroll County, 100 Md.App. 60, 639 A.2d 223 (1994). An appellate court upheld a decision that a female student assumed the normal risks of injury in choosing to play tackle football. The girl was the first female football player for the school and was injured in the first full scrimmage. She had her spleen removed and was hospitalized for days. The record showed that there were multiple times where the potential for injury was discussed, the parent had signed a consent form, and the girl participated in practices where coaches instructed all players about techniques that should be used to avoid injury.

Spears v. Jefferson Parish School Board, 646 S0.2d 1104 (La.App.1994). A school district was found liable for damages for an intentional act by a teacher resulting in emotional harm to a student. A teacher/coach was supervising a P.E. class that was watching a movie indoors due to inclement weather. When three kindergarten students were disruptive, they were moved near the coach, who told them if they didn't stop annoying him, he would "kill them." He then took two of the boys into an adjacent office, and he had the boys play a trick on the boy left behind. They pretended to be dead, and when the plaintiff was brought to the office, he was horrified at what he saw. The plaintiff suffered psychological trauma for weeks and was diagnosed with posttraumatic stress disorder (PTSD).

Johnson v. School District of Millard, Neb. Sup. Ct. 573 N.W. 2d 116 (1998). A court held that a reasonably prudent teacher could have foreseen possible injury to a student. A music teacher had first-grade students play "London Bridge" where they clasped hands and "captured" a student during the song and game. When the formal instruction ended, she allowed students to play this on their own, and a student was grabbed and flung against a bookcase, causing an injury that required fifty stitches near his eyebrow and later resulted in blurred vision and headaches.

Stowers v. Clinton Central School Corporation, 855 N.E.2d 739 (Ind. Ct. App. 2006). A jury trial and subsequent appeals by parents of a deceased football player were not accepted for review by the state Supreme Court. The student died after football practice in extreme heat. Testimony was provided that measures were taken in practice related to the heat. The trial court determined that the school was not negligent while the parents asserted that their son did not contribute to his death through his own negligence.

Kerns v. Independent School District No. 31, 984 F. Supp. 2d 1144 (N.D. Okla. 2013). On the day of prom, a student was on school grounds during decorating and consumed alcohol. At least one teacher became aware that he was intoxicated and notified the superintendent, who confirmed he was intoxicated. He immediately suspended the student for the remainder of the school year. He directed two other students to drive him home but did not contact the parents.

After leaving the school, the students allowed the intoxicated student to drive, and he later was killed in a traffic accident. The court held that under the state-created danger doctrine, the affirmative actions of the superintendent placed the student in greater danger than he was before the actions were taken.

Rogers v. Christina School District No. 45, 2012 (Del. July 16, 2013). The Delaware Supreme Court found the school district not liable under the state's Wrongful Death Act for teen suicide that occurred off-campus, but parents had a valid claim of negligence per se because the district allegedly violated mandatory requirements to notify parents of a crisis situation.

Weinberger v. Solomon Schechter School of Westchester, 961 N.Y.S 2d 178 (N.Y. Sup. Ct. 2013). A freshmen softball player assumed the risk of injury during a pitching drill that resulted in her getting hit in the face with a softball.

Jahn v. Farnsworth, 617 Fed. App'x 453 (6th Cir. 2015). In a tragic case, a student committed suicide after being suspended for the theft of a school computer. The student was told he would be suspended for the remainder of the school year and he subsequently left school and drove his car into a concrete pillar. The court held that his due process rights were not violated and parents were aware of the Code of Conduct procedures. In addition, the state-created danger doctrine did not apply because the student committed suicide off school grounds after being released to his parents.

Sperry v. Fremont County Sch. Dist. No. 6, 84 F. Supp. 3d 1277 (D. Wyo. 2015). In a tragic case, a student was hit and killed by a vehicle after a bus driver motioned to the girl to cross the two-lane highway. The court granted immunity in some claims, but left it for a jury to determine negligence claims as to whether the driver breached his duty to the student.

Duffy v. Long Beach City Sch. Dist., 22 N.Y.S. 3d 88 (N.Y. App. Div. 2015). A student was injured before football practice when unsupervised, several football players used a blocking sled to catapult themselves into the air. The plaintiff broke both wrists after he went ten feet into the air before hitting the ground. The unsupervised actions allegedly lasted at least twenty minutes. The appellate court reversed a lower court decision that favored the school, noting that the school had a duty to supervise students at the time of the accident and that the presumption of risk doctrine did not apply.

Safon v. Bellmore-Merrick Central High School District, 22 N.Y.S. 3d 233 (N.Y. App. Div. 2015). A student was injured during lacrosse practice after his foot hit a goal without a net in place. An appellate court ruled that even though the net was not in place, the student assumed risk inherent in the sport.

L.R. v. Sch. Dist. of Philadelphia, 836 F.3d 235 (3rd Cir. 2016). An appeals court upheld a decision against a teacher and school district in a case where the teacher released a five-year-old student from the classroom with an unidentified adult who later sexually assaulted the girl. The case met the elements to support the claim under the "state-created danger" exception to the general rule that there is no duty on states to protect citizens from private harm.

Slane v. City of Hilliard, 59 N.E.3d 545 (Ohio Ct. App. 2016). A student was hit by a vehicle while crossing a busy street where the school zone flashing light was not yet activated due to the fact she was arriving to school for a "zero" hour class. Additionally, traffic lights at the intersection had not worked for several months prior to the accident. An appellate court affirmed a ruling that the city and school district were entitled to qualified immunity. The injuries occurred on a public roadway and not within the grounds of the school district.

Boatright v. Copeland, 783 S.E.2d 695 (Ga. Ct. App. 2016). A student injured his hand while assisting with shooting a cannon owned by the school district used during football games. He sued under the theory that the school board and administrators were negligent in allowing a cannon to be used in a school safety zone. The district argued that firing the cannon should be considered "classroom work" which was an exception to the statute regarding the prohibition of weapons on school property. The court held that the defendants were not entitled to qualified immunity because complying with a criminal law is a ministerial duty and not discretionary.

Swank v. Valley Christian School, 374 P.3d 245 (Wash. Ct. App. 2016). A high school football player sustained a concussion during a game. He was cleared by his doctor to play the next week. During the game, he showed signs of injury but remained in the game. He was later hit hard and left the game, and died two days later. An appeals court determined that violation of the relevant state law by someone the law imposes a duty upon may be evidence of negligence, and even though the doctor cleared him to play, there was evidence during the game that the player suffered continued signs of injury but was still allowed to continue.

Barnett v. Atlanta Independent School System, 792 S.E. 2d 474 (Ga. Ct. App. 2016). An appeals court held that supervising students was a discretionary act entitled to official immunity, even when actions violated specific policies designed to supervise students. The case concerned a teacher who left a class unsupervised, and while students engaged in horseplay, a student was fatally injured when multiple students fell on top of him.

Doe v. Berkeley County School District, 189 F.Supp.3d 573 (D.S.C. 2016). A principal had received word that a student was sexually assaulting female classmates but took no action. The next school year, the plaintiff was in the same classroom as the alleged perpetrator student and was later sexually assaulted. The plaintiff claimed that the principal violated the doctrine of a state-created danger, but the court noted how difficult the standard is to meet. The action by the principal neither created nor increased the pre-existing risk of being harmed by the student. The plaintiff argued that by not taking action maintaining the status quo, but the court noted that maintaining the status quo is not a state-created danger. The court did note that it did not endorse the conduct of the principal, but that the plaintiff failed to state a claim of a due process violation.

Morgan v. East Baton Rouge Parish School Board, 215 S.3d 442 (La. Ct. App. 2017). A parent sued after her kindergarten student was left locked on a school bus. The driver failed to notice the sleeping child, who was later discovered in the bus. The court awarded damages for the child's medical expenses and general damages, but denied relief for economic loss of the parent.

Ella T. v. California, Case No. BC685730 (Superior Court CA 2017). It is a case that was the California counterpart to *Gary B. v. Snyder* that resulted in a historic settlement agreement to introduce legislation to provide sufficient literacy support in seventy-five schools that received the most students who scored the lowest on state proficiency tests. Ten students argued that although California had created a plan for literacy, the state had never implemented it, and students in disadvantaged communities attended schools that could not provide an opportunity to achieve basic literacy.

Munn v. Hotchkiss School, 165 A.3d 1167, 326 Conn. 540 (2017). The Supreme Court of Connecticut upheld a jury award of $41 million in a case where the plaintiff's parents alleged the school failed to properly warn of the foreseeable risks presented during a school trip to China. The student developed life-long disabling affects after contracting tick-borne encephalitis.

Guerriero v. Sewanhaka Central Sch. Dist., 150 AD 3d 831 (N.Y. App. Div. 2, 2017). A court held that an injury to a student who was punched in the face by another student was foreseeable. One month prior to the incident, the student reported to his teacher that he was slapped and his head was pushed repeatedly to his desk. On the day in question, the teacher glanced up but took no action as students were entering the classroom. Over a period of a few minutes, the plaintiff was blocked from the classroom door, pushed into a desk, followed to his own desk, and despite his pleas for the other student to stop, he was punched in the face. The court held that the incident did not occur so quickly and even the most intense supervision could have prevented it.

Dextraze v. Bernard, No. 2020-48-Appeal (R.I. June 28, 2021). The Rhode Island Supreme Court upheld the trial court's finding of school district negligence and proximate cause of plaintiff's injuries involving a student-on-student assault in the high school's hallway. The school district's motion to dismiss was denied because the school had a common-law duty to adequately supervise students. In this case, a student punched another student in the hallway, breaking his jaw. The student was being followed and was sworn at while passing several classrooms without seeing a teacher. After he was punched, he fell to the ground and was hit again. When he got up, a teacher came to the hallway, yet after he told the teacher he was hit in the head, he was told to get to class. The plaintiffs also alleged the school district did not follow their progressive discipline policy regarding the offending student, and reasonably should have known the student posed a threat of physical harm.

Meyers v. Ferndale Sch. Dist., No. 98280-5 (Wash. Sup. Ct. 2021). The Washington Supreme Court agreed with an appellate court decision that material issues of fact existed concerning proximate cause in a case where a student was killed by a vehicle while walking off-campus with his physical education class.

Moore v. Tyson, No. 1190547 (Ala. 2021). The Alabama Supreme Court affirmed a lower court judgment in favor of defendants based on immunity. A student was seriously injured in a fall in an unsupervised classroom after the teacher left to use the restroom. The court held that no rule existed that prohibited the teacher from leaving the classroom unattended in order to use the restroom where she acted beyond her authority.

CHAPTER 4

Students' Rights

Schools, by their very nature, must encourage free inquiry and free expression of ideas. Such expression should include the personal opinions of students relevant to the subject matter being taught, school activities, services, policies, school personnel, and matters of broad social concern and interest. In expressing themselves on such issues, students have a responsibility to refrain from using defamatory, obscene, or inflammatory language and to conduct themselves in such a way as to allow others to exercise their First Amendment rights as well.

The courts have affirmed that students' free speech rights are protected by the Constitution—so long as they do not present a "clear and present danger" or threaten a "material disruption" of the education process, as noted in *Gitlow v. New York* (1925) and *Tinker v. Des Moines* (1969). In the event that students' activities *threaten the effective operation of the school*, principals are given clear authority to limit or ban students' activities.

School districts face a dilemma as they attempt to balance the issues of school safety, orderly operation of the school, and student rights. How restrictive must school officials become to fulfill their obligation to lead an orderly school and to protect students? Principals grapple with the issue in the same way our entire nation asks how much freedom must be limited in order to protect the citizenry from violence. It is a challenge for school administrators to find the appropriate balance between individual student civil liberties and the rules that keep a school orderly and safe. Unfortunately, there is no single intersection that balances student liberties and student safety that ensures the complete safeguarding of both.

There are also concerns that the responses to violence by educators, legislators, and others involved with public education may, in fact, make students less safe. There is obviously a natural response for parents and educators to err on the side of safety—but what if the action taken actually makes everyone less safe?

These questions are not necessarily new to educators, but they have become more pressing due to the severity of school violence. Imber and Van Geel (1993) state there is a "tension between the school's need to maintain an orderly environment and the student's right as a citizen and human being" (p. 151). The complexity of the issue has also increased. "Many of the most difficult questions in education law concern the conflict between individual rights of students and the corporate needs of the school" (p. 152).

School safety is not the only concern principals must consider when dealing with matters of student rights. Attempting to create a balance between allowing students to freely express themselves against the obligation to maintain an orderly environment is not easy. Schools must allow some degrees of freedom in order to prepare students to become productive citizens in our democracy; yet with a high degree of polarization that has taken place most recently outside of schools, there are greater challenges brought into the schools now than perhaps any other time.

SUGGESTED GUIDELINES FOR PRACTICE

There are essentially seven landmark SCOTUS cases that principals should understand as the foundational basis regarding student rights. Although many other court cases influence what principals can do in practice, these cases guide the majority of other decisions. In 2021, the case of *Mahanoy Area School District v. B.L.* was the first major Supreme Court case that centered on student speech, social media, and off-campus speech. The ruling had the potential to carve additional limitations to student speech rights, but in an 8–1 decision, the Court held in favor of the student. The case will be further discussed in Chapter 5.

Those listed here don't include cases related to religion or special education, which are discussed in other chapters.

Tinker v. Des Moines Independent Community School District (1969). School officials use the findings in this case to limit or restrict speech that either disrupted school, has the potential to disrupt school, or invades the rights of others.

Bethel v. Fraser (1986). When expression is not disruptive, but is deemed lewd or vulgar, school officials may limit or restrict student speech.

Hazelwood v. Kuhlmeier (1988). Schools may exercise control over school-sponsored speech as long as their action was reasonably related to a pedagogical concern. (*Note:* some states have affirmed student rights in this area regarding student publications.)

Morse v. Frederick (2007). School officials may prohibit schools from displays promoting illegal drug usage.

New Jersey v. T.L.O. (1985). Students retain Fourth Amendment protections, but school officials may conduct student searches based on reasonable suspicion. Such searches must be justifiable at inception and reasonable in scope.

Safford v. Redding (2009). Searching of students must be "reasonably related to the objectives of the search and not excessively intrusive in light of the age and sex of the student and the nature of the infraction." The case involved the strip searching of a student.

Goss v. Lopez (1975). Students facing suspension must at a minimum receive some kind of notice and be afforded some kind of hearing.

SECTION A. SYMBOLIC EXPRESSION

In *West Virginia Board of Education v. Barnette* (1943), the U.S. Supreme Court heard its first freedom of expression case that involved public schools. The case was brought against a West Virginia public school system by the parents of children who refused to participate in saluting the American flag because they were Jehovah's Witnesses. Although the parents objected to this requirement as a

Symbolic expression is nonverbal expression that conveys the personal ideas, feelings, attitudes, or opinions of an individual. People exhibit symbolic expression in a variety of forms, for example, physical gestures, clothing, hair-style, buttons, jewelry, and tattoos. Symbolic expression contains an element of subjectivity, and in determining whether or not a form of expression is, in fact, symbolic, some consideration must be given to the intention of the persons who are expressing themselves.

violation of their religious beliefs, the Supreme Court decided this case on free speech grounds. The Court ruled that "the flag salute is a form of utterance. Symbolism is a primitive but effective way of communicating ideas . . . a short cut from mind to mind." Therefore, the students could not be required to salute the American flag.

During most of the twentieth century, students were routinely disciplined for engaging in forms of expression that displeased school authorities. A major turning point in the courts' interpretation of the First Amendment occurred in the landmark case of *Tinker v. Des Moines* (1969). In that case, the U.S. Supreme Court declared that students are "persons" under the Constitution who must be accorded all its rights and protections, especially the right to freedom of expression, and that the school board's subjective fear of some disruption was not enough to override students' right to express their political beliefs. The Supreme Court further noted that students possess fundamental rights that schools must respect. However, a controlling principle of *Tinker* was that conduct by a student, in class or out, that for any reason disrupts class work or involves substantial disorder or invasion of the rights of others is not protected by the constitutional guarantee of freedom of speech.

Policy in the area of student expression is difficult to develop and even more difficult to defend. Assuming that rules and regulations regarding student expression have been developed and are maintained as official policy by local boards of education, individual schools may build on these policies and regulations to set standards. Such standards generally will be upheld as long as the rules are in accord with board policy and are reasonable and specific. School officials may restrict freedom of expression if there is evidence of material and substantial disruption, violation of school rules, destruction of school property, or disregard for authority. The key questions to determine whether the rules are reasonable and specific are the following:

- Does the expression targeted cause a health, safety, or disruptive hazard?

- Are the rules based on objective needs?

- Will the rules constitute an arbitrary infringement of constitutionally protected rights? (Unsubstantiated fear and apprehension of disturbance are *not* sufficient grounds to restrict the right to freedom of expression and should not be the basis for the development of standards.)

Items Students Wear

Students' rights to wear insignia, buttons, jewelry, armbands, and other symbols of political or controversial significance are firmly protected by the Constitution and the courts. Like other student rights, this right may be forfeited when wearing such symbols causes a material disruption of the education process. A federal appeals court, in *Gusick v. Drebus* (1971), held that school authorities may establish policies regulating these activities when the rule is not arbitrary and is applied, without exception, to all insignia and not just one type of insignia. When students' insignia is unlikely to cause material disruption of the education process, courts have generally ruled that students cannot be deprived of their basic right to express themselves (see, e.g., *Burnside v. Byars,* 1966).

In what may seem like a minor problem compared to others, schools have faced challenges with the popularity of "I ♥ Boobies" bracelets and attire worn in support of breast cancer awareness, as well as similar attire supporting other causes. Courts have not been in agreement on such bans. In 2013, a federal district court upheld a ban in *J. A. v. Fort Wayne Community Schools* stating that breast cancer awareness does not eliminate the "vulgar meaning behind the I ♥ Boobies" message and also expressed the reluctance to have the court interfere with a school decision. However, the Third Circuit prohibited a ban in *B. H. v. Easton Area School District* in part because the school district did not consider the bracelet message lewd but instead considered them a disruption, even after having waited months to reach that conclusion. The age and grade level of students involved in these and similar circumstances are additional considerations that may change the context of how administrators and courts weigh their options.

Cases involving messages on clothing have long been issues for schools. "T-shirt" cases can run the gamut on free expression issues. T-shirt challenges related to controversial issues such as abortion, LGBTQ+ rights, the Confederate flag, and racial issues are frequent occurrences, and current local and school climate often determines whether or not a particular shirt is prohibited. Restrictions are more likely to be upheld where a history exists of increased conflict or violence. Given national attention to racial and other issues, it's to be determined if such consideration becomes wider in scope.

Hardwick ex rel. Hardwick v. Heyward (2013) is an example of a federal appellate court decision that considered whether a high school student has a First Amendment right to display a Confederate flag on the student's clothing while at school. In *Hardwick,* applying the *Tinker* "substantial disruption" test, the court ruled that there was ample evidence that the Confederate flag image could excite racial tensions at the school and create a substantial disruption of the school environment. Hardwick wore several different shirts over a period of years, including "Southern Chick" and "Honorary Member of the FBI: Federal Bigot Institutions."

According to the court record, at times she followed school officials' requests to change her shirt, and at other times she served in-school suspension for refusing to change. Most of the shirts depicted a Confederate flag. She also wore a shirt displaying the American flag with the words "Old Glory" and "Flew over legalized slavery for 90 years." Her parents finally requested that she be allowed to wear the shirts because of her heritage and religious beliefs. When the school district refused to relent, the parents sued. After she lost twice on different points in the trial court, in March 2013, the Fourth Circuit ruled against her, relying on *Tinker.*

This case differs in some respect to many cases because the court ruled that school officials could reasonably forecast a disruption due to the shirts, rather than agreeing that there was, in fact, a disruption. Hardwick argued that there was no disruption in the three years she wore the shirts, but the court rejected her position.

Other controversial issues have resulted in "T-Shirt" cases. When a student wore a shirt that said "Be Happy, Not Gay" in counterprotest to a gay rights "Day of Silence," school officials reached too far in their attempt to prohibit the shirt. In *Zamecnik v. Indian Prairie School District No. 204* (2011), the court held that a school that permits the advocacy of the rights of homosexual students cannot silence the views of students who hold a different view. This is a tricky area for educators because during the expression of an opposing view, a line can be crossed at which the expression may be demeaning, derogatory, or even "fighting words." Crossing that line is subject to interpretation and often triggers other legal arguments concerning freedom of speech and/or expression.

Such issues involve issues that go beyond the freedom of expression, because such freedom may actually be a form of harassment to other students or adults. This issue will be more fully addressed in Chapter 7 on sexual harassment.

Additional Dress Codes and Hairstyles

Many schools have grooming policies intended to improve school discipline and bring order to the classroom environment. Among the items prohibited by various school dress codes have been articles of clothing associated with gang activities, shorts, tight or immodest clothing, undergarments worn outside of clothes, sweat pants and jogging suits, torn clothing, baggy pants, night clothes, muscle shirts, halter tops, open-back blouses, and fur coats. Although some of these items of dress have been banned as a matter of taste, others have been outlawed to protect the students from becoming the victims of theft or violence. Mandatory school uniforms have also been upheld as constitutional, as in *Canady v. Bossier Parish School Board* in 2001.

Dress code and hairstyle policies have come under scrutiny due to concerns about racial and gender bias, with schools banning hairstyles predominantly worn by students of color, or having policies clearly directed at female students because their clothing items are described as "distractions." Supporters of these students question the origins of the policies, challenging the basis of the rationale that Black hairstyles are somehow disruptive or unhygienic or that female student attire should be regulated because they are deemed a "distraction" instead of placing the focus on those who may be "distracted." Principals should strongly consider the validity of their dress code policies regarding the potential of such racial and gender bias.

The issue rests between the balance of the interest of the school to mandate a dress code to keep "decorum" with any fundamental interest the student has to personal appearance, free expression, a right to privacy, and equal protection. The courts have not always agreed regarding the authority schools have to control students' appearance. A federal court of appeals, in *Richards v. Thurston* (1970), ruled against a school dress policy, deeming that it was not a justifiable part of the education process. The next year, another federal court, in *Smith v. Tammany*

Parish School Board (1971), upheld the right of elementary and secondary schools to promulgate dress codes. The majority of decisions, including *Karr v. Schmidt* (1972), have recognized a constitutional protection for students to regulate their own appearance within the bounds and standards of common decency and modesty. Students have a constitutional right to wear clothing of their own choice, as long as their clothing is neat and clean and does not cause a material disruption of the education process. To be constitutional, a dress code must be reasonably related to the school's responsibility or its curriculum. The courts have tended to distinguish hairstyles from clothing and have indicated that restrictions on hairstyles are more serious invasions of individual freedom than are clothing regulations. However, courts do give schools wide discretion to regulate appearance in the interests of health, safety, order, or discipline.

There may be increased awareness of Title IX implications with dress codes. In *Hayden v. Greensburg Community School Corporation* in 2014, a hairstyle policy that applied to a boys basketball team, but not the girls team, was struck down by the court. The court held that the policy to maintain a "clean cut" image was gender discrimination.

Physical Acts of Protest and the Right to Freedom of Assembly

Most people are familiar with a variety of physical gestures used by groups or individuals to express an idea, concept, opinion, or contempt. Although most would agree that obscene, disrespectful, or obviously annoying gestures should be banned from schools, policy should be based on the degree to which such gestures impinge on the rights of others and their likelihood of creating substantial disruption.

Students' freedom-of-assembly rights are protected by the First Amendment; however, the Tinker decision made it clear that students' First Amendment rights are protected only so long as they do not substantially disrupt the education process. Schools are well within the scope of their authority to adopt rules that restrict student gatherings to nondisruptive times, places, and behaviors.

A school that allows students to gather, even peacefully, whenever they wish may not function efficiently or effectively. On the other hand, a school that does not allow adequate time for students to meet and discuss relevant issues, or that denies use of school facilities for such assemblies outside regular school hours, clearly discourages one of the most fundamental perquisites and options of good citizenship.

The key to distinguishing between the use and abuse of the students' right to assemble peacefully, then, lies in balancing the fundamental nature, necessity, and usefulness of the freedom itself with the duty to carry out the education process effectively.

In the wake of national protests surrounding civil rights issues, including students "taking a knee" before school events, principals must recognize that such protests, absent some actual substantial disruption of school, are likely to be upheld as permissible should principals attempt to restrict the speech. The "taking of a knee" is controversial and provoking to many people, but principals should be wary of the use of prior restraint when attempting to restrict such speech. Merely because someone may be offended or does not like the speech in question is not a valid reason to prevent the speech, and such action may not be enforceable. The concept of the "heckler's veto" is discussed later in the chapter.

Likewise, student activism raising awareness of school violence led to a National Walkout Day in 2018. Many school districts offered proactive guidance on how the day would be handled in their school districts, informing parents of procedures that would be in place to excuse their students should they wish to participate in the walkout. Many school districts took those measures not in support of the walkout, but to avoid a potential clash with First Amendment concerns. Perhaps instructive for any such events in the future comes from a settlement made by a Kansas school district, which apologized to several students who participated in the walkout and were removed from a stage during student speeches. The district had originally agreed that although they would not sponsor the walkout, they would not punish students for participation, but at one school, administrators began to silence student speakers if they mentioned gun violence. One student was sent home for her speech, and the protest was stopped. After facing litigation, the district agreed to apologize to the students, provide First Amendment training for administrators and teachers, and adopt policies to prevent such action in the future (ACLU, 2019).

School Mascots

With the changing awareness of the importance of symbols in communicating values, a number of school districts have found their mascots the targets of community attacks. For example, in *Crosby v. Holsinger* (1988), the principal of a Virginia high school decided to discontinue the use of a cartoon figure named Johnny Reb as the school's mascot because of complaints that it offended Black students. A group of students protested the principal's decision as a violation of their First Amendment rights. Although the lower court ruled in favor of the students who wished to retain Johnny Reb as their mascot, a federal appeals court ruled in favor of the principal. The appeals court recognized that school officials need not sponsor or promote all student speech and that because a school mascot may be interpreted as bearing the school's stamp of approval, the principal was justified in mandating a change that would not offend a segment of the student population.

A decades-long effort to eliminate Native American mascots, branding, and imagery has recently gained momentum and relates to student rights because these mascots and imagery in schools intersect and clash with school antibullying policies and the rights of students to be free from the hostile learning environment such imagery creates. For over fifteen years, the American Psychological Association (APA) has recommended removing Native American mascots, symbols, and imagery from schools (APA, 2005).

Efforts should not be limited to changing names considered by some to be the most offensive, as research has demonstrated negative effects on all students even when imagery and branding is intended to be honorable and positive (KANAE, 2021). Perhaps the issue is becoming more into focus, as leadership and mascot literature in research have not been fully in concert in the past (RedCorn, 2017). Principal awareness should be raised regarding this issue, acknowledging that their own school and district mission statements and policies promoting "inclusion" or "culturally responsible curriculum" are at odds with what the research has shown with the negative effects of such imagery. Native American mascots are harmful for all students, not just Native American students (Kim-Prieto, Goldstein, Okazaki & Kirshner, 2010).

Some school districts that have moved from Native American imagery have considered the issue from an antidiscrimination policy approach, which is a proactive approach to avoid potential litigation alleging bullying and harassment or equal protection claims (RedCorn, 2021). The issue meets bullying and harassment policies as well as social–emotional learning head on. As with other issues that intersect with school and society as a whole, principals should consider how the continuance of Native American mascots violates the core values of the school and community.

Gang-Related Regalia and Behaviors, Cults, and Satanism

Many communities have to contend with gang activity that can cause substantial interference with school programs and activities. Because students announce their membership in a gang by wearing certain colors or emblems, students in some communities in which gang activity is a serious problem have responded by wearing only neutral colors. Many school administrators have revised their student dress code policies to prohibit the wearing of gang colors or emblems. In doing so, these administrators have re-raised the legal questions regarding whether students have the right to choose their own dress styles and whether schools can limit that right. Those school districts that have adopted rules prohibiting the wearing of gang symbols and jewelry believe that the presence of gangs and gang activities threatens a substantial disruption of the schools' programs.

In a suit challenging the constitutionality of an antigang policy, a high school student claimed that the policy violated his right of free speech under the First Amendment and his right to equal protection under the Fourteenth Amendment. The court, in *Olsen v. Board of Education of School District 228, Cook County, Illinois* (1987), affirmed the district's right to enforce the dress code, saying that school boards have the responsibility to teach not only academic subjects but also the role of young men and women in a democratic society. It went on to say that students are expected to learn that, in our society, individual rights must be balanced with the rights of others. The court's decision indicated that the First Amendment does not necessarily protect an individual's appearance from all regulation. When gang activities endanger the education process and safety of students, schools have the right to regulate students' dress and actions during school hours and on school grounds.

Regulations in the areas of gangs and other groups must be specific. Courts have found some districts' policies unconstitutionally vague. One court, in *Stephenson v. Davenport* (1997), held that the absence of important definitions for terms including *gang* provided administrators with too much discretion in determining how to *define* a symbol. As a result, the school district's rules did not adequately define those terms that would alert students and others to prohibited symbols.

Students' rights to exercise freedom of expression in the school environment have undergone several major transformations. Court decisions upholding schools' rights to set certain limits on student speech reflect a changing interpretation of the First Amendment. Historically, there has been disagreement over the way this amendment should be applied. Some believe that the First Amendment was written primarily to protect citizens from being punished for political dissent. Others take the broader view that the First Amendment extends protection to all expression except overt, antisocial, physical behavior. Oliver Wendell Holmes's "clear and present danger" doctrine, as declared in Gitlow v. New York *(1925), states that speech loses its First Amendment protection when it conflicts with other important social interests. Even proponents of a "full protection" theory of freedom of speech set limits on speech. For example, obscene telephone calls, threatening gestures, disruptive heckling, and sit-ins have been classified as "actions" rather than protected expression.*

Oral Communication

The Supreme Court has relied primarily on two tests to determine whether schools may control freedom of speech or expression. The first is the "clear and present danger" doctrine handed down through *Gitlow*. The second is the "material and substantial disruption" doctrine that derives from the *Tinker* decision. More recent courts have expanded the rationale for schools to limit students' freedom of speech when obscenity is involved.

In a landmark SCOTUS case, a student was suspended for delivering a speech nominating another student for elective office and including a graphic sexual metaphor. Two teachers had warned the student not to deliver the speech, but he proceeded to do so anyway. The student brought suit on First and Fourteenth Amendment grounds. The Court, in *Bethel School District No. 403 v. Fraser* (1985), said that although students have the right to advocate unpopular and controversial rules in school, that right must be balanced against the school's interest in teaching socially appropriate behavior. The Court observed that such standards would be difficult to enforce in a school that tolerated the "lewd, indecent, and offensive" speech and conduct that the student in this case exhibited.

Written Communication

Student Writing in Journalism Classes and Productions

Student journalists have the same rights and responsibilities as any other journalists. There are limits on what adult journalists can write and identified consequences for such actions as copyright infringement and plagiarism, false advertising and the advertising of illegal products, inflammatory literature, obscenity, libel, invasion of privacy, fraud, and threats. Unlike regular newspapers and magazines, school newspapers are considered to be nonpublic forums and are thus subject to reasonable censorship by school officials.

Just as the right of students to express themselves orally has undergone recent modification, their right to freedom of written expression has also been modified, most notably in the landmark case of *Hazelwood School District v. Kuhlmeier* (1988). The *Hazelwood* case involved a principal who deleted two full pages from the student newspaper produced in the journalism class. In his view, the deleted pages contained two "objectionable" articles that he characterized as "inappropriate, personal, sensitive, and unsuitable." The U.S. Supreme Court held that the First Amendment does not prevent school administrators from exercising editorial control over the style and content of school-sponsored student newspapers. The Court reasoned that high school papers published by journalism classes do not qualify as "a public forum" open to indiscriminate use but one " reserved . . . for its intended purpose as a supervised learning experience for journalism students." School officials, therefore, retain the right to impose reasonable restrictions on student speech in those papers, and the principal, in this case, did not violate students' speech rights.

The "public forum doctrine" was designed to balance the right of an individual to speak in public places with the government's right to preserve those places for their intended purposes. Although there is considerable doctrinal conflict in recent public forum cases, the *Hazelwood* court placed school-sponsored activities in the middle ground of a "limited public forum." Although speech cannot be regulated in a public forum, it can be regulated in a nonpublic forum, and school-sponsored speech may be regulated if there is a compelling reason.

The Court also drew a "two-tiered scheme of protection of student expression; one for personal speech, and the other for education-related speech." According to the *Hazelwood* decision, personal speech of the type discussed in *Tinker* is still protected by a strict scrutiny under the material and substantial disruption standard. However, speech that is curriculum related, whether in a class, an assembly, a newspaper, or a play, may be regulated. Such speech is protected only by a much less stringent standard of reasonableness.

Some states have affirmed student press rights in light of *Hazelwood*, which for some principals may actually be welcomed. Being legally permissible is not the same as being an advisable, necessary, or mandated practice. Certainly there may be valid reasons for school administrators to intervene at times when certain topics may become highly disruptive to the school environment. Principals should ask themselves if they truly want to add the responsibility of newspaper editor to their list of duties. It is a slippery slope once a principal decides to be the content editor because such action will ultimately raise questions of why one story was included while another was not; why one sports team received a longer story than another sports team; or whether the school newspaper was expressing the viewpoint only from the perspective of the principal. Such decisions are better left to the instructor or sponsor of the student publication.

In states that have not guaranteed additional protections for student publications, the involvement of school administrators as publication gatekeepers may create unintended consequences that put into question the action taken. A school principal in Texas censored articles, imposed a highly restrictive prior review policy, banned student editorials, and justified the decision by stating that the school newspaper reflected badly on the school (Dieterich & Greschler, 2018). In addition, the contract of the highly recognized advisor was not renewed. After a year of negative national backlash, the principal reversed the policy and would no longer require students to submit their stories prior to publishing. Student journalists from the school felt that in the end the policy was changed before the negative publicity became even worse.

In Nebraska, a high school journalist published an article in the local newspaper after the school principal would not allow a story to be published in the school newspaper. The story involved student reactions to the theft of a Confederate flag displayed on a truck in the school parking lot (Schatz, 2021). The principal would not permit the story to be published due to what he called "inaccuracies," but the student was steadfast in defending her reporting. After multiple revisions and attempts to gain approval, the student decided instead to have the article published outside of school.

In what some viewed as ironic, the initial efforts to ban displays of the Confederate flag were viewed as censorship by the administration. Instructive from this incident is how quickly free speech issues can become seemingly inconsistently regulated; how is the removal of Confederate flags from school grounds deemed a form of censorship, while it is not considered censorship to ban the publication of a school newspaper article about Confederate flags?

Many schools permit students to solicit advertisements to be placed in school-sponsored publications. Problems can arise when school authorities determine that the content of an advertisement is inappropriate for a school paper. A federal court, in *Williams v. Spencer* (1980), found that protecting students from unhealthful activities was a valid reason to justify the deletion of a paid advertisement for drug paraphernalia in a student newspaper. The court affirmed the right of the school to prevent any conduct on school grounds that endangers the health and safety of students and upheld the prior restraint of material that encouraged actions that might endanger students' health or safety. Based on this decision, schools may restrict advertisements that promote unhealthy or dangerous products or activities.

Schools have also been concerned about advertisements that promote controversial points of view. In *San Diego Community Against Registration and the Draft v. Governing Board of Grossmont Union High School District* (1986), the court ruled that a school board cannot, without a compelling interest, exclude speech simply because the board disagrees with the content. Specifically, the school board cannot allow the presentation of one side of an issue but prohibit the presentation of another viewpoint. Because a school newspaper is clearly identified as part of the curriculum rather than a public forum, the school has greater latitude in regulating advertisements.

Courts that have supported schools' rights to regulate student newspapers have made a distinction between off-campus and on-campus publications. Courts have generally held that school authority is limited to school grounds, and school officials do not have the power to discipline students for distributing underground newspapers off-campus (see, e.g., *Thomas v. Board of Education*, 1979).

However, some of the rules that apply to sponsored publications also apply to unofficial student publications. Unofficial publications must not interfere with the normal operation of the school and must not be obscene or libelous. Although students have the right to express themselves, schools retain the right to regulate the distribution of materials to protect the welfare of other students.

Prior restraint is generally defined as official government obstruction of speech prior to its utterance. As agents of the state, school districts or their agents may not exercise prior restraint unless the content of the publication or speech

- Would result in substantial disruption of the education process
- Is judged to be obscene or pornographic
- Libels school officials or others
- Invades the privacy of others

Courts have ruled that a school board is not required to wait until the distribution of a publication takes place to determine whether any of these criteria have been met. Schools have the right to establish rules on prior review procedures as well as standards regulating the times, places, and manner of distribution of student publications. If a school chooses to establish rules that govern the distribution of student publications, these rules must be reasonable and relate directly to the prevention of disruption or disorder.

The concept known as the "heckler's veto" should be recognized by school authorities as they take actions against students when there are free speech issues. The heckler's veto takes away the rights of the speaker and gives greater power to anyone who may be offended by the speech. This is an important concept when administrators attempt to determine whether student speech or actions have caused or have the potential to cause a disruption of the school. Is the potential or actual disruption the fault of the speaker or those who are creating the disruption? Student speech cannot be suppressed for the sole reason that someone may be offended or create an outburst in response to the speech.

As principals try to sort out incidents in their schools, they must consider both sides of a controversy and decide whether the heckler's veto is relevant to the circumstances. Although the courts recognize the difficulty for school authorities as they try to maintain school climate, protected student speech under the *Tinker* standard remains protected unless there is an actual disruption or there are specific facts to reasonably conclude that there would be disruption. Such was the case in *West v. Derby Unified School District No. 260* (2000), in which the court ruled that given the school's history of racially charged fights, a student could be punished for drawing the Confederate flag during class.

Speech cannot be suppressed by being labeled disruptive simply because it attracts attention or invites disagreement. In *Barber v. Dearborn Public Schools* (2003), there was some concern that Barber's shirt calling President George W. Bush an "International Terrorist" would offend Iraqi students, but no evidence to that effect was presented. In *K. D. ex rel. Dibble v. Fillmore Central School District* (2005), school officials were told they could not ban a shirt that said "Abortion Is Homicide" until "such time, if ever" they could demonstrate that the shirt caused a disruption.

School officials must be sensitive to the arguments surrounding the heckler's veto concept. For school authorities concerned with potential or actual disruption, in order to side on speech protection, one court offered,

The "heckler's veto" rule does not limit Defendants' authority to maintain order and discipline on school premises or to protect . . . students and faculty. *Tinker* [is] designed to prevent Defendants from punishing students who express unpopular views instead of punishing the students who react to those views in a disruptive manner. (*Boyd County High School Gay Straight Alliance v. Board of Education*, 2003)

Similarly, in a vigorous dissent in *Harper v. Poway Unified School District* (2006), Ninth Circuit Judge Alex Kozinski wrote, "I must also mention the incongruity of prohibiting speech because others respond to it with violence. . . . Maybe the right response is to expel students who attack other students on school premises." Further, he stated, "Any speech code that has at its heart avoiding offense to others gives anyone with a thin skin a heckler's veto—something the Supreme Court has not approved in the past."

SECTION C. PRIVACY, SEARCH, AND SEIZURE

Principals must be as equally aware of the importance of student rights related to privacy, search, and seizure as they are to those related to student expression. As complex as speech issues can be, principals may find that those related to search and seizure create even greater dilemmas, especially due to the fact that the searching of students may yield contraband that requires the involvement of law enforcement.

Because of school safety concerns, principals are frequently confronted with decisions related to searching for weapons and drugs. Principals may also find themselves needing to search for other reasons not related to school safety, and all searches have their own circumstances that bring layers of complexities to consider such as the age and gender of the student and whether the search involves the possessions of the student or the student themselves. Principals frequently must make immediate judgments because the gravity of the situation could result in serious harm to the student or others. But principals may also be responsible for conducting suspicionless or random searches mandated by local policy.

Principals must also recognize that not only is the Fourth Amendment concerned just with search rights but it also involves the concept of *seizure*—and detaining or restraining students must also be done in a manner that does not run afoul of that right. These rights are considered within the general idea of a student's right to privacy, which is balanced against the legitimate needs of the school to provide a safe and orderly environment.

The *in loco parentis* concept—namely, that school officials act in place of the parents and not as agents of the state—is used as the basis for some court rulings regarding search and seizure. However, in some more recent cases, courts have rejected the *in loco parentis* argument as being out of touch with contemporary reality, affirming that schools act as representatives of the state and not as surrogate parents.

Principals acting with malice toward a student or in ignorance or disregard of the law may be held liable for violating a student's constitutional rights. Absent these conditions, the principal has general immunity.

Students may willingly waive their rights of privacy under the Fourth Amendment. However, this waiver must be given free of even the slightest coercion. Principals are not protected from liability because students give permission for any kind of search. Courts have determined that students cannot freely give consent to a search because they are expected to cooperate in a school setting.

In an emergency situation, when school authorities are faced with a situation that demands immediate action to prevent injury or substantial property damage, the requirements of the Fourth Amendment are relaxed.

Proper or Improper Search and Seizure

The Fourth Amendment to the Constitution guarantees the right of people to be secure in their persons, houses, papers, and effects, against unreasonable searches and seizures without probable cause. In *Mapp v. Ohio* (1961), the U.S. Supreme Court ruled that the Fourth Amendment protects citizens from the actions of state as well as federal governments.

The U.S. Supreme Court ruled, in the case of *New Jersey v. T.L.O.* (1985), that the Fourth Amendment applies to school searches and seizures. In this case, although the student herself lost her individual case, the *T.L.O.* decision affirmed that students have Fourth Amendment protections at school. Although this decision left some questions unanswered, it did give educators some guidance, and that guidance is required, not merely suggested.

Prior to conducting any search, principals must adhere to the two-part legal standard required by *T.L.O.*, asking themselves if the search is both (1) *justified at its inception and* (2) *permissible (reasonable) in scope*. In practice, this means principals must determine whether they have a legitimate (reasonable) reason to initiate a search (inception), and then they must determine how intrusive their search will be (scope).

Therefore, whenever a principal or other government actor (school official) decides to search a student, the person conducting that search—or asking that the search be conducted—must mentally ask themselves "Why am I doing this search? . . . Is this justified? . . . Do I have a valid reason to do this search?" If the answer is "no," then a search should not be conducted.

If the answer is "yes," then the next questions to be asked could include "How far am I going to take this search? . . . Am I going to need to pat down (touch) the student? . . . Am I going to ask the student to remove a clothing item? . . . Am I going to reach inside a bookbag the student won't empty?"

Expanded further, answering the following questions prior to conducting a search helps school officials in particular situations determine whether a search is justified at its inception and reasonable in its scope:

1. *Is there reasonable suspicion that a student has violated a law or school policy?* Before conducting a search of a student's person or property, including school lockers, a school official must have a reasonable suspicion that a student has violated a law or school policy and, in conducting the search, the school official must use methods that are reasonable in scope. The search must be reasonably related to the objectives of the search and

not excessively intrusive in light of the age and gender of the student and the nature of the infraction. Considerations of student age, gender, and emotional condition are directly applicable as inhibitions to searches that must be justified by reasonableness.

2. *Was the source of information suggesting the need for a search* reliable *and* credible? A school official's good judgment applies to the determination of whether the information recommending the need for a search came from a reliable source. The courts have generally agreed that school officials may reasonably rely on information by school personnel or by a number of students, but information from a single student or from an anonymous source should be weighed more carefully before any action is taken.

3. *Does the school official's experience or knowledge of the student's history provide reasonable suspicion to justify a search?* Reasonable suspicion would be based on the details of the information and whether those details are credible in the current overall situation. Reasonable suspicion may be based on the school official's knowledge of the student's history or on the official's experience.

4. *Is the intended search method reasonable in relation to the objectives of the search and the nature of the suspected infraction?* Once the school official has met the standards of reasonable suspicion, reasonable scope is considered. The place or person identified through reasonable suspicion has a direct bearing on the scope of the search.

5. *Is the intended search method not excessively intrusive, given the nature of the suspected infraction?* The closer the searcher comes to the person, the higher the intrusiveness and, as a result, the stronger that reasonable suspicion must be to justify a search. The highest degree of intrusiveness would be the strip search of a person. The lowest degree of intrusiveness would be the search of an inanimate object such as a locker.

A school official's reasonable suspicion that a search will reveal evidence that a student has violated or is violating a law or school policy is a less rigorous test than the probable cause required for a police officer to obtain a search warrant. In an education setting, a school official may rely on their good judgment and common sense to determine whether there is sufficient probability of an infraction to justify a search. Furthermore, the level of suspicion may vary depending on the circumstances of the particular situation. In emergency situations that are potentially dangerous or where the element of time is critical, less suspicion is necessary to justify a search (e.g., the suspected presence of a weapon or explosive device or of drugs that might be quickly disposed of).

School Employee Versus School Police Searches

Although both public school employees and law enforcement officers are considered government actors and therefore are required to follow the Fourth Amendment protections, school administrators follow the lesser standards of "reasonable suspicion" rather than the "probable cause" standards required of law enforcement. Courts will still scrutinize the conditions surrounding any search. To determine whether a search is reasonable, the courts consider the magnitude of the suspected offense and the extent of the intrusiveness to the student's privacy. To establish reasonable suspicion, a school administrator must have some evidence regarding a specific suspicion that would lead a reasonable person (experienced school administrator) to believe that something is hidden in violation of school policy. In addition, the Fourth Amendment clearly states that the issuance of a warrant must "describe the place to be searched and the persons or things to be seized." Even though school administrators may conduct a warrantless search, they must be guided by a degree of specificity, for example, What is the suspected offense? Do I have definitive knowledge of where the suspected contraband is located? Do I know who the subjects in question are?

The most common searches principals conduct are personal searches of an individual student, the possessions or property of an individual student, or the property of the school district assigned to an individual student. Becoming more common are searches of electronic devices such as cell phones, tablets, and computers. In addition, some school district policies or special circumstances call for searches that do not have individualized suspicion, such as locker sweeps or sobriety checks before entry to an activity. Drug testing of students involved in sports or other extracurricular activities has long been routine in many school districts across the nation.

In 2017, a court held that the search of a student after he arrived thirty minutes late to school did not meet the requirements under *T.L.O.* The fact that all late-arriving students were uniformly subjected to suspicionless searches was not persuasive to the court. Student tardiness, standing alone, does not establish the requisite reasonable suspicion required to conduct a search (*State v. Williams.*, 521 S.W.3d 689 Mo. Ct. App. 2017).

Searches Based on Individual Suspicion

Nearly every principal may frequently be faced with a decision to conduct some type of search based on individual suspicion—from actual knowledge they have themselves having witnessed some action by a student; through information gained from other sources; or by the circumstances related to some type of incident involving the student. Among the most common of these searches are the following:

Pocket and pat-down searches. When a school employee actually touches a student's clothing while engaged in a search, the search becomes more invasive. The risks of this type of search increase if it is conducted by a person of the opposite gender. Courts have warned that because this type of search may inflict indignity and create strong resentment, it should not be undertaken lightly. Even though the search of a student may be justified at its inception, principals should strongly consider and evaluate the scope of search of any student.

Strip searches. The most controversial search of students is the strip search. There have been situations in which school officials have ordered students to remove their clothes down to or including the undergarments in a search for stolen money, illegal drugs, or weapons. Although *T.L.O.* did not directly address strip searches of students, the two-part legal standard from the case was used in a U.S. Supreme Court case in 2009 involving the strip search of a thirteen-year-old female student. In *Safford Unified School District #1 v. Redding* (2009), the

Court held that a strip search of a student requires three distinct elements of justification:

1. A significant and immediate danger to students
2. Individualized suspicion based on reliable, specific evidence
3. Reason to believe the strip search will yield the contraband

Even though in most strip search cases, the boys and girls were placed in separate rooms and searched by school personnel of the same gender, the courts have generally condemned strip searches in the public schools as impermissible and, since *Safford,* school officials have been put on notice as to the denial of immunity under Section 1983.

In 2018, a Fifth Circuit opinion held that the strip searching of twenty-two pre-teen girls in an attempt to find missing money was a violation of their Fourth Amendment rights and that the school district acted with deliberate indifference by failing to train administrators regarding the constraints of strip-searching students (*Littell v. Houston Independent Sch. Dist.*).

A body cavity search is the most intrusive type of search and should *not* be conducted by school employees. Such a standard has even applied to school medical personnel. A school nurse was denied qualified immunity for conducting an examination of the genitals of an elementary student after learning the child possibly had a urinary tract infection. The court agreed with the parents that the examination was an unreasonable search and not within the purview of the nurse's duties (*Hearring v. Sliwowski,* 2012).

Some states have recently passed legislation requiring some type of "genital inspection" to "verify gender" of students, specifically transgender students, when their participation is questioned for athletic participation. Challenges to these recent laws will surely be made in the courts based on the privacy issues involved.

Student-owned devices such as cell phones. When a principal is considering conducting a search that involves a student-owned device, most typically a cell phone, a distinction to keep in mind is that there is a difference between searching *for a device* and searching *the contents of a device.* Searching *for* a student bookbag and then searching *the contents* of a bookbag is not entirely analogous to the searches related to cell phones or other devices.

Confiscation of student cell phones and other devices fall under the Fourth Amendment, and the standards of *T.L.O.* apply when considering the taking of a device from a student. As with any search of a student, the decision to search for an electronic device must be justifiable at its inception and reasonable in scope. The search for electronic devices conducted by school police would require the higher standard of probable cause. Except in cases of imminent danger, strip-searching a student for an electronic device would be prohibited.

The decision to search the *contents* of a student-owned device also falls under the standards of *T.L.O.,* however; the additional scrutiny in deciding to initiate the search as well as the scope of the search must be undertaken. The justification to search the contents of a cell phone must be based on a reasonable suspicion that the search would yield necessary information related to whatever is being investigated. A student arriving tardy to class or causing a disruption of some type in class is not a proper justification to initiate a search of the contents of a student-owned device. Although there may be circumstances where searching the contents of a device is justifiable when there is a possible imminent danger to others, it should be remembered that a cell phone in and of itself causes no imminent danger.

Principals should not search the contents of a confiscated cell phone in an attempt to catch violations by other students. A federal court in *Klump v. Nazareth Area School District* (2006) ruled against a school administrator who searched the phone of a student who was caught in violation of school policy that prohibited the display or use of a cell phone during school hours. The administrator searched messages and the directory in the phone and contacted several students in order to determine if other students were also in violation of the policy. The court determined that the confiscation of the cell phone was justified, but the search of the phone was not reasonable in scope because the administrator had no reason at the outset to suspect the student had violated any other policy.

Although this area of law is still emerging, demanding social media usernames and passwords to student accounts and searching the contents of students' devices without their knowledge or permission is likely to be prohibited, as found in *R. S. v. Minnewaska Area School District No. 2149* (2012).

In 2014, the U.S. Supreme Court in *Riley v. California* was emphatic in their decision that police could not conduct warrantless searches of the contents of cell phones of criminal suspects in their custody. Although the case was not related to an educational setting, the unanimous decision of the Court may be an indication of how the Court might apply such searches in an educational setting. The Court concluded that cell phone and other devices were such a major aspect of life that their contents should be considered different from searching occasional items. Therefore, returning to the comparison between bookbags and cell phones, there is a clear recognition that cell phones are more personal in nature and not tantamount to a container. For that reason, principals must very carefully weigh their justifications when deciding to search the contents of a cell phone.

There may be some circumstances in which the search of an electronic device is reasonable based on information provided by a student, for example, in cases of potential imminent violence, threats, or other circumstances that may cause harm to individuals.

In a case that illustrates numerous student search guidelines, a Virginia court in 2014 upheld a pat-down search of a student but ruled that searching the contents of his cell phone constituted an illegal search (*Gallimore v. Henrico County Sch. Bd.*). After receiving a tip from parents that a student was seen smoking marijuana on a bus, the student was searched by a group of administrators. His pockets, shoes, and backpack were searched, uncovering food wrappers and a Vaseline jar. Another administrator searched the contents of his cell phone. The court held that under *T.L.O.*, the search of the student and his backpack was justified at its inception, based on their knowledge of the student, the parental tip, and the fact that marijuana could have been hidden in those places. However, searching the contents of the cell phone exceeded the scope of a reasonable search initiated to find drugs, because the cell phone could not have contained the drugs.

The judge stated that "common sense" dictated that the administrator could not claim to be looking for marijuana by searching the contents of the cell phone.

In a more recent decision, the Eleventh Circuit affirmed a lower court decision that held that the search of a student cell phone contents did not violate clearly established law. In *Jackson v. McCurry*, the court determined that even if the search of messages on a student cell phone was an improper search, the administrator would have qualified immunity because such search guidelines are not clearly established law. The phone was searched after a student had been accused of making threats and harassing another student. The administrator asked the student to unlock the phone, and once she did, he searched numerous messages from different individuals. This was justified as reasonable in scope because the messages were under emojis rather than identifiable names. The search did not result in finding any offending messages and the phone was returned to the student.

The parent of the student claimed the search was illegal, but the court held that the search was justified at its inception because of the allegations involved, and that the scope of the search was allowed because the contacts included emojis and nicknames, and expanding the search was reasonably related to the objectives of the search. The court distinguished the case from *Riley* by holding that the case did not involve search warrants, and that other student cell phone search cases where the search was held as impermissible were also distinguishable due to the elements of the cases.

School district-owned devices. There is typically no expectation of privacy when students are using district technology, and students typically agree to an acceptable use policy each time they sign on to district-owned devices either distributed to students to use off-premises or devices accessed on campus.

Locker searches. There is some question about whether a search of a student's locker falls within the protection of the Fourth Amendment. The Fourth Amendment protects only a person's reasonable expectation of privacy. Therefore, some courts have ruled that because students know when they are issued a locker that the school administrator keeps a duplicate key or a copy of the combination, their expectation of privacy in the locker is so diminished that it is virtually nonexistent. Courts have noted that students have use of the lockers, but the lockers remain the exclusive property of the school. School authorities, therefore, have both the right and duty to inspect a locker when they believe that something of an illegal nature may be stored in it or simply to remove school property at the end of the school year. Therefore, locker searchers may be conducted with a fairly low degree of suspicion.

Before police or other law enforcement officials may search students' lockers, they must have a search warrant. They must demonstrate "probable cause" as the basis to justify the issuance of a search warrant. This also holds true when a law enforcement official requests that school personnel do the actual searching. By acting with the police, the school official becomes an "arm of the state" and subject to due process requirements and illegal search and seizures sections of the U.S. Constitution; therefore, a search warrant is necessary. Evidence seized without a warrant will not be admissible in court.

Whether uniformed or plain clothed, school security personnel are generally considered by the courts to be law enforcement officers. As such, they must apply the higher standard of "probable cause" (as opposed to "reasonable suspicion") in conducting searches.

Student vehicles. The search of a student's car, even when the car is on school grounds, is highly controversial. Because a car is privately owned, the search of a car is a greater invasion of privacy than the search of a locker. However, because the car is parked on school property, in public view, the expectation of privacy is reduced. Courts have, however, identified degrees of privacy. For example, objects in open view are less protected than objects in the trunk or glove compartment. Generally, principals will want to avoid searching a student's car unless there is clear reason to believe that there is imminent danger either to the student or to others, should the student come into possession of the items.

Searches Without Individualized Suspicion

Some school districts conduct searches of students when there is no individualized suspicion of wrongdoing or policy violation, but conduct such searches as preventive or deterrent measures.

Metal detectors. In an effort to reduce the number of guns, knives, and metal weapons carried into schools, some school districts use metal detectors. School districts that use these devices argue that they are one of the less intrusive search techniques for searching for dangerous items, and the compelling need for school safety overrides the privacy concerns expressed by opponents of such searches. The use of metal detectors also raises the additional issue of whether or not faculty and staff will be subjected to the same search.

While not related to the legality of such searches, principals are cautioned that the use of metal detectors is not foolproof, and their use should not be relied upon as the sole means to prevent school violence.

Searches before activities. In their effort to prevent drug and alcohol use at proms or other activities, many school districts attempt to search all students prior to entry to activities. While principals are cautioned regarding these types of searches, a more defined clear line exists when the search may include pat downs or other touching of students without individualized suspicion. In New Mexico, suspicionless pat downs of prom attendees were prohibited from taking place after students brought suit (*Herrera v. Santa Fe Public Schools*, 2013).

Surreptitious video surveillance. The use of video surveillance conducted without the knowledge of those being observed is not recommended and has been struck down by courts. In an effort to improve school security, a Tennessee middle school installed video cameras throughout their building, including locker rooms. The locker room cameras were unnoticed for over six months and captured images and video of students from their school and competing schools changing clothes. In *Brannum v. Overton County School Bd.* (2008), the Sixth Circuit ruled that the scope of the search was not reasonable, and the use of secret surveillance significantly invaded the students' reasonable expectation of privacy.

Dog sniff searches. A U.S. Supreme Court case has placed some question regarding the use of trained dogs used during law enforcement searches. In *Florida v. Jarines* (2013), the Court ruled that a trained dog taken by police without a warrant to the porch of a house that subsequently sniffed drugs amounted to an illegal search.

Because the case was decided on property rights rather than privacy rights, the application of the case to schools is not yet clear.

The Eighth Circuit Court of Appeals held in *Burlison v. Springfield Public Schools* (2013) that a random lockdown policy in Springfield, Missouri, was a reasonable procedure to maintain safety and security at school. As part of the policy, students are prohibited from leaving the classroom until directed by law enforcement, after which their belongings left behind are searched by drug-sniffing dogs. The case was appealed to the U.S. Supreme Court, but the Court chose not to hear the case.

In previous cases, the courts have been split on the legality of using dogs in a dragnet search of students. In the case of *Horton v. Goose Creek* (1982), the court held that because the canine actually touched the students while sniffing, the students' Fourth Amendment right to be free from unreasonable searches was violated. The court also found that the school district failed to establish an individualized suspicion of the students searched.

In *Doe v. Renfrow* (1979), the court held that the use of dogs to sniff out drugs was not a search within the meaning of the Fourth Amendment and, therefore, not a violation of the Fourth Amendment. This court's opinion seems to suggest that if a school district clearly establishes an individualized suspicion of certain students, then a use of dogs might be appropriate.

When school authorities find the use of dog sniffs necessary to combat a drug problem, it is suggested that they coordinate the proposed search with law enforcement officials who have search warrants. In addition, the use of dogs should be subject specific rather than a dragnet of all students and should be done in private.

Drug Testing of All Students

The Carlstadt-East Rutherford, N.J., School District was the first in the United States to adopt a policy under which all the students at a high school would be required to submit to a chemical test for the identification of illicit drugs. The test was part of a more comprehensive physical examination required of all students. A state superior court judge ruled the proposed program unconstitutional. In *Odenheim v. Carlstadt-East Rutherford School District* (1985), the court ruled that drug testing was an unreasonable search, and the school's interest in discovering student drug use did not justify the interference with student privacy that the testing program involved. The court also held that the school district's program violated the students' right to due process because of the possibility that the results of the test could lead to suspension or expulsion from school without following the usual rules for such actions.

Drug Testing of Students Involved in Extracurricular Activities

In the fall of 1998, the U.S. Supreme Court refused to hear *Todd v. Rush County Schools*, a case in which a lower court had held that it was constitutional for the district to test all students involved in extracurricular activities for drugs. Consequently, some school districts have adopted policies that require all students who wish to participate in extracurricular activities to agree to submit to a drug test. In 1999, the Court refused to hear the *Anderson Community Schools v. Willis by Willis* case in which a high school's policy required all students who were suspended for fighting to be tested for drugs.

A 2002 U.S. Supreme Court decision illustrates the trend of the Court to place school safety over the Fourth Amendment protection of students. In *Board of Education of Independent School District No. 92 of Pottawatomie County v. Earls,* a group of Oklahoma high school students and their parents challenged a district's policy that required all middle and high school students to consent to urinalysis testing for drugs in order to participate in any extracurricular activity. They argued that this policy resulted in an unconstitutional suspicionless search in violation of the Fourth Amendment. The Court held that the policy was a reasonable means of furthering the school district's important interest in preventing and deterring drug use among its students and therefore did not violate the Fourth Amendment. The Court reasoned that there is a limited expectation of privacy in extracurricular activities generally, and that drug testing and the use of the results were minimally intrusive.

Drug Testing of Athletes

Schools that test student athletes for drugs argue that the tests are preventative, not punitive. Most drug-testing procedures are similar in that they make participation in athletic programs conditional on consent to drug testing at the beginning of each season. Typically, a district randomly selects athletes for testing each week throughout the athletic season. Selection is made from the entire athletic team regardless of whether the student has already been tested that season. Once selected, students who refuse to be tested are treated as if they had tested positive for drugs.

In 1995, the U.S. Supreme Court considered the constitutionality of a school's program of mandatory drug testing for athletes. In *Vernonia School District 47J v. Acton,* the Court held that the Fourth Amendment permits school districts to randomly search high school athletes without cause through drug testing. The Court held that the standard for the search was reasonable and that future balancing tests include the reduced privacy expectations for athletes, appropriate safeguards for testing, and the compelling governmental interest demonstrated by the school to combat drug use and abuse.

Seizure of Property

Seizing property that belongs to students is covered by the Fourth Amendment. Recently the trend has been toward an increase in cases involving illegal seizures, some of which center on students with disabilities. There have also been challenges to random lockdowns of classrooms and challenges when school authorities have physically restrained students using force or devices such as handcuffs (*E. C. v. County of Suffolk,* 2013) or specially designed desks (*Ebonie S. v. Pueblo School District 60,* 2012).

Restraint of Students

The restraint of students also falls under the Fourth Amendment, and principals are under strong advisement to adhere to all statutes, policies, and regulations regarding student restraint and to ensure that their staff is properly trained in restraining techniques when the decision is made to restrain a student. Detaining students is also a seizure, but does not have the same physical implications of student restraint.

In a 2017 case, a court allowed a case to proceed to trial against a school district where an employee allegedly dragged a first-grade autistic student across the classroom floor after de-escalation attempts failed to calm the student. The student suffered carpet burns as a result of the dragging by his ankles, which the court concluded was precisely done to restrain his freedom of movement (*K.G. v. Sergeant Bluff-Luton Community Sch. Dist. et al.*).

Putting hands on a student to restrict their movement is frequently challenged. Summary judgment for a teacher was denied in a case where a teacher was alleged to have forcibly grabbed the wrist of a student to prevent him from using a drinking fountain (*Young v. Mariscal*, 2017). In another case, an elementary student refused to sit at a table with a student who had previously bullied him and argued with a staff member. When the student tried to leave, the staff member blocked the student, bumped his chest, and knocked the student backwards. The student was then grabbed by the wrist, dragged to the table, and "slammed" onto the chair. A court allowed a Fourth Amendment claim to move to discovery in the case (*Jaythan E. v. Board of Education of Sykuta Elementary School et al.*, 2016).

SECTION D. GENDER IDENTITY

In light of recent efforts by legislatures that challenge the rights of transgender students, such rights should be highlighted. There are ongoing cases where teachers refused to use preferred pronouns of students, with teachers asserting such use violates their personal or religious beliefs. Still being weighed by the courts, a teacher filed suit in Indiana alleging discrimination and forceful resignation because his sincerely held religious beliefs prevented him from following a school policy that required him to address students by their preferred pronouns (*Kluge v. Brownsburg Cmty. Sch. Corp.*, 2020). In a similar case in Virginia, the courts have yet to rule on a case where a teacher was fired for refusing to call students their preferred name (*Vlaming v. West Point Sch. Bd.*, 2020).

For the purpose of this text, principals are reminded that such rights often clash, but framing that issue in a different light may help inform practice. Is any name absolutely gender specific or "belong" to a specific gender? Is the name of a student the criterion used to judge or determine the gender of a student, or are other criteria used? The question of which rights take precedence will likely take time to work through the legal system.

Several courts have made decisions regarding the use of restrooms by transgender students, with some noting that schools cannot punish a student for their nongender conformity. (See *Grimm v. Gloucester Cty. Sch. Bd.*, 2019; *J.A.W. v. Evansville Vanderburgh Sch. Corp.*, 2019; *Whitaker v. Kenosha Unified Sch. Dist. No. 1 Bd of Educ.*, 2017).

In 2020, the U.S. Supreme Court declined to hear a lawsuit aimed at barring transgender students from bathrooms and locker rooms that matched their gender identity (*Parents for Privacy v. Barr,* 2020). In 2021, the Court declined to review the appeal from Virginia in the Gavin Grimm case, which signaled a victory for the student in the case. These outcomes indicate an unwillingness by the Court to side with restrictions related to limitations of transgender rights.

Principals must be mindful that transgender students have the same rights as other students including protection against bullying and harassment; the right to same educational opportunities; and the right to present themselves according to their gender identity. A school cannot force a student to identify as the gender the school chooses. Their rights, as with all other students, are protected through Title IX, which bans sex discrimination in schools; through the Equal Access Act, which requires student organizations such as a Gay-Straight Alliance to be treated equally; and through FERPA, which protects their transgender status in terms of privacy. Protecting the privacy of the student is paramount, and it is up to the student, and not the school, to inform or not inform others about the gender identity of any student.

In the most recent developments in 2021, the U.S. Department of Education issued a "Notice of Interpretation" stating that the Office for Civil Rights (OCR) will enforce the Title IX prohibition on discrimination on the basis of sex to include discrimination based on sexual orientation and discrimination based on gender identity. This interpretation is based on the 2020 SCOTUS decision in *Bostock v. Clayton County* that held that discrimination against a person based on their sexual orientation or gender identity is discrimination on the basis of sex, which is prohibited under Title VI of the Civil Rights Act of 1964 (U.S. Department of Education, 2021a).

SUGGESTED GUIDELINES FOR PRACTICE

Finding the proper balance between maintaining a safe and orderly school while safeguarding the rights of students is not a simple task, and often there are no existing bright lines to help resolve those dilemmas. In general, however, some of the following suggestions may be good rules for practice.

Take precautions to ensure that efforts to avoid controversy or disruption do not result in silencing or muzzling sides of issues. A school climate in which ideas are suppressed may result in undesirable outcomes.

However, you must also ensure that while allowing more freedom of expression, other students are not targets of harassment or other victimization. Educators have not only a moral but a legal obligation to respond to as well as prevent such harassment.

Student expression cannot be banned merely because it may conflict with the personal views of school officials. As long as the actions of school officials are not coercive or threatening, educators can advise students about such issues, but to summarily suppress student viewpoint expression that would fall under *Tinker, Fraser, Hazelwood,* or *Morse* guidelines would be prohibited.

When making decisions regarding student expression that is disruptive, school officials must be able to establish proof of an imminent or substantial disruption. Student expression that has taken place for an extended period of time that did not cause actual disruption but has instead merely tested the patience of the administration cannot later be justified as "disruptive." Similarly, principals should make certain that it's not their response to the expression and their actions that are the actual disruption of the school.

Preparation for the potential of peaceful student protest as well as potentially disruptive unauthorized protest is a proactive step that helps to minimize the likelihood of making mistakes when responding

(Continued)

to such protests. Even when schools don't formally "sponsor" or "endorse" peaceful student protests, providing avenues to do so may help prevent the potential for disruptive student protest.

Ensure that any acts by school officials to censor student expression are reasonable in light of the context in which the communication is expressed. There are differences between the classroom, clubs, assemblies, or other ceremonies. An invited graduation speaker may not be considered in the same light as a student speaking to a large assembly of students in the cafeteria during lunchtime.

Involve multiple parties in the development of school dress codes, including students, faculty, and staff. Paying careful attention to avoid dress codes that are overly focused on "female" attire helps to limit potential discriminatory practices. Reasonable dress codes generally supported by the courts are those that focus on health, safety, order, and decency, rather than those that focus solely on style, fashion, and personal taste.

Always consider if a student search is even justified to be undertaken in light of the circumstances and then always seriously consider how far you are willing to proceed in your search. If you have no justifiable reason to conduct a student search of any kind, to proceed with the search could be found to be an unreasonable search. Even fully justifiable searches could be prohibited if the scope of the search goes beyond what is reasonable in light of the circumstances.

Absent sufficient reason to search the contents of a student-owned device such as a cell phone, such a search would be ill-advised. Mere possession of a cell phone is not generally, in and of itself, a reasonable cause to search the contents of the device. School handbook policies should clearly state that the school may conduct a search of a device if there is reasonable suspicion that a search of the device will reveal a school policy violation.

Strip searching of students should not be undertaken; in the rare instance when such a search may be considered, it should only be conducted if there is reason to believe the search would protect the health and safety of the student or others. This language indicates that a strip search might be supported when searching for weapons, but not supported for searching for material items such as missing money.

Principals should always turn over to law enforcement any device where there is suspicion that pornographic images of minors may be involved. Should a principal discover such evidence, under no circumstances should the principal copy, share, store, or distribute such images, as doing so may be in violation of child pornography laws regardless of the motive of the principal.

There should be written policy and guidelines regarding student publications that are school sponsored and nonschool sponsored. Make sure such policies adhere to school board policy. Such policy should include the procedures that are to be followed in the event any prior review is deemed necessary.

Principals should be wary of becoming "editors" of school publications. Entrusting those responsibilities to qualified staff members is the best practice. Principals don't have the time to add such responsibilities to their job description, and doing so opens them up to criticism of their editorial decisions.

All school officials must recognize that all students, regardless of their sexual orientation or gender identity, enjoy the same rights as other students, which include the right to be free from harassment and discrimination. Although states have taken measures to restrict transgender students from restroom and locker room access, the courts have trended toward nullifying those restrictions. Although the courts will likely be asked to weigh in on transgender student athlete bans, in 2021 the OCR has indicated they will consider discrimination a violation of Title IX.

ADDITIONAL CASES OF INTEREST TO EDUCATORS

FREEDOM OF EXPRESSION

Blackwell v. Issaquena County Board of Education (363 F.2d 749, 5th Cir. 1966). In a case that today provides context for discussion, this case predates *Tinker* and involved Black students in Mississippi in 1965 who were suspended for wearing "freedom" buttons and others in support of the Student Nonviolent Coordinating Committee (SNCC). The school claimed the buttons caused disruption in the school, and the federal courts upheld their action by saying the interest of the school to prevent interference with school policies trumped the student speech rights.

Alabama and Coushatta Tribes v. Big Sandy School District (817 F.Supp. 1319 Tex. 1993). A school policy regarding the length of hair male students could wear was challenged by Native American students, who testified that their hair length was guided by their religious beliefs. The court was persuaded that the school interest in dress codes is not so compelling to overcome religious practice and belief.

Chandler v. McMinnville School District (U.S. Ct. of App., 9th Cir. 1992, 978 F.2d 524). Students filed suit after the school district prohibited the wearing of buttons in school supporting their striking teachers. The buttons were in protest of hiring replacement teachers and referred to them as "scabs." An appeals court sided with the students, noting that the buttons should have been analyzed using a *Tinker* analysis because *Fraser* and *Hazelwood* precedents did not apply.

Palmer ex rel. Palmer v. Waxahachie Independent School (79 F.3d 502, 5th Cir. 2009). The U.S. Supreme Court declined to review a case involving a student who challenged school policy banning printed messages on t-shirts. Among the shirts the student wore was a shirt that said "Free Speech" on one side and the text of the First Amendment on the other. School officials may restrict speech that is considered content neutral. Although the student lost the case, the school district later relaxed the restrictions in its policy.

BWA v. Farmington R-7 School District (554 F.3d 734, 8th Cir. 2009). A court upheld a ban on Confederate flag clothing, citing a history of racially based discrimination and violence at the school.

Defoe ex rel. Defoe v. Spiva (625 F.3d 324, 6th Cir. 2010). Justified a ban on displaying Confederate flags at school.

Scott v. School Board of Alachua County (324 F.3d 1246, 11th Cir. 2003). Upheld decision to prohibit students from displaying a Confederate flag at school.

Bystrom v. Fridley High School Independent School District No. 14 (822 F.2d 747, 8th Cir. 1987). Underground newspapers can be controlled by school.

Rivera v. East Otero School District R-1 (721 F.Supp 1189, D.Colo. 1998). Students were determined to have a right to engage in political and religious speech in their distribution of an independent newspaper that advocated Christian principles for living.

Hedges v. Wauconda Community Unit Sch. Dist. No. 18, 1991 U.S. Dist. LEXIS 14873 (N.D. Ill. 1991). A court upheld a school policy that prohibited distribution of materials that were not primarily prepared by students. Allowing distribution of student self-expression enhances the educational mission, but to permit outside groups access to students uses the school as a convenient target audience.

DRESS CODE

Hines v. Caston Sch. Corp., 651 N.E.2d 330 (Ind. App. 1995). A court held that a policy banning males from wearing earrings served a valid educational purpose.

Littlefield v. Forney Independent Sch. Dist., 268 F.3d 275 (5th Cir. 2001). Mandatory school uniform policies do not violate free speech rights even though the policy may limit expression. Such policies enhance the school district interest in the educational process.

Canady v. Bossier Parish School Board., 240 F.3d 437 (5th Cir. 2001); *Littlefield v. Forney Independent School District.,* 268 F.3d 275 (5th Cir. 2001). These decisions upheld school district school uniform policies.

FOURTH AMENDMENT

Beard v. Whitmore Lake School District, 402 F.3d. 598 (6th Cir. 2005). The strip search of twenty-five students—in an attempt to find missing money—lacked individualized suspicion, and a search undertaken to find money serves a less weighty government interest than one undertaken for items that pose a threat to student safety.

Camreta v. Greene, 131 S.Ct. 2020 (2011). Although the U.S. Supreme Court discarded a Ninth Circuit Court of Appeals ruling on technical grounds, it did not rule on the merits of the case as to whether authorities needed a search warrant to interview students at school regarding sexual abuse allegations. The question concerns whether police or social worker interviews absent a warrant, parental consent, or a court order constitute a "seizure" under the Fourth Amendment.

Cornfield v. Consolidated High School District No. 230, 991 F.2d 1316 (U.S. Ct. of Appeals, Seventh Cir., 1993). In an exception to many strip search decisions, a court held that the strip search of a student believed to be in possession of drugs due to a noticeable bulge in his pants was not illegal. The court noted that as the intrusiveness of a search intensifies, so does the standard for reasonableness of the search. Therefore, a less intrusive search may be based on justifiable grounds that could be insufficient for a strip search.

DesRoches v. Caprio and School Board of Norfolk, 156 F.3d 571, 129 Educ. L. Rep. 628 (U.S. Ct. of Appeals, Fourth Cir., 1998). The school had reasonable suspicion to search student's backpack for stolen tennis shoes.

Hough v. Shakopee Public Schools, 608 F. Supp. 2d 1087 (D. Minn. 2009). Daily searches of students and belongings, including student pat downs, were considered overly intrusive and prohibited under the Fourth Amendment.

In the Matter of T. A. S., 713 S.E. 2d 211 (N.C. Ct. App. 2011). Daily searches of students at an alternative school were allowed, but strip-searching without individualized suspicion was prohibited.

Isiah B. v. State of Wisconsin, 176 Wis. 2d 639, 500 N. W. 2d 637 (S.C. of Wisc., 1993). A student does not have a reasonable expectation of privacy when storing personal items in a school locker.

Oliver v. McClung, 919 F.Supp. 1206 (N.D. Ind. 1995). A strip search for money was found not reasonable, but the same search for drugs or weapons may have been reasonable.

R. S. v. Minnewaska Area School District No. 2149, 894 F. Supp. 2d 1128 (D. Minn., 2012). Although this case could continue through the judicial system, principals should take notice of the issues. Because of incidents in the school, administrators demanded Facebook and e-mail user names and passwords from a middle school student. School officials searched the accounts of a middle school student without permission, and the court deemed this to be a violation of privacy and a prohibited search.

State v. Polk, 78 N.E.3d 834 (Ohio 2017). The Ohio Supreme Court reversed a lower court decision and upheld the search of an unattended bookbag. School employees searched the bag to determine who owned the bag and to ensure the contents of the bag were not dangerous.

State of Louisiana in the interest of K. L., 217 S.3d 628 (La. Ct. App. 2017). The court held that reaching into the pocket of a student by a staff member after he observed a drug transaction constituted a legal search. The student was evasive when asked to empty his pockets, and because the staff member observed the hand-to-hand transaction, the search was not a random, suspicionless drug search.

Mendoza v. Klein, No. H-09-3895, slip op. at 2 (S.D. Tex. Mar. 15, 2011). A teacher confiscated the cell phone of an eighth-grade student after she was observed looking at her phone surrounded by friends. Because the teacher suspected inappropriate behavior based on the reactions of the students, she decided to search through text messages and photos on the device and discovered nude photographs of the student. The student was suspended and assigned to a disciplinary program. A court held that the teacher was justified in checking the contents of the phone to see if she violated policy, but denied summary judgment for the school district, holding that a jury might conclude that opening the texts was not reasonable in light of the original justification to search the phone.

G. C. v. Owensboro Public Schools, 711 F.3d 623 (6th Cir. 2013). A court held that the school had insufficient reasons to search the contents of the cell phone of a student even though in the past the student had expressed suicidal thoughts and admitted to smoking marijuana. The court ruled they had no reason to search the phone to attempt to determine if he had violated other school rules.

J. W. v. DeSoto County School District, Civil Action No. 2: 09-CV-155-MS (N.D. Miss. Mar. 18, 2010). School officials confiscated a student's cell phone after he was observed looking at text messages in class. Several school officials searched through private and personal pictures stored on the phone and, after claiming they were gang related and indecent, turned the phone over to law enforcement. The student was suspended and expelled. The photos primarily depicted the student dancing in the bathroom of his home. The district court ruled in favor of the school, noting that because the student was caught violating school policy by using the phone, there was a diminished expectation of privacy that resulted. Qualified immunity was granted.

Jones v. Latexo Ind. Sch. Dist., 499 F.Supp 223 (E.D. Tex. 1980). A court held random drug dog sniffing of students' person as impermissible. The court held that such searches were too intrusive and unreasonable. Similarly, because students did not have access to their vehicles during the day, the interest of the school to conduct dog sniff searches of student vehicles was also unreasonable.

Robertson v. Anderson Mill Elementary School, No. 19-2157 (4th Cir. 2021). The Fourth Circuit held, under standards in *Hazelwood v. Kuhlmeier,* that a fourth-grade student's rights were not infringed when her essay regarding the topic of LGBTQ+ equality was not included in the class essay booklet after the school judged the essay as age inappropriate.

CHAPTER 5

Technology and Social Media

There may be no area of school law in which principals find themselves searching more often for guidance than the issues surrounding the student use of technology. The bad news for principals is that rapidly changing technology is nearly always accompanied by new ways for that technology to be misused, and the entire arena of cyber-related law remains unsettled. The good news is that many of the problems that occur with the student misuse of technology fall under what principals should already know about student speech rights, student search guidelines, and how they should respond to disruptions at school and to student bullying and harassment.

THE INTERRELATIONSHIPS BETWEEN ONLINE ISSUES AND STUDENT RIGHTS WITH ON- AND OFF-CAMPUS BEHAVIOR USING TECHNOLOGY

Issues involving the misuse of student technology are often complicated because it is frequently unclear where the misconduct falls within established student rights. When student behavior done off-campus, not during school hours or during a school activity, finds its way to the school through technology, there is often a dilemma to determine if or when school discipline should occur. More than ever before, each day principals face the reality that off-campus student misbehavior will require some type of intervention on their part. Although it is understandable that principals can become frustrated dealing with internet-related issues that inevitably invite challenges from a myriad of conflicting court rulings and opinions, applying known standards and rules can help them navigate through most scenarios they face.

For example, regardless of the type of social media a student used to send a message, there may be a *nexus* between the conduct and any school impacts. The elements of *Tinker* (1969) could apply regardless of the type of social media used, if the behavior caused or would likely cause imminent and substantial disruption or invade the rights of others. Messages deemed lewd, indecent, or vulgar may fall under the guidelines established in *Fraser* (1986). When the message can be reasonably attributed to the school, or connected to the curriculum, and the school has a legitimate pedagogical reason to regulate it, *Hazelwood* (1988) may provide the necessary guidance. In a narrow sense, drug use messages may bring the *Morse* (2007) decision into the picture.

In 2021, the Supreme Court delivered a less than bright-line decision regarding student expression using social media that originates off-campus. In *Mahanoy Area School District v. B.L.* (2021), the Court held that student speech on social media that originated outside of school may have First Amendment protections when the speech is not disruptive. The decision may not alter the practice of principals to a great degree, because the Court also stated that speech that originates off-campus that is threatening or bullying may still be regulated, which should have already been what principals were doing in practice.

SUGGESTED GUIDELINES FOR PRACTICE

School policy can be made that restricts possession and use of student-owned devices at school. Principals are urged to review the practicality of prohibiting possession of devices at school, because enforcing such provisions may be more time consuming and problematic than attempting to reasonably enforce the usage of the devices.

Technology, social media, and online behavior of students create an intersection between off-campus behavior and on-campus ramifications. Principals should not want to monitor all student behavior twenty-four hours per day, seven days a week, but there are situations where off-campus behavior causes enough disruption or invades the rights of others where principals may be forced to take action. These include social media threats, or bullying and harassment of students. However, similar to other student speech rights, even while on social media, students do retain some First Amendment protections.

Principals may be aided during their investigations of social media messages and their potential impacts by considering the elements involved as where messages were launched and where messages eventually landed. Such messages may have originated from outside of school, but may have major effects inside of school based on who received the messages. Conducting investigations, when warranted, should include discovering as much information as possible surrounding the origin of the message, including intent, intended audience, and content of the message (i.e., protected speech or not protected speech)—as well as the impact of the message—the viral nature of the message, what actual or imminent disruption the message created, and whether the message invaded the rights of others.

Principals should recognize that searching for a device is not the same as searching the contents of a device. Cell phones or other devices are not inherently dangerous. Searching the contents of a confiscated student-owned device after the student is suspected of a rules violation may be found to be an unreasonable search.

Student sexting, even when consensual, is not only a rules violation but also likely violates state or federal law. When there is a suspicion that pornographic images of minors may be on a student-owned device, principals and other school officials must also take precautions to protect themselves by avoiding the copying, sharing, or possessing of such images as they conduct any investigation. School officials are also obligated to educate all students, in an age-appropriate manner, of the dangers and potentially life-long negative consequences of being involved with sexting.

SECTION A. STUDENT TECHNOLOGY MISCONDUCT ON AND OFF SCHOOL GROUNDS

Discipline for conduct and speech that occur off school grounds must have a nexus to the school. Courts have upheld school discipline in cases where criminal acts occurred off school grounds, and are more likely to support the school when threats of violence are involved. There are differing court results when offensive remarks were made about staff or when students or staff were demeaned on social media. Courts will generally not support discipline for behavior or speech that has no connection to or effect on the school.

School officials have broad authority to control the conduct of students, to take responsibility for conduct, and to punish misconduct that has a negative impact on the school where school-related activities are concerned. The authority to control student conduct is implied by state statutes and has developed over time through court cases. The courts generally uphold school officials' authority to discipline students for misconduct off the school grounds when the students are engaged in school-sponsored activities.

Student misuse of technology while at school during the school day may be no more complicated than other school rule violations. If there are limitations to the possession or use of a device during class time, such a violation would be little different than breaking other school rules. In order to access school-owned devices, acceptable use policies make enforcement of rules violations easier as well. Using technology while at school to bully or harass another student signals an issue that must be addressed just as bullying or harassment without technology would.

Before the advent of the internet and the use of social media, student behavior that occurred off-campus had far fewer avenues to become connected to the school. As noted in Chapter 6, there may be instances where school officials may wish to respond to student misbehavior off school grounds that never has a true nexus to the operation of the school. In establishing how far schools can extend their reach, a case from the 1980s had the chance to perhaps establish a clear rule that conduct occurring outside of the school is off limits for school officials to address. Although the court did not go that far in *Klein v. Smith* (1986), they did rule that Maine school officials went too far in disciplining a student for giving the finger to a teacher in a restaurant parking lot. School policy called for disciplinary action for inappropriate language or conduct directed to a staff member, and the student was suspended for ten days. But a court felt there was no nexus between the act in a parking lot far from the school and the operation of the school.

Even before *Klein*, a Second Circuit opinion in *Thomas v. Board of Education, Granville Central School District* (1979) limited the reach of school district officials when they attempted to punish students for their involvement with an off-campus publication that was aimed at the school community. The court stated that although school officials should be given substantial discretion to execute their responsibilities, the "arm of authority does not reach beyond the schoolhouse gate." In *Thomas*, students were suspended for publishing and circulating a magazine off-campus that contained sexually graphic material, but none of the magazines made it to campus, a fact that made the conclusion of the court easier to reach.

As far back as 1969, a federal district court in Texas wrote, "School officials may not judge a student's behavior while he is in his home with his family nor does it seem to this court that they should have jurisdiction over his acts on a public street corner" (*Sullivan v. Houston Independent School District 307*, 1969). This decision implies that the standard should be that it is parental authority, not school authority, that deals with the behavior of a student who is off campus.

Times have obviously changed. The rise of social media gives new meaning to the language in *Tinker v. Des Moines* (1969) that stated, "Conduct by the student, in class or out of it, which for any reason—whether it stems from time, place, or type of behavior—materially disrupts class work or involves substantial disorder or invasion of the rights of others" is not protected speech. "In class or out of it" certainly has a different meaning now than when *Tinker* was decided. And the concern of protecting the rights of others breathes different and new life into the "invasion of the rights of others" concept, helping to lead to the conclusion that it is the message rather than the method of delivery that is important.

Where and how these messages originate may be thought of as where the messages are launched. Eventually, no matter from where a message was launched, it will inevitably land at some point, and in the case of social media, messages are likely to be "launched" multiple times over. When school administrators have time to investigate and move deliberately, consideration should be given to the circumstances and manner of how the speech or message was communicated. This is extremely important as administrators deal with the increased frequency of cyber-related threats. However, antibullying laws and other civil rights protections require that educators respond where the message was received (the victim)—it does not matter how the message originated. Of course, even when using the "launched vs. landed" metaphor, there are always exceptions.

Coy v. North Canton City Schools (2002) is a case that illustrates the dilemma for school officials, where an eighth-grade student in Ohio was punished for accessing a website at school that he had created at home. On his website, the student had posted pictures of himself and friends, including some pictures of himself and others giving "the finger" and others in which he labeled some of his classmates "losers." The student accessed the website while at school and was subsequently suspended from school for eighty days. Because the student was both the sender of the message and the receiver of the message, he was suspended either for "sending a message to himself or receiving a message from himself" (Graca & Stadler, 2007, p. 125). Ulti-mately, the student prevailed in court under the *Tinker* standard, but it illustrates the circumstances some schools and students have created.

When school officials are not successful demonstrating a direct connection to the school, whether it is a disruption or another standard, students could prevail in a challenge to any discipline applied to them. In *J.C. ex rel. R.C. v. Beverly Hills Unified School District* (2010), a high school student sued the school district and school administrators for suspending her for posting a video clip on a website in which students made derogatory, sexual, and defamatory statements about another student. The fact that the video was made outside of school and was seen by other students was considered by a federal district court and would have been acceptable reason for punishment. The court ruled, however, there was no substantial disruption or reasonably foreseeable risk of disruption of school activities as a result of the video. Having to address the concerns of an upset parent, and having some students miss classes, along with a fear that students would "gossip" or "pass notes" in class did not amount to a substantial disruption.

Once speech in any form reaches campus, the line becomes blurred. At what point does off-campus speech become on-campus speech? There has not been a consensus from the courts answering that question. Unsettled is the issue of speech that never makes it to campus but still causes disruption or compromises an educational interest, such as shared information that constitutes cheating of some sort.

Court cases involving the use or misuse of technology or social media that somehow reaches campus frequently relate to or are a combination of bullying and harassment, threats, racism or sexism, criticism of the school or individuals, parody of the school or individuals, inappropriate jokes, rants about the school, or other inappropriate video or image content. Principals may be conflicted with the outcomes of many of these cases, but many also take some satisfaction that student expression off-campus has not been limited, and others may find relief that they are not obligated to monitor or regulate all off-campus speech. Unfortunately, few bright lines exist for principals to always know how to respond to each. However, by using foundational knowledge about basic student rights, direction from the case law, and administrative common sense about their school and knowledge of students, principals are more likely to make proper decisions when dealing with these issues.

The following circumstances are not necessarily limited in their own category; for example, messages that are bullying and harassing may also be threatening.

Use of Technology to Bully or Harass Others or Is Racist or Sexist

School officials are obligated both legally and morally to make efforts to prevent, and respond to, acts of bullying and harassment regardless of whether such acts are done through social media or through some other means. Misuse of social media by posting racist or sexist content may accompany other issues such as threats or harassment, but highlighting the issue is warranted because such postings may also violate Title IX or other antidiscrimination laws and policies. Athough the case decided by the Supreme Court in *Mahanoy Area School District v. B.L.* (2021) was not a bullying and harassment case, the opinion of the Court noted that schools may have a substantial interest in regulating off-campus conduct such as severe bullying and harassment aimed at students or teachers.

Antibullying laws have been in effect for several years, and states are developing new or strengthening existing antibullying and antiharassment laws. Cyberbullying is a form of bullying that is becoming ever more prevalent and difficult to monitor. Districts that encourage, tolerate, ignore, or fail to adequately address harassment may violate civil rights laws. A school is responsible for addressing harassment incidents about which it knows or reasonably should have known. This means that educators must take positive steps both to prevent and punish acts of bullying and harassment and to *know* about bullying and harassment that occur in their school.

The goal of every principal should be to eliminate bullying and harassment, and although technology has provided another avenue for bullying behavior, a written or digital record exists that principals don't have with purely verbal bullying.

When other students are targets, courts have generally supported disciplinary action of the schools even when technology may have originated off-campus. The Fourth Circuit in *Kowalski v. Berkeley County Schools* in 2011 concluded that a high school student's First Amendment rights were not violated when the school suspended her for creating a website on which other students had posted defamatory comments about a female student, including an insinuation that she had a sexually transmitted disease. The plaintiff knew that her website would impact the school environment, which eventually occurred.

In 2012, a court reversed an earlier decision and upheld the suspension of students following their posting of offensive and racist comments as well as sexually explicit and degrading comments. In *S.J.W. v. Lee's Summit R-7 School District* (2012), the twin brothers created the website that included sexually explicit and degrading comments about a female student identified by name. Records showed that school computers were used to access the website, although it could not be determined who had accessed the site. The students claimed they created the site to satirize and vent about events at their high school, and they intended their audience to be only their friends. The site became known to the general student body and was quickly connected to the brothers. An appeals court rejected their claim that their speech was protected and determined that there was enough of a significant disruption of the school to warrant their suspension.

Use of Technology to Make Threats

The obligation of schools to protect the safety of students and staff must be balanced against the obligation to protect the rights of students. It is this tension that educators must weigh in each case. When principals are faced with a situation involving the use of technology and social media that has elements of a threat, they should focus first on the threat, and not the means of the communication. There is also guidance from case law involving threats against students or teachers without the use of social media that likely would apply in similar cases that do involve social media.

Reasonable discipline against students who make threats through social media is likely to be supported by the courts. *Wisniewski v. Board of Education of Weedsport Central School District* (2007) involved the suspension of a student who created an instant messaging icon depicting his teacher being shot. The icon was created by an eighth-grade student who sent the message to fifteen people, some of whom were classmates. The icon depicted a pistol firing a bullet at a person's head, with dots representing blood and the words "Kill Mr. [name withheld]." The discipline of the student was upheld based on the disruption of the school, with the Second Circuit holding that it was clear that off-campus conduct could create a substantial disruption of the school. In 2011, a court determined that the online expression that mentioned acquiring a gun and shooting students posed a risk of substantial disruption, and were deemed a true threat (*D.J.M. v. Hannibal Public School District 60*). The school was not required to determine if the student would take further steps to carry out the threat. A court in 2013 did not rule on the threat aspect but instead focused on the disruption where online comments were initiated off-campus about committing a school shooting spree (*Wynar v. Douglas*).

There are fine lines where threats may not be considered an actual threat and may in fact be expression better described as venting. In 2015, a court sided with a student in *Burge v. Colton* who filed suit to have his disciplinary record expunged after he served a 3.5 day in-school suspension. The student had posted on a Facebook page intended for his friends to see his comments about his math teacher, who he was angry with after a grading period in the class. He made statements about starting a petition to get her fired, called her a bitch, and after his friends expressed laughter at his post, he said, "She needs to be shot." It took six weeks for the school to learn of the post through an anonymous printout that was placed in the office. A magistrate judge decision in favor of the student based on *Tinker* was affirmed by a district court. Although the teacher was visibly upset and even fearful, the court stated that alone was not sufficient to assert there was a disruption of the school.

In another case where a perceived threat may have been more inappropriate or considered parody, a court sided with a student who created an "unofficial" webpage of their school where they noted the page was for "entertainment purposes only." In *Emmett v. Kent School District* (2000), the students were inspired by a creative writing class assignment about writing their own obituaries, and their posting of fake obituaries of students proved so popular they began taking requests and added a feature to enable voting for who the next obituary should be for. Eventually this was picked up by the local news and characterized as a "hit list" and who would "die" next. Although the intended audience was clearly those connected to the high school, the speech was entirely outside of the control of the school, and the website was not actually threatening, according to the court.

Summary judgment was granted to a student who was disciplined after posting a webpage that talked about, in a joking manner, him hating school and killing fellow students (*Mahaffey v. Aldrich*, 2002). The court held that there was no disruption to the school and that the website was not a true threat because no reasonable person would conclude the student wanted to kill the students listed under "people I wish would die."

What is important in practice for principals is to consider if the threat is not serious enough to act upon, for example by staff or students missing classes, or stopping excessive talk among the students about the incident during class time, that may not be enough to make a claim that there was a substantial disruption of the school. It would be difficult to claim that a threat was serious if the school did not treat it as one. Additionally, as applied to situations involving jokes and parody, having staff hurt, embarrassed, or angered by student postings may also not be enough to assert a disruption of the school.

Use of Technology for a Parody of the School or Individuals

Using social media to parody, criticize, or demean school officials or students may in some circumstances be classified as cyberbullying and harassment; however, the prevalence of such messages that are not actually bullying or harassment, yet potentially disruptive to the school, may be more common. Free speech issues are relevant when students use social media to criticize school policy and school officials and also when they parody or otherwise make fun of principals and teachers.

A student was arrested, interrogated, and suspended for logging onto a Facebook page that parodied the principal. He was not the creator of the webpage, nor did he access the page from school. He was accused of disrupting school activities, disruptive behavior, malicious defamation of school personnel, bullying, harassment, threats, and intimidation. Originally the school district assigned him to an alternative school but later reversed its decision (Courthouse News Service, 2011).

A Washington court, in *Beidler v. North Thurston School District* (2000), ruled in favor of a student who created a website depicting his assistant principal drinking beer and participating in a Nazi book burning. The judge in this case predicted the future by stating that "schools can and will adjust to the new challenges created by . . . students and the internet, but not at the expense of the First Amendment." If the court was trying to predict a smooth course of adjustment, it was inaccurate, but it was certainly correct to claim there would be challenges.

Principals must be mindful that generations of students have criticized and made fun of their principals and teachers—it is the means of delivering the messages that has changed. In this day and age, students will perhaps be more likely to voice their opinion against a school or a teacher through social media. Absent an actual threat of violence, school officials would be wise to grow thicker skins when they run across such postings. Calvert (2001) properly predicted the future when he stated, "Students create Web sites that give a metaphorical middle finger to teachers and administrators. Just as Jason Klein [*Klein v Smith*, 1986] flipped off a teacher in a parking lot, students today are doing the same in cyberspace" (p. 275).

These cases exemplify how the internet changed the nature of a behavior that has taken place for generations. School officials are frequently the target of jokes and comments that are free from school punishment, but with the widespread use of technology those jokes and comments can spread rapidly and out of control. In *J.S. v. Blue Mountain School District* (2010), the court noted this, holding that off-campus speech that causes or threatens to cause a disruption "need not satisfy any geographical technicality in order to be regulated pursuant to *Tinker.*" The court clarified that, in their view, this is distinguishable from a potential comment made outside of school because "we are expressively not applying *Fraser* to conduct off school grounds; there is no risk that a vulgar comment made outside the school environment will result in school discipline absent a significant risk of a substantial disruption of the school."

Principals may find no comfort knowing that social media platforms such as Twitter allow the use of parody and fake accounts, and in the case of Twitter do not monitor and will not remove accounts unless they are in violation of their terms of service. This does not mean that principals are powerless when dealing with such social media, but the lines are blurry as to how far their reach can be.

Unlike cases of bullying, in which definitions are more clearly defined and principals are required to respond to acts of bullying and harassment, there is less guidance in cases in which the target of the speech is the object of parody, impersonation, or criticism.

Courts have been split on the issue, and, in what may be viewed as a victory for students in terms of off-campus social media expression, the U.S. Supreme Court declined to review two cases from the Third Circuit in 2010. *Layshock v. Hermitage School District* (2010) and *J.S. v. Blue Mountain School District* (2010) are separate cases dealing with the aftermaths of students creating social network profiles of their school principals. In the first case, Justin Layshock was disciplined after he used his grandmother's computer to create a fake MySpace profile of his high school principal. In the second, middle school student J.S. was disciplined after creating a MySpace profile of her principal.

Layshock was a high school senior in December 2005 when, during nonschool hours, he sat at his grandmother's computer and created a "parody profile" of his principal. He copied a picture of his principal from the school district website and created a bogus profile. Providing answers to the MySpace profile questions, he, according to the court record, included among several things,

> Birthday: too drunk to remember. In the past month have you gone skinny dipping: big lake, not big dick. Ever been called a tease: big whore. Under "interests" he listed "Transgender, Appreciators of Alcoholic Beverages."

The profile was made available to other students by listing them as "friends" on the MySpace website, and shortly thereafter word spread quickly at school about the profile. A few days later, three other students also posted profiles of the principal, each more "vulgar and more offensive" than Layshock's. The principal then learned of the profiles from his daughter who attended the same high school. He believed the profiles to be "degrading," "demeaning," "demoralizing," and "shocking."

On December 15, Layshock accessed the website from a class at school and showed it to other classmates. The next day, he accessed the profile from school, purportedly to delete it. One teacher briefly saw the profile when he saw a group of giggling students in class huddled around a computer. Although the district was able to determine on investigation how many students accessed MySpace before it was disabled, there was no way to determine how many actually viewed the profile.

On December 21, after school officials learned of Layshock's role, Layshock and his mother met with administrators. After the meeting and without prompting, Layshock apologized to the principal, which the principal later testified he believed to be respectful and sincere. On January 3, 2006, Layshock received notice of an informal hearing to determine charges against him, including "Disruption of the normal school process; Disrespect; Harassment of a school administrator; Gross Misbehavior; Computer Policy Violation (use of school pictures without authorization)."

Layshock was given a ten-day out-of-school suspension and was placed in an alternative education program for the remainder of the school year, banned from extracurricular activities and from graduation ceremonies. He subsequently sued the school district on the grounds that his speech was protected under the First Amendment.

The school district asked the court to reject Layshock's claim that his speech was protected by asserting that his actions created a disruption of the school, and although he created the profile off campus, he effectively entered the campus when he accessed the district website to copy the picture of the principal. The circuit court rejected that argument because it "equates Layshock's act of signing onto a website with the kind of trespass he would have committed had he broken into the principal's office or a teacher's desk." The court referred to *Thomas v. Board of Education* (1979) and felt that the relationship between his action and the school was even less than that in *Thomas*. "We will not allow the School District to stretch its authority so far that it reaches [Layshock] while he is sitting in his grandmother's home after school." The court also distinguished his situation from *Morse* by stating it would be a "dangerous precedent" to reach into a home the same way they can control behavior at school activities.

When the federal district court denied the school district's original position on appeal, the school district did not dispute that finding. Accordingly, the speech was then protected by *Tinker* and not related to *Morse*. That left the district to argue that the speech fell under *Fraser* standards. The school district argued that guidelines of *Fraser* and others applied to their case. But the court rejected those arguments, stating,

> We believe the cases relied upon for the District stand for nothing more than the proposition that schools may punish expressive conduct that occurs outside of school as if it occurred inside the "schoolhouse gate," under certain very limited circumstances, none of which are present here.

J.S. v. Blue Mountain School District (2010) was originally decided on the premise that school authorities could reasonably forecast a substantial disruption of the school. In the spring of 2007, J.S. was a middle school student. Upset over how she was disciplined for a dress code violation, J.S. and her friend K.L., working from their separate homes, created a fake MySpace profile. The girls took turns adding to the profile as they messaged each other.

Court records show that the actual URL for the page was http://myspacecom/kidsrockmybed. Similar to Layshock, they copied a picture of their principal from their school website. They did not identify him by name, school, or location, but they created the page to appear to be by a middle school principal named "m-hoe=]." He was made to be a bisexual forty-year-old man living in Alabama with his wife and child. His "interests" section included the following:

> General: detention. being a tightass. riding the fraintrain. spending time with my child (who looks like a gorilla). baseball. my golden pen. fucking in my office. hittin on students and their parents. Television: almost anything. i mainly watch the playboy channel on directv. OH YEAH BITCH! Heroes: myself. of course.

Another section was titled "About me" and stated,

> HELLO CHILDREN Yes. It's your oh so wonderful, hairy, expressionless, sex addict, fagass, put on this world with a small dick PRINCIPAL. I have come to myspace so I can pervert the minds of other principal's to be just like me. I know, I know, you're all thrilled. Another reason I came to myspace is because—I am keeping an eye on you students (who I care for so much). For those who want to be my friend, and aren't in my school I love children, sex (any kind), dogs, long walks on the beach, tv, being a

dick head, and last but not least my darling wife who looks like a man (who satisfies my needs) MY FRAINTRAIN so please, feel free to add me, message me whatever.

The reference to "fraintrain" appeared to be a reference to the principal's wife, a counselor at the school.

The profile was made accessible for anyone who knew the URL or found it by searching MySpace for a term contained in the profile. The next day at school, students approached J.S. to talk about the profile, and after school she went home and made the profile "private," meaning it could only be viewed by those invited by J.S. or K.L. Approximately twenty-two students were invited, and because MySpace was blocked from access at school, they could only view it from off-campus locations.

The principal first learned of the profile the same day as the students. He was informed of the profile by a student, and he asked the student to find out who made the profile. When he could not access it himself, he contacted MySpace, who told him they needed the entire URL. Later that day, the student returned with information that J.S. had created the website, and two days later the student brought him a printed copy.

After investigation and discussion with district administrators, the principal called J.S. and K.L. to his office where they eventually admitted their role. MySpace was contacted with the appropriate information to have the profile removed. Both students were suspended for ten days and were warned by the police of the seriousness of their actions.

The court record reflects some of the events that occurred at the school, both before and after the suspensions. A teacher reported that two students had come to her concerned about some of the comments in the profile. The testing of some students had to be rescheduled during the investigation. Upon their return to school from their suspensions, J.S.'s and K.L.'s school lockers were decorated with construction paper, ribbons and bows, and words of congratulations. The locker decorations caused the congregation of twenty to thirty students in the hallway, who had to be dispersed. Additionally, at least one teacher had to quiet his class numerous times when students began discussing the profile and suspensions during class time. Later, these incidents were described as brief, lasting only a few minutes, and there were only general "rumblings" about the incident.

The principal later testified that he noticed a deterioration of school discipline after all of the events, and he attributed this to a new culture rallying against the administration. He also stated that he had stress-related health problems as a result of the profile and litigation.

J.S.'s parents filed suit against the district, claiming that her free speech rights were violated by suspending her for creating the profile. Although the court ruled against J.S. using a *Fraser* standard, the circuit court declined

> to decide whether a school official may discipline a student for her lewd, vulgar, or offensive off-campus speech that has an effect on-campus because we conclude that the profile at issue, though created off-campus, falls within the realm of student speech subject to regulation under *Tinker*.

The court reasoned that the *Tinker* standard would apply because the school could meet the burden of showing a substantial disruption through evidence of a belief future disruption would occur.

Citing a case (*Lowery v. Euverard*, 2007) that supported a coach for kicking players off the team for circulating a petition against the coach, the court said, "*Tinker* does not require school officials to wait until the horse has left the barn before closing the door. . . . [I]t does not require certainty, only that the forecast of substantial disruption be reasonable." In fact, the court reasoned that there was no actual disruption of the school from the MySpace profile and deemed the disruption that did occur as "minor inconveniences." But the court found sufficient evidence that had the school not acted swiftly, there was a likelihood of future disruption.

The legal history of *Layshock* and *J.S.* is a story in itself, with the cases having differing outcomes through the courts. Ultimately, the cases were merged together and were heard *en banc* in the Third Circuit Court of Appeals, where the students emerged victorious. The appeals court concluded that *Fraser* does not authorize schools to limit off-campus lewd and vulgar expression and that expression that interferes with the rights of others under the *Tinker* standard cannot be prohibited unless there is a substantial disruption of the school. Furthermore, they concluded that the parodies were so outrageous that no one would believe they were serious. The U.S. Supreme Court declined to review the cases.

Use of Technology That Is Critical of the School or Individuals

Social media parodies of school officials or others may oftentimes not have any purpose other than, in the best case, to poke fun at others, or in the worst case demean others. A motivation to create a parody could have an underlying motive to be critical of the school or school officials. There are also times when social media may be used to directly criticize, and such criticism may create tensions between freedom of speech and school disruption, regardless of whether the message involved social media or originated off-campus.

Even when there is no actual criticism involved, the naming of individuals can easily create a situation that becomes a story of its own. A principal in Mississippi called a student into his office to confirm if a Facebook message encouraging students to wear jeans with holes in them to school to intentionally anger the principal was written by the student. Once confirmed, he informed the girl she would face punishment if other students wore such jeans to school, which would be in violation of the dress code. Her parent met with the principal and expressed that it would not be fair to hold her accountable for the behavior of other students. The meeting in the office became heated, and law enforcement became involved.

In a lawsuit (*Cash v. Lee County School District*, 2012), a court held that the First Amendment rights of the parent were violated because he had the right to express his views about the potential punishment of his daughter. In addition, the court held that his Fourth Amendment rights against unreasonable seizure were violated when he was later informed by law enforcement that a warrant was out for his arrest and he should voluntarily report to the police station. Once at the police station, he was taken via police car to the home of a municipal judge who served him with a notice that he was no longer allowed on school district property. Even though he was not in handcuffs, the court determined that a reasonable person in similar circumstances would conclude they were not free to leave.

In *J. S. v. Bethlehem Area School District* (2002), a student-authored website entitled "Teachers Sux" included audio and visual statements casting teachers and the principal in an unflattering light. The site also included a portion captioned, "Why Should She Die?" (referring to an algebra teacher), called her a "fat fuck," "stupid bitch," and "fat bitch," and then asked for donations to hire a hit man. The FBI and the police declined to file charges against the student. At the end of the school year, the student was informed that he would be expelled for the next school year. Although the court found that no serious threat to the teacher existed, it upheld the school's punishment based on the substantial disruption the website caused.

However, in another student website case, *Beussink v. Woodland R-IV* (1998), the court ruled that a student's website did not cause a material and substantial interference with school discipline. Brandon Beussink created a personal website on his home computer away from school. He made highly critical remarks of his teachers and the school, and it was brought to the attention of school officials by another student intent on getting Beussink in trouble. He was first suspended for five and later ten days for using vulgar language. Because of the school absence policy, the suspension resulted in a lowering of his grades. The federal district court in Missouri overturned the suspension, in part because there was no disruption of the school, but also because the school could not show the suspension was something other than "a mere desire to avoid the discomfort and unpleasantness that always accompany an unpopular viewpoint."

In *Evans v. Bayer* (2010), Katherine Evans was suspended for a Facebook posting that stated, "Ms. [name withheld] is the worst teacher I've ever met." The court overturned the suspension and ruled that the student expressed an opinion about a teacher that "was published off-campus, did not cause any disruption on-campus, and was not lewd, vulgar, threatening, or advocating illegal or dangerous behavior." In a case that did not result in litigation, a Mesa Verde High School (CA) student had his suspension rescinded after school officials decided his Facebook posting did not disrupt the school environment. The student's post had described his teacher as a "fat ass who should stop eating fast food, and is a douche bag" (National School Boards Association, 2011).

In another case, a court held that off-campus speech can be regulated under *Tinker* but not under *Fraser*. In determining there was not substantial school disruption nor a true threat, the court held in favor of students in *Neal v. Efurd* (2005). The students created websites highly critical of their school that contained violent illustrations, but the court stated the school failed to show a nexus between the websites and school disruption. Neither bullying nor school disruption was stated as the reason for the discipline until after the suit was filed.

Another school criticism case was not decided on off-campus elements, but instead on overbroad and vague language in school policy. Such a decision may be instructive for other principals in their school handbooks. Students posted internet messages on a website message board from home and school that negatively critiqued the boys' volleyball team by making fun of their performances and likelihood of a successful season. The court held that their speech was protected by the First Amendment, and there was not sufficient disruption of the school by the speech that brought negative publicity and attention to the school (*Flaherty v. Keystone Oaks School District*, 2003).

Use of Technology to Post Inappropriate Jokes

Using social media to post or express jokes or joking statements may be similar or relate to parody, and in some instances could potentially intersect with *Fraser* or *Hazelwood* standards. Principals should take caution, however, when considering discipline that could reasonably be interpreted as a joke. Taking action under *Tinker* standards may be a difficult hurdle when a message is merely juvenile or in poor taste.

In 2014, a high school senior was suspended, expelled, and forced to withdraw from the final four months of high school after he posted a two-word tweet response to a post. The student sarcastically tweeted, "Actually yes," in response to an anonymous message that asked if it was true he "made out" with a named teacher. The student had always maintained it was a joke, but the school disciplined him for "posting inappropriate comments online about a staff member" (*Sagehorn v. Independent School District No. 728*). The case reached the level of law enforcement involvement, where newspaper accounts quoted officials as saying the student could face multiple felonies for committing a crime. Investigations never found evidence of any relationship between the student and the teacher. The court sided with the student, noting that it was protected speech posted off-campus and outside of school hours. In a settlement agreement that included the city where the school district was located, the student received $425,000.

In *Killion v. Franklin Regional School District* in 2001, a student made a derogatory "top ten list" about the athletic director of the school and e-mailed the list to his friends. The list included statements about his appearance and references to the size of his genitals. The student e-mailed the list and insisted he made no copies; however, printed copies of the list made it to school. A court concluded that *Tinker* applied because the printed list made it to school, but because the list did not contain threats or cause a disruption, the suspension of the student was not proper. Although the court found portions of the list to be lewd, abusive, and derogatory, it would not ignore the fact that the relevant speech occurred off-campus in the confines of the student's home.

Use of Technology to Express Venting or Anger

In 2021, the U.S. Supreme Court ruled in favor of a student who posted a Snapchat that vented her frustration after not being selected for the varsity cheerleading team (*Mahanoy Area School District v. B.L.*, 2021). The case was widely anticipated as having the potential to redefine student speech rights and the prongs of *Tinker* in deciding how to apply student speech rights to off-campus expression. Brandi Levy was a 14-year-old high school freshman when she posted a private Snapchat message intended for her 250 followers that showed an image of herself and another student giving the finger and captioned with "Fuck school fuck softball fuck cheer fuck everything." The image was created at a local store, not during a school activity, and without wearing any identifiable school clothing.

She testified that she did not intend the message to be directed at anyone and that she would not use similar language at school because she knew she could face discipline for doing so.

The message was made available for twenty-four hours, and although it was created on a Saturday, the school did not become aware of the message until the next Thursday, when a copy was brought to the attention of a cheerleading coach. The school responded by suspending her from cheerleading for one year, citing a violation of cheerleading policy that included a statement that there would be "no toleration of any negative information regarding cheerleading, cheerleaders, or coaches placed in the internet." The school also placed a focus on the profanity expressed in the message and stated they would have applied discipline for that reason regardless of whether the message was on social media.

B.L. (Brandi) and her parents filed suit claiming that her speech rights were violated by disciplining her for off-campus expression. A district court held in her favor, and that decision was upheld in the Third Circuit of Appeals. In their ruling, the court stated that *Tinker* does not apply to off-campus speech and cannot be used to punish speech that is "outside of school owned, operated, or supervised channels and that is not reasonably interpreted as bearing the school's imprimatur" (*B.L. v. Mahanoy Area School District*, 2020).

The U.S. Supreme Court granted review of the case to determine if schools could regulate speech that occurs off-campus. In an 8–1 decision that numerous observers felt to be a middle-ground determination, the Court held that the special characteristics that normally give schools additional license to regulate speech do not always disappear when speech is made off-campus, which reversed the broad language of the Third Circuit (*Mahanoy Area School District v. B.L.*). The decision specified bullying or threats aimed at teachers and students, or while participating in online activities as examples.

But the Court also held that the school went too far in their discipline of B.L., noting that if she was an adult, such speech would be protected, and that there was limited evidence of any disruption to the school. The decision stated that although some might regard the substance of the message too trivial to be speech worthy of First Amendment protection, "sometimes it is necessary to protect the superfluous in order to preserve the necessary."

The decision also outlined three features of off-campus speech that make schools less likely to have an interest in regulating it. First, a student's off-campus speech is generally the responsibility of the parents. Second, any regulation of off-campus speech would cover virtually anything a student says or does outside of school. Third, the school does have an interest in protecting unpopular speech and ideas.

The Court left it for future cases to decide where, when, and how the three features mean the speaker's off-campus location make a critical difference, leaving such guidelines open to debate. Schools are not *prohibited* from taking actions against off-campus speech, but school officials must understand that the regulation of such speech invokes First Amendment principles. Justice Alito, in a concurring opinion, noted that "school officials should proceed cautiously before venturing into this territory." Perhaps the middle-ground decision was foreshadowed during oral arguments, when Justice Breyer, who subsequently authored the decision, stated, "I'm frightened to death of writing a standard" (Oyez, 2021).

Of note is a similar case decided prior to *B.L.* in 2019 where a cheerleader was dismissed as the head varsity cheerleader after coaches discovered a series of posts on her personal Twitter account containing profanity and sexual innuendo. Her claim against the school district was dismissed and qualified immunity given to defendants because there was no clearly established law that placed the constitutionality of their actions into question (*Longoria v. San Benito Ind. Sch. Dist.* 942 F.3d 258 (5th Cir. 2019)).

In an earlier case where a student vented against her school, in *Doninger v. Niehoff* (2009), Avery Doninger, a student council member and junior class secretary at her high school, became upset over the rescheduling of a student council event. She set into motion a mass email, blog message, and phone call protest, and in her blog referred to school personnel as "douchebags" and encouraged people to keep contacting the superintendent to "piss her off more." When school officials became aware of her involvement, she was banned from running for senior class secretary, and she brought suit against the district to force a new election or be installed as an additional class secretary. The decision of the school was upheld, but the court noted that because courts had difficulty determining First Amendment concerns in off-campus speech, it was unreasonable to expect school administrators to do so in the digital age.

Use of Technology to Post Inappropriate Images or Video Content

Sexting

The sending of nude images via various social media has been labeled "sexting," and it has been estimated that as many as one in five teens has either seen or sent their own sexting message. Emerging technology has made sexting easier to send and more difficult to track.

Child pornography laws written before the use of social media by minors do not account for the reality of the circumstances surrounding teen sexting, and many states have modified those laws to avoid life-long legal consequences for minors who may be involved in a consensual act without thinking about the potential consequences. Without modification of those laws, students sending even one consensual image could be found guilty of the distribution of child pornography if the student involved was a minor. And once such an image goes "viral," potentially an unlimited number of individuals could also be guilty of distribution and possession of child pornography. It is also possible that one could be charged with possession of child pornography even if the recipient of the images did not give consent.

Additionally, it is not uncommon for a person who at one time did not object to the images being distributed no longer wishes for that to be the case. Sexting images are sometimes used to bully, harass, and even blackmail other students.

The social consequences can be life-long because images posted via social media can never be completely eliminated from circulation. Tragedies have also resulted as a consequence of sexting, as teens have committed suicide after images of themselves have been posted in various forms.

When principals suspect or discover sexting, there are many legal implications to consider. Specifically, the following must be considered:

- Principals must take all precautions to avoid violating child pornography laws by immediately involving law enforcement when they suspect or discover pornographic images of minors. Do not copy, distribute, or possess any images. Although some states have modified laws to protect both adults and minors from prosecution when dealing with such images in good faith, not all states have done so. In a case where sexting was a new phenomenon, an administrator took a photo of a pornographic image for record-keeping purposes and was charged with possession of child pornography. Although he was eventually vindicated, the reputational damage was done (Martin, 2009). The bottom line is that you must investigate, but also take precautions to protect yourself.

- Recognize that not all sexting is bullying or harassment, but investigate the possibility that it is. Failure to respond to sexting that is bullying or harassment may be a violation of Title IX.

- It is possible that sexting may trigger the need for mandatory reporting, and although not all sexting may qualify for such reporting, the possibility must be considered.

- It does not matter if the sexting originated off-campus. It must still be addressed, and not doing so may be determined to be an act of deliberate indifference if the elements involve bullying and harassment.

- In addition to any moral and legal obligations principals have, there are also professional career implications. To dismiss or entirely ignore potential sexting that you know about, only later to have additional incidents come to public light, is hard to defend—the headline "Principal knew of student sexting but chose to ignore it" could be a career-ending moment.

Having said that, although it may seem obvious, school policy should reflect differences between images that include nudity that may be illegal and those that may be in poor taste that don't rise to the level of involving law enforcement. A sexting case from Pennsylvania demonstrated early attempts to deal with the issue. In *Miller v. Skumanick* (2009), school officials confiscated student cell phones and discovered photographs of nude or partially nude students. The images were given to District Attorney George Skumanick, who promised to prosecute those possessing the images and those posing for the images under child pornography laws unless they enrolled in a six- to nine-month education program and wrote an essay explaining why their actions were inappropriate and "what it means to be a girl in today's society." Although some parties complied to the agreement, others filed suit, claiming that their First and Fourteenth Amendment rights were violated by being compelled to complete the program. On appeal, their position was upheld. The appellate court prohibited the prosecution of the students, noting there was no evidence that they knowingly distributed the photos.

In another case where student participation in activities was included in the discipline of the students involved, in *T.V. ex rel. B.V. v. Smith-Green Community School Corporation* (2011), two female students posted photos of themselves taken during a summer sleepover. The pictures included depictions of themselves sucking on a phallic-shaped lollipop and another with the lollipop positioned between their legs. Although the postings were made only available to Facebook and MySpace "friends," a parent reported the images to the superintendent. The students were initially excluded from fall volleyball, but had their suspension reduced by visiting a counselor and apologizing to the team.

In a court decision, it was noted that the photos themselves were not obscene because they did not involve sexual conduct as defined by either federal or Indiana state law. The school argued that the photos caused divisiveness among the team, with some members supportive of the students, while others were not. The court noted that the evidence provided showed two complaints from parents, and "petty sniping" that could not have been what the Supreme Court had in mind when it was describing a "substantial disruption" of the school. Although there is no right to participate in extracurricular activities, the case was not decided on those grounds, but instead on freedom of speech. The handbook policy regarding out-of-school conduct was deemed so vague and overbroad that it violated the Constitution. Although the action of the school violated the student speech rights, the principal was entitled to qualified immunity because the circumstances surrounding the case involved rights not clearly established at the time of his decision.

What may be instructive in this case is that the school argued that they were not punishing the students for *posting* the pictures, but instead for the *activity* in the pictures—taken during the summer, outside of school. Principals who may make this argument when faced with a similar incident should consider the foundation of that position. It's essentially arguing that it's permissible to post what you wish, but the school will police what you are doing in the pictures you post and determine the acceptability of your activity. For many, that is a slippery slope inviting the monitoring of all student activity done in the privacy of their own homes.

Postings of Videos, Images, or Other Media

Students may also post videos, music, or nonsexting images that may require consideration for action by principals. In some cases, such postings could include many of the elements listed earlier.

One noteworthy case that began in 2011 and took four years to proceed through the courts was *Bell v. Itawamba County School Board* (2015). A student recorded a rap song that accused two coaches at his school of engaging in sexual misconduct with female classmates. The rap used vulgar language and allegedly suggestions that the coaches may face some type of retaliatory violence. The rap was sent to Facebook friends and posted on YouTube. The school accused the student of making up the allegations, but the student claimed his speech was an attempt to bring sexual harassment to the attention of the public, and that the issue was a matter of public concern. He was suspended and assigned to an alternative school.

A district court held in favor of the school district, but a panel of judges from the Fifth Circuit Court of Appeals reversed and held in favor of the student. Later, the Fifth Circuit reheard the case and ruled in favor of the school district, noting that the rap caused a substantial disruption of the school through threatening, harassing, and intimidating the teachers. The student and his supporters had argued that overbroad decisions against a student's well-meaning criticism of school officials could prevent any criticism of school officials and deny a safe space for students.

In *Latour v. Riverside Beaver School District* (2005), a thirteen-year-old student posted four rap songs, three with violent themes and one about a fellow student. He was arrested and spent a weekend in a juvenile detention center as well as weeks under house arrest. He was allowed to return to school after a court determined there was no substantial disruption of the school. The songs were determined to not be a true threat. Later the student received a cash settlement from law enforcement related to his arrest. The position of his supporters was that law enforcement did no investigation surrounding the songs and he was arrested without any evidence that he posed a clear or imminent threat.

A case from Washington involved the posting of a video of a teacher made without her awareness. A student posed behind the teacher making bunny ears and making pelvic thrusts, and it came to the attention of school officials after being contacted for comment by a news outlet doing a story about YouTube. The students involved were suspended and one later sued the district. A court determined that the student was not likely to prevail on his claim that the punishment was for his speech and not his conduct. The school district successfully argued that it was not punishing him for the off-campus posting of the video, but instead for the fact that the video was taken during school time on-campus. The court applied both *Tinker* and *Fraser* standards in holding against the student.

SECTION B. USE OF TECHNOLOGY TO MONITOR STUDENTS

Advances in technology coupled with increased pressure to ensure student safety have led to some school districts using assorted student monitoring practices. Technology is available and used to scan social media posts, track student location on school property and student IDs, and use facial recognition programs. Seemingly less-invasive tracking includes tracking the location of school-owned devices, although such tracking can also lead to questionable practices. There has sometimes been opposition from parents and students regarding the use of such tracking devices as well as student pushback when they believed security certificates they were required to download to access WiFi were instead a way for the school to monitor student browsing history and text messages (EFF, 2020).

There may perhaps be no better example of what could go wrong for school districts than what transpired in Lower Merion Township, Pennsylvania. On February 18, 2010, the Lower Merion School District (LMSD) superintendent released a statement regretting if a "situation caused concern or inconvenience" to anyone in the "LMSD community" (McGinely, 2010). The situation he referred to was the fact that his school district had installed and activated webcams in laptop computers checked out to students. The webcams were installed to help locate laptops that may have been lost or stolen. After an assistant principal confronted a student about what was seen on one webcam, that student filed suit against the district and the story became national news. The district came under fire when it was revealed the district had at least forty-two times, without the knowledge or consent of students or parents, activated the webcams, some of which had been in student bedrooms. Student B.R., with his parents, filed a civil action against the district in federal court after the assistant principal claimed B.R. was witnessed taking drugs, which B.R. claimed were "Mike and Ike" candy (Robbins, 2010). A judge ordered the district to shut off the webcams and the involved parties eventually reached a $610,000 settlement (*Robbins v. Lower Merion School District,* Civil Action No. 10-665 E.D. Pa. Aug 30, 2010).

Clearly the actions in that case are outside reasonable boundaries for school officials to take. However, given the technological capabilities available, the chance for overreaching into student tracking, whatever good intentions may exist, is a real possibility. It would be advisable that school districts proceed with caution when student tracking of any type is proposed, and group decisions are made in order to prevent potentially misguided action from taking place. Ensuring student safety is, of course, paramount, but simply monitoring student device usage without valid and justifiable reasons could be questioned.

Circumstances differ, and the use of surveillance cameras may be justifiable, and most students today are accustomed to such surveillance. However, microphones installed throughout the school or using facial recognition software may not face similar approval by a large number of students or their parents.

Suggested Risk Management Guidelines

- Develop, widely distribute, and implement a responsible use policy regarding use of electronic devices by students.

- Develop and implement the appropriate use of electronic devices in school curriculum to demonstrate the positive use of technology.

- Develop clear and reasonable guidelines for off-campus (out-of-school, off-school-grounds) behavior that is related to the order, safety, discipline, or general welfare of the school. Schools have no authority to control behavior or speech that has no relationship to or effect on the school.

- Have clear guidelines in school policy and handbooks stating that off-campus behavior, especially through the use of social media, may be subject to disciplinary action if the behavior violates bullying and harassment policy and law or if the behavior causes a disruption of school.

- Ensure that any and all students who frequently or infrequently are involved in school-sponsored field trips understand that the rules for away-from-school activities are the *same* as for in-school activities, including teacher and administrator authority.

- Describe what is considered to be an *educational purpose* and outline what activities are considered acceptable and unacceptable. For example, *acceptable activities* might include class assignments and career development activities for students, and professional development and communication. And *unacceptable activities* might include materials that contain racist, profane, or obscene language; using the network for financial gain or political or commercial activity including attempting to send anonymous or threatening messages of any kind; and using the network to provide addresses or other personal information that others may use inappropriately.

- Inform all users that the technical system administrators and technical services personnel have the ability to access personal files and monitor online use.

- School officials should ask themselves how much control they really want regarding off-campus student speech or student behavior. There is a trade-off that may not be worth it for educators—the more control they seek, the more potential liability they assume.

- Address problems from an educational perspective first and as a punitive measure second.

- Administrators should avoid becoming cyber censors.

- Policy should focus on the impact of expression and not the content of the expression.

- If students are disciplined, principals must keep the standards of *Tinker, Fraser, Hazelwood, Morse,* and *Mahanoy* in mind throughout the process.

- When punishment for disruption of the school is considered, it must be administered within a reasonable time frame. Principals should not wait weeks or months to decide that school was disrupted.

- Students should be educated, through programs and district responsible use policy, that there is no expectation of privacy and that schools have the authority to regulate and monitor use of school resources intended for educational use.

- When dealing with threats against staff or students delivered by social media, concentrate first on the receiving end of the message rather than the sending end of the message. In other words, concentrate on where the message landed rather than from where it was launched.

- Be aware of what constitutes a threat, but don't summarily dismiss what comes to your attention without investigation.

- Knowing your students and developing strong positive relationships helps during investigations of threats.

- Involve parents in the process.

- Address cyberbullying as a part of the entire antibullying curriculum.

- Cyberbullying should be defined and included in the district and school handbooks.

- Investigate complaints and take disciplinary action appropriate to the facts. Be consistent in how investigations are conducted.

- Create a supportive school climate to lessen the likelihood of bullying and to also empower students to report being victimized.

- When sexting is discovered, inform all parents, involve law enforcement, and follow all required mandatory reporting laws.

- Place sexting policies in responsible use policies and educate all students, in an age-appropriate manner, about the dangers of sexting.

- Include sexting as part of the school bullying and harassment prevention program.

- Educate and train all staff regarding the issues surrounding the problem of sexting.

CHAPTER 6

Student Discipline

One of the most difficult issues facing principals is the question of how to deal with unacceptable student conduct. Principals must be able to balance the school's interest in maintaining a safe and orderly environment against the rights of individual students to be free from unreasonable discipline. Although the doctrine of in loco parentis *has been eroded by the courts, it still supports reasonable disciplinary control by school officials. The courts typically uphold school personnel in matters of student discipline unless a student's liberty or property rights are threatened or the punishment is unreasonable or arbitrary.*

School officials have a long-established right to make and enforce reasonable rules of student conduct. As long as the rules are necessary to carry out the school's education mission, the courts recognize the school's authority to adopt reasonable regulations for maintaining order. Rules and regulations for student conduct, the foundations of which should be adopted as official board policy, need to be specific enough so that both students and their parents know what actions will not be tolerated at school and school-related activities. These rules must not be vague and must be applied uniformly to all students. Punishments need to be appropriate to the offense and the circumstances.

School discipline of students is under continuous court review. In recent years, the courts have chosen to defer to school board decisions on the assumption that school boards reflect the values of the community. Nevertheless, students and their parents continue to litigate when they believe that their rights have been violated, the school failed to follow proper procedures in taking disciplinary actions, or the punishment was unreasonable and arbitrary under the circumstances. For example, current zero-tolerance practices are bringing the question of one-size-fits-all policies into the courts' scrutiny in the area of reasonableness and fairness. When schools are careless, unreasonable, or arbitrary regarding discipline actions, students tend to prevail.

Schools are permitted by both statute and common law to regulate the conduct of students and have generally been given broad latitude in the areas of rules, control of misconduct, determination of guilt, and prescription of discipline and punishment. However, state statutes and the Constitution limit schools to rules that control behavior in ways that are reasonably related to legitimate education goals.

School administrators are also unfortunately aware of tragedies that have occurred after disciplinary action was taken against students. In 2011, a seventeen-year-old student returned to school a short time after being suspended and shot and killed the assistant principal who had suspended him (Cordes & Ferak, 2011). Although this tragedy is an extreme example, it demonstrates why principals must be mindful of, and responsive to, the highly emotional reactions that can accompany the imposition of student discipline.

CONSIDERATIONS RELATED TO COVID-19

COVID-19 has created unique challenges especially related to any disciplinary issues related to virtual learning. What should be done (or can be done) when a student does not follow rules when they are "attending class" virtually when located in their own home? In a hybrid situation, if a student is suspended from school, are they permitted to attend virtually during their suspension? Is a mask policy merely an extension of the dress code?

School districts have been forced to examine how policies written for in-school instruction apply to virtual instruction. For example, how should school officials respond to acts they may view on camera that would not be allowed at school? Under what circumstances should a student face punishment should a weapon be viewed in a virtual classroom (Canicosa, 2020)?

Although virtual learning has created some new considerations, much of what applies to all school behavioral issues will in most cases apply to a virtual setting. However, as you will see in this chapter, discretion is always advised in order to maintain the safest and most productive learning environment while simultaneously preserving the most rights for students.

SUGGESTED GUIDELINES FOR PRACTICE

Ensuring the protection of due process rights for students is imperative for principals. The degree of due process required in a given situation is dependent on the level of punishment being considered, not necessarily on the seriousness of the violation.

Issues of disproportionality in student discipline must be addressed. School policy and practice should be aimed at addressing disproportionality in not only the frequency of discipline for students of color and students with special needs, but also the level of punishment more frequently applied to students.

Principals should avoid turning over their responsibilities of school discipline to law enforcement. The criminalization of school rules is a serious problem, where behaviors once deemed rule book violations have turned into criminal code violations. This problem has far-reaching implications for the lives of students in the future.

SECTION A. DISCIPLINE CONSIDERATIONS FOR PRINCIPALS

School officials have broad authority to control the conduct of students, to take responsibility for conduct, and to punish misconduct that has a negative impact on the school where school-related activities are concerned. The authority to control student conduct is implied by state statutes and has developed over time through court cases. The courts generally uphold school officials' authority to discipline students for misconduct off the school grounds when the students are engaged in school-sponsored activities.

This section will highlight longstanding as well as emerging issues for principals as they carry out their significant responsibility to administer student discipline when students violate school rules or state and local laws. The question of when the schools must respond to student behavioral issues that occur off school grounds has taken place for decades. Since the 1980s and 1990s, many school districts implemented zero-tolerance policies, which brought their own set of implications. More recently, concerns have been raised regarding the criminalization of school behaviors as well as disproportionality in school discipline. These are essential considerations for principals and are highlighted due to their importance.

Disproportionality in Student Discipline

Student misbehavior is caused by a host of factors that work together, and principals are strongly urged to not adopt the idea that student conduct is a simple matter of following "the rules," and when broken, there must always be a consequence applied to rule breakers. As with disproportionate enrollment in special education, years of research point to inequities in school discipline practices for students of color, students with disabilities, and students from low-income backgrounds. Students from those groups are not only disciplined at higher rates than their peers; they are also more likely to face more serious punishment, even for the same infractions (NCLD, 2020).

Some studies indicate that students of color are more likely to receive office referrals and exclusionary discipline, with Black students three times more likely than white students to be expelled (NEA, in NCLD, 2020). Additionally, such disparities to even a greater degree exist for students with disabilities. The Obama administration issued new guidance regulations designed to help school districts address such disparities, including implementing a standard methodology to determine if and when those disparities may exist in a school district. The Trump administration delayed the implementation of that guidance.

However, even without such guidance, the moral imperative for principals is to make every effort to ensure that they themselves, their teachers, and their staff do all they can to dismantle conditions that increase the likelihood of disproportionality in discipline, as the effects harm students and lead to other societal inequalities.

Awareness of the problem is the first step, as well as learning personal implicit biases. Careful examination of school district policies and handbooks seeking inequities that exist in policies and rationale for the existence of some rules is another step. For example, most student dress codes disproportionately affect one gender, typically females. Hairstyle and other attire is another example. Resorting to suspending students for absenteeism are counterproductive and address the problem by "punishing" the student with the same action as their behavior.

Creating positive learning environments and increasing the use of alternatives to suspension strategies makes significant differences. Providing training and implementing systems such as MTSS (multi-tiered systems of supports) and culturally responsive teaching (CRT) are impactful (Advancement Project, 2014).

The Criminalization of School Behaviors

Related to the problem of disproportionality is the disturbing trend of criminalization of school behaviors. It's perhaps understandable, as schools face increased demands of ensuring school safety. "School based policing is the fastest growing area of law enforcement (*E.W. ex rel T.W. v. Dolgos,* 884 F.3d 172 188, 4th Cir. 2018). The resulting "broken windows law enforcement" is not just the response of the school and police officials, as in 2021 at least thirty-one states have some form of state or municipal statutes pertaining to conduct that occurs in or around schools (Rivera-Calderon, 2019). Such laws could colloquially be termed as school disturbance laws. This section is not promoting a case against law enforcement in schools, but instead urges school districts and principals to fully outline differences in roles and responsibilities of school employees and law enforcement in their MOU agreements between school districts and law enforcement agencies.

Studies have demonstrated that differences exist in the numbers of student arrests between schools staffed with full-time law enforcement and those schools that do not have such a presence. Schools with full-time law enforcement have higher arrest frequency for minor infractions or misdemeanors in schools, yet similar arrest numbers for serious offenses as those schools that do not have such a presence (ACLU, 2017). One cannot conclude that these statistics mean arrestable violations do not occur in schools without full-time law enforcement, nor can it be assumed that violations are ignored in those schools. Instead it may indicate a difference between viewing student misbehavior as violating school rules instead of breaking the law.

With law enforcement working within the educational space and with schools essentially a microcosm of society at large, there will inevitably be interactions between students and law enforcement, many times with school employees and law enforcement having similar goals and objectives but conflicting means to reach those goals. By necessity, educational employees have different training and mindsets from those who were trained in law enforcement. Interactions with law enforcement, from school police to school resource officers (SROs), impact all students, but particularly students of color and students with disabilities. This may sometimes lead to problems, especially if officers assigned to schools are not properly trained regarding the special characteristics related to youth, to students with special needs, or to students from communities of color. There is a danger when students are continually viewed as suspects or perpetrators or when the education space of a school is viewed and treated as equivalent to the streets.

Unfortunately, a trend has emerged with educators willing to cede that space to law enforcement, which many times is in effect an abrogation of their administrative duties and responsibilities to school police. Many violations that were at one time a breaking of rules has now become a breaking of a law, and rule enforcement has become law enforcement.

This resulting shift, however, may be less of a law enforcement problem, but instead one often created by school officials willing to let it happen. The practice of using school police to enforce low-level school policy violations deserves serious scrutiny. Students have been charged for offenses such as eating food off another's lunch tray, throwing candy, and doodling on a desk (Merkwae, 2015).

An illustrative case began in 2011 when a seventh-grade student in New Mexico was arrested under state law for "interfering with the education process" (N.M. Stat. Ann. § 30-20-13(D)). His offense was disrupting his physical education class for repeatedly burping and laughing during class time. The arresting officer was called to the class by the teacher who told the officer the student needed to be "removed" from the class. After his removal, the officer eventually decided to arrest the student. He was suspended and did not return for the rest of the school year. The next year, he was involved in an unrelated incident that included a search for marijuana, after which his parent filed a suit that included claims surrounding his arrest for burping.

The student lost all claims against individual defendants, and qualified immunity was granted to all defendants. Of note regarding the case was the dissenting opinion of Neil Gorsuch, who would later become an associate justice on the Supreme Court. Gorsuch stated in his dissent:

> [I]f a seventh grader starts trading fake burps for laughs in gym class, what's a teacher to do? Order extra laps? Detention? A trip to the principal's office? Maybe. But then again, maybe that's too old school. Maybe today you call a police officer. And maybe today the officer decides that, instead of just escorting the now compliant thirteen-year-old to the principal's office, an arrest would be a better idea. So out come the handcuffs and off goes the child to juvenile detention. (*A.M. v. Holmes*, 830 F. 3d 1123 1169, 10th Cir. 2016)

Courts have been critical of law enforcement actions where officers have asserted their authority when they believe students are not showing them proper respect. When an SRO was called to counsel a group of seventh-grade girls who had been involved with incidents of bullying and fighting, he decided that the assembled group in the classroom were being unresponsive to him and disrespectful. He told them he was "not playing around" and taking them to jail was the easiest way to prove a point and make them "mature a lot faster." Qualified immunity was not given to the arresting officers after they were sued for unlawful arrest and violation of the Fourth Amendment (*Scott v. County of San Bernardino*, 2018).

In *E.W. ex rel T.W. v. Dolgos* (2018), an officer was granted qualified immunity for handcuffing a calm and compliant ten-year-old student who had been in a confrontation on a school bus three days prior. An SRO called to the school felt that the student acted as though she did not think the situation was "a big deal" and decided to take the student into custody. An appellate court held that no reasonable officer confronted with a similar situation would have determined the handcuffing was justified; however, qualified immunity was granted because it would not have been clear that such handcuffing would give rise to a Fourth Amendment violation. The court emphasized that moving forward their excessive force holding is clearly established for any future qualified immunity cases involving similar circumstances. The court stated, "[W]hile the officers' presence surely keeps the nation's children safe, officers should not handcuff young students who may have committed minor offenses but do not pose an immediate threat to safety." (*E.W. ex rel T.W. v. Dolgos*, 884 F.3d 172 187, 4th Cir. 2018).

There should be clear guidelines in place between what is the responsibility of school employees and those in law enforcement, as well as under what circumstances who "takes charge" when necessary. There should be proper training on de-escalation techniques; when the use of restraints may be necessary; and the special characteristics of youth. In addition, while keeping within privacy rights of students in mind, it may be a good proactive step to include law enforcement on an informational basis regarding some students with special needs. Frequently law enforcement engages with students who to the officer appear like every other student, but who do not properly respond to officer requests, resulting in an avoidable escalated confrontation. *Scott v. City of Albuquerque* (2017), *Love v. Penn-Harris-Madison Sch. Corp.* (2016), and *S.R. v. Kenton County* (2017) are examples of cases which raise the questions to the degree that problems may be avoided if SROs were given more specifics about student behavior interventions or accommodations.

Principals must be mindful of the potential overreach of filing criminal charges against students for violations of school rules. A Florida case illustrates a common occurrence when a student faces suspension. In *H.W. v. State* (2012), a student was charged with assault after verbally lashing out at the administrative assistant for student discipline who suspended him for rules violations. Along with some profane name-calling, the student said, "You're going to die today, bitch. Something is going to happen to you after school; you watch." He also told a police officer he would make sure the administrator was "put to sleep." Although the suspension of the student was upheld, the appeals court held that the evidence was not sufficient to support a guilty verdict of assault in a criminal court.

Institutional Authority Off School Grounds (Not Related to Off-Campus Use of Social Media)

The common law basis for the school's authority to control student conduct or activities off school grounds is based on the assumption that the authority of school officials extends to any student acts that are detrimental to the good order and best interests of the school, whether the acts are committed during school hours, while students travel to and from school, or after the student has returned home. Schools can make rules and regulations governing students' extracurricular activities in athletic competitions, musical organizations, dramatic organizations and productions, social activities, class and school trips, cheerleading, school and class elective offices, literary and service clubs, scholastic activities, and honor groups. These rules and regulations are enforceable when student activities take place off school grounds as officially sanctioned school activities or when it can be shown that the off-campus activities have a *detrimental effect* on the school.

Students are not deprived of constitutional rights of free speech and property interests when disciplined for behavior that is detrimental to the school, regardless of whether the incident took place on or off school property. A *reasonable* school regulation is one that is essential in maintaining order and discipline on school property and that measurably contributes to the maintenance of order and decorum within the educational system, as ruled in *Blackwell v. Issaquena County Board of Education* (1966).

In *Fenton v. Stear* (1976), a federal court in Pennsylvania held that lewd comments made about a teacher on Sunday off school premises were sufficiently detrimental to the school to warrant disciplinary action. In this case, while a teacher was in a shopping center on a Sunday evening, a student shouted, "There's Stear." A second student loudly responded, "He's a prick." On Monday morning, when confronted about the incident by school authorities, the student admitted calling teacher Stear a prick. The student was given an in-school suspension (ISS), not allowed to participate in the senior trip, not permitted to attend any extracurricular activities, and placed on other restrictions at school. The student challenged the disciplinary action as a violation of his freedom of speech and denial of a property right to an education. The *Fenton* court stated:

> The First Amendment rights of the plaintiff were not violated. His conduct involved an invasion of the right of teacher Stear to be free from being loudly insulted in a public place by lewd, lascivious or indecent words or language. . . . It is our opinion that when a high school student refers to a high school teacher in a public place on a Sunday by a lewd and obscene name in such a loud voice that the teacher and others hear the insult, it may be deemed a matter for discipline in the discretion of the school authorities. To countenance such student conduct even in a public place without imposing sanctions could lead to devastating consequences in the school. Furthermore, because the student continued his education while serving the in-school suspension, he was not deprived of any property right.

In a case in which a student sold cocaine to an undercover police officer on three occasions while not on school property, the student was arrested at the high school and suspended by the principal and subsequently expelled. The student challenged the expulsion, claiming the school board lacked authority to expel him for a nonschool activity off school grounds. The court, in *Howard v. Colonial School District* (1992), upheld the school board, agreeing that the student was a threat to the safety and welfare of other students, even if he was an off-campus drug dealer.

In a case in which a student was expelled from school for committing battery on another student on a public street after school, the student challenged the school's authority to discipline him for off-school-grounds behavior. The court, in *Nicholas B. v. School Committee* (1992), upheld the school's action, observing that imposing discipline off school grounds was not arbitrary or capricious.

When the safety of students is compromised, school-based discipline clearly extends to activities beyond the school grounds. Two students, one in a Jeep and the other in a pickup truck, blocked the progress of a school bus loaded with children traveling to school. The driver of the Jeep positioned his vehicle in front of the bus while the pickup truck followed behind, and, by alternately slowing and speeding up, they obstructed the operation of the bus. On arriving at the school, the students in the Jeep and the pickup truck were cited by the highway patrol and suspended by the school. They challenged the disciplinary action by school authorities. The court, in *Clements v. Board of Trustees of Sheridan County School District No. 2* (1978), stated,

It matters little that the proscribed conduct occurred on a public highway. It is generally accepted that school authorities may discipline pupils for out-of-school conduct having a direct and immediate effect on the discipline or general welfare of the school. This is particularly true where the discipline is reasonably necessary for the student's physical or emotional safety and well-being of other students.

The following cases are important for school administrators to be familiar with as they deal with violent essays and verbal threats and the question of whether they are the cause of enough disruption of the school to be prohibited speech. Administrators must consider what constitutes an actual disruption of the school, as well as the intent of the speaker when dealing with potential threats. Restricting all speech because of a fear of potential disruption would not be permissible. With the widespread common use of technology, administrators must become aware that even more clashing points are created where they must balance student rights and school safety. Even though courts are not in full agreement about what defines a threat, principals must frequently make that determination.

The U.S. Supreme Court, in *Watts v. United States* (1969), held that a true threat is a type of speech that is not protected by the First Amendment. A threat must be a realistic, actual threat and not mere hyperbole. The Court further defined a true threat in *Virginia v. Black* (2003) as statements "where the speaker means to communicate a serious expression of an intent to commit an act of unlawful violence to a particular individual or group of individuals." The Court stated that the actual intent to carry out the threat was not required. The speaker must intend to convey or communicate the threat, and the lack of intent to communicate the threat makes it protected under the First Amendment.

Lower courts have adopted differing standards regarding what is considered a true threat, with most circuits adopting a reasonable person standard; however, circuits are split as to whether the speech should be analyzed from the viewpoint of the speaker or of the recipient. Some jurisdictions have adopted an approach from the viewpoint of the speaker—whether a reasonable person would conclude that a statement could be interpreted by someone as a threat. Another approach, adopted by the Second Circuit, uses a "reasonable listener" test, analyzing whether the listener believed that the threat would be carried out. The Eighth Circuit outlined a list of factors or considerations regarding how a reasonable recipient would view a purported threat in *United States v. Dinwiddie* (1996). Consider (a) the reaction of those who heard the alleged threat; (b) whether the threat was conditional; (c) whether the person who made the threat communicated it directly to the object of the threat; (d) whether the speaker had a history of making threats against the person purportedly threatened; and (e) whether the recipient had a reason to believe that the speaker had a propensity to engage in violence.

Controversies have arisen as a result of what students have written even if they never intended someone else to see it. An example of a case determined from the viewpoint of the recipient would be *Doe v. Pulaski* (2002), in which the recipient of the message could reasonably conclude it was a threat. Although this case did not involve social media, it has implications regarding both written threats and the threshold issue of where the reach of the school begins and ends. An *en banc* decision of the Eighth Circuit Court of Appeals reversed an earlier three-judge ruling and determined that an eighth-grade student could be expelled from school for a threatening letter he wrote about his former girlfriend, even though he never intended to give it to her. Because it was shown to another classmate, it was viewed as communicating a threat.

A student wrote two letters about a girl after she broke up with him that talked about raping, sodomizing, and killing her. In one letter, he used words such as "bitch," "slut," "ass," and "whore" more than eighty times and used the f-word no fewer than ninety times. He also warned her not to go to sleep because he would be lying under her bed waiting to kill her with a knife. Another student found one of the letters, and initially the writer tried to take it back, but then allowed the other student to read it. Later the girl found out about the letters and persuaded the second student to get them for her, which he did. After the letter was shown to a student resources officer and the principal, the writer was suspended for the remainder of the school year. The writer's parents filed suit in November 2000, and the U.S. District Court for the Eastern District of Arkansas found that the letter was not a true threat and ordered the writer reinstated in school.

Initially this ruling was upheld under appeal until the full Eighth Circuit ruled against the writer. The court ruled that because the writer had allowed another student to read the letter and because he had discussed it with the victim, he intended to communicate the threat. The court did note, "Had we been sitting as the school board, we might very well have approached the situation differently, for it appears to us that the action taken . . . was unnecessarily harsh." Expressing the view that other options existed that may have protected students as well as aided in the understanding of the inappropriateness of the conduct, the court nevertheless stated,

> It is not the role of the federal courts to set aside a decision of school administrators which the court may view as lacking a basis in wisdom or compassion. Those judgments are best left to the voters who elect the school board.

The *Doe* case involved a unique element respecting the communication of a threat, but there are other cases in which violent narratives of some sort came to the attention of school officials. Again, although not involving social media, the aspect of the threat and off-campus behavior can be seen as similar to situations involving social media. In 2008, the Eighth Circuit Court of Appeals ruled in *Riehm v. Engelking* (2007) that a Minnesota high school student's essay depicting a student's murder of a teacher and suicide was not protected speech because it was reasonable to conclude it was a threat.

Riehm wrote three essays in his high school creative writing class that his teacher found disturbing. The first essay contained sexually graphic descriptions, and the teacher returned it to him with written comments that she found it offensive and a suggestion that he change teachers or change his "obsessive focus on sex and potty language." Later Riehm submitted a two-part essay in which he wrote that "life is not G-rated . . . there is violence, language, sexual content everywhere." His essay further went on to criticize a fictitious English teacher named "Mrs. Cuntchenson," whom he described as "narrow minded, uncreative, and paranoid." In the third essay, titled "Bowling for Cuntchenson," Riehm referred to the teacher as a "bitch . . . who is way out of line." The story ends with the student getting a gun and shooting the teacher in the eye and with the narrator fading to a movie theater and discussing the film *Bowling for Columbine*. After being reported to the school principal, Riehm was suspended and the essays were given to law enforcement.

Another case, *Ponce v. Socorro Independent School District* (2007), that considered whether the First Amendment protected student speech that threatened a Columbine-style attack, could also apply to situations involving social media threats. In this case, E.P., a high school student in Texas, kept a personal journal in which he wrote a first-person account of creating a pseudo-Nazi group at his high school and other schools in the district, as well as plans to commit an attack at his school and others. School officials learned of the journal from a concerned student with whom E.P. had shared the contents. Upon questioning, E.P. insisted that the writing was fictional and consented to a search of his backpack where the journal was found. He was subsequently suspended for making a "terroristic threat," and it was recommended that he be placed in an alternative education program.

After his parents brought suit against the district, a U.S. district court ruled in his favor, determining that the school had not proven a disruption would occur. However, the Fifth Circuit reversed on appeal, determining that the speech was not constitutionally protected. Relying on the U.S. Supreme Court ruling in *Morse v. Frederick* (2007), the circuit court concluded that "speech advocating a harm that is demonstrably grave and that derives that gravity from the 'special danger' to the physical safety of students arising from the school environment is unprotected." The court stressed that school officials must take threats such as those in E.P.'s journal seriously or they may miss signals that lead to tragedy. They must be able

> to react quickly and decisively to address a threat of physical violence against their students, without worrying that they will have to face years of litigation second-guessing their judgment as to whether the threat posed a real risk of substantial disturbance.

The court fell short, however, of allowing schools to expel students just because they are loners, wear black, or play video games.

In the previous cases, it was clear who the target of the potential threat was. What has been less clear in some cases is whether there was actual intent to carry out the threat. In 2001, a telling case became national news that Hudson (2005) describes as "the epitome of overreaction in the Columbine age" (p. 1). A.P. was fourteen years old in 1999 when he drew a picture of his Louisiana high school. His picture depicted the school being attacked by a missile launcher, explosives, and people with weapons. The principal was also a target in the drawing, with derogatory remarks including a racial epithet. A.P. showed the drawing to his mother, who later recalled that he told her he was "just playing." The sketchpad was thrown into a closet in his bedroom, where it stayed for two years.

In March 2001, his younger brother discovered the sketchpad, drew an animal on it, and took it on the bus to school to show his teacher. When he showed it to another student on the bus, the student flipped through the sketchpad and saw the drawing A.P. had made two years earlier. The student then showed the drawing to the bus driver.

The younger brother received a three-day suspension for bringing an inappropriate drawing to his middle school, and word was sent to the high school A.P. was then attending. A.P. was searched by school officials, and they found a box cutter that he used for his job at a local market. They also found fake identification and notebooks that contained references to gangs, drugs, death, and sex. A.P. was arrested and spent four nights in jail. He was allowed to re-enroll at an alternative school after his mother waived his right to an expulsion hearing.

A.P. and his brother filed suit against the school district, claiming that school officials violated their First Amendment rights by punishing them for the content of the drawing. In *Porter v. Ascension Parish School Board* (2004), the district court concluded that the brothers did not have constitutional protection because the drawing represented a true threat and that the drawing constituted a substantial disruption of the school. This court relied, in part, on the decision in *Doe v. Pulaski* (2002) and reasoned that the drawing and its language could reasonably be construed as a serious threat. It was immaterial whether A.P. had intended to ever bring the drawing to school; what mattered was the fact that the drawing did make its way onto the campus.

Upon appeal, the Fifth Circuit supported the district court in upholding the suspension, but it did not agree with the First Amendment analysis.

> A.P. did not intentionally or knowingly communicate his drawing in a way sufficient to remove it from the protection of the First Amendment. . . . Because A. P.'s drawing cannot be considered a true threat as it was not intentionally communicated, the state was without authority to sanction him for the message it contained.

Porter is an important case because it dealt with the issue of First Amendment protection for off-campus student speech, and although it did not deal with off-campus speech brought onto campus through technology, there are elements of the decision relevant to those circumstances. With social media, it is very common for messages to be received by parties the sender never intended to see. Learning the background of what legally is a "true threat" and what constitutes "on-campus" speech may help administrators make better decisions as they deal with students and social media, cell phones, instant messages, and other technologies.

Zero-Tolerance Policy Development and Implementation

Many school districts adopted zero-tolerance policies in the wake of the Gun-Free Schools Act of 1994. The act mandates that all states receiving federal funds for education must require school districts to expel a student for at least a year for possessing a gun on school grounds. Many states have gone farther and require students to be expelled for possession of any weapon—not just a gun. But even before this, school districts had other zero-tolerance policies and regulations in place to ensure consistent handling of situations involving such issues as drugs and alcohol, threats, and harassment.

Zero-tolerance policies emerged from federal drug enforcement policy dating back to the 1980s, during the administration of President Ronald Reagan. Zero-tolerance policies in schools are an attempt to send antiviolence or antidrug messages by treating both minor and major incidents severely. And despite controversies surrounding that attempt, zero tolerance is a widely used response to school violence and school disruption. Zero tolerance has been defined as "the policy or practice of not tolerating undesirable behavior, such as violence or illegal drug use, with the automatic imposition of severe penalties even for first offenses" (Potts, Njie, Detch, & Walton, 2003, p. 16).

The prevalence of zero-tolerance legislation and similar school board policy increased during the 1990s. Examples of zero tolerance went well beyond the mandates of the federal government and included a range of offenses—from threats to swearing in school. By the late 1990s, zero tolerance in some form was the norm in public schools, and 94 percent had zero-tolerance policies for weapons, 87 percent for alcohol, and 79 percent mandated suspension for violence or tobacco (Heaviside, Rowand, Williams, & Farris, 1998). As zero-tolerance policies were being phased out in law enforcement, school districts expanded their policies, with nearly 91 percent of schools having some zero-tolerance policy for something other than firearms. It is also common for school districts to have zero-tolerance policies for noncompliance and disrespect (Molsbee, 2008).

A task force created by the American Psychological Association (2006) to study the effects of zero-tolerance programs noted among several findings that zero-tolerance policies challenge the developmental stages that adolescents normally experience.

When a violated policy does not threaten safety, the task force noted it is better to weigh the importance of the particular consequence against the potential long-term negative effects of zero-tolerance policies, especially when applied to situations in which juveniles may be acting *as juveniles*.

Before a school district attempts to develop or refine zero-tolerance policy, the primary question that should be asked is how does the proposed or current zero-tolerance policy define prohibited actions, substances, and possessions and what, if any, room for interpretation of individual events does the policy permit? Secondary questions should include what kinds of situations present a clear violation of policy; what constitutes a weapon, prohibited substance, threat, or harassment under the policy; and does the current or proposed policy offer any flexibility for interpretation?

Every school district needs tough policies that deal with weapons, drugs, threats, and so forth, but a zero-tolerance policy can be difficult to enforce if (a) the policy is not well written and (b) those who administer the policy don't have some "interpretation" room. For example, any reasonable educator recognizes a gun or a knife as a weapon. A sharpened stick could be a weapon but, then, so could a pencil. Zero-tolerance policies need to be written in such a way that school district credibility is not going to be damaged by enforcement. Does the specific policy use the words *shall* or *will* (the policy dictates the decision and individual cases cannot be evaluated by onsite administrators) or *may* (onsite school administrators have some decision-making power and can consider the merits of individual cases)?

School district attorneys have a tendency to advise school boards to develop zero-tolerance policies that treat students as if one size fits all. Attorneys are sensitive to the demonstration of fairness in any policy. They are aware of the historical patterns of apparent inequitable disciplinary treatment of minority students as reflected in suspension and expulsion rates. One of school districts' responses in recent years to address this apparent inequity in the meting out of discipline has been to create zero-tolerance policies based on the assumption that all circumstances and all students are exactly equal. Yet, on the other hand, schools commit to individualizing instruction and, in some cases, are legally mandated to do so. For example, the Individuals with Disabilities Education Act requires that school districts provide an individualized education plan—an IEP.

Applying the letter of the zero-tolerance law to cases like the following one often makes school officials appear ridiculous. A school district in Pennsylvania suspended a kindergartner for bringing a plastic hatchet to school as part of his Halloween costume. A Chicago fourth grader who forgot to wear his belt was suspended for violating the school dress code. A thirteen-year-old Texas student was suspended for carrying a bottle of Ibuprofen in her backpack instead of giving it to the school nurse. In Louisiana, an eight-year-old girl was suspended for bringing a family heirloom to show and tell: she brought a gold-plated pocket watch and fob with a one-inch knife attached to it. A New Jersey school district suspended four kindergartners who allegedly pointed their fingers like guns and shouted "Bang!" at other pupils during recess. A school district in Colorado expelled an honors student for accidentally packing a knife with her lunch. A school district in Virginia suspended a model student for writing in a note to her girlfriend that she was upset about the grade she was going to receive from a particular teacher, her parents would ground her "forever," and she "felt like killing herself and the teacher." In this case, the teacher discovered the note, and the school suspended the student for threatening a teacher, pending a hearing for expulsion (in accordance with a zero-tolerance policy). Although the school board considered it a threatening note, they found it *not threatening enough to keep her out of school* and ordered her reinstated—but at a *different* school in the same district. (*Our note*: Apparently, she was much less threatening at a different school?) The student and her parents appealed, community pressure heightened, the press had a heyday debating the issue, and then, quietly, the girl was allowed to return to her home school without any permanent record of the incident. Results? Do incidents like these demonstrate unfair treatment of students or examples of management decisions by school administrators hamstrung by zero-tolerance policies that don't allow for leadership in decision making? All these examples caused substantial embarrassment to the school districts. The Virginia example, which was destined to be played out in the courts at the expense of the taxpayer, focused on the girl's alleged threat but ignored the girl's purported desire to kill herself. One threat was taken seriously to an illogical extreme and the other was ignored. The conundrum that school districts find themselves in is to create zero-tolerance policies that ensure consistent, fair, reasonable, and equitable treatment of all students in all circumstances.

In developing a zero-tolerance policy, giving school administrators the opportunity to exercise their professional judgment and common sense in individual situations, may provide the balance desired between the policy and individualization of discipline. The policy, like other aspects of instruction, should provide that the onsite administrator can be overridden, when necessary, through standard due process procedures—the classic checks and balances tenet of democracy. The following suggested policy statements include the provision that onsite school administrators retain final authority in determining what constitutes a weapon, threat, prohibited substance, harassment, and so forth—and whether the situation constitutes a potential danger. Consider the following examples.

Weapons Policy

A policy statement such as the following balances the district's responsibility to act consistently and strongly with its responsibility to consider students as individuals:

> The school district strictly prohibits the possession, conveyance, use, or storage of weapons or weapon lookalikes on school property, at school-sponsored events, or in or around a school vehicle. This policy applies to students, employees, and visitors, including those who have a legal permit to carry a weapon. *Onsite school administrators retain final authority in determining what constitutes a weapon and evaluating potential danger.*

If the problem of defining what constitutes a weapon surfaces, a policy statement might include the following definition:

> All the following are considered weapons: knife blades, razor blades, cutting instruments, martial arts hardware, lasers, BB guns, shockers, brass knuckles, metal pipes, sharpened sticks, stun guns, firearms, ammunition, mace, pepper spray, acid, explosive devices, fireworks, pyrotechnics, slingshots, cross or noncross bows or arrows, or any other instrument capable of inflicting serious injury. The brandishing of *any* instrument, piece of equipment, or supply item in the form of a threat of bodily harm to another will cause such instrument to be considered a weapon. Weapon lookalikes, such as toy guns, may also be considered weapons under this policy.

Drugs Policy

A policy statement such as the following is suggested to balance the need for a strong and consistent response with the importance of viewing students as individuals:

> The school district strictly prohibits the possession, conveyance, use, or storage of drugs on school property, at school-sponsored events, or in or around a school vehicle. This policy applies to students, employees, and visitors. *Onsite school administrators retain final authority in determining what constitutes a prohibited drug and in evaluating potential danger.*

Now, again, the problem arises in defining which drugs are prohibited and what the district considers to be a drug, so a policy statement should include examples (e.g., "All of the following are considered to be drugs and are strictly prohibited: . . .").

Using these areas as examples, zero-tolerance policies could include threats to others, sexual harassment, child molestation or abuse, and a multitude of other areas that school districts believe need to be closely monitored. Whatever a school district decides, all zero-tolerance policies should include, at a minimum, the following components:

- Exceptions to the policy (e.g., in a weapons policy, "Law enforcement officials may carry weapons on school property . . . principals may issue exceptions for items such as cutting instruments used in a specific class or lookalikes for school drama productions"). Delineate exceptions in all other zero-tolerance policies. Define the use of the words *shall* or *will* as opposed to *may*.

- Include a description of where and when such policies will be enforced. Any policy should specify the areas in which the policy will be enforced and the events—outside school hours—at which students, employees, parents, or visitors are subject to the policy (e.g., field trips, school-sponsored events, school buses, and other school vehicles).

- Establish guidelines (local and state regulations) for notifying other authorities (e.g., police, social welfare).

- Provide disciplinary rules and procedures that include students, employees, and parents and other visitors. It is suggested that school districts include a statement such as, "The district will vigorously pursue prosecution through law enforcement agencies."

- Include an explanation of due process rights.

Any zero-tolerance policy must comply with existing state laws, should be reasonable but tough, and should be designed in such a way that both district credibility and exposure to liability are not compromised. To preserve credibility, any zero-tolerance policy should state that the principal has the right to make the final judgment on what constitutes a weapon, a drug, abuse, harassment, and so forth. Exercising professional judgment is part of a principal's job as an effective leader.

SECTION B. DUE PROCESS

The right to due process of law is the cornerstone of civil liberty. It guarantees fairness for all citizens. The primary source of this guarantee is the Fifth Amendment, which protects individuals against double jeopardy and self-incrimination and guarantees that no person can be deprived of life, liberty, or property without due process of law. This protection is further defined in the Equal Protection Clause of the Fourteenth Amendment. In addition, all fifty states have some form of due process language in their constitutions.

The states have total authority for education, and under state laws, schools are required to provide students and teachers with due process before they can be deprived of any right. Courts view due process in two ways:

- *Substantive* due process requires that the rules or policies be fair in and of themselves.

- *Procedural* due process requires that the policies, rules, and regulations be carried out in a fair manner.

Rather than defining an inflexible due process procedure universally applicable to every situation, the courts prefer to decide the required elements of due process on a case-by-case basis. The most commonly accepted elements of due process are

- Proper notice of the charges

- A fair and impartial hearing

However, courts generally follow precedent. This means that when a court rules a certain way, the same court or a lower court is obliged to rule the same way in similar cases. A court is not bound by precedent if it can show that the case before it is significantly different from the precedent-setting case, despite an apparent similarity.

In general, the more severe the punishment, the more formal the due process requirements are. The degree of due process that is required is not directly related to seriousness of the offense, but instead to the seriousness of the consequences being proposed. In *Goss v. Lopez* (1975), the Court prescribed a ten-day limit to separate short-term suspensions from long-term suspensions and expulsions. Because students who are suspended for more than ten days or expelled from school altogether are deprived of certain constitutional rights, the courts require a more stringent due process to ensure the penalty is both deserved and fair. Under these more stringent due process requirements, students have, at a minimum, the following rights:

- To receive written notice of the charges and the school's intent to long-term suspend or expel, as noted in *Strickland v. Inlow* (1975)

- To receive prior notice of a hearing that specifies the time, place, and circumstances

- To be represented by legal counsel or other adult representative, as noted in *Black Coalition v. Portland School Dist. No. 1* (1973)

- To see adverse evidence prior to the hearing, as noted in *Graham v. Knutzen* (1973)

- To be heard before an impartial party (the hearing officer may be the school principal, unless it can be shown that the principal cannot be fair and impartial), as noted in *Dixon v. Alabama State Board of Education* (1961)

- To compel supportive witnesses to attend the hearing

- To confront and cross-examine adverse witnesses, as noted in *Morrison v. City of Lawrence* (1904)

- To be protected from self-incrimination

- To testify on their own behalf and present witnesses

- To receive a transcript of the proceedings for use on appeal

In *Goss*, students alleged that they had been suspended for up to ten days without a hearing. They claimed that their suspensions were unconstitutional on the grounds that they were deprived, without a hearing, of their right to an education—procedural due process under the Fourteenth Amendment. In ruling in favor of the students, the district court declared that minimum requirements of notice and hearing must take place before students can be suspended.

On appeal, the school district contended that the Due Process Clause does not protect students from expulsion from a public school because there is no constitutional right to an education at public expense. The Supreme Court disagreed and affirmed that the Due Process Clause forbids deprivations of liberty. The *Goss* Court stated that "when a person's good name, reputation, honor, or integrity is at stake because of what the government is doing to him, the minimal requirements of the due process clause must be satisfied."

The *Goss* decision affirmed that education is one of the most important functions of state and local governments. It recognized that because of the complexity of public schools, discipline and order is essential for the education function to be performed. However, the Court required schools to set up hearing procedures that must be followed before students are suspended. These hearing procedures must include the following:

- An oral or written notice of the charges against the student
- An explanation of the evidence the authorities have to support the charges
- The opportunity for the student to present their side of the problem

The Court noted, however, that if the continued presence of a student in a school poses a danger to persons or property, the student can be removed from school immediately. In this case, the notice and hearing must follow as soon as possible.

In *Wood v. Strickland* (1975), the Supreme Court held, in the context of student discipline, that school board members can be held liable for damages if they knew, or reasonably should have known, that the disciplinary action taken by the school would violate the constitutional rights of the affected student. Traditionally, educators and school board members enjoyed good faith immunity from liability for damages, and educators who acted with no intent to commit a wrongful act were not held liable for their errors of judgment. The *Wood* decision demonstrates how far the pendulum has moved, from the earlier, hands-off policy that left education to the educators to a policy that demands strict legal accountability on the part of educators. However, *Wood* also noted that "it is not the role of the federal courts to set aside decisions of school administrators which the court may view as lacking a basis in wisdom or compassion." Principals should understand that taking actions against students when they know they are violating, or should have known they are violating, student rights may be held liable for their actions.

However, courts continue to be reluctant to become involved in the day-to-day operation of schools, and in the majority of short-term suspension cases, schools have been successful when they have followed the procedures required by *Goss*. The intent of the *Goss* and *Wood* decisions was to respect both the discretionary powers of educators and the constitutional rights of students. These decisions formalized the requirement of fairness in the relationship between students and educators.

SECTION C. APPLYING DISCIPLINE TO STUDENTS

Principals frequently hear the statement "I sent the student to the office and nothing happened!" Such a conclusion based on perception may in fact be true; however, perhaps the more honest statement would be "I sent the student to the office and the principal didn't do what I wanted to see happen to the kid."

"What happens" to a student who is referred for discipline is a decision that principals make which takes into consideration multiple elements which can include the nature of the violation; the age and abilities of the student; the past history of the student; and how the punishment fits the offense and is allowed by law and in school policy. The overall climate of the school is also important in context. But "what happens" to a student referred to a principal is also based on what the goal of the suggested punishment is. Is the goal to apply a punishment to lead the student to cease the misbehavior and not commit a similar violation in the future, or is the goal to actually inflict some form of "pain" to the student?

The principal must act as a fair and reasonable party in the process and ensure that any discipline applied to a student isn't done to simply "extract a pound of flesh" but instead to meet the educational needs of the student, benefit the school climate and culture, support the teachers, and at times serve as a deterrence to other students. The use of any extreme measures of punishment such as expulsion carry the risk of life-long enduring consequences and have been linked to contributing to the "school-to-prison" pipeline; on the other hand, measures deemed too minimal to change student behavior create a revolving door of the "classroom to the office and back" that is disruptive to everyone.

These considerations frequently create right versus right dilemmas, where the concepts of justice and mercy conflict, where potentially either direction in the final decision is the "right" decision—but opening up the "nothing happened" door.

State statutes and school policy may mandate some punishments, particularly related to weapons offenses. Other school policies use point systems that allow for long-term suspension or expulsion after the accumulation of a given number of points assigned to various infractions. No matter the system in place, discipline should be based on some progressive system designed to correct and address basic causes of misbehavior, with increasing severity based on the level of the offense or repeated violations.

Of note, make certain that such policies do not have unintended consequences. Consider the example of a high school that had in place a tardy and unexcused absence policy where the same progressive discipline applied to both violations. The problem with the policy was that for some student situations, the consequence for skipping class could be less than if a student arrived late—defeating the purpose of the policy and encouraging students to skip the class to avoid the tardy consequence. The policy was eventually revised.

Minimal Consequences—Conferences, Detentions, Time-outs

The first level of discipline for students is often being sent to the office, where the consequence may amount to no more than a conference or verbal warning. The use of time-outs, even at higher grade levels, can not only provide a "cooling off" period for a student but also remove the student from a situation where further escalation is a risk. Caution is in order to avoid overusing time-outs because of the loss of instructional time.

Although not "punishments," consequences could also include meeting with parents; attending counseling interventions; and doing reflective activities such as writing essays about their misbehavior.

The use of detentions, when reasonable, does not violate due process rights.

Restorative Justice

Restorative justice may be applied in conjunction with other consequences or may be applied on its own. The purpose of restorative justice is to repair harm to others due to the misbehavior of the student. Students may be required to participate in resolution activities including restorative counseling and some type of skills building (social–emotional, etc.) and may even include some type of community or school service.

In-School Suspension

ISS may also be called in-school detention and could take place during lunchtime or during school time. Because of the loss of instructional time when students are removed from the class, caution is in order to ensure proper due process was implemented during the placement of the student and to ensure educational opportunity for the assigned student. This is extremely important when assigning students with an IEP to ISS and even more important when multiple days or a series of days of ISS are considered for any student.

Academic Discipline

Violations of academic policies such as cheating can carry consequences that include grade reductions and a denial of credits. Academic discipline is typically upheld if challenged as long as schools ensure some level of due process in their decision, and their actions did not "shock the conscience" as being unreasonable.

Lowering grades or imposing other academic penalties for behavior violations has been challenged with mixed results. A court noted that reducing grades for nonacademic conduct results in an inaccurate measure of student performance (*Smith v. School City of Hobart,* 1993).

The lowering of a grade at times carries additional implications, such as losing credits toward graduation or even the ability to qualify for graduation. Such circumstances would also trigger diligent due process, but have at times been upheld as permissible. In a Seventh Circuit case, two senior students were caught drinking alcohol on a senior class outing and both students were suspended for the remaining three days of school, with both students unable to take their final exams (*Lamb v. Panhandle Community Unit School District No. 2,* 1987). Both students were allowed to take the required "Flag and Declaration of Independence" test, which they passed. However, one of the students was able to pass his required classes in order to graduate even without taking the final exams. The other student filed suit because at the time of his suspension, his grades were not high enough to survive the loss of credit by not taking the final exams.

The court ruled against his Equal Protection claim, holding that the differences in grade point averages do not violate the Equal Protection Clause. The court did note that the consequence of failing to graduate may have been harsh.

In a case where zero-tolerance and academic penalties intersected, an appellate court upheld the zero-tolerance expulsion of a student in possession of marijuana who also had his grades computed with zeros factored in for the remaining portion of the semester after his removal. He was to be given credit if he still was passing with the zeros factored in. The appellate court reversed that finding, noting that it was not for the courts to set aside decisions of school administrators (*South Gibson School Board v. Sollman*, 2002).

The Texas Court of Appeals held that the evidence demonstrated there was no adverse impact from academic penalties assigned to each day of the suspension of students, noting that at the time of a hearing, they had already been admitted to the university of their choice. The students had been suspended for consuming alcohol on a school trip, with the additional consequence of receiving zeros on all graded classwork for each day of the suspension as well as having grade points deducted for each day from their six-week grade averages. The major disagreement between the parties was that although the students acknowledged that school policy could suspend them for their violation, there was no expressed policy regarding the reduction of grades. The court disagreed with the student plaintiffs, holding that school policy relating to discipline need not be in writing in order to be legally enforceable, and rules or policies may be informal as long as the school fairly apprises students of prohibited conduct (*New Braunfels Ind. Sch. Dist. v. Armke*, 1983).

Once a student has completed the requirements for graduation, the withholding of a diploma is a ministerial act that the school must perform. Schools may deny the participation in graduation ceremonies as a consequence but not withhold the diploma.

Short-Term Suspension

Suspensions of up to ten days are considered short-term suspensions. Requirements for short-term suspensions are derived primarily from *Goss v. Lopez*. The due process required for such suspensions may differ by state and school policy. For example, some school districts may require more than just an "informal" hearing process before suspending a student, where the student has the right to schedule a hearing regarding the proposed suspension. In other school districts, an "informal" hearing may be no more than a principal or designee informing the student of the violation and the evidence against them, providing a chance to explain their side of the story, and determining the consequence.

Although the suspension from school is a temporary removal, the use of repeated school suspension carries significant negative implications for students through lost instruction and school time. For students with IEPs, no services need to be provided for students suspended up to ten days; however, after the accumulation of ten days of suspension, services must be provided, which would be determined in an IEP review, manifestation determination review, and other procedural requirements. Note that these requirements are not for each time a student with an IEP is suspended for up to ten days, but for the accumulation during the school year of any suspensions that add up to ten days.

Long-Term Suspension and Expulsion

When violations occur where long-term suspension or expulsion is considered, because of the severity of the consequence and what students stand to lose educationally, proper due process afforded the student is both morally and legally required. Definitions may differ with what is a long-term suspension or expulsion, but generally any suspension longer than ten days is a long-term suspension.

The two most important considerations for principals would be ensuring all due process requirements are met and ensuring all procedures for students with IEPs are followed, including providing all required services during the suspension.

Due process hearings or tribunals where long-term suspension or expulsion are proposed may vary by state and local policy, but should include at a minimum (1) adequate notice of the charges or allegations; (2) the use of an impartial decision maker; (3) an opportunity for the student to present their side of the story; (4) an opportunity to present evidence and witnesses; (5) an opportunity to challenge witnesses and evidence used against them; (6) the right to legal counsel; and (7) a record of the decision and rationale made available to the student.

Corporal Punishment

Although we believe that corporal punishment should not be allowed under any circumstances, it remains an acceptable action in some school districts across the country.

Corporal or physical punishment continues to be a highly controversial issue in public education, and perhaps no other issue has drawn as much criticism. A majority of states now ban corporal punishment, and in other states in which it is allowed, a substantial number of school districts prohibit it. However, the courts still view corporal punishment as an acceptable form of discipline when administered in a reasonable manner.

The constitutionality of corporal punishment was confirmed in *Ingraham v. Wright* (1977), a landmark case in which the U.S. Supreme Court ruled that even severe corporal punishment may not violate the Eighth Amendment prohibition of cruel and unusual punishment. In its decision, the Court noted, however, that the use of corporal punishment deprives students of liberty interests protected by the Constitution, and as a result, *rudimentary* due process must precede its use. When corporal punishment is allowed, due process is satisfied with a brief explanation of the reason for the discipline coupled with an opportunity for the student to comment. However, reasonable school administrators take parents' wishes concerning this form of punishment into consideration and require an adult witness to be present when administering corporal punishment.

The common law rule on the subject of corporal punishment allows school administrators, standing *in loco parentis*, to use *reasonable* force they reasonably believe to be necessary for a child's proper control, training, or education. The following factors, as identified in *Hogenson v. William* (1976), are generally considered in determining whether the amount of force used was reasonable:

- Age, gender, and condition of the child

- Nature of the offense or conduct and the child's motives

- The influence of the student's example on other students

- Whether the force was reasonably necessary to compel obedience to a proper command

- Whether the force was disproportionate to the offense, unnecessarily degrading, or likely to cause serious injury

THE PRINCIPAL'S QUICK-REFERENCE GUIDE TO SCHOOL LAW

Minimum Due Process

Before administering corporal punishment, school officials should develop, publish and disseminate rules that provide students and their parents with *adequate notice* that specific violations may result in corporal punishment. The student to be punished should be informed of the rule violation in question and provided with an opportunity to respond. A brief but thorough informal hearing is a good way to give the student the opportunity to present their side of the issue. Because the student's property rights are not involved, an extensive, full due process procedure is not necessary. However, the courts have identified the following as the minimal due process standards:

- Specific warning is given about what behavior may result in corporal punishment.

- Evidence exists that other measures were attempted that failed to bring about the desired change in behavior.

- Administration of corporal punishment takes place in the presence of a second school official.

- On request, a written statement is provided to parents explaining the reasons for the punishment and the names of all witnesses.

Reasonable Punishment, Excessive Punishment, Intentional Torts

Poor decisions regarding the use of corporal punishment may result in civil damage suits or even criminal prosecution of assault and battery. Excessive punishment occurs when the punishment is inflicted with such force or in such a manner that it is considered to be cruel and unusual. Excessiveness also occurs when no consideration is given to the student's age, size, gender, physical condition, or ability to bear the punishment. Assault and battery charges are normally associated with allegations of excessive punishment, and both are classified as intentional torts. Excessive corporal punishment may be actionable under the Due Process Clause when it involves "arbitrary, egregious, and conscience-shocking behavior" (*Neal v. Fulton County Bd. of Educ.*, 229 F.3d 1069, 1075 (11th Cir. 2000)).

Privileged Force

Sometimes school employees need to use physical force to control a potentially dangerous situation. School personnel have an affirmative duty, for example, to break up a fight between or among students. When the use of physical force is necessary, the *Hogenson* court stated that school officials should use only the amount of force *reasonably* necessary to control a specific situation. The amount of force used should be proportionate to the prohibited activity.

ADDITIONAL CASES OF INTEREST TO EDUCATORS

Clements v. Board of Trustees of Sheridan County School District No. 2 (585 P.2d 197 Wyo. 1978). Discipline is reasonably necessary for the student's physical or emotional safety and the well-being of other students. The case involved a student who used the vehicle he was driving to impede and harass a school bus full of students. He challenged his suspension, claiming there was no evidence his continuation in school would create any negative effects on other students, but the court held that even though they agreed with his conclusion, there was no exception written into the law he could use.

Clinton Municipal Separate School District v. Byrd (477 So.2d 237, Miss. 1985). A court held that "staying after school was a viable form of punishment and mandatory school discipline rules are not unconstitutional."

McClain v. Lafayette County Board of Education (U.S. Ct. of App. 5th Cir. 1982, 673 F.2d 106). The "indefinite suspension" for carrying a knife to school was upheld by the court. The parent had challenged the due process procedures of the school. The court held that the issue was whether the student in fact brought a knife to school, rather than what due process he was provided, noting that procedural due process is a flexible concept.

Nicholas B. v. School Committee (412 Mass. 20, 587 N.E.2d 211, 1992). A student filed suit after being expelled for assaulting a fellow student on a public street near, but not on, school property. He claimed that the school had no authority to discipline him for conduct that occurred off school grounds. The court held that imposing school discipline off school grounds is not arbitrary or capricious and that the student knew the behavior was wrong and in violation of school policy.

Price v. New York City Board of Education (N.Y. Sup. Ct. May 7, 2007). A court upheld the ban on possession of cell phones and suggested that it would be unlikely there would be constitutional claims upholding the right to possess a cell phone at school.

Wiemerslage v. Maine Township High School District 207 (U.S. Ct. of App. 7th Cir. 1994, 29 F.3d 1149). A court determined that school district policy regarding "loitering" was not unconstitutionally "vague" or a violation of the First Amendment.

Muschette v. Gionfriddo, 910 F.3d 65 (2nd Cir. 2018). An appellate court granted qualified immunity to an officer who tased a profoundly deaf twelve-year-old student who communicated primarily in American Sign Language. The student was reported to law enforcement as "out of control." When confronted, the student was verbally warned he would be tased and the message was relayed by sign language by two different staff members. When the student did not comply, he was tased two times.

Walsh Ex rel. J.W. v. Katy Independent School District, 390 F. Supp. 3d 822 (S.D. Tex. 2019). An emotionally disturbed and intellectually disabled seventeen-year-old student attempted to leave the building after the room he normally went to in order to calm himself down was occupied. A security officer eventually tased the student, who subsequently urinated and defecated on himself. The court held that alleging excessive force under the Fourteenth Amendment does not preclude the same assertion under the Fourth Amendment. However, facts of the case were disputed and there was no finding of summary judgment for either party.

Ruiz De Gutierrez v. Albuquerque Public Schools, 2019 U.S. Dist. LEXIS 7871 (D.N.M 2019). A thirteen-year-old autistic student told his teachers he was walking home and left school without permission. He was pursued by teachers and security on foot and in vehicles. He was tased by an SRO but the student continued to flee until he reached the car of a teacher aide. The court held that because the student continued to move to the car after being tased, there was no "seizure" of the student.

Warren v. NASSP, 375 F.Supp 1043 (N.D. Tex. 1974). An honors student was observed by a staff member drinking a beer at a local establishment. Contrary to the policy in place regarding the removal of students from the National Honor Society, he was removed without any hearing. A court held that this was a violation of his due process rights and ordered that his removal be expunged from the record.

Cole v. Newton Special Municipal Separate School District, 853 F. 2d 924 (5th Cir. 1988). The court held that due to the loss of significant instruction, a hearing to place a student in ISS may be required.

Campbell v. BOE of New Milford, 475 A.2d 289 (Conn. 1984). A court denied a due process claim made by a student who had his grade reduced and credit withheld after missing twenty-four class periods. The student handbook had an explicit policy that stated absences would result in grade reductions, which made the penalty due to academics and not discipline.

Seamons v. Snow, 84 F.3d 1226 (10th Cir. 1996); *Hebert v. Ventetuolo,* 638 F.2d 5 (1st Cir. 1981). Two examples of cases where courts held that no due process hearing is required for denial of placement in extracurricular programs.

Wooten v. Pleasant Hope R-VI School District, 270 F.3d 549 (8th Cir. 2001). A student sued for denial of due process after being dismissed from her softball team for missing a game with an unexcused absence. The appellate court affirmed the lower court ruling that she failed to state a claim for which relief could be granted.

Orange v. County of Grundy, 950 F. Supp 1365 (E.D. Tenn. 1996). Students were denied due process when they were assigned to spend two days in a custodial closet.

Hinterlong v. Arlington Independent School District, 2010 Tex. App. LEXIS 1010 (Tex. App. Feb. 11, 2010). A court upheld the placement of a student in an alternative school after he was found to have a thimbleful of liquid that smelled like alcohol in his car. While the court noted that "zero tolerance policies, as a whole, have promoted consistency over rationality," the student could not "escape application of the zero tolerance policy."

Seal v. Morgan, 229 F.3d 567 (6th Cir. 2000). The Sixth Circuit held in favor of a student who violated the zero-tolerance policy against weapons brought to school property because it failed to investigate whether the student knowingly or unknowingly brought the weapon to campus. Although the court acknowledged and did not wish to minimize the obligation of the school to ensure safety, it did not agree with the argument that because it is difficult to determine what the student's state of mind is, there is no need to attempt to determine if the student had in fact known he was in possession of a weapon before expelling him.

Peterson v. Baker, 504 F.3d 1331 (11th Cir. 2007). A court held in favor of defendant teacher in a case filed after a physical altercation between the teacher and a student. The confrontation began when the teacher blocked the student at the door, preventing him from leaving. It was undisputed that the student initiated the physical contact which resulted in the teacher responding by grabbing the student by the neck. The plaintiff claimed that the teacher administered corporal punishment by choking him. The appellate court concluded that it was unimportant whether the teacher acted in self-defense or imposed corporal punishment because her conduct was not a constitutional violation, noting that all student injuries caused by a teacher amount to corporal punishment.

Lillard v. Shelby County Bd. of Educ., 76 F.3d 716, 725 (6th Cir. 1996). A court held that "it is simply inconceivable that a single slap [to the face] could shock the conscience," even though the conduct had no legitimate disciplinary purpose.

Kirkland v. Greene County Bd. of Educ., 347 F.3d 903 (11th Cir. 2003). Qualified immunity was not granted to a principal who repeatedly struck a thirteen-year-old student with a metal cane, including one on the head as the student doubled over protecting his chest. The student was not armed or behaving in a threatening manner, and the court held that the amount of force used was excessive and presented a foreseeable risk of serious bodily injury.

Dunn v. Fairfield Community High Sch. Dist. No. 225, 158 F.3d 962 (7th Cir. 1998). In direct defiance of rules related to music performance, two students violated the policy by performing solos during their performance. As a result, they were assigned "F" grades for the class, which prevented one student from graduating with honors. The court noted that although the school may have overreacted, there was nothing illegal about assigning the students grades of "F" for violating school rules, and they did not violate substantive due process or shock the conscience in doing so.

Williams v. Morgan, 652 Fed. Appx. 365 (6th Cir. 2016). A middle school student had earlier in the day been suspended and, upon leaving the office, angrily tore posters off the wall in a hallway, an action an SRO testified as having "crossed the line to criminal disorderly conduct." She was later confronted by an SRO in a stairwell where the officer felt her posture was defiant and decided to seize her by pushing her into lockers and bending her arm behind her back. Video evidence confirmed that this action by the SRO picked the student up off the floor. It was later determined her arm was broken. In an excessive force claim, the officer was not given qualified immunity because although the force used is considered a low-level force tactic, it could still be misused or misapplied as alleged in the complaint.

Metzger By and Through Metzger v. Osbeck, 841 F.2d 518 (3rd Cir. 1988). Although a teacher was motivated by a legitimately disciplinary desire and his intent was not to injure a student, the appellate court reversed a lower court decision and could not conclude that a reasonable jury would not find in favor of the plaintiffs. The teacher overheard profanity from the student and as a result stood behind the student with his arms around the student's neck and shoulders while telling him his language was not acceptable. He then moved his arms higher, causing the student to rise on his toes, and unknown to the teacher, the loss of consciousness. When he released his hold, the student fell face down, suffering lacerations, a broken nose, fractured teeth, and other injuries that required hospitalization.

Carter v. Pointe Coupee Par. Sch. Bd., 268 Sl. 3d 1064 (La. App. 1 Cir. 2018). Twenty-two elementary school children were awarded $5,000 in damages in a suit filed after they were forced by an SRO to kneel on gravel for between ten and forty minutes. The students had been identified as bullies. Testimony indicated the uniformed officer would push students back down when they attempted to get up.

Mirich v. State ex rel., Board of Trustees of Laramie County School District Two, No. 20-1034 (Wyo. 2021). The Wyoming Supreme Court affirmed the judgment of the state district court that upheld the decision to dismiss a teacher who disciplined his daughter on school grounds after school hours. The daughter was also a student at the school. At issue was whether school policies and conduct standards applied to the teacher while disciplining his own child.

T.O. v. Fort Bend Independent Sch. Dist., No. 20-20225 (5th Cir. 2021). The Fifth Circuit has upheld dismissal of claims against a teacher and school district where, after the teacher was kicked by a student, she threw him on the floor and held in a choke hold for several minutes. The teacher told the student he "had hit the wrong one" and needed "to keep his hands to himself." The Court noted the actions of the teacher were ill-advised and inappropriate because they were not arbitrary or capricious.

L.G. v. Edwards, No. 20-2161 (8th Cir. Mar. 18, 2021). The Eighth Circuit reversed a lower court opinion, holding that it was not clearly established that the school setting makes no difference for Fourth Amendment purposes when a seizure occurs at the behest of law enforcement. In this case, a student claimed she was unconstitutionally seized when an SRO escorted her to an office for questioning in a closed office with police officers. The court held that it is not necessarily clear at what point a student is considered seized for constitutional purposes.

Kenny v. Wilson, 885 F.3d 280 (4th Cir. 2018). A group of former and current South Carolina students and a nonprofit organization filed suit under 42 U.S.C. § 1983 challenging S.C. Code Ann. § 16-17-420 (the "Disturbing Schools Law") and S.C. Code Ann. § 16-17-530 (the "Disorderly Conduct Law") as unconstitutionally vague. The district court dismissed the complaint for lack of standing. It reasoned that plaintiffs' fear of future arrest and prosecution under the two statutes does not rise above speculation and thus does not constitute an injury in fact. The appellate court held that some of the students did not rely on conjecture or speculation because they attended school where they were previously arrested and criminally charged, and they did not know which of their actions may be a violation in the future. They also alleged the laws chilled free expression, forcing them to refrain from exercising constitutional rights or face arrest. The court vacated the decision of the lower court and remanded the case.

CHAPTER 7

Sexual Harassment

Sexual harassment is a serious offense. It's not about flirting, humor, raging hormones, or horseplay. It's about power and the harasser's need to exert it over a victim. Many targets of sexual harassment would rather try to deal with incidents informally, but many do not have the necessary skills. In the workplace, victims of sexual harassment are just as likely to change jobs as a result of sexual harassment as they are to take formal action. Students usually do not have the option of leaving school. Consequently, they often suffer in silence (Shoop, 2004). The concepts of sexual harassment as described and discussed in this chapter are equally applicable to adults as employees and children as students under expected duty and standards of care. The use of the terms bullying *and* harassment, *as well as* sexual harassment, *may be used interchangeably, because not only are there legal obligations required to prevent and deal with each, there are strong moral obligations to do so as well.*

Since publication of the third edition of this book, many significant changes have taken place in laws, regulations, and even societal attitudes regarding sexual harassment. Increased awareness of the rights of LGBTQ+ and transgender students, as well as the #MeToo movement overall, has impacted all of society as well as the schoolhouse. Although significant changes impact higher education and college campuses, the focus in this chapter will be on pre-K through twelfth-grade public schools. It is nearly certain that additional changes along with new guidance will be in place between the writing of this chapter and after the publication of the fourth edition, so the intent of the chapter is to provide foundational information that should be applicable no matter what changes may be made by the administration of President Biden.

SUGGESTED GUIDELINES FOR PRACTICE

Sexual harassment (and bullying) is a problem that *must* be addressed by school principals, from not only a legal standpoint but a moral one as well.

Guidance under Title IX has changed and is currently under further review. Principals should always seek the current guidance from not only the federal government but also their own state and local laws and policies as well.

This chapter will primarily focus on sexual harassment rather than sexual assault, and although much of the same sources of law and regulations come from the same statutes, due to the seriousness of incidens of sexual assault, when such incidents occur, consulting law enforcement and legal authorities for guidance is essential.

SECTION A. ORIGINS OF SEXUAL HARASSMENT PROHIBITIONS

Sexual harassment is a violation of Title VII of the Civil Rights Act of 1964 and Title IX of the Education Amendments of 1972. An outline of amendments to Title IX is provided in Section C of this chapter. Title VII prohibits employers of more than fifteen people from discriminating on the basis of race, color, religion, gender, or national origin in all aspects of employment. Subsequent amendments permit employees and applicants to file suit in federal court if they are not satisfied with the employer's disposition of their complaints. This act covers all aspects of employment including pay, promotion, hiring, dismissal, and working conditions.

In 1980, the Equal Employment Opportunity Commission (EEOC) issued guidelines that declared sexual harassment a violation of Title VII, establishing criteria for determining when unwelcome conduct of a sexual nature constitutes sexual harassment, defining the circumstances under which an employer may be liable, and suggesting affirmative steps an employer should take to prevent sexual harassment. The EEOC guidelines were reinforced in 1986 by the U.S. Supreme Court in *Meritor Savings Bank v. Vinson,* the Court's first decision regarding sexual harassment in the workplace. So effectively did the Supreme Court clarify the nature of sexual harassment and the responsibility employers have for preventing or remedying harassment that, in 1988, the EEOC published definitive guidance for employers, victims, EEOC officials, and attorneys. These guidelines have shaped all subsequent interpretations of both Title VII and Title IX in the area of sexual harassment. According to these guidelines, unwelcome sexual advances, requests for sexual favors, and other verbal or physical conduct of a sexual nature are harassment if

- Submission to such conduct is made either explicitly or implicitly a term or condition of an individual's employment.

- Submission to or rejection of such conduct by an individual is used as the basis for employment decisions affecting that individual.

- The conduct has the purpose or effect of unreasonably interfering with an individual's work performance or creating an intimidating, hostile, or offensive working environment

Title VII was amended in 1991 to allow sexual harassment plaintiffs to sue for monetary damages. This amendment limits recovery of compensatory damages to cases of intentional discrimination and punitive damages to nonpublic employers who act with malice or reckless indifference. In general, Title VII is enforced by the EEOC. In 1993, the U.S. Supreme Court ruled, in *Harris v. Forklift Systems,* that employees alleging sexual harassment on the job do not have to prove psychological injury to collect damages under Title VII. In 1998, the U.S. Supreme Court, in *Oncale v. Sundowner Offshore Services, Inc.,* ruled that same-sex sexual harassment in the workplace is actionable as sex discrimination under Title VII.

Every state has some form of gender discrimination law. In some state statutes, sexual harassment is specifically prohibited; in others, sexual harassment is included under the prohibition against sex discrimination. Individual state statutes reinforce federal law and often define harassment more specifically. It's clear, however, that school districts and individual schools are required to take all steps necessary to prevent sexual harassment. Specifically, school districts must *formulate and disseminate* a strong, clearly stated policy and *implement an effective procedure* for resolving complaints that does not require the victim to complain first to the offending supervisor or, in the case of a student, the adult offender. School districts and individual schools are required to investigate thoroughly every complaint of sexual harassment, deal appropriately with offenders, and resolve the problem.

Title IX prohibits discrimination on the basis of sex in education programs or activities that receive federal financial assistance. Title IX covers both employees and students and virtually all activities of a school district. The prohibition covers discrimination in employment of teachers and other school personnel as well as discrimination in admissions, financial aid, and access to educational programs and activities of students. Title IX states,

> No person in the United States shall on the basis of sex be excluded from participating in, be denied the benefits of, or be subjected to discrimination under any education program or activity receiving federal financial assistance.

Under Title IX, school employees and students may sue to collect monetary damages from the school, or the school may lose federal funds. In general, the EEOC enforces Title IX for the Office for Civil Rights (OCR) of the U.S. Department of Education. OCR defines the education program of a school as *all* of the school's operations: (a) academic, (b) educational, (c) extracurricular, (d) athletic, and (e) other programs of the school. The school is responsible for ensuring a safe place to learn whether the education activity takes place in (a) the facilities of the school; (b) on a school bus; (c) at a class, on a field trip, athletic event, or training program sponsored by the school at another location; or (d) anywhere else if the activity is school related.

Teacher-to-Student Sexual Harassment

In 1992, the U.S. Supreme Court confirmed that damages might be awarded in sex discrimination action under Title IX. In the case of *Franklin v. Gwinnett County School Board,* the Court ruled that schools owe their students protection from sexual harassment, a form of discrimination, by school employees and by other students. A student in a high school in Georgia filed a complaint in a federal district court against the school district under Title IX. In her complaint, the student alleged that (a) she was subjected to continual sexual harassment and abuse, including coercive intercourse, by a male teacher at the school; (b) teachers and administrators were aware of the teacher's conduct but took no action to halt it; and (c) the school closed its investigation of the teacher's conduct after the teacher resigned on the condition that all matters pending against him be dropped. The district court dismissed the complaint on the grounds that Title IX did not authorize an award of damages. Although an appeals court upheld the district court, the U.S. Supreme Court reversed the decision and ruled that money damages can be awarded for an action brought to enforce Title IX.

In 1998, the U.S. Supreme Court ruled, in *Gebser v. Lago Vista Independent School District,* that school districts may be held liable under Title IX of the Education Amendments of 1972 (20 U.S. § 1681–88) for sexual harassment of a student by an employee in which (a) an official representative of the educational institution who had authority to take constructive steps to stop the harassment actually knew of the harassment and (b) the educational institution responded with deliberate indifference. The case involved an eighth-grade student who, after joining a book discussion group led by a teacher, began to have sexual intercourse with the teacher. This relationship continued until her sophomore year, when a police officer discovered them having sexual intercourse in a car and arrested the teacher. The school district terminated his employment, and the state revoked his teaching credentials.

The student brought suit against the school district, claiming that the school should be liable under Title IX. She also argued that the court should follow Title VII's imposition of liability for "constructive knowledge": "If one by exercise of reasonable care would have known a fact, he is deemed to have had constructive knowledge of such fact" (*Black's Law Dictionary,* 1979, p. 477). Both a district court and an appeals court ruled in favor of the school district. The U.S. Supreme Court also rejected the constructive knowledge argument and ruled that the district could only be found liable in the case of actual knowledge.

A school district would be held liable for sexual harassment if a teacher abuses delegated authority over a student to create a hostile environment, for example, if a teacher explicitly or implicitly threatens to fail a student unless the student responds to the teacher's sexual advances, even though the teacher fails to carry out the threat. Often the line between *quid pro quo* and hostile-environment discrimination is blurred, and the employee's conduct may constitute both types of harassment.

Janitors or cafeteria workers may be considered to be in positions of authority— or appear to have authority if authority is actually given to the employee (e.g., in some schools, a cafeteria worker or paraprofessional may have authority to impose discipline or report infractions). The age of the student is an important factor. Generally, the younger the student, the more likely it is that they will consider any adult employee to be in a position of authority.

Student-to-Student Sexual Harassment

In 1999, the U.S. Supreme Court, in *Davis v. Monroe County Board of Education,* ruled that school boards could be held liable under Title IX for "deliberate indifference" to known student-to-student sexual harassment that is "severe, pervasive, and objectively offensive." In this case, a fifth-grade student alleged ongoing verbal and physical sexual harassment at the hands of a male classmate. The male classmate was charged and pled guilty to sexual battery. The girl's mother had reported each incident of harassment to a teacher. One teacher had reported the matter to the school's principal. When the student had attempted to report the event directly to the principal, a teacher had told her that if the principal "wants you, he'll call you." When the girl's mother spoke to the principal, he said, "I guess I'll have to threaten him a little bit harder." The principal then asked the mother why her daughter was the only one who was complaining. The family sued the school district under Title IX. The district court rejected their claim. On appeal, the circuit court reversed the district court's holding. The U.S. Supreme Court ruled that schools may be held liable for student-to-student sexual harassment if (a) the school exercises substantial control of both the harasser and the context in which the known harassment occurs, (b) the school is deliberately indifferent to peer harassment or its response or lack of response is clearly unreasonable under the circumstances, and (c) the harassment is so severe, pervasive, and objectively offensive that it deprives the victims of a school's educational benefits.

Employee Sexual Harassment

Related to adults in the workplace, EEOC guidelines describe sexual harassment as unwelcome sexual conduct that is a term or condition of employment. In *Meritor Savings Bank v. Vinson* (1986), the Supreme Court clarified this definition by identifying two kinds of sexual harassment: *quid pro quo* (this for that) and *environmental*. Several other courts have expanded the definition of environmental sexual harassment to include nonsexual conduct (physical or verbal aggression or intimidation) that creates a hostile environment that would not exist but for the gender of the employee. The EEOC guidelines also identify a third type of sexual harassment, *"sexual favoritism,"* that is a possible result of *quid pro quo* harassment. Incidents of *quid pro quo* and hostile education environment are daily occurrences in schools (American Association of University Women, 1993). Although it is sometimes difficult to distinguish between the two categories, it is important to do so because school districts are held to different standards for each.

Quid pro quo sexual harassment exists whenever a supervisor makes unwelcome sexual advances toward an employee and implicitly or explicitly threatens that the victim's continued employment and advancement are contingent on submission. Once the fact of the sexual (or sex-based) conduct of the supervisor is confirmed, the next question to be determined is whether the conduct was unwelcome. In this inquiry, the question of whether the victim voluntarily submitted to the supervisor's advances is irrelevant. The court will not fault a victim who has made a clear protest for submitting to an offending supervisor rather than face real or perceived job-related consequences. When an employment opportunity or benefit is granted because of an individual's submission to sexual advances, other employees have grounds to sue on the basis of sexual discrimination under Title VII (sexual favoritism).

Sexual activity between two consenting adults as coworkers is not illegal. Sexual activity is not sexual harassment unless it is unwanted. However, sexual activity between an adult and a minor student is always illegal. Because of the special relationship between the school and the student, schools have a duty to protect students from sexual abuse by school employees. Sexual activity between an adult employee and a student, or propositions for such activity, is grounds for dismissal and for criminal action against the adult. In addition to qualifying as sexual harassment, sexual assault, sexual battery and rape, and sexual activity with a minor are forms of child abuse and violations of criminal law and must be reported.

Title IX and its administrative regulations prohibit an education program or activity that receives federal funds from denying any individual admission to, participation in, or the benefits of any academic, extracurricular, research, occupational training, aid, service, or other education program or activity on the basis of gender. Programs that receive federal funds are specifically prohibited from

- Preferentially ranking applicants by gender

- Applying numerical quotas based on gender

- Administering any preadmission tests that have a disproportionately adverse effect on persons on the basis of gender unless the test is a valid predictor of success in the program and alternative tests are unavailable

- Applying any rule concerning parental, family, or marital status or making any preadmission inquiry regarding the marital status of an applicant

- Subjecting any person to separate or different rules of behavior, sanctions, or other treatment on the basis of gender

- Measuring skill or progress in a physical education class in any manner that has an adverse effect on members of one sex

As on-site representatives of a school district's central administration, principals are responsible for preventing and remedying sexual harassment in their schools. Principals must clearly understand what constitutes sexual harassment and what they must do to protect their teachers, students, and other staff members from this kind of discrimination.

In addition, programs that receive federal funds may not exclude any student from any class or extracurricular activity on the basis of pregnancy, childbirth, termination of pregnancy, or recovery therefrom unless the student requests to participate in a separate program or activity and the separate program is comparable to that offered to other students. It is permissible to require a doctor's certification that the student is physically and emotionally able to participate in the normal program or activity. Furthermore, the program or activity must treat the pregnancy, childbirth, or termination of pregnancy in the same manner that it treats any other temporary disability under its medical or hospital benefit, service, plan, or policy.

Title IX does not prohibit an education program or activity from

- Grouping students in physical education classes by ability as assessed by objective standards

- Separating students by gender within physical education classes or other activities that involve body contact

- Conducting classes in elementary and secondary schools that deal with human sexuality in separate sections for boys and girls

- Making requirements based on vocal range or quality that result in a chorus of one or predominately one gender

SECTION B. DEFINITIONS

The 2020 amendments to the Department of Education Title IX regulations define sexual harassment to include certain types of unwelcome sexual conduct, sexual assault, dating violence, domestic violence, and stalking. Sexual harassment means conduct on the basis of sex that satisfies one or more of the following:

1. An employee of the (school) conditioning the provision of an aid, benefit, or service of the recipient on an individual's participation in unwelcome sexual conduct;

2. Unwelcome conduct, determined by a reasonable person to be so severe, pervasive, and objectively offensive that it effectively denies a person equal access to the school's education program or activity; or

3. "Sexual assault" as defined in 20 U.S.C. 555 U.S. 246 (2009).1092(f)(6)(A)(v). This also includes references to laws related to dating violence, domestic violence, and stalking.

Under the new amendments, the first category is referred to as *quid pro quo* sexual harassment. It is perhaps the easiest type of harassment to recognize in schools. It occurs when sexual demands are made on a student or a school employee in exchange for education participation, advancement, or other benefits; or under the threat of punishment. OCR defines an employee as any agent of a school district. In addition to certified and classified staff, anyone with whom the school contracts to provide services for the school is considered an employee. Student teachers who are given authority to assign grades may be considered employees. An incident of sexual bribery or sexual intimidation is considered *quid pro quo* sexual harassment even if it happens only once. Because of the age and vulnerability of students, in the case of a student who "consents" to the sexual attention, both the school and the adult employee are liable for sexual harassment.

The second category uses the definition of sexual harassment found in *Davis v. Monroe County Board of Education*. Schools are not required to adopt a specific definition of consent, but instead are provided flexibility to define consent that best serves their own "unique needs, values, and environment" of their own community.

It is important to note that prior to the new 2020 amendments, the guidance language was related to conduct determined to be sufficiently "severe, persistent, or pervasive" to limit a student's ability to participate in or benefit from the education program. Such a definition was broad enough to include a variety of conduct that could interfere with the ability to participate in school. The language of the new guidance, similar to that used in *Davis,* is considered by some to be a narrowed definition. Additionally, language from previous guidance prohibiting conduct that limited the ability to benefit from an educational program or activity was eliminated. Critics of the amendments fear that the changes in the language could mean it will become more difficult for victims to successfully claim sexual harassment. The narrowed scope of the new regulations makes it less expansive than the workplace standards under Title VII.

The third category refers to definitions in the Clery Act (20 U.S.C. §1092(f)(2018)) and the Violence Against Women Act of 1994 (Pub. L. 103-322). This category is particularly important for requirements in higher education, but also applies to schools in primary and secondary education. Unfortunately, principals finding a need to respond to sexual assault, dating violence, or stalking are not a rare occurrence.

Environmental sexual harassment exists when a pattern of unwelcome and offensive conduct, which would be considered abusive by any reasonable person under the same circumstances, creates a hostile work environment that inhibits the work performance of an employee. The court views similarly offensive conduct that is sexual in nature and aggressive nonsexual conduct that is focused on an employee because of their gender.

In the workplace, this type of harassment is called *hostile work-environment sexual harassment*. In a school setting, it is referred to as a *hostile education environment*. A hostile education environment is the most frequent type of sexual harassment in schools. This form of harassment is less tangible and less discrete, and it often occurs over a period of time. Although one inappropriate touch, comment, or joke may be offensive, to cross the threshold into sexual harassment, the behavior must either be very severe (e.g., touching the breast, crotch, or buttocks) or be persistent and pervasive (e.g., a teacher making sexual comments to or about a student on a regular basis). Hostile-environment harassment may be the conduct of an employee or another student and may include unwelcome sexual advances, requests for sexual favors, and other verbal or physical conduct of a sexual nature. If this behavior is sufficiently severe, persistent, or pervasive and limits a student's ability to participate in or benefit from an education program or activity, a hostile or abusive education environment exists.

Sexual favoritism occurs when a less qualified applicant receives employment opportunities or benefits as a result of the individual's submission to the employer's sexual advances or requests for sexual favors. Sexual favoritism is often a form of harassment claimed by employees or students when another employee or student has benefited from *quid pro quo* harassment.

The Title IX prohibition against sexual harassment does not extend to nonsexual touching or other nonsexual conduct. There are legitimate reasons for an employee to touch a student or another employee, or for one student to touch another student. For example, a vocal music teacher showing a student the correct way to breathe, an instrumental music teacher demonstrating the proper way to hold a musical instrument, a basketball coach demonstrating the proper way to block out another player, or an elementary school teacher comforting a student with a skinned knee by putting an arm on the child's shoulder to console the child are appropriate forms of physical contact.

Some school districts are so worried about having an employee charged with sexual harassment that they have adopted policies prohibiting school employees from having any physical contact other than a handshake. This may be an overreaction to the problem. There is a clear difference between appropriate and inappropriate touching.

Conduct is unwelcome when an adult or a student being harassed did not solicit or incite it and regarded the conduct as undesirable or offensive. The fact that the victim does not complain or report the harassment does not mean that the conduct is welcome.

Although a single instance of *quid pro quo* harassment is a violation of Title IX, hostile-environment sexual harassment must be sufficiently severe, persistent, and pervasive to limit an employee's ability to work or a student's ability to participate in or benefit from the education program, or it must create a hostile or abusive educational environment. Everything sexual is not sexual harassment. If a student drives by another student and shouts a sexual comment out the window or makes an obscene gesture, this is certainly inappropriate. However, usually, one isolated incident does not cross the threshold into sexual harassment.

Hostile-environment sexual harassment may result from either one incident of intense, aberrant behavior or a number of lesser behaviors that take place over a period of time. For example, a single incident of a severe behavior, such as grabbing a female's breast, crotch, or buttocks, or threats of rape or assault would constitute a hostile environment as well as be a criminal action. On the other hand, a situation that may not appear to be too serious may be sexual harassment when it is pervasive and persistent. For example, when one person (student or employee) is the target of name calling, taunting, propositions, rumors, or graffiti, and the offensive behavior occurs almost every day or is initiated by several people, there is a serious cumulative impact.

The context of the behavior is also an important factor. For example, it is not sexual harassment to ask someone for a date. However, it can become sexual harassment if the request is continually rejected to the point that a reasonable person would understand that the behavior is unwanted.

Sexual harassment is not just something that happens to those who identify as female. According to Uggen (2004), "All women are at some risk of sexual harassment, but males are also likely to be targeted if they seem vulnerable and appear to reject the male stereotype." Uggen found that if a man refuses to go along with sexual joking, wears an earring, or engages in activity typically attributed to women, he is more likely to be harassed. The harassers tend to be men who are flaunting their heterosexual masculinity over all forms of femininity. Victims therefore are not just women but also men who seem to challenge stereotypical male ideals. Sexual harassment of males appears to be underreported. School policy, practice, and culture should be in place to encourage and provide safe reporting of sexual harassment, regardless of the gender identity of the target.

SECTION C. TITLE IX AND CHANGING GUIDANCE

The Department of Education Title IX was first issued in 1975 and has been reissued and amended since then, with the latest issued in 2020. Before 2020, the regulations set out requirements under Title IX for educational programs and activities that receive federal funding, but did not include specific requirements related to sexual harassment. The OCR provided guidance documents to assist schools, sometimes in the form of a "Dear Colleague Letter," with such documents designed to inform schools how the OCR interpreted and would enforce the regulations. The 2020 amendments added specific and legally binding obligations schools must follow in response to notices of sexual harassment. The amendments took effect on August 14, 2020, and were not made retroactive, meaning that incidents that occurred prior to that date would follow the previous guidance. Interestingly, such guidance was rescinded in 2017 by the Trump administration, with additional guidance rescinded in 2020. As noted, although the 2020 amendments are now in place, they are currently under review and likely headed toward some type of revision in 2022.

The 2020 amendments focus on requirements for how schools respond to sexual harassment, but also note that efforts should be made to prevent sexual harassment from occurring in the first place, and such efforts should be based on their own educational communities.

In 2021, guidance was provided to help schools determine whether sexual harassment effectively denied equal access to the educational program or activity under the "unwelcome conduct" category. As stated in the preamble to the amendments and in subsequent guidance, principals should try to determine whether a reasonable person in the complainant's position would be effectively denied equal access to education compared to a similarly situated person who is not suffering the alleged harassment. Evidence to consider may include missing class to avoid a harasser, declining academic performance, difficulty concentrating in class, or quitting a certain activity while remaining in others. Other examples may include changing behavior in the home.

Guidance also notes that educational loss does not have to occur before a complaint is made, and effective denial of equal access does not need to require that a person's total or entire educational access has been denied. This is an important element for principals to understand, as a student may be suffering from sexual harassment in one context or space and therefore be denied equal access, yet could be performing satisfactorily in a different context or space. Merely because a person enjoys success in one area does not mean they do not suffer in another. Additionally, more serious outcomes such as failing classes, dropping out of school, or exhibiting other signs of trauma symptoms do not need to occur in order to be denied equal access. School officials cannot simply waive away or ignore a complaint because they determine the victim was not "harmed enough" to have merit in their claim.

Previous to the 2020 changes, the Department of Education enforced sexual harassment and bullying on a known or should have known basis, meaning school officials were legally expected to take action on allegations they knew about in addition to those they should have reasonably known about. The new regulations limit the enforcement in K-12 to sexual harassment known by any school employee and deliberate indifference. Keeping the previous guidance in mind, being continually aware of not only actual harassment, but the potential for harassment, is a proactive measure that decreases the likelihood of student harassment and provides another layer of protection, even if the "should have known" mandate does not exist in the 2020 amendments.

The new amendments trigger obligations in certain situations with new mandatory reporting obligations for all employees. In order for the obligations to apply, the following elements must exist:

- *Actual knowledge* in the form of some notice to *any employee of an elementary or secondary school*; and

- *Sexual harassment* as defined in the new amendments; and

- *Educational program*—locations, events, or circumstances over which the recipient (of the complaint) exercised substantial control over both the respondent and the context in which the sexual harassment occurs.

If any of these elements does not exist, there is no obligation under Title IX regulations, but just because it's not covered by Title IX does not mean principals cannot or should not deal with the matter.

Actual knowledge does not necessarily trigger obligations to conduct formal investigations, but the Title IX coordinator (many times the principal) must promptly reach out to alleged victims and offer supportive services once informed of possible sexual harassment. Supportive measures must also be provided when a formal complaint is made.

SECTION D. HOW TO HANDLE ALLEGATIONS AND COMPLAINTS

The 2020 Title IX amendments detail the requirements for handling sexual harassment allegations (Title IX and Sex Discrimination, 2022). What follows are guidelines provided by the Department of Education in July 2021 and should serve only as foundational guidance on procedures. The Biden administration has signaled that changes may be made which will be delayed until 2022. As always, check current Department of Education updates as well as your own local policies, should you become involved in a sexual harassment claim.

The preamble to the 2020 amendments note that Title IX is not the exclusive remedy for sexual misconduct or traumatic events for students. Schools are given the discretion to respond appropriately to misconduct that does not fall within the definitions and scope of Title IX. For example, schools may respond to misconduct that occurs outside of the educational program or activity or causes harm in the school environment that does not fit within the definitions. School policy and codes of conduct may go beyond what is spelled out in the 2020 amendments.

In elementary and secondary school settings, a school must respond whenever any school employee has notice of sexual harassment. This includes principals, support staff, teachers, cafeteria workers, custodians—effectively any adult employee within the school. A school may also accept reports of sexual harassment from any person, even if they are not associated with the school.

A school must respond promptly and appropriately when it receives notice of alleged facts that could be considered sexual harassment as defined in the 2020 amendments. Once they are notified, the school must

- Contact the complainant (victim) to discuss the availability of supporting measures and
- Explain the process of filing a formal complaint.

Supportive measures are designed to restore, provide, or preserve equal access to the education program; protect safety; or deter further sexual harassment. Supportive services can include, among other things, counseling, modification of timelines, class schedules, or restrictions on contact with others. The Title IX coordinator is the person responsible for implementing the supportive measures.

These are designed to support the victim and are not disciplinary or punitive with respect to other students. The formal complaint does not actually have to be filed in order to receive supportive services.

A formal complaint is a document filed by the victim alleging sexual harassment that requests the school to investigate the allegation. The complaint may be a hard copy or in digital form, but must include a signature. An e-mail from a student to the Title IX coordinator with the signature of the student would suffice. Parents and guardians may also file formal complaints.

Schools must accept the formal complaint if the student is attempting to participate in the educational program or activities at the time of the formal complaint. Upon receiving a complaint, there must be written notice between all parties including the names, dates, and locations of the alleged misconduct and a description of the alleged misconduct. Investigations must include meeting with the complainant and the respondent. Such meetings shall be conducted after written prior notice is given, as well as the opportunity to have parents present.

After gathering appropriate evidence, a written report must be provided to the parties, and such report must include physical evidence and witness statements. The investigator (Title IX coordinator) has the power to dismiss a complaint and *must* do so when the allegations do not constitute sexual harassment, did not occur in the school's education program or activity, or did not occur in the United States. The investigator *may* dismiss the complaint when requested in writing by the victim to do so, the respondent is no longer enrolled or employed by the school, or when special circumstances prevent a sufficient gathering of relevant evidence.

Once this step is completed, there must be some form of grievance procedure that takes place. The Title IX coordinator does not have the authority to make a final determination or to assign punishment to the respondent. The grievance process must include due process protections, including the use of a neutral decision maker who oversees a hearing on the matter. All parties have equal rights during the procedure, including the right to call witnesses. In the K-12 setting, there is no requirement for a live hearing but instead may rely on written answers. The grievance procedure is based on the presumption that the respondent is not responsible, so the school bears the burden of proof.

Following the outcome, the decision maker must send both parties a written determination, and the school must implement remedies should the respondent be found responsible for the sexual harassment.

School Liability for Sexual Harassment

School districts and individual schools are always liable for *quid pro quo* harassment because the action (promotion, demotion, transfer, termination) taken by an employee is an exercise of authority delegated by the district. School districts and individual schools are liable for environmental harassment if the district has no strong, widely disseminated, and consistently enforced policy against sexual harassment and has no effective complaint procedure in place. Without these clear protections in place, employees and students can reasonably assume that a superior has "apparent authority" (tacit approval) to practice sexual harassment. School districts and individual schools are also liable for environmental harassment if senior management does not take immediate and appropriate steps to terminate harassing conduct and discipline the offending party. (*Note*: When immediate and appropriate action has not been taken in response to a complaint, school districts have been found liable for sexual harassment by independent contractors, e.g., by roofing, electrical, and plumbing contractors and those who provide contracted services such as custodial and food preparation.)

Section 1983 applies to student sexual harassment because it can violate a student's Fourteenth Amendment right to bodily integrity (*Doe v. Taylor Indep. Sch. Dist.*, 15 F.3d 443 (5th Cir. 1994, *cert denied*)). Although school districts cannot be held liable merely because an employee commits an illegal act (*Jett v. Dallas Indep. Sch. Dist.*, 491 U.S. 701 (1989)), a school district could be liable when the school board acts with deliberate indifference by adopting an unconstitutional policy or knowing or acquiescing in a deeply imbedded custom or practice that causes an unconstitutional violation (*Gonzalez v. Ysleta Indep. Sch. Dist.*, 996 F.2d 745 (5th Cir. 1993)). What this means in practical purposes is that "toleration" of harassment directed toward LGBTQ+ students or staff, or others, could meet Section 1983 liability head on and must always be considered by school principals.

Affirmative Response to a Complaint

To avoid liability for sexual harassment of students or employees, a school must take immediate and appropriate corrective action when it is notified of or has suspicion of an incident of alleged harassment. In the case of an allegation of sexual harassment, the accused person should be separated from any contact with the victim until an investigation has been completed and a finding reached. A school is considered to be on notice as soon as an agent or responsible employee of the school receives notice. Notice occurs when

- A student or employee files a grievance.
- A student or employee complains to an administrator or other school employee.
- A parent or other responsible individual contacts a school employee.
- A responsible employee of the school witnesses the harassment or finds some other evidence of harassment.

All reports of sexual harassment (superior to employee, employee to employee, employee to student, student to employee, student to student) should be taken seriously and promptly investigated. Even unsubstantiated reports of possible sexual harassment should heighten scrutiny by a principal.

In attempting to determine if harassment occurred or if the behavior was welcome or unwelcome, the totality of the circumstances must be taken into consideration. For example, in attempting to resolve a dispute, the following should be considered:

- Statements by any witnesses to the alleged incident

- Evidence about the relative credibility of the allegedly harassed victim and the alleged harasser

- The level of detail and consistency of each person's account and of corroborative evidence

SECTION E. ADDITIONAL ESSENTIAL TOPICS OF FOCUS

Harassment Based on Sexual Orientation and Gender

Harassment of students based on sexual orientation, including harassment directed toward transgender students, is a serious concern, especially since LGBTQ+ students suffer increased levels of bullying and harassment, and such youth attempt suicide at a rate five times that of heterosexual youth (CDC, 2021). Adding complexity to the issue, there are those who claim that policies in place to prohibit harassment of LGBTQ+ students restrict their freedom of speech; infringe on their religious freedom and beliefs; and are viewpoint discrimination.

Throughout this text there has been an emphasis placed on not only legal obligations for principals but moral obligations as well. Even though courts throughout the country have provided mixed legal decisions regarding the intersection of the First Amendment and allegations of sexual harassment targeting LGBTQ+ students (such as in T-shirt cases), there are legal realities that support the argument that all homophobic expression is not protected speech. In *Bostock* in 2020, the Supreme Court affirmed that discrimination based on sexual orientation, which would include transgender students, is prohibited. Courts are also being asked to apply the second prong of *Tinker* to such cases, where speech can be prohibited that invades the rights of others.

Homophobic speech should be treated no differently from racist or other hostile speech and should not be regarded by principals as some kind of viewpoint speech. This touches on controversy, but viewpoints can be expressed without using denigrating, demeaning, or hateful speech. Speech that is intended to denigrate others could perhaps be restricted using elements of *Hazelwood, Fraser,* and *Morse*. Eckes (2017) argues that if student speech right exceptions can be made for illegal drug use as in *Morse,* for offensive speech as in *Fraser,* or for speech that is counter to the educational mission of the school, there perhaps should be an exception as well for speech that attacks members of historically marginalized groups. Eckes does note to narrowly tailor such restrictions, and suggests the questions to ask are whether the speech attacks the core being of a minority person, and if the speech is inconsistent with the goals of public education.

Political and religious viewpoints should not shield and protect those who use speech to attack others, and principals should not allow themselves to be an additional weapon against any group of students. Homophobic speech is not political speech, but instead should be viewed as sexual harassment and subject to discipline following student code of conduct policy.

Antigay bias has been referred to as "the last 'acceptable' form of discrimination in the United States" (Walker, 2002). There have been two significant federal cases that have affirmatively held that school districts have a legal obligation under the Equal Protection Clause of the Fourteenth Amendment to protect students from discrimination, harassment, and abuse based upon their sexual orientation.

In a 1996 case, *Nabozny v. Podlesny,* Jamie Nabozny, a gay man, was awarded $900,000 in the first federal trial against a school for not protecting gay students. In this case against the Ashland School District in northern Wisconsin, Nabozny alleged that he had been harassed from the time he entered middle school in 1988 until he dropped out of high school as a junior in 1993. Nabozny said that abuse by other students ranged from name calling to being shoved, beaten, spat upon, and even having his head pushed in a urinal. He said he was kicked in the stomach so many times that he later required surgery.

The award in the *Nabozny* case was ground breaking in that it affirmed that a school district's failure to protect a gay student from peer harassment violated the federal Equal Protection Clause. The case also affirmed that the student was protected by Title IX's prohibition on sex discrimination because he alleged that the harassment was based on his failure to conform to male stereotypes.

Experts generally agree that sexual harassment directed at gay or lesbian students that is sufficiently serious to limit or deny a student's ability to participate in, or benefit from, the school's program constitutes sexual harassment prohibited by Title IX. An important point to keep in mind is that school boards may be held liable for harassment of students by their peers if the harassment—verbal or physical—has been severe and persistent, and the school took no action after learning of the misconduct. As in any other case of alleged sexual harassment, a trained investigator should investigate complaints of harassments based on sexual orientation thoroughly and promptly.

In *Flores v. Morgan Hill Unified School District* (2003), the U.S. Court of Appeals for the Ninth Circuit held that local school officials who didn't take formal action when consistent discrimination and abuse were evident could be held liable. The plaintiffs sued the school district, administrators, and school board members under Section 1983, claiming the defendants' response or lack of response to complaints of student-to-student antihomosexual harassment denied them equal protection. The plaintiffs alleged that, during their time as students in the Morgan Hill Unified School District, they suffered antigay harassment by their classmates. The case settled in early 2004 after a five-year court battle, with the district agreeing to make extensive policy changes, provide training for all district staff on how to appropriately respond to harassment, and pay a total of more than $1.1 million.

Student Pronouns

An emerging issue relates to preferred pronouns of students balanced against some teacher sentiment that requiring them to use certain pronouns violates their religious beliefs. Although arguments can be made regarding how any pronoun is absolutely connected to a specific gender, and an even greater argument how the preferred name of a student is somehow gender specific, the issue is nevertheless growing and unsettled. In an ongoing dispute, in 2020, a court dismissed most claims in a suit filed by a teacher, but allowed Title VII claims of failure to accommodate and a retaliation claim made by a teacher who was forced to resign after he refused to use the preferred names and pronouns of students based on his strongly held religious beliefs (*Kluge v. Brownsburg Cmty. Sch. Corp.* 432 F.Supp.3d 823 (S.D. Ind. 2020)). As of the summer of 2021, this and other cases are still ongoing (*Vlaming. V. West Point Sch. Bd.*).

Student Organizations and Clubs

LGBTQ+ students are guaranteed equal protection under the Fourteenth Amendment and freedom of speech and association under the First Amendment. Like other student clubs, LGBTQ+-related student groups are guaranteed equal treatment and access under the Equal Access Act (1984).

Questions about the legal rights of LGBTQ+ students generally focus on (a) student organizations and clubs, (b) student dress codes, (c) curriculum and LGBTQ+ issues, (d) student involvement in school events, and (e) harassment of LGBTQ+ students.

In *Westside Community Schools Board of Education v. Mergens* (1990), the courts found that the Equal Access Act requires schools to treat student clubs that address LGBTQ+ issues the same as other student groups. When students establish a club in a public school that both receives federal money and provides an "open forum," the Equal Access Act requires the school to allow LGBTQ+-oriented clubs the same access to school facilities that other student groups enjoy.

It is important to note that courts have not looked favorably on school districts that have changed the rules regarding "non-curriculum" clubs in attempting to exclude LGBTQ+ clubs (*Boyd County High School Gay Straight Alliance v. Board of Education of Boyd County,* 2003). Students had initially petitioned to form a Gay-Straight Alliance (GSA), and after initially refusing to approve the club, and subsequently delaying the approval process, the district took the step to suspend all student clubs rather than allow the formation of the GSA. A settlement agreement required the allowance of the formation of the club, as well as mandatory antiharassment training for students and staff.

Student Dress Codes

Since the *Tinker* case in 1969, courts have recognized that school districts must balance their interest in maintaining a safe and orderly learning environment against the rights of students to freedom of speech and expression. *Bethel School District No. 403 v. Fraser* (1986) and other cases have allowed schools to prohibit spoken, written, or symbolic speech that is deemed to be lewd, vulgar, indecent, or clearly offensive, and speech contrary to the school's educational mission. Some courts have held that messages or images that are at odds with values such as civility were contrary to a school's educational mission (*Boroff v. Van Wert City Board of Education,* 2000). Speech that does not fall into one of the above-mentioned categories may be regulated only if it substantially disrupts or interferes with the work of the school (*Sypniewski v. Warren Hills Regional Board of Education,* 2002). Courts have made it clear that mere disagreement or dislike of a message does not meet the disruption test. In order to prohibit expression, the school does not need to wait for a disruption but must have *well-founded* concerns. Consequently, prohibiting clothing that conveys a message that might be construed as pro- or antigay, but is not likely to disrupt the learning environment or interfere with other students' rights, risks legal challenge.

Although some courts have supported the actions of schools that restricted clothing based on a student's gender and on the basis that such clothing distracted from learning, such actions are open to challenges on the basis of sexual discrimination. For example, prohibiting a boy from wearing a dress to school might be viewed as a disruption in one community and be seen as permissible in another. Schools with sex-specific dress codes should consider making a measured exception for transgender students.

Curriculum and LGBTQ+ Issues

Courts have consistently ruled that parents do not have the right to control the content of a curriculum. As long as the curriculum is based on sound education rationale such as age appropriateness, relevance, and currency of the information, school districts have great leeway. School districts should provide complaint and review procedures for resolving challenges to school curriculum and advise all parents of their right to use this process.

Some states require written parental consent before students can participate in classes in which topics such as sex, sexuality, and AIDS are discussed. The federal Protection of Pupil Rights Amendment of 2004 gives parents the right to limit their child's participation in surveys or questionnaires that may contain controversial and/or sexual subject matter (PPRA, 2004).

Student Involvement in School Events

Increasingly, student groups are asking permission to take part in such events as "Diversity Days" or a "Day of Silence." Unless the activity will substantially disrupt the work of the school, such activities as remaining silent for all or part of a day to raise awareness for LGBTQ+ students must be accorded the same rights that would be given to any other school group.

Adult Sexual Harassment

Sexual harassment in the employment relationship is definitively described in the Supreme Court's ruling in *Meritor*. The employer's responsibility for preventing and dealing with sexual harassment is clearly outlined in the EEOC guidelines.

Workplace sexual harassment related to employees can occur in a school setting just as it can in other arenas of employment, and principals have obligations to prevent and respond to employee sexual harassment. All forms of sexual harassment can occur between employees, with a key element nearly always being unwelcome conduct. Principals must also be equally aware of conditions that could give rise to a hostile environment, which depend on the particular circumstances of the incidents. Such considerations include, but are not limited to, the degree of adverse effects on daily performance; the type, frequency, and duration of the conduct; the relationship between parties involved; the number of individuals involved in the harassment; and the context in which they occurred.

To establish a Title VII *quid pro quo* claim, a plaintiff must show that the acceptance or rejection of a supervisor's alleged sexual harassment resulted in a tangible employment action. Such actions include a significant change in employment status, such has hiring, failure to promote, firing, reassignment, or a loss of benefits. There must also be a demonstrated "causal nexus" between the acceptance or rejection of sexual advances and the tangible employment action.

Suggested Risk Management Guidelines
Compliance

School principals have an affirmative duty to ensure and enforce compliance in accord with school district policy and procedures. To ensure that your procedures are prompt and equitable, the school district should be sure that

- One employee is delegated to coordinate the school district's efforts to comply with and carry out its Title IX responsibilities.

- One district office employee is designated to be responsible for coordinating the compliance activities at each school.

- The policy and procedures are widely publicized to all students, parents, and employees (also see Shoop, 2004).

- The policy and procedures are written in language appropriate to the age of the school's students.

- All students and employees are notified of the name, office address, and telephone number of the employee responsible for receiving complaints.

- All complaints are taken seriously and are promptly investigated.

- The investigation is conducted by an impartial investigator.

- The investigation is conducted by a trained investigator.

- The due process rights of students and employees charged with sexual harassment are protected.

- The investigation is completed in a timely manner.

- All parties are told of the outcome of the investigation.

- Accurate records are kept to ensure that the school can and will identify and resolve recurring problems and the problem of repeat offenders.

- Training is instituted to prevent recurrence of any harassment.

SECTION F. PREVENTION

The clearest way a school district can demonstrate that it takes sexual harassment prevention seriously is to have a comprehensive board-adopted policy regarding sexual harassment prevention. *However, individual building principals must affirmatively enforce such a policy.* A formal policy provides a structure under which everyone in the school district can understand their individual rights and responsibilities. Furthermore, having such a policy will help prevent sexual harassment, provide guidance in how to respond to incidents of sexual harassment, and provide some protection from liability in the event of a lawsuit. *The policy should be written in nonlawyer language that is user friendly and should include a separate section for staff and a separate section for students.* In developing, implementing, or enforcing a policy, remember that a school will be held to be liable for hostile-environment sexual harassment by its employee if the employee

- Acted with apparent authority (i.e., because of the school's conduct, the employee reasonably appears to be acting on behalf of the school, whether or not the employee acted with authority)
- Was aided in carrying out the sexual harassment by their position of authority within the institution

A comprehensive sexual harassment prevention policy should include

- A statement prohibiting sexual harassment, indicating that sexual harassment is illegal
- A definition of sexual harassment, with examples
- A description of who is covered by the policy
- A description of the complaint procedures
- A time frame for filing and responding to formal complaints
- A description of the appeals process
- A list of consequences
- A statement prohibiting retaliation
- A statement about confidentiality
- A statement about coverage of off-campus violations
- Identification of the school employee who should be notified if there is a complaint
- A statement about false charges
- A statement about other legal remedies available to complainants
- An indication of how the school community will be notified about the policy
- A statement regarding the ongoing training of school staff and students
- A requirement for an ongoing review, evaluation, and improvement

Policy Implementation and Enforcement

- Ensure that administrators are thoroughly familiar with the policy.
- Include a copy of the policy in faculty and staff handbooks.
- Train all certified and classified staff members in how to recognize and prevent sexual harassment.
- Train investigators in investigation protocols.

- Include a comprehensive presentation of sexual harassment prevention in student handbooks.

- Inform off-campus sites about the school district's sexual harassment prevention policy.

- Integrate information about sexual harassment prevention across the curriculum.

- Display posters in prominent places in district buildings that explain what people should do if they believe they are being sexually harassed.

- Include questions regarding sexual harassment in any surveys conducted to assess school climate.

Codes of Conduct and Training to Support Policy

- There should be a code of conduct for teachers, other school staff members, and volunteers. This document should explicitly state that all romantic and sexual relationships between students and teachers, regardless of the student's age, are prohibited and what the consequences will be if the code is violated.

  - If the allegations involve improper language or a nonphysical form of sexual harassment, it may be possible to allow the teacher to remain in the classroom. However, if the complaint involves sexual intimidation, inappropriate contact, stalking, sexual propositions, or sexual intercourse, the school has a duty to remove the teacher to ensure student safety. A range of options, including suspension or reassignment to non-classroom duties, may be considered.
  - If the complaint was false, there must be serious consequences for the accuser. The punishment must be strong enough to make it clear to employees and all others that a false complaint is a very serious matter.
  - In the event of a false complaint, the employee should be reinstated, and efforts must be made to rehabilitate the employee's reputation.

- There should be a code of conduct for students. This document should explicitly state what types of conduct are not permitted and what the consequences will be if the code is violated (e.g., suspension, expulsion, transfer, criminal charges).

- If a false complaint is filed, there must be serious consequences for the accuser. The punishment must be strong enough to make it clear to students and all others that a false complaint is a very serious matter.

- Provide training in prevention strategies. Specific training is necessary to reduce the confusion between appropriate and inappropriate physical or verbal contact.

For Teachers and Other Employees

The best way that teachers can protect themselves from false accusations is to avoid behaviors that can be misconstrued. Teachers and other school employees should not

- Be alone with a student in a schoolroom, outside of the regular school day, without informing the principal.

- Be alone with a student behind a closed door. If a room door does not have a window, request that one be installed.

- Make a habit of meeting students outside of school.

- Counsel students in nonacademic matters.

- Regularly transport students in your own vehicle or allow students to have access to it.

- Give students hall passes to come to your room on nonschool-related business.

- Allow students to engage you in conversations regarding their romantic or sexual activities. Don't discuss your personal problems with students.

- Entertain students in your home unless it is a school-sponsored activity.

- Make sexual comments, comments about their bodies, tell sexual jokes, or share sexually oriented material with students.

- Put your hands on a student in a manner that a reasonable person could interpret as inappropriate.

Cautions for Principals

- Don't assume that otherwise "good teachers" will not harm children.

- Don't assume that only certain types of students engage in sexual harassment.

- Don't assume that only certain types of students can be victims of sexual harassment.

- Don't confuse sexual harassment with flirting or giving someone a compliment.

- Don't assume that sexual harassment did not take place if there are no witnesses.

- Don't assume that sexual harassment is an isolated incident.

- You have an affirmative duty to
    - Protect students and employees from potential harm.
    - Ensure that no retaliation is taken against a person who reports abuse.
    - Promptly investigate all complaints.
    - Report the suspected abuse to the appropriate state agency if required.
    - Report the suspected abuse or complaint of abuse to the appropriate school district person (e.g., Title IX compliance officer).
    - Document the investigation process.
    - Evaluate the circumstances in the case of an unsubstantiated complaint to determine if any actions could be misconstrued, and eliminate these actions.
    - Provide ongoing education about sexual harassment by (1) reminding all staff members of the importance of appropriate behavior; (2) reminding all staff members of the state statutes and school district policy; (3) reminding all students that no one has the right to touch them in a sexual manner; (4) reminding all students how to complain if they believe they have been touched inappropriately; (5) reminding

all students that if they have any concerns or questions, they are strongly encouraged to talk to the principal.

The following guidelines are based on Justice Sandra Day O'Connor's explanation of the Supreme Court's decision in *Davis v. Monroe County Board of Education* (1999), as reported by Schimmel (2000). It should be remembered that the following are guidelines of legal liability, *not necessarily guidelines for best education practice*. Even though there may not be legal liability for some actions, it is hoped that school administrators will work to eliminate all forms of sexual harassment. The "operative statements" included in the guidelines later (based on Justice O'Connor's explanation) should provide administrators with the tools to set policy in the areas of (a) "deliberate indifference," (b) accusations that an administrator's "response is clearly unreasonable," and (c) "denying victims equal access to education."

- Administrators are not required to purge their schools of peer harassment.

- Schools are not required to suspend or expel a student accused of harassment nor are administrators required to take any particular disciplinary action in response to harassment charges.

- Victims of peer harassment do not have a right under Title IX to make any particular remedial demands.

- Courts should not second-guess the disciplinary decisions made by administrators.

- Schools are not liable for the sexual harassment of their students (but only for their own acts of deliberate indifference).

- Administrators should not be considered deliberately indifferent to peer harassment unless their response is "clearly unreasonable."

- Schools are not required to take disciplinary action that would expose them to constitutional or statutory claims.

- Damages are not available simply by showing that a student has been teased or called offensive names—even if gender specific.

- Damages are not available unless the harassment is severe, pervasive, and objectively offensive and denies its victim equal access to education.

Protecting Teachers' Reputations

The fear of false accusations of sexual harassment and abuse has a negative impact on educators. It is important to recognize that a false allegation of harassment may significantly damage an educator's reputation and destroy their career. This is another reason that every allegation of sexual harassment should be quickly and thoroughly investigated and disposed of. If an accusation is proved to be true, then definitive action to punish must be demonstrated. If the accusation is proved false, then definitive action should be taken to punish the false accuser. Include *prohibition against false complaints* in any sexual harassment prevention policy. Including such a prohibition is an important component in protecting the reputation of innocent victims. Students and employees must understand the damage that can be done by a false complaint and that serious punishment will be given to any person who makes a false complaint.

ADDITIONAL CASES OF INTEREST TO EDUCATORS

KD v. Douglas Cnty. Sch. Dist. No. 001, No. 20-1772 (June 16, 2021). The Eighth Circuit has affirmed a district court's ruling concerning the sexual abuse of an Omaha student by a teacher, upholding default judgment against the teacher and summary judgment in favor of the principal and school district. The court found that the principal did not have actual notice of the abuse as required by Title IX and § 1983, nor did he aid or abet any intentional infliction of emotional distress by the teacher. Although there were numerous occasions where the behavior of the teacher and his relationship with the student was called into question, the principal never had actual knowledge of a sexual relationship between them.

Doe v. Fairfax Cnty. Sch. Bd., No. 19-2203 (June 16, 2021). The Fourth Circuit has reversed and remanded a district court's denial of a new trial where a jury found in favor of the school district in a case alleging that the school's administrators acted with deliberate indifference to a student's reports of sexual harassment by another student. The appeals court found the evidence did not support the jury's finding that the school board lacked actual notice, and it remanded the case for a new trial to determine deliberate indifference and if sexual harassment standards were met under Title IX.

Adams v. Sch. Bd. of St. Johns Cnty. Florida, 968 F.3d 1286 (11th Cir. 2020). The appellate court held in favor of a transgender student ruling only on equal protection grounds for the student, who challenged a school board policy that barred him from the boys' restroom. In an earlier ruling, the same court held in favor of the student on both equal protection grounds and Title IX discrimination. However, the ruling was delayed through a procedural step and the court reconsidered and held on the narrower grounds. The language in the decision of the majority and dissent represented a sharp divide on the issue.

C.C. v. Harrison Cnty. Bd. of Educ., No. 20-0171 (W.Va Sup. Ct. App. 2021). The West Virginia Supreme Court of Appeals reversed a lower court and allowed two of eight claims related to an incident between a high school assistant principal and a transgender student. The assistant principal confronted a transgender male student in a restroom who demanded he expose his genitalia and use a urinal instead of a stall, and after blocking his exit from the restroom yelled loudly down a hallway "you freak me out." The assistant principal was suspended but later reinstated. Among the surviving claims was one based on the district's failure to adopt an antiharassment policy.

Deminski v. State Board of Education, No. 60A20 (N.C. Sup. Ct. 2021). North Carolina's Supreme Court unanimously held that the right under the state constitution's education clause to a sound basic education protects individual students from bullying, placing an affirmative duty on the government to protect that right. The deliberate indifference to a hostile, abusive classroom environment that inhibits a student's ability to learn constitutes a constitutional claim.

Jauquet v. Green Bay Area Catholic Education, Inc., No. 20-2803 (7th Cir. 2021). The Seventh Circuit has upheld the dismissal of a student's Title IX lawsuit against her private school. The school, which is subject to Title IX because it receives federal funding, was found to have responded properly to peer-to-peer sexual harassment by responding promptly through disciplinary action, and the actions appeared to have been successful in stopping the bullying behavior.

Fitzgerald v. Barnstable School Committee, 504 F.3d 165 (1st Cir. 2007). The Court held that Title IX does not "make an educational institution the insurer either of a student's safety or of a parent's piece of mind." The Supreme Court on appeal noted that Title IX was not meant to be an exclusive mechanism to address gender discrimination.

Estate of Olsen v. Fairfield City Sch. Dist. Bd. of Educ., 341 F.Supp.3d 793 (S.D. Ohio. 2018). The parents of a middle school student who committed suicide after experiencing several years of bullying, harassment, and physical assault filed multiple claims against a school board and school district employees. The girl experienced extreme bullying and harassment at her intermediate school, and the same mistreatment continued at her middle school. The parents alleged that their requests for intervention were ignored or insufficiently acted on by numerous school administrators or other employees.

Multiple administrators, counselors, and a Title IX coordinator were denied summary judgment on the plaintiff claim that they failed to investigate complaints, meet with the parents, or notify each other of the bullying and harassment. The superintendent and two principals were denied immunity under Section 1983, with the court determining they indeed had final policy-making authority when dealing with bullying and harassment. Summary judgment was also denied regarding Title VI claims, with the court noting that the level of bullying and harassment was far beyond teasing, and was in fact persistent and pervasive; school officials had sufficient knowledge of the incidents; and they demonstrated repeated deliberate indifference to the suffering of the girl. The harassment included verbal, physical, and threatening assaults, in both a racial and sexual manner. The girl was told to "kill herself" on more than one occasion.

Cass v. Town of Wayland, 383 F.Supp.3d 66 (D. Mass 2019). In a case related to Title IX concerns and a state whistleblower act, a court determined that the dismissal of an athletic director was in retaliation for his reporting allegations of Title IX violations. After being hired as the athletic director, he discovered what he felt were significant issues related to equal funding and other issues within athletic programs, and at one time reported that the high school athletics program was a "walking Title IX violation." He filed suit after his dismissal. A federal jury also awarded the former athletic director $250,000, determining that the school violated the state act when he was dismissed from his position.

Sanches v. Carrollton Farmers Branch Ind. Sch. Dist., 647 F.3d 156 (5th Cir. 2011). An appellate court affirmed the dismissal of a case and described it as a "petty squabble, masquerading as a civil rights matter" that had no place in any court. The court concluded that the behavior was better described as bullying or teasing than sexual harassment. The case involved a cheerleader, another female student, and the ex-boyfriend of the female student. Name calling, rumor spreading, and slapping the buttocks of the boyfriend was determined in the whole as not severe, pervasive, or offensive for Title IX remedies. Although the inappropriate and immature behavior caused hurt feelings and embarrassment, it was deemed "the sort of conflict that takes place every day in high schools, and it is not the proper stuff of a federal harassment claim."

Campbell v. State of Hawaii Dept. of Educ., 892 F.3d 1005 (9th Cir. 2018). An appellate court affirmed the judgment of a lower court that dismissed claims brought by a teacher who alleged sexual harassment claims against her employer. The teacher alleged that she was repeatedly sexually harassed by students at the school, but the court determined that the evidence showed that the school took sufficient action in response to those claims. At the same time of her allegations, she was also involved with complaints against her regarding inappropriate confrontations with students, among other claims. The court determined that the district did not cause her any adverse employment action and the appellate court concluded that both her Title IX and Title VII claims failed to state a proper claim.

Alamo Heights Indep. Sch. Dist. v. Clark, 544 SW 3d 755 (Tex. Sup. Ct. 2018). The Texas Supreme Court reversed a lower court decision that had favored the plaintiff in a sexual harassment suit that was based on whether sexual harassment can occur when the allegations were based on parties of the same gender. Although the U.S. Supreme Court has held that sexual harassment can be based on gender stereotypes even if the harasser is not LGBTQ+ and the lower court based their finding on that interpretation, the Texas Supreme Court held that the Texas equivalent of Title VII does not. A new female coach was harassed from nearly the beginning of her employment by two senior female coaches, including comments about her body. The majority opinion found it didn't matter if the harassment was motivated by homosexual behavior or not, and was merely horseplay. In a dissenting opinion, it was noted that if the offending parties were male, there would be no doubt it was sexually harassing behavior.

Neshaminy Sch. Dist. v. Neshaminy Federation of Teachers, 171 A.3d 334 (Commw. Ct. 2017). A court overturned an arbitrator decision to reinstate a teacher who continually sexually harassed a female first-year teacher who worked with him in a ninth-grade classroom. The teacher testified that he made sarcastic and sexually explicit comments to her "all day, every day" including comments such as inviting her to sit on his lap in front of students. The decision of the school district to terminate the employment of the male teacher was upheld by the superior court.

Does v. Southeast Delco Sch. Dist., 272 F.Supp 3d. 656 (Dist. ED Penn. 2017). The case stemmed from actions filed after a teacher was convicted of the sexual assault of elementary school students. The teacher assaulted students at school and served prison time and is on a sex offender registry. The court rendered a partial decision for the plaintiffs as to state-created danger claims and Title IX claims against the district.

CHAPTER 8

Special Education Services

Special education law, regulations, and procedures are very precise. School administrators should seek day-to-day guidance on such important (and potentially litigious) areas as disciplining students with disabilities, determining eligibility for services, changing educational placement, and providing an appropriate education in the least restrictive environment, from experts in their school district and, in problematic situations, from legal counsel.

CONSIDERATIONS RELATED TO COVID-19

While all students, teachers, and parents have been affected in some way by COVID-19, perhaps no student group has been impacted as greatly as students who qualify for special services. As with all guidance regarding policy and practice, state and local policy must always be considered, so what follows in this chapter is general guidance and not specific to any one school district. However, equally important is federal guidance, and since the start of pandemic, the Office of Civil Rights (OCR), the Centers for Disease Control and Prevention (CDC), and the U.S. Department of Education have all recognized that schools have authority to take necessary actions to protect the health and safety of students and staff.

There are several key concepts to keep in mind as schools attempt to meet the needs of students who qualify for special services.

- Students receiving special services remotely have the same free, appropriate public education (FAPE) rights as those who receive in-person services.

- Virtual individualized education plan (IEP) meetings are allowable.

- In what may appear to be counter to educational missions, a school district is not required to provide services to a qualified student with an IEP if it is not providing services to the general education population. Such a situation would be for a short-term period of time in the event a school is closed. However, if a district is providing any services to the general population, it must also provide services to those with special needs.

- When a school district moves to remote learning, school districts must have a plan to accommodate

(Continued)

and provide equal access for students with special needs. Special services may be allowed in-person even when other students are required to learn remotely, but that may depend on local policy.

- Access means more than the mere possession of a device such as a tablet or computer. What is posted for students must be accessible for those who are hearing or vision impaired as well as for those with mobility issues who cannot operate screens in the same manner as those without such disabilities. There are students who do not use keyboards; others cannot use a touchscreen or a computer mouse. For videos with audio files, they should always be closed captioned.

- When services are not provided, schools and IEP teams must consider what "compensatory" services may be required. If there is a denial of FAPE, students have a right to compensatory services. What is unsettled is whether good faith efforts to continue services during the pandemic even if they don't fully comply with the IEP will be permitted.

- Also unsettled may be "stay-put" provisions where the question is whether IEP services must remain exactly the same between "in-person" instruction and remote learning.

- Children sent home to quarantine or with an illness who are out for an extended period of time have a right to instruction at home as long as certain requirements are met. IEP teams should determine how to continue to provide services and in what form.

- Some experts are predicting a potential "perfect storm" of COVID-19-related litigation related to what services were or were not provided during school closures and virtual learning, and despite the difficulties and challenges, every effort to continue "normal" services to all students, and especially those identified requiring special services, must not only be the goal, but one that is met as much as possible.

- School districts should assess if children have regressed due to school closures and virtual environments, and if the child has not regressed, have they instead met meaningful progress toward their IEP goals. What additional or different services may need to be provided in order to bring the student back on track to make meaningful progress?

SUGGESTED GUIDELINES FOR PRACTICE

Principals don't need to be special education experts, but should strive to be special education advocates. Principals must advocate for all of their students, and everyone else's for that matter, but should especially be aware of the needs of students who qualify for special services under IDEA or accommodations under Section 504.

Thinking in terms of what a FAPE truly means for students and parents helps to frame many challenges they face. The laws surrounding special education helped to remedy those challenges, but no serious issue or problem can be fully solved without creating new or perhaps controversial questions.

Principals should familiarize themselves with the essential differences between special education law and IDEA compared to civil rights laws under Section 504. The IDEA is a special education law that protects students identified with a disability that adversely affects their educational performance sufficiently enough to require special services; Section 504 is a civil rights law that protects an individual who has a physical impairment that substantially limits a major life activity. IDEA protects students up to age 21, and Section 504 provides protections throughout the lifespan.

Principals face major challenges related to special education. Among these are ensuring access for students; adhering to statutory processes and procedures while safeguarding parental and student rights; making decisions related to the discipline of students on IEPs; and recently a new definition of what constitutes an "appropriate" education. These challenges are addressed in the chapter.

The recognition of parental rights in special education and fostering genuine involvement of parents in the IEP process would provide better outcomes for students as well as reduce the possibility of litigation initiated by parents against the school. IDEA provides rights not only for the identified student, but also for the parents or guardians. As has been a recurring theme in this book, principals are reminded that collaboration with parents is more likely to produce positive results for children and is much easier to accomplish than trying to work through an adversarial process in the judicial system.

Principals are urged to seek and support proper training for SROs, especially for encounters with students who have disabilities. Students with disabilities frequently have negative encounters with law enforcement in schools oftentimes due to a lack of awareness of differences in behaviors that such students may exhibit. This problem and those related to the use of restraint and seclusion are discussed more fully in Chapters 4 and 6.

SECTION A. THE PURPOSE AND HISTORICAL CONTEXT OF SPECIAL EDUCATION

By necessity, this chapter can provide only a general overview of this critical area of the law and does not purport to give detailed guidance for every dilemma involving special education. Nor does it attempt to address every difficult situation and every procedural question that may arise in educating students with disabilities. Instead, we explain the key terminology and principles underlying federal special education law and describe, in a general manner, the related procedures mandated by such law. In this fourth edition, we have also chosen to highlight what might be among the most common special education challenges and dilemmas that principals face. We do not present specific state laws and regulations, which in many cases go further than federal laws and regulations in requiring specific actions and procedures, and principals are reminded to always follow local policy and procedures.

The Purpose of Special Education

Nearly 14 percent or over 7 million public school students qualify for special services and have an IEP. On a daily basis, principals make a number of significant decisions involving educating students with disabilities, and often questions and challenges arise in individual cases about what is required and what is best for each student. The dynamic nature of special education law makes it difficult for administrators to stay well versed on the changing federal and state statutes and regulations. However, children with disabilities did not always have the educational entitlements that are currently guaranteed under federal law.

A disability can impact a child's educational experience in a variety of ways. Sensory disabilities such as hearing impairments and visual impairments can limit a student's access to certain instructional formats such as large group discussions and instructional materials such as textbooks. Other limitations resulting from a specific learning disability (SLD) or traumatic brain injury can severely impact a child's ability to read, write, or do math at the same level as their peers without disabilities.

The basic principles of IDEA are access and equality. The idea of access for students is contrasted with the exclusion of students. Excluding students from receiving a public education is not only a moral violation but a legal one under IDEA. The concept of equality of treatment for students with disabilities is sometimes more difficult to define, because uniformity is often in tension with the ideals of diversity and individualization. Often the decision to place a student in special education is not clear cut and is a dilemma, having to choose between being identified as a student who could benefit from additional services or being treated like every other child and not labeled as "different." However, the point is that without such support, millions of students could not enjoy the benefits and privileges students without identified disabilities always have at their disposal. Special education and services should not be viewed as a way to "fix" children who have disabilities, but instead be seen as providing a chance at an equal floor and ceiling to help kids become who they want to be.

Historical Context of Special Education

Almost a half century has passed since students with disabilities were given the right to an education in the United States. Court cases that grew out of the racial desegregation movement of the 1950s and 1960s, such as *Brown v. Board of Education of Topeka (Brown I)* in 1954, affirmed that all children had a constitutional right to equal educational opportunities. Prior to this landmark case, educational decisions had been made at the state or local court level. The *Brown* case served as a foundational case for later litigation both at the federal level and in locales across the nation seeking to guarantee equal educational opportunities for all children.

In the early 1970s, numerous parents of students with disabilities went to federal courts when their local school districts did not provide services to meet their children's educational needs. In *Pennsylvania Association for Retarded Citizens (PARC) v. Commonwealth of Pennsylvania* (1971, amended 1972), a Pennsylvania court ruled that all children, regardless of disability, have a basic right to an education under the Fourteenth Amendment. The decision also established that children should be offered education that is appropriate to their learning capacities. The court further stated that no law could postpone, terminate, or deny children access to a publicly supported education and described a basic order of preference for placement starting with the regular public school class, if possible:

> Placement in a regular public school class is preferable to placement in a special public school class. Further, placement in a special public school class is preferable to placement in any other type of program of education and training.

THE PRINCIPAL'S QUICK-REFERENCE GUIDE TO SCHOOL LAW

Soon afterward, in *Mills v. Board of Education of the District of Columbia* (1972), a federal court ruled that the District of Columbia schools could not exclude children with disabilities from the public schools and that the lack of necessary funds claimed by the school district was unacceptable justification for not providing services. In essence, the decision means that school districts are constitutionally prohibited from using lack of resources as the reason to withhold services to children with disabilities. (Of course, the fact that IDEA has never been fully funded places significant burdens on school budgets when they are also mandated to fully provide services.)

Court decisions and social and political pressures resulted in landmark federal legislation that boldly addressed the educational rights of children with disabilities. Two resultant laws—the Rehabilitation Act of 1973 and the Education for All Handicapped Children Act of 1975 (commonly known as Pub. L. No. 94-142)—provided federal funds and established regulations to protect equal access to a FAPE for students with disabilities. Before enactment of the law, millions of students were excluded from school entirely or only provided limited or minimal services. In addition, the Americans with Disabilities Act of 1990 (ADA) protects individuals with disabilities from discrimination and guarantees equal access and opportunities.

The IDEA is the main federal statute authorizing state and local aid for special education for children with disabilities. The IDEA is an education statute based on the basic principles of access versus exclusion and the equality of treatment for students with disabilities.

The Americans with Disabilities Act Amendments Act (ADAAA) and Section 504 of the Rehabilitation Act serve to improve access to accommodations for students and adults with learning disabilities. Section 504 is a civil rights law that prohibits discrimination against people with disabilities by any agency that receives federal funding.

The Elementary and Secondary Education Act (ESEA) challenges states and school districts to improve student academic achievement. The eighth authorization, 20 U.S.C. § 6301 (2015), is known as the Every Student Succeeds Act (ESSA).

SECTION B. KEY TERMINOLOGY AND PRINCIPLES IN SPECIAL EDUCATION LAW

When considering the issues involved in educating students with disabilities, it is critical to understand specific terminology and key principles that have been defined both in legislation and through litigation. These terms and principles may sound straightforward, and their definitions may seem obvious. But frequently there are conflicting interpretations as to exactly what the law means by a certain term—and the courts often serve as the arbiters of such disagreements over definitions. Certain words have very specific meanings in the special education arena. Knowing the meanings of terms used in the context of special education is a prerequisite for being able to meet both the requirements of the law and the educational needs of students with disabilities.

Common Terms and Essential Concepts

There are essential terms and concepts that all principals must know and understand in order to navigate through the policies, procedures, and practices required to provide services for students with special needs or who qualify for services under Section 504. This is not intended to be comprehensive, but instead to provide a review of what you may most likely become presented with on what may seem to be a daily basis. Additional information related to some of these terms is included in the chapter.

Accommodations: Measures taken to "level the playing field" in order for qualified individuals to have an equal opportunity to demonstrate knowledge.

Assessment: The methods of obtaining information to determine eligibility for services.

Behavior intervention plan (BIP): A plan within the IEP that includes positive interventions when behaviors interfere with learning or that of others.

Change of placement: An IEP team determines the placement of a student with disabilities; a change in placement occurs if a child is removed from school for disciplinary reasons longer than ten consecutive school days or for a series of days that add up to more than ten days. States vary in policy but a change in placement may also occur due to extended illness or a modified school day.

Child Find: The requirement that all students with disabilities are identified and evaluated, and those qualifying receive special education and related services.

Consent: A procedural safeguard for parents and students and requires that the parent be fully informed of all information that relates to actions taken with the child. Consent is voluntary and can be revoked at any time.

Cumulative file: The general student file maintained by the school. Parents have the right to inspect and make copies of all information contained in the file.

Disability: An impairment that substantially affects one or more major life activities and/or impairment that has been established in records, or when a person has been regarded as having an impairment.

Disproportionality: Related to the concern that students of color are overrepresented in identification for special education, placement in special education, and matters of school discipline.

Due process: Procedures in place to resolve disputes between parents and school authorities. Such procedures may be required to be exhausted prior to attempted resolution through the courts.

Free, appropriate public education (FAPE): All eligible students have the right to a free and appropriate public education that is in conformity with their IEP.

Functional behavior assessment (FBA): A process to determine reasons for student behavior. The central idea is that the behavior of a student serves a purpose and is done for a reason. The FBA attempts to determine those reasons.

Individualized educational plan (IEP): The individualized education plan.

Inclusion: The practice of educating students with special needs in regular classrooms, preferably at their home school. Related term to LRE and mainstreaming.

Local Education Agency (LEA): A public board of education or typically an authorized "LEA representative" who is qualified to provide and supervise the administration of services for children with disabilities. Typically the LEA representative is a school administrator.

Least restrictive environment (LRE): The student with a disability should have the opportunity to be educated with nondisabled peers to the greatest extent appropriate and have access to the general curriculum, extracurricular activities, and any other program nondisabled peers have access to.

Manifestation determination review (MDR): An IEP team meeting that reviews whether the behavior of a child was a manifestation of the disability when determining proposed disciplinary action that would result in a change of placement.

Mediation: A procedural safeguard for parents and students to resolve disputes. Cannot be used to deny a due process hearing and must be conducted within the law by qualified mediators.

Modifications: Changes not limited to what is expected of the student; of changes in instructional level, content, or performance.

Other health impairment (OHI): An umbrella term that encompasses a wide range of health conditions that may qualify a student for educational services.

Prior written notice: Required notices to parents when the school proposes to initiate changes, identification, evaluation, or educational placement of the child.

Public Law (P.L.) 94-142: The Education for All Handicapped Children Act (1975).

Reasonable accommodations: Provide modifications or adjustments to lessons, tasks, the environment, or other areas that allow a person with a disability to have an equal opportunity to participate in school or work. Such accommodations could include note takers, interpreters, recorded lessons, or other measures that do not create undue administrative or financial burdens.

Related services: IDEA defines related services to include any transportation, developmental, corrective, or other supportive services necessary to enable a student with disabilities to benefit from special education. In order for a student to receive related services, that child must first be found eligible for special education.

Response to intervention (RTI): Research-based instructional and intervention strategies used with students who have or are suspected of having SLDs.

Section 504: Part of the Rehabilitation Act of 1973 and a civil rights law that prohibits discrimination against people with disabilities by recipients of federal funding. Section 504 protects both students and employees.

Stay put: A provision that parents may invoke that requires the student to remain in the current placement while awaiting due process or other proceedings.

Supplementary aids and services: This describes the aids, services, and supports necessary to provide to the maximum extent appropriate needed for disabled students to be educated with nondisabled students in regular education classes.

Transition services: A requirement in the IEP designed to facilitate movement from school to work or postsecondary education.

Zero reject: Federal law makes it clear that all state agencies must implement a zero-reject policy; that is, they must provide special education and related services to meet the needs of all children with disabilities.

SECTION C. IDENTIFICATION AND PROCEDURES FOR STUDENTS WITH DISABILITIES

All children with disabilities are guaranteed a FAPE. The zero-reject provision of the law is the premise on which special education is provided and all additional procedures and safeguards are based. Although the level of services provided is not guaranteed, all qualified students are unconditionally guaranteed services, including what are known as related services. IDEA guarantees that students with disabilities have equal access to education provided at public expense, under public supervision and direction, and without charge.

Furthermore, the school and district or agency must make available all levels of schooling—preschool through secondary school education—to students with disabilities. Eligible students with disabilities are entitled to receive special education and related services from ages three through twenty-one or until they graduate from high school, whichever comes first. In addition, under Part C of IDEA, states that accept federal funding must provide federally assisted early intervention services to infants and toddlers (from birth through age three) who would be at risk of experiencing a substantial developmental delay if early intervention services are not provided.

For children to qualify for special education services under IDEA, having a disability is not enough to qualify for services. There must be evidence that a child's academic performance has been adversely affected by the disability. Every public school is required to identify, locate, and evaluate children with disabilities. Children with disabilities as defined under the latest reauthorization of IDEA are between the ages of three and twenty-one who have one or more of the following conditions:

- SLD, including in reading, math, and writing

- Speech or language impairment (SLP), including stuttering or other expressive language issues

- OHI that includes ADHD and other medical conditions

- Autism spectrum disorder (ASD), which is a developmental disability

- Intellectual disability (ID), which is characterized by low intellectual ability

- Emotional disturbance (ED), which could include anxiety, depression, and bipolar disorder

- Developmental delay, which includes delays in cognitive, social, emotional, physical, or cognitive development up to age nine

- Multiple disabilities where more than one disability is qualifying

- Traumatic brain injury, which includes those caused by brain injury or physical force

- Orthopedic impairment, including difficulties with body control, cerebral palsy

- Visual impairment, including blindness or other eyesight problems

- Deafness, which includes lack of hearing even with assistance of hearing aids

Implementing Required Procedural Safeguards

Throughout the span of public education for all students, parents and children have specific rights, and IDEA delineates additional protections and safeguards that exist to preserve those rights. These procedural safeguards are complex and were developed to hold the school and district accountable for complying with the law's provisions. Parents and students of majority age have specific rights even before a student may be determined to be eligible for services. Preserving and adhering to these rights isn't just a legal and moral requirement, but also serves as a means for the school and parents to work together to improve outcomes for the student.

Notification rights: Examples of these rights include the right to receive written notice about the procedural safeguards delineated under IDEA; advance notification of evaluations and IEP meetings; the educational placement of the student; and provisions of a FAPE for their child with a disability. Prior written notice is intended to inform parents about all actions school systems are proposing to take, or even declining to take, regarding the student. Parents of students with disabilities must be provided with prior written notice of procedural safeguards (at least once annually) and of actions proposed or refused by the school.

Consent rights: Parents have the right to informed consent (and the right to decline) any evaluation proposed to be conducted; the initial placement of a child in a program providing special education and related services; and any change in the identification, evaluation, program, or placement of a child with a disability. If parents do not consent to proposed evaluations that school personnel believe are necessary to provide the student with a FAPE, then the LEA may choose to pursue consent for the evaluation via the mediation or due process hearing procedures.

Other rights: Parents and students have other specific rights, including the right of the transfer of parental rights at the age of majority (depending on state law); the right to inspect, review, and amend educational records related to the child; the rights involving disciplining students with disabilities; the rights of surrogate parents; and the right to appeal any placement or education issue through requesting an administrative review, mediation, impartial due process hearing, and award of attorney fees. A due process hearing can be requested by the parents or the school for any disagreements related to a child's educational evaluation, placement, or FAPE.

Any notice provided to parents must be written in clear language that is understandable to noneducators (i.e., free of jargon). If the native language of the parent is not English, or if the parents' mode of communication is not a written language, school districts must ensure that the notice is translated orally or by other means into the parents' native language or other mode of communication.

Methods for contacting parents may include making telephone calls, mailing a letter, sending a letter home with the student, making a home visit, or contacting the parents through a friend or relative. It is important to document efforts made to notify parents of IEP meetings, in case the parents do not attend and the school determines that an education surrogate parent must be assigned to advocate for and represent the student's interests in the IEP process.

A final note is that throughout all processes in special education, IDEA was written taking into account the recognition that there would potentially be disagreements between school authorities and parents/guardians regarding educational decisions. For that reason, administrative due process hearings as well as the right to appeal in state and federal courts were placed into the law. However, a key element is that all administrative remedies must be exhausted before seeking court action.

Disproportionality in Special Education

The issue of disproportionality related to students placed in special education as well as related to the discipline of students must be considered by all school principals. Research has significant disproportionality for students of color or low-income backgrounds in three major areas: the identification or eligibility of students, the placement of students in more restrictive settings, and higher rates of exclusionary discipline of students of color (NCLD, 2020). The misidentification of students into more restrictive educational settings and subjecting students to harsher discipline policies can negatively affect the educational outcomes for students.

Students of color are identified for special education at a higher rate than their white peers, and Black students are 40 percent more likely to be identified with a disability than all other students (Harper, 2017; cited in NCLD, 2020). Although some argue that the disparities in identification exist because students of color may indeed have higher rates of disabilities, others point to evidence of systemic biases that may lead to the misrepresentation (NCLD, 2020). Research has demonstrated that although both race and income play a role in the disparities, even within the same income levels, students of color are more likely to be identified as needing special education services (Grindal et al., 2019).

A deeper discussion of disproportionality is beyond the scope of this text. However, principals should be mindful of the issue and should support efforts to have in place positive school environments and culture to minimize discipline issues in their schools such as MTSS, PBIS, and restorative justice practices, and should also support educational practices that benefit all students through culturally responsive teaching and genuine efforts to hire a diversified faculty and staff.

Determining Eligibility for Services Under IDEA

Special education law not only specifies eligibility criteria that must be met in order for a student to receive special education and related services, but also mandates that certain procedures be followed in determining who is eligible for services, deciding on the appropriate placement for a student, and developing an IEP for each student with disabilities. In addition, the law contains provisions guaranteeing that parents be involved and informed in the process of making decisions regarding their child's education.

At times, administrators, teachers, and school support staff may disagree with parents about what type of placement, instructional approach, support services, and accommodations are appropriate for the students involved. School personnel must comply with procedural safeguards and notification requirements that are guaranteed to students with disabilities and their parents by law. Although students and parents have due process rights to appeal decisions with which they disagree, it is to everybody's advantage to prevent disagreements from escalating into adversarial relationships or, worse yet, litigation.

Conducting Prereferral Interventions

The prereferral intervention process is often confused with the referral process defined in IDEA. The prereferral intervention is more than providing temporary accommodations for students, with the purpose to identify and implement alternative strategies for students who are having academic or other difficulties in the classroom before the student is referred to special education. Prereferral represents a school-based intervention process that allows educational professionals and stakeholders to brainstorm ways to improve educational outcomes. Members of the prereferral team typically include the teacher or teachers of the student, the parents/guardians, an administrator, and school support staff such as counselors, nurses, school psychologists, and social workers. The name of the team varies, among others being a student-centered team, student referral team, or student intervention team.

It is important to note that not all students who experience difficulty learning have disabilities. There are numerous other reasons why children are unsuccessful in school. While the purpose is to assist the student with their needs, the prereferral process also serves to decrease the number of inappropriate referrals to special education and hopefully reduce the problems associated with disproportionality; provide multidisciplinary perspectives for working with a student with learning difficulties; potentially discover strategies and accommodations that benefit the student to see if that level of support is sufficient for the student.

It is at this stage that many states and school districts implement their RTI process. It is through the tiered levels of intervention that the team can determine if the interventions can help a student achieve success without entering special education. Most often these interventions are conducted within the parameters of the general education class. An important component of prereferral intervention is communicating with the parents about the student's difficulties and how the school is trying to support the child. Teachers document the strategies they employ and how the student responds to the interventions. Even if the interventions are unsuccessful, the data collected during the intervention can prove valuable when others work with the same student in the future. Prereferral interventions may not be used by a school or district to postpone or delay evaluation for special education eligibility when there is a strong reason to suspect that a child has a disability that is impeding learning.

Early Intervening Services

The passage of IDEA 2004 introduced a new term to special education known as *early intervening services*. The purpose of early intervening services, similar to prereferral interventions, is to reduce the need to identify and label children as disabled; however, unlike prereferral interventions, IDEA allows school districts to use a portion of the federal money (not more than 15 percent) received each year out of Part B of IDEA to develop and implement interventions for students who have not been identified as needing special education or related services but who would benefit from additional academic and behavioral support to be successful in the general education classroom. Furthermore, early intervening funding allows school districts that have a pattern of identifying a significant number of children from culturally diverse backgrounds as disabled to offer professional development to their teachers on the delivery of academic instruction and behavioral interventions, as well as the use of adaptive and instructional technology. Unlike prereferral interventions, data on early intervening services must be reported to the state annually and include information about the number of students who received services and the number of students who subsequently became eligible for special education and related services.

Determining Next Steps After Prereferral Interventions

If after prereferral interventions in general education classrooms do not appear to improve the difficulties the student is experiencing, children suspected of having a disability that affects their learning may be referred for evaluation to determine whether they have a qualifying disability. Such referrals may be made by teachers or other school personnel, the parents or guardians of the child, or any other person involved in the education or care of the child. This referral begins the formal process of determining the eligibility for special services. Once the referral is made, the school must obtain consent from the parents or legal guardians to begin the evaluation process.

According to IDEA 2004, the evaluation process involves educators and related service providers using a variety of assessment tools and strategies to gather relevant functional, developmental, and academic information, including information provided by the parent, that may assist in determining (a) whether the child has a disability and (b) the content of the child's IEP, including information related to enabling the child to be involved in and progress in the general education curriculum or, for preschool children, to participate in appropriate activities. The evaluation committee should not use any single measure or assessment as the sole criterion for determining whether a child has a disability or determining an appropriate educational program for the child.

Assessments must be administered within a sixty-day time frame (some states may have shorter time frames) from the receipt of parental consent and with the student's native language, if using that language is most likely to yield accurate information about the child's academic, developmental, and functional status. Districts must also ensure that the assessments used are not discriminatory on a racial or cultural basis. In addition, assessment or measures must be valid and reliable and be administered by trained professionals.

IDEA directs schools to use sound evaluation procedures (and to eliminate unnecessary tests and assessments) to ensure that the performance of all students suspected of having disabilities is appropriately measured and analyzed to determine whether the student is eligible to receive special education; to determine the extent of the students' educational needs; and to rule out as causes for learning difficulties the lack of appropriate instruction in reading or math, or limited exposure and proficiency in usage of the English language.

Eligibility for FAPE and Making Placement Decisions

Any student with a disability who is found eligible to receive special education and related services is entitled to receive an IEP. The IEP describes the special education and related services specifically designed to meet the unique educational needs of a student with a disability and is a legal contract between the parents and the school district. The IEP should be considered a "living document" that can be modified throughout the year (following all required guidelines). An IEP provides both a structure for identifying and addressing individual student needs and a written plan for ensuring that students with disabilities receive a FAPE. A team consisting of multidisciplinary professionals and the student's parents develop the IEP in a collaborative process at a meeting that takes place at least once a year (or more often if needed).

Members of the IEP team: The parent(s) or guardian(s); the student when appropriate; at least one special education teacher or provider; at least one general education teacher if the student will also be participating in the general education environment; an LEA representative, typically a school administrator or special education director; a member qualified to interpret evaluation results, such as a counselor, school psychologist, or social worker; and any other individuals with special knowledge of the student, including related service specialists.

The basics of the IEP include a profile of the student describing the background of the student; the strengths and needs of the student; performance information; and the reason for the need for special services. The IEP should also include all effective dates; measurable annual goals; how the goals will be measured; details of what special education and related services need to be provided; a description of any supplementary aids that are necessary including transportation; where applicable, statements to what extent the student will not participate with nondisabled students in the classroom or other activities; a statement regarding any individual accommodations that are necessary for the student to participate in state and district assessments; and an explanation if the student is exempted from such assessments.

There must also be a postsecondary goal statement for students aged sixteen or older, as well as a notification to students within one year of reaching majority age that the rights associated with the IEP transfer to the student upon reaching the majority age.

The IEP team must meet at least annually—or more often as needed or as requested by any member of the IEP team—to review and revise the IEP. The law requires that the IEP must be completed and that the parents must agree with it before special education services can begin. In developing an IEP, the various IEP team members typically have certain responsibilities based on their areas of expertise.

To maximize parent involvement in developing the IEP, some educators solicit parent input or send draft goals for parents to review prior to the IEP meeting. Doing so gives parents time to think about the draft IEP and about what contributions they want to make before the large group meeting—often conducted on a tight time schedule—is convened.

Students should understand the purpose and significance of the IEP meeting and understand their rights under IDEA as much as possible. Severe disabilities and chronological or developmental immaturity may prevent some students from participating as a contributing IEP team member. To prepare students to participate in IEP meetings, school personnel and parents can assist them in understanding their disability and helping them to be aware of their educational challenges.

Placement and the Least Restrictive Environment

After an IEP team has developed and reached consensus on a student's annual goals, they then consider the optimum setting in which the child will receive the special education and related services specified in the IEP. That is, first the IEP team determines what the child needs to make academic and functional progress, and then they decide how to meet that child's special needs. The IEP specifies what is needed—and how the needed services will be delivered. The guiding principle in determining a student's placement is the legal mandate for placement in the LRE. Placement in the general education classroom is the first option the IEP team must consider. Removal of students with disabilities from the general education classroom should occur only when the nature or severity of the disability of a child is such that education in the general education classroom cannot occur satisfactorily with the use of supplementary aids and services. Schools must offer students with disabilities a continuum of services to ensure that students' education needs are met.

IDEA mandates that students with disabilities be educated with their peers without disabilities to the maximum extent appropriate and that removal from the regular educational environment can only occur when the nature or severity of their disability is such that education in regular classes with the use of supplementary aids and services cannot be achieved satisfactorily. If it is determined that the general education classroom is the LRE for a child, it is equally important to ensure that the child is accessing the curriculum within that classroom rather than simply being *included*. "Access to the general education curriculum means more than simply being present in a general education classroom. Access requires that students with disabilities be provided with the supports necessary to allow them to benefit from instruction" (Nolet & McLaughlin, 2000, p. 9). Such an environment must be consistent with students' academic, social, and physical needs. While the general education classroom is most often the LRE, additional settings must be available along a continuum from least to more restrictive.

Examples of additional settings include resource rooms, special classes, special schools, and hospitals or institutions.

IDEA 2004 includes an additional requirement related to LRE regarding states funding formulas for placement of students with disabilities. IDEA 2004 states,

> [A]State shall not use a funding mechanism by which the State distributes funds on the basis of the type of setting in which a child is served that will result in the failure to provide a child with a disability a free appropriate public education according to the unique needs of the child as described in the child's IEP. (2678[i][A])

Therefore, student placement is based on educational needs rather than streams of funding.

Unless the IEP requires other placements, the child should be educated in the school they would attend if not disabled. Each student with a disability has access to a continuum of placement options that include the following alternative settings, starting from the least restrictive setting and ending with the most restrictive placement:

- Regular class
- Special class
- Special school
- Home instruction
- Instruction in a hospital or institution

The student can receive different supplementary aids and services at different points on the above continuum during the same time period, to enable the student with disabilities to learn in that environment. For example, the student may spend part of the day in a general education classroom (regular class) with supportive, special education services and part of the day in a separate classroom (special class) receiving special education services.

Supplementary Aids and Services and Determining Related and Supplementary Services

Special education is instruction that is specially designed to meet the unique needs of students with disabilities, including instruction conducted in the classroom, the home, hospitals, institutions and other settings, and instruction in physical education. Instruction that is specially designed is tailored to each eligible child's needs and may differ in presentation, pacing, content, methodology, and mode of delivery, as appropriate. Such instruction must ensure that the child accesses the content included in the general education curriculum to meet the educational standards within the local school district and state that apply to all children.

IDEA defines related services to include any transportation, developmental, corrective, or other supportive services necessary to enable a student with disabilities to benefit from special education. In order for a student to receive related services, that child must first be found eligible for special education.

Related services include speech-language pathology and audiology services; interpreting services; psychological services; physical and occupational therapy; recreation and therapeutic recreation; social work services; school nurse services; counseling services; orientation and mobility services; diagnostic and evaluative medical services; or early identification services.

Supplementary aids and services include aids, services, and other supports that are provided in regular education classes or other education-related settings to enable children with disabilities to be educated with their peers without disabilities to the maximum extent appropriate. These include devices, materials, modifications, adaptations, and accommodations to instruction that are required to meet the educational needs of the student with disabilities.

Such aids and services include technology on which to complete written assignments; communication devices for students with severe speech and language disabilities; books on tape; books in Braille; instructional delivery accommodations; or homework and test administration accommodations.

Adaptations to materials might include providing chapter outlines of textbook content or a different version of a classroom reading assignment (such as a novel) that is written at the student's reading level.

Accommodations that might be specified in a student's IEP include seating the student at the front of the classroom (to address visual impairments or poor attention) or providing a desk with a slant top to facilitate a student's completion of written work (to address certain fine motor difficulties).

What Is "Appropriate" in FAPE?

Under the Education for All Handicapped Children Act of 1975, and now under the ESSA authorized in 2015, children eligible for IDEA services have a right to a FAPE including special education and related services in the LRE. IDEA includes extensive procedural safeguards to protect parent and student rights and to ensure that appropriate placement decisions are made. Under *Honig v. Doe* (1988), and as clarified in the 1997 amendments to IDEA, certain procedural and placement protections also apply when a child with a disability is disciplined for behavior that was a manifestation of the student's disability. In addition, reasonable attorneys' fees may be awarded to parents who prevail in court review, under IDEA (20 U.S.C. § 1415[i][3][B]).

In 1982, in *Board of Education of the Hendrick Hudson Central School District v. Rowley*, the Court established the standard of review to be applied in determining the appropriateness of an eligible child's educational program. The standard is used to determine whether the school has complied with the procedures identified in IDEA and whether the student's IEP is reasonably calculated to enable the student to receive educational benefit from the special education and related services provided.

In 2017, the Supreme Court issued a unanimous opinion in *Endrew F. v. Douglas County School District Re-1*, where the Court held that for a school to meet its substantive obligation under the IDEA, the school must offer an IEP reasonably calculated to enable a child to make progress appropriate in light of the child's circumstances. The decision clarified the standards that must be present in an IEP, focusing on what is "appropriate" in FAPE. The Court held that a child was entitled to an educational program that allowed the student to make more than minimal (*de minimis*) progress. Before *Endrew F.*, courts relied on *Rowley*, which was interpreted to mean that the child received FAPE if the IEP was reasonably calculated to enable the child to make progress, without specifying any single test to determine educational benefit.

In *Endrew F.*, his parents were seeking tuition reimbursement after they removed their autistic son from his public school after which his behavior improved, and he thrived after his academic goals were strengthened. Endrew's parents had argued that the IEP proposed by the public school was mostly unchanged from his previous IEPs, under which he made "minimal progress." The decision of the Court is significant because each child's educational program must be appropriately ambitious and the child should have the opportunity to meet challenging objectives, as opposed to mere minimal goals and objectives. The standard in *Endrew F.* applies regardless of the child's disability, the age of the child, or the child's current placement.

There has been disagreement regarding the degree to which the decision changed educational practice in school districts, as many strongly believe they were already providing services to students beyond minimum goals and objectives. Although surely school districts that previously used a "some benefit" standard would likely need to change their IEP standards, those that provided a "moderate benefit" standard may not change their practice much at all. In any case, as with other aspects of education law, the lower courts will eventually further refine the requirements as they interpret the broad language of the *Endrew F.* decision.

Determining Eligibility for Services Under Section 504 of the Rehabilitation Act of 1973

Some students with physical or mental disabilities who have difficulty learning are not found eligible for special education services under IDEA—they do not meet the eligibility criteria. For such students, Section 504 of the Rehabilitation Act of 1973 may apply. Section 504 and the American with Disabilities Act (ADA) are both civil rights laws that prohibit discrimination based on disabilities and apply to all schools that receive federal funds. Although the ADA is applicable to schools, the greater focus should be on Section 504 for students. Section 504 is enforced by the Office for Civil Rights (OCR) of the U.S. Department of Education.

Students may be eligible for services under Section 504 if they have a physical or mental disability that substantially limits one or more major life activities which include the following: eating, walking, seeing, hearing, breathing, concentrating, thinking, speaking, learning, working, caring for oneself, and performing manual tasks. Congress has added to and created a nonexhaustive list of examples of "major bodily functions" that are major life activities, such as functions of the immune system or other body systems. To be protected under Section 504, a student must be determined to have a physical or mental impairment that substantially limits one or more major life activities, or have a record of such an impairment, or be regarded as having such an impairment.

In contrast to IDEA, where services for eligible students are required to be provided under FAPE, Section 504 requires nondiscrimination and providing reasonable accommodations to the eligible student. Generally speaking, such accommodations are far less costly than the services required for eligible students under IDEA.

Eligibility for services under Section 504 may also be considered for students who return to school after a serious illness or injury. Unlike IDEA, Section 504's implementing regulation does not limit coverage to specified and defined categories of disabilities.

In determining eligibility for services under Section 504, a team composed of persons knowledgeable about the student's needs, including the parents, should meet to determine eligibility and develop an educational plan. This team should base its eligibility decision on whether the student is substantially limited by a physical or mental impairment that affects at least one major life activity, and would the student be qualified to participate in the academic and extracurricular program under discussion if they did not need an accommodation or specialized services? If the student is otherwise qualified to participate, then that student cannot be denied to participate in the program.

A 504 plan is a document describing the services and modifications the school district commits to provide to a student with a physical or mental impairment. Section 504 applies to all students whether they are in special education or general education. Section 504 requires procedures for evaluation, a written plan, as well as prescribed parent rights, but is less prescriptive than the requirements under IDEA.

Some advocates believe that if there is a close call between qualifying for services under IDEA or Section 504, taking the IDEA approach better serves the needs of the student and also potentially avoids later claims that the student should have been in special education all along, thereby also potentially avoiding legal action for compensatory damages and services.

Considerations for Principals and Teachers

There are obviously clear legal obligations surrounding students with disabilities, and while all students retain rights while at school, students with special needs have additional rights and protections. IDEA provides rights not only to the eligible student, but to the parents as well. But there is also the moral obligation principals and teachers have related to all students, and especially to those students with disabilities.

Working with families of students with a disability is more important than ever, and building a strong relationship with families serves to improve the processes involved and more importantly the outcomes for the student. Families and students should never be viewed as adversaries, but instead partners. Parents recognize that their child requires extra time and may at times create additional challenges. What they do not need is to feel as though they or their child is an extra burden. The prevention of that perception is dependent on how they are treated by school officials. One way to avoid that is for educators to always consider the needs of the student, as opposed to viewing the student as merely an IEP or a diagnosis.

This speaks to the dilemma of difference (Minow, 1990), where the "I" in IDEA stands for "individuals" placed within a key component of access versus exclusion, and equal treatment versus recognizing and celebrating diversity and individualization.

Once a student has been identified and placement has been made, every effort by the school to avoid negative stigma and isolation of the student must be of primary importance. The school-age years are difficult enough for most kids, but once they have a "label," the risk of being known as "different" increases significantly. Many if not most students with a disability already have self-esteem issues, feel as though they are bad students, know that they don't learn like others, and perhaps have already been marginalized in other ways by their peers or even teachers. The fact that they are now eligible for services doesn't change that, and efforts must be made to connect with each student in new and better ways. Clearly, online and hybrid learning has made that an even greater challenge.

But the larger point is this—the determination of eligibility and placement of a student may be the end of the referral process, but is only the beginning of a new journey for the student, the family, and the school.

SECTION D. DISCIPLINING STUDENTS WITH DISABILITIES

Disciplining students with disabilities is as necessary as disciplining students who do not have disabilities. The challenge for teachers is how to create a classroom environment and culture that reduces the frequency and severity of discipline issues, and that goal is easier to achieve when principals lead and help sustain a school culture that grows in that classroom environment.

When a student with an IEP requires discipline for serious misconduct, educators need to exercise great care to ensure that they comply with the law. Any exclusionary discipline such as an extended in-school suspension, office isolation, and especially out-of-school suspension may amount to a change in placement or reduction of services, neither of which can be arbitrarily done without an IEP change. The keys regarding discipline include whether the behavior was a manifestation of the disability of the student and, in serious infractions, the amount of time a student may be excluded from school through suspension.

Students with disabilities may be punished similarly as those without disabilities especially for minor infractions such as tardies. Behavior management strategies used for all students such as restrictions, detentions, and even timeouts may be implemented as long as such implementation follows otherwise legal and required guidelines and do not amount to any change of services for the student. Also assuming that all other aspects of the punishment follow appropriate laws and guidelines, students with IEPs may also be suspended for serious violations for up to ten consecutive days without the need to still provide services.

But when out-of-school suspension is considered for serious infractions, IDEA due process rights are triggered, and students with IEPs cannot be suspended for longer than ten days, whether those ten days are all at once or a part of the sum of a series of suspensions over the school year that constitute a pattern. In such circumstances, the rules of "stay put" and "change in placement" come to the forefront. Some students not yet in special education may also assert their rights under IDEA.

In such circumstances, an MDR must take place before the student can be suspended. The purpose of the MDR is to determine if the behavior in question was something beyond control of the student because the behavior was not within the volition of the child due to the disability.

The MDR team consists of members of the IEP team, and in general the MDR must take place within ten school days of any decision to change the placement of the student. The MDR team attempts to determine

- If the conduct in question was caused by, or had a direct and substantial relationship to, the disability of the child OR

- If the conduct was the direct result of a failure to implement the IEP.

If the MDR determines the behavior WAS NOT a manifestation of the disability: The student may be subjected to the same discipline as a nondisabled student including suspension of up to ten school days with no services required. However, any future proposed suspension of the student beyond ten days would constitute a change in placement and would trigger due process protections under IDEA. When a student with an IEP is facing a suspension beyond those ten days, mandated processes must take place and services must be provided beginning on the eleventh day should it be determined the suspension beyond the ten days is warranted.

If the MDR determines the behavior WAS a manifestation of the disability: The team must implement a BIP and return the student to the placement they were removed from unless the parent and team agree to a change in placement. If the student already has a BIP, then that plan must be modified to meet the changing needs of the student.

Unfortunately, there are other more serious circumstances that occur where the removal of the student may be required due to the severity of the behavior or to ensure the safety of the student and others. If a student is found to be in possession of a weapon at school or at a school activity; knowingly possesses, uses, sells, or distributes illegal drugs while at school or at school functions; or has inflicted bodily injury to another person at school or on school premises, the student may be removed to an alternative education setting for not more than forty-five school days without an MDR. Services must be provided during that placement. Although it is true that schools cannot cease providing services to students with disabilities, regardless of the severity of the misconduct, principals and other administrators have the necessary authority—and the responsibility—to remove students with disabilities from immediate situations in which they pose a danger to themselves or others. Mandated services can be provided in alternative placements, and contrary to what some believe, school personnel can take action in such circumstances. In addition, although these students' rights to a FAPE and to certain procedural safeguards are protected by IDEA, the law also protects the safety and learning of all students.

SECTION E. SUGGESTED ADDITIONAL RESOURCES

The following suggested website information is a very small sample of the information available for educators and parents. All links were valid at press time.

Government Resources

www.ed.gov The main page of the U.S. Department of Education; from this site you will find links to the OCR, the Office of Special Education Programs, and other information from the federal government related to all aspects of education.

www.air.org American Institute for Research Center for Special Education Finance

https://ncd.gov/resources National Council on Disability provides advice to government agencies and not direct advice or services to individuals, but does provide a host of valuable resources to assist individuals seeking those services most likely found at the state and local level.

Educational Advocacy, Organizations, and Resources

www.nasdse.org National Association of State Directors of Special Education (NASDSE)

www.naset.org National Association of Special Education Teachers

www.nrcpara.org National Resource Center for Paraprofessionals

www.napcse.org National Association of Parents with Children in Special Education

www.projectidealonline.org Project IDEAL is a teacher education program intended to better prepare students to work with students with disabilities.

www.theinternetisforeveryone.com This group assists with ADA website compliance.

www.tash.org TASH is a paid membership organization that advocates for human rights and inclusion for people with significant disabilities. They also provide training; provide access to research and publications; and hold conferences, webinar series, and more.

www.understood.org Understood provides resources to help parents, educators, employers, as well as young adults better understand disability issues to help those with disabilities thrive at home, in school, and in the workplace.

www.ideapartnership.org Idea Partnership reflects the collaborative work of national organizations, technical assistance providers, and state and local agencies.

Parental Resources

https://www2.ed.gov/parents/needs/speced/edpicks.jhtml Parent resources from the U.S. Department of Education www.parentcenterhub.org The Center for Parent Information Resources serves families of children with disabilities.

www.cbirt.org The Center on Brain Injury Research and Training

www.exceptionalchildren.org The Council for Exceptional Children (CEC) is dedicated to improving the educational success of children and youth with disabilities.

www.hanen.org The Hanen Centre focuses on early language intervention for children with language delays, ASD, Asperger syndrome, and language and literacy development.

www.disabilityresource.org The Disability Resource Community is a platform designed to ask questions, share resources, and build a community.

www.aph.org The American Printing House for the Blind provides accessibility tools for individuals with visual impairments.

www.ncbegin.org BEGINNINGS for Parents of Children Who Are Deaf or Hard of Hearing helps parents and families who experience hearing loss.

ADDITIONAL CASES OF INTEREST TO EDUCATORS

Schaffer v. Weast, 546 U.S. 49 (2005). The burden of proof in an administrative hearing challenging the IEP is placed on the party seeking the relief. In this case, it was the student making the challenge, but the court held that the rule would have equal effect if it was the school district making the claim.

Arlington Central School District BOE v. Murphy, 548 U.S. 291 (2006). The Supreme Court held that IDEA did not authorize reimbursement of expert fees in a case where parents sought reimbursement for fees they had paid to an educational consultant during proceedings.

Van Duyn v. Baker School District 5J, 502 F.3d 811 (9th Circ. 2007). The court noted that to provide a student FAPE, a school district must deliver education and related services "in conformity with" the IEP and cannot decide on its own to no longer implement part or all of the "clearly binding" IEP.

M.R. v. Ridley School District, 744 F.3d 112 (3rd Cir. 2014). The Third Circuit Court of Appeals held that when a hearing officer determines a placement is appropriate, the student is entitled to the stay-put provision in that placement during all federal disputes regarding the placement.

National Federation of the Blind v. Scribd Inc., 97 F.Supp.3d 565 (D. Virginia 2015). The court held that those receiving services remotely are entitled to the same protections as those who physically receive services, and to conclude otherwise would be "absurd."

Miller v. Monroe School District, 159 F. Supp. 3d 1238 (W.D. Wash. 2016). A parent filed discrimination claims against the school district related to interventions used with her autistic son where the district responded to his autism-related hitting and kicking by repeatedly using five minute or less time-outs in a seclusion room. The parties could not agree on the appropriateness and frequency of the interventions. The court allowed the case to proceed to trial.

C.C. v. Hurst-Euless-Bedford Independent School District, 641 Fed. App'x 423 (5th Cir. 2016) *cert denied.* A student eligible for services under IDEA and protected by Section 504 was placed in an alternative disciplinary placement for sixty days after an MDR concluded that his taking a photograph of a student in a school bathroom stall was misbehavior that was not a manifestation of his disability. Courts supported the school and an appeal to the U.S. Supreme Court was denied.

M.C. v. Antelope Valley Union School District, 858 F.3d 1189 (9th Cir. 2017). In the first case decided by a federal court of appeals after the *Endrew F.* decision, the Ninth Circuit reversed a lower court and held that a school district's procedural violations of IDEA prevented a parent from challenging alleged substantive violations. The U.S. Supreme Court denied an appeal by the district.

Wade v. Dist. of Col. Pub. Sch., 322 F.Supp.3d 123 (D.D.C. 2018). Summary judgment was granted to the parent of a student who appealed as inadequate a damage award granted by a hearing officer who determined the school district did not follow the required hours of service on an IEP. The school district admitted that it did not provide the full number of required instructional hours stated on the IEP, but a hearing officer determined that the district was only liable for two years of denial of FAPE and that it was the social maladjustment of the student, and not his disability, that accounted for his lack of progress. A hearing officer determined that FAPE was indeed denied for two years but that the failure was *de minimus* and his low grades were due to his failure to attend school rather than the school not following the IEP.

The court determined that the student was improperly placed at the high school from the beginning, noting that missing 7.5 hours of service was not *de minimus*. The court stated the DCPS may not fail to implement the student's IEP and then demand the student shoulder the full responsibility for the subsequent, and likely, behavior attendance issues.

Had they fully implemented the IEP and the student refusal then occurred, the analysis might be different. In this case, the district placed a student in a school that could not accommodate his needs and then changed the IEP to match the placement.

A.R. v. Connecticut State Board of Education, No. 20-2255 (2nd Cir. 2021). The court held that the state board violated IDEA by denying FAPE to students with disabilities aged twenty-one to twenty-two while providing a FAPE to students without disabilities in the same age range.

SAMPLE OF COVID-19-RELATED LITIGATION ONGOING AT PRESS TIME

L.V. v. City of New York Department of Education, No. 19-CV-05451 (AT) (KHP) (S.D. NY 2020). From the start of the pandemic, a parent claimed her autistic child was not receiving consistent services. The student was provided a tablet for remote learning but could not sit still long enough to use it, and there were unresolved technical issues. A magistrate judge recommendation that the mother be granted an injunction to order immediate in-person instruction was granted by a federal court. Services were ordered to be provided in-person to the extent they can be performed safely and within allowable health department guidance.

Parent on Behalf of Student v. L.A. Unified School District, No. 2020050465 California Office of Administrative Hearings (2020). The District was required to provide compensatory services. The California Office of Administrative Hearings determined that moving to all distance learning was inadequate in implementing the IEP. The circumstances were somewhat uncommon because the student was a twenty-two-year-old who continued to be eligible for services due to her autism.

Hernandez v. Grisham, No. CIV 20-0942 JB/GBW, WL 6063799 (D.N.M. Oct. 14, 2020). Parents of a child with learning disabilities filed suit challenging the state's school closure orders due to the pandemic. The state Department of Education advised districts that if they provided educational opportunities for the general student population, they must also provide equal access for students with disabilities. The parent alleged that many IEP services were not provided since schools were closed, causing her child to regress. State officials stated that flexibility should be allowed regarding FAPE due to the circumstances. The court held that the parent did not need to exhaust administrative remedies due to the circumstances, and despite the ongoing pandemic, the state must provide a FAPE as required by IDEA and should amend the IEP in order to provide FAPE.

J.T. ex rel. D.T. v. de Blasio, No. 20 Civ. 5878 (CM), 2020 WL 6748484 (S.D.N.Y. Nov. 13, 2020) *appeal filed,* case No. 20-4128 2d Cir. Dec. 14, 2020. Several parents filed suit alleging that FAPE was denied due to school closings related to the pandemic. Parents alleged that the school closures denied FAPE, even though all students were offered a choice between completely remote learning or a blended format. The parents sought a reopening of schools and other claims. The court held that the parents failed to exhaust remedies on their FAPE claim. The court also held that during a health crisis, an order shutting down schools, if applied equally to all students, did not amount to a change in placement.

CHAPTER 9

Program Management

A school administrator's affirmative responsibilities in program management are as diverse as they are difficult. Program management covers the entire spectrum of duties for principals and some are covered in other chapters in the book. This chapter will focus on some program areas that principals are likely to encounter, and they are ever changing, often challenged, and frequently driven by politics. Redefining the boundaries of separation of church and state is taking place, particularly in terms of school funding, and although principals must be aware of those issues involved, school funding related to religion is not addressed. School administrators need to continuously update their personal knowledge and skills in program management issues to be able to effectively reduce the risk of litigation.

CONSIDERATIONS RELATED TO COVID-19

Still unresolved are ongoing concerns regarding immunization guidelines for both adults and students. Prior to publication, vaccines for children ages 12–17 had been approved, with vaccinations for those ages 5–12 being approved months later. At the time of publication, boosters for the older group had also been approved.

At some point, there will likely be discussion (and probably controversy) about COVID-19 vaccinations being added to the list of required vaccines in schools. At the present time, this has not been raised.

SUGGESTED GUIDELINES FOR PRACTICE

The topic of religion is raised in a section of this chapter, and at this time as it relates to religion in the public school setting, the U.S. Supreme Court appears to be poised to change the current boundaries that exist between the obligation of the school to prevent violations of the Establishment Clause and the rights given under the Free Exercise Clause. Many believe that the Court will lean toward redefining free exercise and allowing greater deference toward those who wish to express religious views or conduct religious practices in public schools and other public settings.

SECTION A. SCHOOL ATTENDANCE

Since the end of the eighteenth century, most states have enacted compulsory attendance laws, and the courts generally have defended compulsory attendance as a duty for the public good. The U.S. Supreme Court held, in Pierce v. Society of Sisters *(1925), that the state's right to require school attendance did not give it the right to limit attendance only to public schools. The Court found that such a law violated parents' rights to control the education and upbringing of their children and was an unreasonable exercise of state power. Thus compulsory attendance can be satisfied in both public and private schools.*

In 1944, the U.S. Supreme Court, in *Prince v. Massachusetts*, reaffirmed the right of the state to regulate school attendance. The court declared that "the family itself is not beyond regulation in the public interest . . . neither rights of religion nor rights of parenthood are beyond limitations."

Each state has enacted its own compulsory attendance laws. Most state statutes include (a) the beginning and ending ages for required attendance, (b) the various ways that compulsory education can be accomplished (i.e., public schools, private schools, homeschooling), (c) the length of the school day and school year and the minimum attendance that is required, (d) any basis for granting exemptions to compulsory attendance, (e) provisions for enforcing compulsory attendance, and (f) any penalties for violation of compulsory attendance laws. The two general exceptions to the compulsory attendance laws are (1) conflicts with religion, as noted in *Wisconsin v. Yoder* (1972); and (2) statutory exemptions (i.e., excusing students who live more than a specified distance from the nearest school).

In addition to affirming the states' right to require compulsory school attendance, courts have also affirmed the right of school districts to require residence requirements for school attendance, as demonstrated in *Martinez v. Bynum* (1983). States have their own specific residency statutes, ranging from open admission to requiring permission from the sending and receiving districts before students are allowed to attend a school outside their home district.

Post pandemic attendance concerns may take time to stabilize—at press time for this book, it is unknown about any degree of hesitancy there may be for those considering a full return to regular classrooms; whether there will be a rush of new students eager to attend school who may have been homeschooled in the past; or how newly created hybrid environments will remain in place in some school districts that will affect classrooms, class sizes, and staffing needs. With the latest surge of COVID-19 variant cases nationwide at the end of 2021 and the beginning of 2022, moving to virtual learning has again been either implemented or discussed by school districts, along with the renewal of other mitigation strategies such as mandatory masks and increased social distancing.

Constitutional Right to an Education

In *Plyler v. Doe* (1982), the U.S. Supreme Court was asked if the Equal Protection Clause of the U.S. Constitution entitled children of illegal immigrants residing in Texas to attend the public schools of Texas free of charge. The Court found,

For purposes of the Fourteenth Amendment's equal protection clause which prohibits states from denying equal protection to any person "within its jurisdiction," undocumented aliens, despite their immigration status, are persons within the jurisdiction of a state entitled to the equal protection of its law. Use of the phrase, "within its jurisdiction," confirming that the protection of the Fourteenth Amendment extends to anyone, citizen or stranger, who is subject to the laws of a state, and reaches into every corner of a state's territory, and that until he [*sic*] leaves the jurisdiction, either voluntarily or involuntarily in accordance with the Constitution and laws of the United States, a person is entitled to the equal protection of the laws that a state may choose to establish.

States may not withhold funds from local school districts for the education of children not legally admitted into the United States, and if states authorize districts to deny enrollment to such children, it is a violation of the Equal Protection Clause. Although public education is not a "right" under the Equal Protection Clause, neither is it merely some government "benefit." Consequently, to deny education to noncitizen children would impose a lifetime hardship on a discrete class of children and such discrimination of the funding statute is not rational.

Homeschooled Students

Although many parents prefer to enroll their children in public, private, or parochial schools, others have sought the right to educate their own children through home instruction. The estimates of the number of students who are homeschooled vary from year to year, but range from 3 percent to 4 percent of all students nationwide in the United States (NCES, 2021), with the long-term effects of the pandemic on those numbers unknown. While principals may feel little need to be concerned about students who are not enrolled in their school, the fact remains that homeschooled students may choose to enroll at any time during a school year; may choose to participate in extracurricular activities; or may also request an evaluation or be eligible for special services.

While homeschooling is permitted in all fifty states, there is considerable variation in how each state regulates this type of instruction. Regardless of the specifics of the various statutes, responsibility for ensuring that the quality of home instruction meets at least the minimum requirements prescribed by state law rests with local school superintendents. The majority of states require that parents notify the state department of education or the local school district that they plan to homeschool their child. However, other specific regulations vary widely from state to state. In close to half the states, there are no means to determine whether students are being homeschooled or are simply not accounted for. When issues relating to home instruction find their way into the courts, they generally focus on either (a) interpretations of the statute or (b) the rights of homeschooled students to receive some of the benefits, that is, participation in coursework, available through the public school system.

In *Wisconsin v. Yoder* (1972), the U.S. Supreme Court modified the state's power to impose regulations on parents. It held that Wisconsin could not require members of the Old Order Amish religious sect to send their children to formal schools beyond the eighth grade. The Court said that even though the state had the power to impose reasonable regulations governing school attendance, the exercise of that power must not inhibit the deeply held religious beliefs of parents. In this case, the parents' right to the free exercise of religion was sufficient to override the state's power to compel formal school attendance to age sixteen. The general application of the Court's ruling is limited because the Amish objected only to post-eighth-grade compulsory attendance of fourteen- and fifteen-year-olds. The fact that the Amish beliefs were of longstanding tradition and an important part of their total religious culture were the key considerations in this case.

Efforts to extend the *Yoder* decision have been unsuccessful. The West Virginia Supreme Court refused to extend the ruling of *Yoder* to Biblical Christian parents who chose to educate their children at home. In *State v. Riddle* (1981), when the Riddle family refused to comply with the state's compulsory attendance laws, they were arrested by a local truancy officer. The court found that even though the family was apparently doing a good job of educating their children and were sincere in their beliefs, the state had the right to require compliance with its attendance laws.

Homeschooled Students' Participation in Public School Programs

Frequently, parents of homeschooled students wish to have their children participate in some public school courses or extracurricular activities. Although a school district may adopt a policy that allows homeschooled students to enroll on a part-time basis, the district may not receive state aid for such students. Generally, parents have no legal rights to insist that their children be permitted to participate in programs in public schools in which they are not enrolled. For example, a New York court, in *Bradstreet v. Sobal* (1996), rejected the argument that denying a homeschooled child the right to participate in interscholastic activities was a violation of the student's right to equal protection under the Fourteenth Amendment. In the case of *Swanson v. Guthrie* (1998), the U.S. Court of Appeals for the Tenth Circuit ruled that not allowing a homeschooled student to attend public school on a part-time basis did not violate the student's rights under the Free Exercise Clause of the U.S. Constitution. However, it should be noted that several states have enacted specific legislation that permits homeschooled students to use school facilities and participate in extracurricular activities.

Parents have also lost claims attempting to "dual enroll" part-time at homeschool and essentially "cherry picking" parts of the public school program they wish to attend. A Fourth Circuit opinion noted that school boards did not need to provide their publicly funded services "like a buffet from which (parents) can pick and choose" (*D.L. v. Baltimore City Board of School Commissioners*, 706 F.3d 256, 264 (4th Cir. 2013)).

Homeschooled Students and Eligibility for Special Services

Whether or not homeschooled students are considered private school students, making them eligible for special services they may qualify for varies by states. In the Ninth Circuit, the Court of Appeals ruled that the "Child Find" provision of Individuals with Disabilities Act (IDEA) does not apply to states that consider homeschool distinct from private school (*Hooks v. Clark County School District*, 2000). School districts may not evaluate homeschooled students without parental consent, according to IDEA regulations, influenced in part by *Fitzgerald v. Camdenton R-III School District* (2006). Although under "Child Find," school districts are obligated to evaluate all students, state laws vary as to whether homeschooled students are provided services as well as whether such services must be provided in the school setting.

Homeless Children and Youth

Because homeless families move frequently, and the length of stay in shelters is often restricted, it is often difficult for homeless children to attend school regularly. In addition, guardianship requirements, delays in transfer of school records, and lack of a permanent address and immunization records often prevent homeless children from enrolling in school. Further, homeless children who are able to enroll in school face another obstacle—the inability to get to school because of a lack of transportation.

The McKinney-Vento Education for Homeless Children and Youth (McKinney-Vento) Program was originally established by Congress in 1987 in response to reports that more than 50 percent of homeless children were not attending school regularly. The McKinney-Vento Program provides formula grants to state education agencies (SEAs) to ensure that all homeless children have equal access to the same free, appropriate education, including preschool education, provided to other children. State and local educational agencies receive McKinney-Vento funds to review and revise laws, regulations, practices, or policies that may act as a barrier to the enrollment, attendance, and success in school of homeless children.

The McKinney-Vento Program defines "homeless children and youth" as individuals who lack a fixed, regular, and adequate nighttime residence. The term includes children who

- Share the housing of other persons due to loss of housing, economic hardship, or a similar reason (sometimes referred to as *doubled-up*)

- Live in motels, hotels, trailer parks, or camping grounds due to lack of alternative adequate accommodations

- Live in emergency or transitional shelters

- Are abandoned in hospitals

- Are awaiting foster care placement

- Have a primary nighttime residence that is a public or private place not designed for, or ordinarily used as, a regular sleeping accommodation for human beings

- Live in cars, parks, public spaces, abandoned buildings, substandard housing, bus or train stations, or similar settings

- Are migratory and qualify as homeless because they are living in circumstances described previously

SECTION B. BILINGUAL AND SPECIAL LANGUAGE PROGRAMS

With each passing year, our nation's student population becomes more diverse. The most recent figures available indicate that language minority students, including culturally and linguistically diverse (CLD) students (sometimes referred to as limited English proficient [LEP] students), are the fastest growing group of students in the United States today. The number of families whose children could be considered CLD continues to grow in school districts across the county. Many of these students need special language programs to overcome the language barriers to an equal education and to equal participation in the life of society.

Court Rulings on the Education of Language Minority Students

A number of federal court cases have defined the parameters of bilingual or special language programs in local school districts and established a legal basis for challenges to school districts that fail to provide bilingual or special language programs or provide inadequate programs. An early test case was *Lau v. Nichols* (1974), a case brought by a group of Chinese CLD students who alleged that they were not receiving any special assistance to learn English. The federal court supported the school district's contention that it had no obligation to specifically respond to the communication difficulties of the non-English-speaking students because the Chinese-speaking students were being taught in the same facilities, by the same teachers, at the same time as everyone else. Because they had equal opportunities, there was no discrimination.

In reviewing the court's decision in *Lau,* the U.S. Supreme Court strongly supported the right to a quality education for language minority students and ruled that the school district had violated the rights of Chinese-speaking students by failing to provide them with an education commensurate with their special language needs. The Court wrote that "merely by providing students with the same facilities, text-books, teachers, and curriculum; for students who do not understand English [they] are effectively foreclosed from any meaningful education." Consequently, schools have an obligation to take action to rectify language barriers that result in the exclusion of linguistic minority children from meaningful participation in educational programs. In addition, the Court noted:

> Basic skills are at the very core of what these public schools teach. Imposition of a requirement that before a child can effectively participate in the educational program he must already have acquired these basic skills is to make a mockery of public education. We know that those who do not understand English are certain to find their classroom experiences wholly incomprehensible and in no ways meaningful.

The *Lau* court further required that action be taken to address the special language needs of the non-English-speaking children. The Court's rationale was based on Section 504 of the Civil Rights Act of 1964, which states,

> No person in the United States, on the ground of race, color, or national origin, shall be excluded from participation in, be denied the benefits of,

or be subjected to discrimination under any program or activity receiving federal financial assistance.

Because the school district in this case was receiving federal funds, it could not discriminate against non-English-speaking students by refusing to provide them with the benefits of public education through meaningful programs.

The Equal Educational Opportunities Act (EEOA) was passed in 1974. Under this act, an education agency's failure to take appropriate action to overcome language barriers that impede equal participation by students in instructional programs is an unlawful practice that gives individuals the right to sue.

Another important result of the *Lau* decision was an intensive evaluation of school districts by the Department of Health, Education, and Welfare (HEW) and the Office for Civil Rights (OCR) to determine the extent of violations identified by the Court's decision in *Lau*. This investigation resulted in administrative guidelines known as the *Lau* Remedies or *Lau* Guidelines issued jointly by HEW and OCR in 1975. Although never enacted by Congress nor officially adopted as federal policy, the *Lau* Remedies have become recognized, even by many courts, as the minimal standards for designing or evaluating an educationally effective program to overcome discriminatory practices against limited-English-speaking students (Teitelbaum & Hiller, 1979). The *Lau* Guidelines require school districts to identify all students who might be limited-English speakers and develop programs to assist them. Students involved in special language programs must remain in them until they can compete on an equal basis with their English-proficient peers.

Castañeda v. Pickard (1981) is generally regarded as the most significant court decision affecting language minority students after *Lau*. In responding to the plaintiffs' claim that their school district's language remediation programs violated the EEOA of 1974, a federal appeals court formulated a set of basic standards to determine school district compliance with EEOA. The tripartite "*Castañeda* test" includes the following criteria:

> *Theory:* The school must pursue a program based on an education theory recognized as sound or, at least, as a legitimate experimental strategy.

> *Practice:* The school must actually implement the program with instructional practices, resources, and personnel necessary to transfer theory to reality.

> *Results:* The school must not persist in a program that fails to produce results.

By applying this test, the court is able to determine the degree to which actions taken by a school district are appropriate. However, the *Castañeda* decision imposed the additional dual obligation to (1) teach students English while taking appropriate action to ensure that English language deficiencies do not constitute a barrier to the acquisition of substitutive knowledge and (2) overcome all barriers to an equal education. (*Note:* Under the Fourteenth Amendment of the U.S. Constitution, as ruled in *Plyler v. Doe* [1982], the state does not have the right to deny a free public education to undocumented immigrant children.)

The *Castañeda* test was applied in *Keyes v. School District #1* (1983), in which a school district had argued that it had asserted a good faith effort to provide services to students in need. The court ruled that "good faith" alone is not an adequate defense and stated, "What is required is an effort which will be reasonably effective in producing the intended result of removing language barriers to participation in instruction programs offered by the district." The *Keyes* court also required programs to include the proper identification of students in need of services at the outset of their educational program and evaluate those services at regular intervals to ensure progress is being made.

Education of Migratory Children

The Migrant Education Program (MEP) is authorized by Part C of Title I of the ESEA. The MEP provides formula grants to SEAs to establish or improve education programs for migrant children. These grants assist states in improving educational opportunities for migrant children to help them succeed in the regular school program, meet the challenging state academic content and student academic achievement standards that all children are expected to meet, and graduate from high school.

The general purpose of the MEP is to ensure that migrant children fully benefit from the same free public education provided to other children. To achieve this purpose, the MEP helps SEAs and local operating agencies address the special educational needs of migrant children to better enable migrant children to succeed academically.

Undocumented Students

Undocumented students cannot be denied enrollment, or have their enrollment delayed in a public school. Neither students nor their parents can be required to provide information regarding their immigration status, and interference with their efforts to attend public schools is not allowed. Parents are not required to submit Social Security numbers and schools must make information available, noting that divulging such information is voluntary.

The Family Educational Rights and Privacy Act (FERPA) prevents the release of information related to immigration status except under court order or other exceptional circumstances, including such information to the U.S. Immigration and Customs Enforcement (ICE). Normally ICE does not conduct enforcement at sensitive locations such as schools without some type of administrative approval, and generally ICE will not surveil, interview, search, or arrest individuals at schools or school activities.

SECTION C. RELIGION IN PUBLIC SCHOOLS

"Congress shall make no law respecting an establishment of religion, or prohibiting the free exercise thereof" (First Amendment to the U.S. Constitution; see Establishment of Religion Clause of the First Amendment). At first reading, these sixteen words appear to be relatively straightforward. However, the appropriate relationship of religion and public schools is a sensitive and controversial issue that has divided Americans and resulted in more contention between community groups than any other issue in school law.

Some have asked if the issue of religion in schools is so often contentious and difficult for principals to effectively navigate through the application of laws and the operation of schools, why doesn't the topic of religion have a chapter solely focused on it? One answer is practicality, because space won't allow for a comprehensive analysis of every aspect regarding the relationship between religion and public schools. But an editorial decision by the author is also important. When principals place too much focus or become hypersensitive to every potential religious issue, they run a serious risk of elevating even minor incidents or events into a full-blown religious controversy.

That is most definitely not saying a principal should have blinders on and ignore what is happening that borders on any aspect of religion in the school. But what it is saying is that principals should learn about and develop a keen sense for not only the bright lines that exist about what is allowable and prohibited in schools and when to take action, but also those times when those lines may be blurry and judgment is needed to avoid having their own actions become what is the bright light.

In other words, using a sports analogy, referees hope to be forgotten when a game concludes such that their decisions have no impact on the final outcome. Principals in public school should strive for a similar goal and not be known either as a principal who promotes religion or as a principal who opposes religion. Unfortunately, just like in a ballgame where decisions by officials lead to accusations of bias toward one team, principals must also make calls that make them appear less than neutral when it comes to religion in schools. This chapter attempts to explain why that is, and will provide guidance to help principals navigate this difficult area.

The first major governmental debate regarding religious freedom occurred in 1789, when the First Amendment to the U.S. Constitution was written. The first part of the First Amendment is commonly known as the *Establishment Clause*, and the second part is known as the *Free Exercise Clause*. Although one might assume that the framers of the U.S. Constitution had a clear understanding of what this phrase meant, it has been the focus of much debate. The origin of the debate is found in the 1946 U.S. Supreme Court decision in *Everson v. Board of Education* that barred a state from levying a tax to support any religious activities or institutions. Much of the contemporary confusion can be traced to the 1962 U.S. Supreme Court decision, in *Engel v. Vitale,* that banned state-sponsored school prayer. Some people have interpreted this to mean that all religious expression is prohibited. In fact, this decision did not preclude individual students, in their personal capacity, from expressing their religious faith. Because of the *Engel* decision, a national debate continues between those groups that favor organized classroom prayer as part of the regular school experience and those who oppose any form of religious speech in the public schools. Much of this debate has taken place in the courts as they have struggled to balance the requirements of the Establishment Clause with the Free Exercise Clause.

Teachers and school administrators, when acting in those capacities, are representatives of the state and are prohibited by the Establishment Clause from soliciting or encouraging religious activity and from participating in such activity with students. Teachers and administrators are also prohibited from discouraging activity because of its religious content and from soliciting or encouraging antireligious activity.

In *Mitchell v. Helms* (2000), the U.S. Supreme Court removed virtually all constitutional barriers that previously prevented the flow of taxpayer dollars to Catholic schools. The Court redefined "neutrality" as meaning that if the tax funds were not used for one religious group over another and the funds used did not discriminate between religious factions, then the statute distributing the funds is constitutional.

There is tension between the Establishment Clause and the Free Exercise Clause because although the underlying concepts appear simple, once applied to real-world situations the interpretation of those clauses is nearly impossible to definitively answer. The Establishment Clause relates to what may appear to be the *endorsement* or *promotion* of any religion, and public school entities and employees are prohibited from such actions. But where are the lines drawn? At the same time, the Free Exercise Clause means that public school entities and employees are prohibited from preventing students (and staff) from exercising their religious freedom. The tension arises when in the process of ensuring the school does not endorse or promote religion, it is not at the same time violating the existing religious freedom rights. The Supreme Court has attempted to guide this tension, noting the difference between government speech endorsing religion, which is forbidden by the Establishment Clause, and private speech endorsing religion, which is protected by the Free Exercise Clause and Freedom of Speech Clause. One court opinion from the Fifth Circuit summed up the complexities of the issue with the following statement regarding the First Amendment and religion: "One wonders whether the Founding Fathers ever envisioned the intense . . . at times, malevolent . . . discourse these simple, instructive words would evoke throughout the land for over 200 years" (*Doe. v. Tangipahoa Parish Sch. Bd.*, p. 825, 2009).

In 1971, the U.S. Supreme Court, in *Lemon v. Kurtzman*, gave schools some direction when it articulated a three-part test, known as the *Lemon* test, to be used to evaluate state statutes and local school board policies under the Establishment Clause. In order for a statute or policy to be constitutional, it must have (1) "a secular legislative purpose," (2) "a primary effect that neither advances nor inhibits religion," and (3) "it must not foster excessive entanglement between government and religion." To satisfy the Establishment Clause, governmental action must pass all three prongs of this test.

Since 1971, subsequent U.S. Supreme Court rulings arguably have modified the *Lemon* test, and courts are now more likely to apply the "endorsement test" or the "coercion test." Pauken (2005) notes,

> The *Lemon* test has not been overturned. However, after 30 years, several courts and commentators have modified it and argued in favor of two newer standards that may reflect a changing balance. The "endorsement test" articulated in Justice O'Connor's concurring opinion in *Lynch v. Donnelly* (1984), rewrites the first two questions of *Lemon* to address the intention of the government's activity or policy and the actual message that the activity or policy conveys. The questions become (1) Is the intent of the government action or policy to endorse religion? (2) Regardless of the intent, does the action or policy actually convey a message of endorsement? (p. 1)

In *Lynch,* Justice Sandra Day O'Connor argued that "endorsement sends a message to non-adherents that they are outsiders, not full members of the political community, and an accompanying message to adherents that they are insiders, favored members of the political community. Disapproval sends the opposite message." Operative in the application of the endorsement test is whether a "reasonable observer" would perceive the government action or policy to endorse religion.

The "coercion test," adopted by the Supreme Court in the landmark graduation prayer decision in *Lee v. Weisman* (1992), holds that a government action is unconstitutional if it has a coercive effect with respect to religious practices. In *Lee,* a student graduating from a public middle school complained that the school's policy of inviting local religious leaders to deliver the commencement ceremony's invocation and benediction violated the Establishment Clause. The Supreme Court agreed and struck down the policy. In the majority opinion, Justice Anthony Kennedy articulated a "coercion" test, under which governmental entities may not coerce anyone to support or participate in a religious exercise. In furtherance of this directive and in application to a public school's use of a religious leader to deliver a graduation prayer, Justice Kennedy stated the following:

> Of course, in our culture standing or remaining silent can signify adherence to a view or simple respect for the views of others. And no doubt some persons who have no desire to join in a prayer have little objection to standing as a sign of respect for those who do. But for the dissenter of high school age, who has a reasonable perception that she is being forced by the State to pray in a manner the conscience will not allow, the injury is no less real.

Each of the three Establishment Clause tests has been applied regularly in cases involving legal challenges and defenses to the inclusion of religion in public schools. And along with the litigation-heavy Establishment Clause also come claims of free speech and free exercise infringement.

Courts attempt to balance the right of free exercise of religion against the right not to have a religion established. Problems arise when these two rights are perceived as being in conflict. In 1995, the U.S. Department of Education's published guidelines regarding religious expression in public schools (Riley, 1999) and updated in 2020 (U.S. Department of Education, 2020). These guidelines reflect two basic and equally important obligations of public school officials: (1) schools may not forbid students acting on their own from expressing their personal religious views or beliefs solely because they are of a religious nature; and (2) schools may not discriminate against private religious expression by students but must, instead, give students the same right to engage in religious activity and discussion as they have to engage in other comparable activity. Generally, this means that students may pray in a nondisruptive manner during the school day when they are not engaged in school activities and instruction, subject to the same rules of order that apply to other student speech. At the same time, schools may not endorse religious activity or doctrine and may not coerce participation in religious activity. Among other things, of course, school administrators and teachers may not organize or encourage prayer exercises in the classroom. Students do not have the right to make repeated invitations to other students to participate in religious activity in the face of a request to stop.

Prayer and Public School Program Management

The tension between the free exercise of religion and the establishment of religion by the state is perhaps best reflected in the issues surrounding prayer. This may be because the practice of prayer is a personal act. However, prayer in schools is also mischaracterized when described as a prohibited act and something that cannot be done in school. The act of praying is not prohibited in schools, nor can it be prohibited in schools. Any "ban on prayer" relates to the fact that in public schools, the school cannot lead prayer, require prayer, approve the prayer, or coerce or mandate anyone to pray or not pray.

In an effort to circumvent U.S. Supreme Court decisions that prohibit schools from conducting prayer, some school districts and state legislatures have enacted policies and statutes that authorize a moment of silence for meditation or silent prayer. The Supreme Court ruled, in *Wallace v. Jaffree* (1985), that such a statute in Alabama violated the first prong of the *Lemon* test that required the statute to have a secular legislative purpose. The Court ruled that Alabama's statute was not motivated by a secular purpose and had the purpose of endorsing religion. When schools conduct moments of silence, no school employees may require, encourage, or discourage participation from praying or joining in the moment of silence. School officials are also cautioned to not take on a "parental role" regarding student participation; for example, a teacher should not advise a student who chooses not to participate that their parents would disapprove of their choice.

Student Prayer

Students may pray at school and may not be prevented from praying as long as students are not disruptive. The same rules designed to prevent disruption of the educational program that would apply to other expressive activities would apply to prayer activities. As examples, students may pray, read religious materials or other scriptures, say grace before meals, or engage in other religious activities that would be allowed for nonreligious activities. Students may also have organized prayer groups, "see you at the pole" prayer gatherings, and religious clubs to the same extent that students are permitted to organize other nonreligious student groups.

School Employee Prayer

It is important for teachers and others in the school setting to remember that they are employees of the government and subject to the Establishment Clause and thus required to be neutral concerning religion while carrying out their duties. Consequently, school employees may not pray with or in the presence of students during the school day. This, of course, does not mean that an employee is prohibited from praying silently or outside the presence of students. Employees are permitted to wear nonobtrusive religious jewelry, such as a cross or Star of David. But employees should not wear clothing with a proselytizing message (e.g., a "Jesus Saves" T-shirt).

Although many teachers prefer not to answer questions about their personal religious beliefs, others choose to answer the question in the interest of an open and honest classroom environment. Before answering the question, however, the teacher should consider the age of the student. The critical issue is, would the student be likely to interpret the teacher's personal view as the official position of the school?

Prayer at School Events and Graduation Ceremonies

In 2000, the U.S. Supreme Court handed down its decision regarding prayer at athletic events in *Santa Fe Independent School District v. Doe*. Prior to 1995, a student elected as Santa Fe High School's student council chaplain delivered a prayer over the public address system before each home varsity football game. A number of Mormon and Catholic students and their families filed a suit challenging this practice under the Establishment Clause. While the suit was pending, the school district adopted a different policy that authorized two student referenda, the first to determine whether "invocations" should be delivered at games and the second to select the spokesperson to deliver them. After the students voted to authorize such prayers and select a spokesperson, the district court entered an order modifying the policy to permit only nonsectarian, nonproselytizing prayer. The federal Fifth Circuit Court held that, even as modified by the district court, the football prayer policy was invalid.

The U.S. Supreme Court affirmed the decision of the circuit court and ruled that the district's policy permitting student-led, student-initiated prayer at football games violates the Establishment Clause. The *Santa Fe* Court ruled that the policy involved both perceived and actual endorsement of religion. For some students, such as cheerleaders, members of the band, and the team members themselves, attendance at football games was mandated, sometimes for class credit.

In its decision, the Court was guided by the principles endorsed in *Lee v. Weisman* (1992). The U.S. Supreme Court has consistently held that invocations and prayers at high school graduation ceremonies violate the Establishment Clause. In *Lee,* the Court had ruled that a prayer delivered by a rabbi at a graduation ceremony violated the Establishment Clause. The Court held that, at a minimum, the Constitution guarantees that the government may not coerce anyone to support or participate in religion or its exercise, or otherwise act in a way that establishes a state religion or religious faith, or tends to do so. Furthermore, the Court ruled that the delivery of a message—such as the invocation, on school property, at school-sponsored events, over the school's public address system, by a speaker representing the student body, under the supervision of school faculty, and pursuant to a school policy that explicitly and implicitly encourages public prayer—is not properly characterized as "private" speech. Although graduation ceremonies may be voluntary, the Court held it is not appropriate for the state to place a student in the position of choosing whether to miss the graduation ceremony or attend and listen to a prayer that the student might find objectionable. The Court reasoned that even though the graduation ceremony is not mandatory, it is still one of life's most significant occasions.

School officials may not mandate or organize prayer at graduation or organize religious baccalaureate ceremonies. If a school generally opens its facilities to private groups, it must make its facilities available on the same terms to organizers of privately sponsored religious baccalaureate services. However, a school may not extend preferential treatment to baccalaureate ceremonies and may, in some instances, be obliged to disclaim official endorsement of these ceremonies.

In a recent case that includes issues of employee speech but also centers on the Establishment Clause and prayer, the U.S. Supreme Court denied review of an appeal by a football coach from the state of Washington who was fired after he continued the practice of praying with players after football games even after directed by the school to cease the practice. The case of *Kennedy v. Bremerton School District*, 880 F.3d 1097 (9th Cir. 2019), is an example of situations where tensions exist in the First Amendment rights of a public employee's freedom of religious expression and the employer's obligation to restrict that expression when it violates the Establishment Clause. There is also an intersection of public employee speech when speaking as an employee and as a private citizen, and some have claimed that the actions of the coach were less about religion and more about trying to make a political statement.

The case gained national notoriety, and although the Supreme Court denied to hear the appeal of the coach, four justices signaled they would be open to hearing similar cases in the future that involve religious speech.

Religion and the Academic Program Management

Student Prayer and Religious Discussion

The Establishment Clause does not prohibit purely private religious speech by students. Students, therefore, have the same right to engage in individual or group prayer and religious discussion during the school day as they do to engage in other comparable activity. Local school authorities possess substantial discretion to impose rules of order or other restrictions on student activities, but they may not structure or administer such rules to discriminate against religious activity or speech.

Generally, students may pray in a nondisruptive manner when not engaged in school activities or instruction—subject to the rules that normally pertain in the applicable setting. Specifically, students in informal settings, such as cafeterias and hallways, may pray and discuss their religious views with each other. Students may also speak to and attempt to persuade their peers about religious topics, just as they do with regard to political topics. School officials, however, should intercede to stop student speech that constitutes harassment aimed at a student or group of students.

The right to engage in voluntary prayer or religious discussion free from discrimination does not include the right to have a captive audience listen or to compel other students to participate. Teachers and school administrators should ensure that no student is in any way coerced to participate in religious activity.

Students have a right to distribute religious literature to other students on the same terms as they are permitted to distribute other literature that is unrelated to school curriculum or activities. Schools may impose the same reasonable time, place, and manner or other restrictions on distribution of religious literature as they do on nonschool literature generally, but they may not single out religious literature for special regulation.

Teaching About Religion

Public schools may not provide religious instruction, but they may teach about religion, including the history of religion, comparative religion, the Bible (or other scripture) as literature, and the role of religion in the history of the United States and other countries. Similarly, it is permissible to consider religious influences on art, music, literature, and history. Although public schools may teach about religious holidays, including their religious aspects, and may celebrate the secular aspects of holidays, schools may not observe holidays as religious events or promote such observance by students. In *School District of Abington Township v. Schempp* (1963), the U.S. Supreme Court found the required reading of verses from the Bible to be a violation of the Establishment Clause. The Court stated:

> It might well be said that one's education is not complete without a study of comparative religion or the history of religion and its relationship to the advancement of civilization. It certainly may be said that the Bible is worthy of study for its literary and historic qualities. Nothing we have said here indicates that such study of the Bible or of religion, when presented objectively as part of a secular program of education, may not be effected consistently with the First Amendment.

As a result of this and other court decisions, the question is not, may teachers teach about religion, but rather, how should religion be taught? The answer is simply that instruction concerning religions may not include religious education or indoctrination.

Teacher Religious Freedom

Teachers have a right to religious freedom, but similar to other freedoms, there are limitations to those freedoms in the public school space. For example, teachers have a right to their religious beliefs, but cannot refuse to teach required curriculum due to their religious beliefs. There is a compelling state interest in the teaching of students, and while teachers have the right to their own beliefs, they cannot require others to submit to their beliefs or deny to students any part of their education they are entitled to (see *Palmer v. Board of Education of the City of Chicago*, 1979).

In a general sense, as long as the exercise of religious freedom of the teacher does not encroach on the rights of students, their actions are seen as permissible. At times that boundary is easy to define, such as a teacher wearing a necklace of a cross. Other circumstances can draw a teacher closer to that boundary, if, for example, the same teacher displayed numerous crosses on the walls of the classroom.

Guest Speakers on Religion

Frequently, teachers invite outside speakers to their classes to supplement their teaching. Many districts have board-approved policies regulating this practice. These policies should be consulted prior to inviting an outside speaker. However, when community members are invited to speak on a religious topic, it is very important that they have appropriate academic credentials and understand that they are to speak about religion and cannot proselytize.

Student Assignments

Students may express their beliefs about religion in the form of homework, art work, and other written and oral assignments free of discrimination based on the religious content of their submissions. Home and classroom work should be judged by ordinary academic standards of substance and relevance and against other legitimate pedagogical concerns identified by the school (e.g., a student writing about their activities at a church camp or a student singing a religious song at a talent show would be permitted).

Teaching About Creationism

Efforts to clarify the interpretation of the Establishment Clause and the Free Exercise Clause have resulted in five major evolution–creationism cases. The first is the well-known 1927 case of *Scopes v. State of Tennessee* (often referred to as the Scopes Monkey Trial). In this case, John Scopes volunteered to be the defendant in a test case challenging Tennessee's antievolution statute. He was charged with teaching the theory of evolution in violation of Tennessee's antievolution statute, was found guilty, and was fined $100. A year later, the decision of the district court was reversed by the Tennessee Supreme Court on a technicality.

The U.S. Supreme Court decided a second case in 1968. In *Epperson v. Arkansas,* the Court invalidated an Arkansas statute that prohibited the teaching of evolution. The Court held the statute unconstitutional on grounds that the First Amendment does not permit a state to require that teaching and learning must be tailored to the principles or prohibitions of any particular religious sect or doctrine.

In 1987, the U.S. Court of Appeals ruled, in *Mozert v. Hawkins,* that a group of fundamentalist Christian students in Tennessee had to participate in classroom use of a basic reading series that exposed students to competing ideas and philosophies, some of which were contrary to the students' religious beliefs. This ruling reversed a lower court's decision to allow those students to opt out of a reading curriculum because of their objection to the textbooks used. The court held that students merely being exposed to materials were not compelled to either do an act that violated their religious convictions or communicate an acceptance of a particular idea or belief. The court recognized the broad discretion of school boards to establish curriculum even in the face of parental disagreements.

In *Edwards v. Aguillar* (1987), the U.S. Supreme Court held unconstitutional Louisiana's Creationism Act. This statute prohibited the teaching of evolution in public schools, except when it was accompanied by instruction in "creation science." The Court found that, by advancing the religious belief that a supernatural being created humankind, which is embraced by the term *creation science,* the act impermissibly endorses religion. In addition, the Court found that the provision of a comprehensive science education is undermined when it is barred from teaching evolution except when creation science is also taught.

In 1997, the U.S. District Court for the Eastern District of Louisiana rejected a policy requiring teachers to read aloud a disclaimer whenever they taught about evolution, ostensibly to promote "critical thinking." The court wrote, in *Freiler v. Tangipahoa Parish Board of Education*, that "in mandating this disclaimer, the School Board is endorsing religion by disclaiming the teaching of evolution in such a manner as to convey the message that evolution is a religious viewpoint that runs counter to . . . other religious views." In 1999, the Fifth Circuit Court of Appeals upheld the lower court ruling, noting that the actual effect of the disclaimer was to establish religion by encouraging them to read about religious "alternatives" to evolution. In June 2000, the U.S. Supreme Court denied the petition for a *writ of certiorari*, allowing the decision of the Appeals Court to stand.

Under the Tenth Amendment to the U.S. Constitution, federal control over education is secondary to the power exercised by the states. Consequently, public school curriculum decisions are delegated to state boards of education. In the late 1990s, the creationism–evolution controversy moved from the federal courts to various state boards of education. For example, a 1999 decision by the Kansas Board of Education to delete any mention of evolution from the state's science curriculum became one of the most far-reaching efforts by creationists in recent years to challenge the teaching of evolution in schools (Belluck, 1999).

Pledge of Allegiance

The issues surrounding the flag salute could be discussed as a religious freedom issue or as a First Amendment freedom of expression issue. The first flag salute statute was passed in 1898, shortly after the United States declared war on Spain. Certain religious groups, most notably the Jehovah's Witnesses, immediately expressed their opposition to any mandatory pledge of allegiance based on their religious teaching that forbade reverence to a national symbol. Various state courts upheld the expulsion of students who refused to salute the flag. In the midst of the nationalistic sentiments just prior to the Second World War, the Supreme Court ruled that national unity and national security take precedence over individual religious liberties (*Minersville School District v. Gobitis*, 1940). However, in 1943, the Court again addressed this issue when a West Virginia state law required all students to recite the pledge under threat of expulsion from school and criminal prosecution. The Jehovah's Witnesses argued, in *West Virginia State Board of Education v. Barnette* (1943), that being required to recite the Pledge of Allegiance forced them to worship something other than Jehovah. They argued that their refusal was not an indication of disrespect or antigovernment sentiments, bolstering their argument by quoting from the *Encyclopedia Americana*: "The flag, like the cross, is sacred."

The U.S. Supreme Court, in a reversal of a lower court decision, affirmed the state's right to adopt a curriculum designed to "inspire patriotism and love of country." The Court concluded that although the state's purpose in requiring a flag salute was valid, its methods overstepped constitutional bounds. It stated that "the actions of the local authorities in compelling the flag salute and pledge transcends constitutional limitations on their power." This decision does not prohibit schools from including a flag salute in a school's daily program. Several courts, for example in *Steirer v. Bethlehem Area School District* (1993), have stated that the Pledge's reference to God does not violate the First Amendment.

During the 2003–2004 term, the Supreme Court had an opportunity to settle the question of the constitutionality of the words "under God" in the Pledge. The Court sidestepped this opportunity. In *Elk Grove School District v. Newdow* (2004), a noncustodial California father argued that his daughter was injured by being compelled to watch and listen as her teacher led her classmates in what he described as a ritual proclaiming that there is a God. Because of the unusual set of facts in this case, the Court's decision focused on procedural issues rather than the substantive issue of the words "under God." The noncustodial father did not inform the custodial mother that he was acting, in spite of the fact that the mother reported that neither she nor her daughter was troubled by her reciting the Pledge. The federal trial court dismissed the case. On review, the Ninth Circuit reversed in favor of Newdow and struck down the 1954 statute that added the words "under God" to the Pledge. The Supreme Court chose to ignore the constitutional issue and decided that since the state courts had yet to clarify issues surrounding Newdow's standing and custodial status, it would have been improper for the Supreme Court to have resolved the merits of his claim. Consequently, although a student cannot be required to recite the Pledge, the Pledge remains intact.

Teachers cannot be required to recite the Pledge of Allegiance but may be required to carry out the ceremony for student participation.

The Ten Commandments

In the event a school leader is faced with an issue surrounding the display of the Ten Commandments, it will very likely be emotionally and politically charged. In 1980, in *Stone v. Graham*, the U.S. Supreme Court overturned a Kentucky law calling for the Ten Commandments to be posted in public schools. Since then there have been a number of lower court decisions pertaining to the display of the Ten Commandments. In 2004, the Supreme Court agreed to review two such cases (Kentucky and Texas) in which the Fifth and Sixth Circuits reached opposite conclusions. In the 1950s and 1960s, the Fraternal Order of Eagles donated monuments of the Ten Commandments to a number of communities. The Texas case involves a six-foot-tall red granite monument of the Ten Commandments that is displayed seventy-five feet from the state capitol building (*Van Orden v. Perry*, 2003). The Fifth Circuit found no constitutional violation in this display. In the Kentucky case, the Sixth Circuit ruled that the display of framed copies of the Ten Commandments in two county courthouses and a school district violated the Establishment Clause (*ACLU v. McCreary County, Ky.*, 2003).

The Distribution of Bibles and Other Religious Materials

Historically, some schools have allowed outside groups, such as the Gideons, to come into schools and distribute Bibles to students. The Fifth Circuit Court, in *Meltzer v. Board of Public Instruction of Orange County* (1977), prohibited this practice, stating that the practice favored the Gideons and consequently was not a neutral act. However, in *Peck v. Upshur County Board of Education* (1996), a federal court in West Virginia ruled that as long as the distribution was conducted in an area that is open to other outside organizations, and the students are free to refuse the Bibles, the distribution is permitted.

The issue of Bible distribution in schools continues to find its way into the courts. For example, in 1997, a case in Alabama concerned a teacher who argued that the distribution of Bibles to public school students during homeroom by an outside group did not violate the First Amendment because no instruction took place during homeroom. The court ruled against permitting the distribution, stating that because the homeroom was surrounded by other school activities, such a practice gave the impression that the school endorsed the religious activity (*Chandler v. James*, 1997).

Accommodation of Student Special Religious Needs

Various religions have practices that may require a student to perform a specific task or refrain from performing a specific task. For example, Muslim students need a quiet place at lunch or during breaks to fulfill their prayer obligation during the school day. At schools attended by Jehovah's Witnesses students, principals are frequently given a brochure that describes the beliefs of Jehovah's Witnesses and requests that these children be excused from singing anthems and school songs; from being involved in elected offices, cheerleading, and homecoming king or queen; and from celebrating birthdays or holidays. As long as honoring these requests is feasible, school officials may do so under the First Amendment. However, schools must not permit school employees to monitor or enforce a child's compliance with a particular religious requirement.

Religious Holidays

There is a difference between teaching about and celebrating religious holidays. Teaching is permissible, celebrating is not. Teachers may not use the study of religious holidays as an opportunity to proselytize or otherwise inject personal religious beliefs into the discussion.

If any religious symbols are incorporated into the teaching unit, they may be displayed only on a temporary basis as part of the academic lesson. When students have the opportunity to work on projects, they may choose to create artwork with religious symbols. However, teachers must not assign or suggest such creations.

Religious Excusals

Subject to applicable state laws, individual school districts have substantial discretion to excuse individual students from lessons that are objectionable to the student or the students' parents on religious or other conscientious grounds. However, students generally do not have a federal right to be excused from lessons that may be inconsistent with their religious beliefs or practices. School officials may neither encourage nor discourage students from opting out of certain activities.

Released Time

Subject to applicable state laws, schools have the discretion to dismiss students to off-premises religious instruction, provided that schools do not encourage or discourage participation or penalize those who do not attend. Schools may not allow religious instruction by outsiders on school premises during the school day.

Student Attire

Schools enjoy substantial discretion in adopting policies relating to student dress and school uniforms. Students generally have no federal right to be exempted from school dress rules based on their religious beliefs or practices. Schools may not single out religious attire in general, or attire of a particular religion, for prohibition or regulation. Students may display religious messages on items of clothing to the same extent that they are permitted to display other comparable messages.

Religion and Public School Access Issues

The Equal Access Act

In response to community demands, many school districts have expanded their programs of community and adult education. These programs have resulted in schools offering a wide range of enrichment, academic, recreational, and social courses and activities. Consistent with the First Amendment, the Equal Access Act (1984) was enacted to ensure that student religious activities are accorded the same access to public school facilities as are student secular activities. Based on decisions of the federal courts, as well as their interpretations of the act, the Department of Justice has advised that the act should be interpreted as providing, among other things, that student religious groups at public secondary schools have the same right of access to school facilities as is enjoyed by other comparable student groups. Under the act, a school receiving federal funds that allows one or more student noncurriculum-related clubs to meet on its premises during noninstructional time may not refuse access to student religious groups.

The Equal Access Act made it unlawful for any public secondary school to deny equal access to school facilities to students wishing to conduct religious, political, or philosophical meetings. It specifically gave students the right to conduct these meetings if the school received federal financial aid and had a limited open forum. The act defines an "open forum" as a school district's action that "grants an offering to, or an opportunity for, one or more non-curriculum-related student groups to meet on school premises during non-instructional time." "Noninstructional time" is defined as that time set aside by the school before actual classroom instruction begins or after instruction ends.

The law specifically states that school districts have the option of not being subject to the provisions of the act. To exercise that option, they must avoid creation of a limited open forum by keeping their facilities closed to all noncurriculum-related student meetings and activities, including religious meetings. Historically, school administrators who sought guidelines for deciding whether or not to allow students to participate in religious-oriented activities on school property could look to the three-pronged *Lemon* test established by the Supreme Court. Strictly following those guidelines, public schools could ban students from conducting religious activities on school property.

In 1989, the Supreme Court ruled for the first time on the constitutionality of the Equal Access Act in *Mergens v. Board of Education of Westside Community Schools.* This case began in 1985 when several students at a high school were denied permission to form a Christian group devoted to fellowship and Bible study. The students filed a suit, arguing that their rights under the Equal Access Act had been violated. They contended that their school had sanctioned several extracurricular clubs on topics ranging from chess to scuba diving. School officials countered that all their clubs were related in some way to the broad goals of the school curriculum. They also argued that the Equal Access Act violated the First Amendment. The Court ruled that the act does not violate the First Amendment's prohibition against government establishment of religion. In its decision, the Court said that if a school sanctions even one student group that is not directly tied to course work, the act comes into play and the school cannot discriminate against other student organizations based on the religious, philosophical, or political views of their members. The decision further stated that "there is a crucial difference between government speech endorsing religion, and private speech endorsing religion, which the free speech and free exercise clause protects." According to the *Mergens* Court:

> A student group directly relates to a school's curriculum if the subject matter of the group is actually taught, or will soon be taught, in a regularly offered course, if the subject matter of the group concerns the body of courses as a whole, if participation in the group is required for a particular course, or if participation in the group results in academic credit.

The Court gave the example of a French club, which would be considered curriculum related if the school offered a French course. However, chess or stamp collecting, for example, would most likely be considered noncurriculum related, and thus their existence would create a limited open forum at the school, requiring the accommodation of religious groups. School districts have three options: (1) drop all extracurricular programs to ensure a closed forum, (2) only permit those groups that directly relate to the curriculum, or (3) open their doors to all student groups.

Lunchtime and Noninstructional Time—Limited Open Forum

A school creates a limited open forum under the Equal Access Act, triggering equal access rights for religious groups, when it allows students to meet during their lunch periods or other noninstructional time during the school day, as well as when it allows students to meet before and after the school day.

Religious Clubs

The critical issue relating to student clubs is, does the school allow other student clubs? Student religious groups at public secondary schools have the same right of access to school facilities as is enjoyed by other comparable student groups. The Equal Access Act is intended to protect student-initiated and student-led meetings in secondary schools. According to the act, outsiders may not "direct, conduct, control, or regularly attend" student religious clubs, and teachers acting as monitors may be present at religious meetings in a nonparticipatory capacity only. A meeting, as defined and protected by the Equal Access Act, may include a prayer service, Bible reading, or other worship exercise.

In addition, a school receiving federal funds must allow student groups meeting under the act to use school media—including the public address system, the school newspaper, and the school bulletin board—to announce their meetings on the same terms as other noncurriculum-related student groups. Any policy concerning the use of school media must be applied to all noncurriculum-related student groups in a nondiscriminatory manner. Schools, however, may inform students that certain groups are not school-sponsored.

According to Fields (2005), one organization, the Child Evangelism Fellowship (CEF) that sponsors Good News Clubs for children, has successfully challenged the limited public forum rulings by arguing that religious speech is "private speech," not "governmental speech," in a number of jurisdictions.

Use of School Facilities by Religious Groups

Under the Equal Access Act, a school district may not deny access to school facilities to religious groups if a school district has made itself a "limited open forum" by permitting other nonreligious groups, for example, recreational organizations, to use its facilities (*Lamb's Chapel v. Center Moriches Union Free School District*, 1992).

SECTION D. THE MARKETPLACE OF IDEAS

A long line of U.S. Supreme Court opinions recognize that schools foster moral, cultural, and intellectual qualities in children in a uniquely important way and identify the classroom as a marketplace of ideas. Justice Oliver Wendell Holmes in the early 1900s argued that the government suppression of ideas in a democratic society would not allow truth to prevail and was later echoed by Justice William O. Douglas when he used the phrase "marketplace of ideas," which has been a prevailing metaphor for freedom of speech. (See Abrams v. United States, 250 U.S. 616 [1919], and United States v. Rumely, 345 U.S. 41 [1953].) Text and library book selection and the use of technology can exert a powerful influence on curriculum. In 2021, political influences have taken legislatures in numerous states to prohibit the teaching of curriculum such as Critical Race Theory in public schools.

In *Meyer v. Nebraska* (1923), the U.S. Supreme Court recognized that there is a substantive constitutional interest in teaching and learning. The Court ruled that a Nebraska law forbidding, "under penalty, the teaching, in any private, denominational, parochial or public school, of any modern language, other than English, to any child who has not attained and successfully passed the eighth grade, invades the liberty guaranteed by the Fourteenth Amendment and exceeds the power of the State." Although this case was decided in 1923, it is still highly relevant because it established the foundational tenet that the freedom to teach may not be interfered with under the guise of protecting the public interest.

Censorship of Print Material

One of the major issues in the selection of textbooks, library books, and other instructional material, including technology, is censorship. Censors may be state appointed or self-appointed. They may be school employees, members of citizens groups, or talk show hosts. They are found on both the right and the left ends of the political spectrum.

The National Council of Teachers of English (NCTE, 2014) suggests that teachers are uniquely qualified to judge their own instructional materials' strengths and weaknesses and that the textbook selection process should always include teachers' evaluations of the books (NCTE, 2014). The process should be shared with parents and other interested members of the community.

The American Library Association (ALA, 2005) asserts that intellectual freedom is the right of every individual to both seek and receive information from all points of view without restriction. The ALA notes that there has been a long debate between acquisition and censorship. Looking at the same material, some may find the contents a reason for its adoption or use, while others may look at the same material and find the contents objectionable enough to either reject the adoption, or have material removed entirely.

Some people claim they are engaged in a battle to determine who will use the schools to indoctrinate young people. Others claim they have a right to remove educational material that fosters sexual stereotypes. Other advocates say they have a right to remove books that are racist, profane, or obscene and replace them with books that present positive role models for racial and ethnic minorities. Whatever the challenge, principals need to follow school district policy and procedures to the letter before removing materials from the classroom, library, or school.

Some states delegate the responsibility for textbook selection to local boards of education, while the others exercise this authority directly. In adoption states, a single text is selected for each subject, and publishers supply them statewide. Typically, local school districts, in adoption states, may not use state funds to buy books that are not on the state list.

Although the courts have ruled that citizens of the community cannot use court action to require a board of education to use a certain textbook, school boards are very responsive to vocal pressure. In some cases, textbooks have been removed from schools as the result of pressure from less than a dozen citizens.

In addition to attacking textbook adoptions, school patrons and individual board members sometimes demand that certain materials they consider objectionable be removed from classrooms or libraries. School boards, faced with such complaints, have often been willing to order school administrators to remove the materials from the schools. In some cases, school officials have ordered not only that materials be removed from schools but also that their content not be discussed in classrooms. School boards have justified their actions by asserting that they have absolute discretion in all curriculum matters in the school and that they must be permitted to establish and apply the curriculum in such a way as to transmit community values. Those who oppose the removal of school curriculum materials or library books from schools argue that the practice is a violation of the First Amendment's guarantee of free speech.

In 1982, in *Island Trees Union School District v. Pico,* the U.S. Supreme Court heard its first school library book-banning case. This case of censorship involved the removal of nine books from a school library within the Island Trees District. The board defended its decision by claiming the books contained "material which is offensive to Christians, Jews, Blacks, and Americans in general," as well as "obscenities, blasphemies, brutality and perversion beyond description." The board's action prompted Pico and four other high school students to sue the school district. They charged that the board ignored the advice of literary experts, libraries, teachers, and publications that rate books for secondary students and based its decision solely on a list of objectionable books put out by a conservative parents' group. In hearing the *Pico* case, the Court affirmed the appellate court's decision that school officials can be taken to federal court if they are challenged about removing books from school libraries. The Court noted that the "right to receive ideas is a necessary predicate to the exercise of speech, press and political freedom."

The *Pico* decision sent the message that board members have discretion in curriculum matters by reliance on the duty to support community values in the schools, but that duty is misplaced when boards extend their discretion beyond the compulsory environment of the classroom into the library, in which voluntary inquiry is paramount. In addition, although school boards have significant discretion to determine the library's content, such discretion cannot be exercised in a narrowly partisan or political manner. The *Pico* Court ruled, "Our Constitution does not permit the official suppression of ideas."

The courts have ruled that books cannot be removed simply because school officials disagree with the ideas. Removal decisions should be based on a book's or other curriculum material's educational suitability, considering such "politically neutral" factors as relevance, quality, pervasive vulgarity, and appropriateness to age and grade level (see also *Hazelwood v. Kuhlmeier,* 1988; *Virgil v. School Board of Columbia County,* 1989).

Prohibitions on Curriculum and Course Content

In 2021, several state legislatures passed prohibitions of curriculum based on teaching of racial history in the United States. As with nearly every issue that principals may be presented in their schools, state and local policy will be different, and principals must adhere to their own state policy. Similarly, principals must also take time to educate themselves around the issues or controversies no matter what their own state or local policy mandates.

School districts have the authority to regulate the course content and teaching methods of their teachers, and teachers may not teach in any method they choose that runs counter to school district policies. The mandate to avoid discussion of sensitive topics related to race creates questions for teachers as to how any topics related to race can be discussed or taught in the classroom. It is very likely that there will be challenges to these policies, as well as actions taken against principals and teachers who may violate the new prohibitions. Because this is somewhat uncharted territory, the best way to avoid legal entanglements is to follow policy guidelines in each state created after the mandates and to discuss ahead of time with teachers how subjects will be taught in classes.

SECTION E. HEALTH AND SAFETY ISSUES

School administrators are responsible for the success of all students by ensuring management of the organization, operations, and resources of the school for a safe, efficient, and effective learning environment. Essentially school employees perform the following major tasks each day related to their students: teaching the curriculum; attending to their social–emotional needs; and taking steps to ensure their safety. Having an overall school safety plan is imperative, and principals are advised to seek additional resources specific to the development of school safety plans and school violence prevention. This section will highlight four important elements of an overall school safety plan: the social–emotional needs of students; protection of students from abuse and neglect; health considerations of students; and privacy rights related to students and families.

Student Social–Emotional Needs

Student success and learning is severely impacted when they are undergoing extreme stress and anxiety, particularly when they are not emotionally equipped or skilled with understanding how to manage their emotions. Challenges students regularly face outside of school have been compounded for some by the isolation of remote learning and other stresses caused by the COVID-19 pandemic, with reports of significant increases in loneliness, anxiety, and grief by children (National Alliance on Mental Illness 2021). Social–emotional learning (SEL) has been shown to have a positive impact on learning as well as school climate.

Having SEL as a core component of a school safety plan and school curriculum adds to what are known to increase overall school safety, with relationship building, positive school climate, effective communication channels, and building communities as key components. There is a wide spectrum of SEL programs that school districts may choose to implement. The key point is that principals should make SEL a priority in the daily practice of their school.

Child Abuse and Neglect

For more than 5 million American children, punishment at home has meant being shot, stabbed, kicked, beaten, poisoned, burned, or bitten by their parents. In addition to suffering abusive punishment, many children are raped, starved, and psychologically damaged by parents or relatives in their homes. According to the CDC at least one in seven children experiences abuse or neglect, with such abuse having life-long impacts on the individual as well as overall societal impacts.

The key federal law addressing child abuse and neglect is the Child Abuse Prevention and Treatment Act (CAPTA), originally enacted in 1974, and has been reauthorized or amended several times. CAPTA provides federal funding to states to support prevention, assessment, investigation, prosecution, and treatment activities and also provides grants to public agencies and nonprofit organizations for demonstration programs and projects.

What Is Child Abuse and Maltreatment?

Child abuse and neglect are defined in both federal and state legislation. The federal legislation provides a foundation for states by identifying a minimum set of acts or behaviors that characterize maltreatment. There are four major types of abuse and maltreatment: physical abuse, neglect, sexual abuse, and emotional abuse. Although state definitions may vary, operational definitions generally include the following:

Physical abuse includes any physical injury that results from punching, beating, kicking, biting, burning, shaking, or otherwise harming a child.

Child neglect is characterized by failure to provide for the child's basic needs. Neglect can be physical, educational, or emotional. Physical neglect includes refusal of or delay in seeking health care, abandonment, expulsion from the home or refusal to allow a runaway to return home, and inadequate supervision. Educational neglect includes the allowance of chronic truancy, failure to enroll a child of mandatory school age in school, and failure to attend to a special educational need.

Sexual abuse includes fondling a child's genitals, intercourse, incest, rape, sodomy, exhibitionism, and commercial exploitation through prostitution or the production of pornographic materials.

Emotional abuse (psychological and verbal abuse and mental injury) includes acts or omissions by the parents or other caregivers that have caused, or could cause, serious behavioral, cognitive, emotional, or mental disorders. In some cases of emotional abuse, the acts of parents or other caregivers alone, without any harm evident in the child's behavior or condition, are sufficient to warrant child protective services intervention. Emotional neglect includes such actions as marked inattention to the child's needs for affection, refusal of or failure to provide needed psychological care, spouse abuse in the child's presence, and permission of drug or alcohol use by the child.

Although any of the forms of child maltreatment may be found separately, they often occur in combination. Emotional abuse is almost always present when other forms are identified. Although injuries can occur accidentally, child abuse should be suspected if the explanations do not fit the injury or if there is a pattern of repeated injury. Also, the existence of several injuries in different stages of healing may demonstrate that they did not happen as a result of one accident. A child who is consistently withdrawn or overly aggressive, who complains of soreness or wears inappropriate clothing for the weather, or who is a chronic runaway may be a victim of abuse.

Because attendance in school is compulsory, educators are often the only professionals to whom a child is exposed on a regular basis. Because of this, educators have an affirmative obligation to be aware of child abuse warning signs and to report suspected cases to proper authorities.

Every state has enacted reporting laws requiring certain professionals, including teachers and administrators, to report suspected cases of child abuse. School personnel are expected to report suspected cases of child abuse "immediately." Typically, immediately is interpreted to mean as soon as there is sufficient evidence from which it is "reasonable" to conclude that a child has been or is being abused. The question then arises: How much information is necessary to establish sufficient evidence from which it is reasonable to conclude that abuse has occurred?

It is not the intent of mandatory reporting statutes to require educators to investigate child abuse cases. These statutes require educators to report if they "have reason to suspect." This language is important because the original standard in most states was some variation of "reason to believe." Several states have changed the standard required of mandatory reporters to that of "reason to suspect," explaining that less evidence is required to establish a suspicion than to establish a belief. Reasonableness invariably is defined with reference to the hypothetical reasonable person similarly situated. In this case, the standard of reasonableness would be the actions of a competent school administrator or teacher. School personnel should use common sense in trying to figure out if a child is being abused. For example, normal, active children get some bruises and bumps from everyday playing. These bruises are mostly over bony areas such as knees, elbows, and shins. However, a child with injuries on other parts of the body, such as the stomach, cheeks, ears, buttocks, mouth, or thighs, or showing black eyes, human bite marks, or round burns the size of a cigarette, should clearly be considered a possible abused child.

Each of these state laws has a clause providing a degree of immunity from prosecution for those reporting, without malice, cases of suspected abuse. Each state statute also specifies the penalties for mandatory reporters who fail to report cases of suspected child abuse. All mandatory reporters should understand that making a report of suspected child abuse means reporting the suspicion to the proper agency responsible for investigating the potential abuse. To simply "report" it to a superior expecting or hoping that person will then make the report is not sufficient, and may not satisfy mandatory reporting requirements.

Child Abduction

School personnel should be very cautious about the physical custody of children. If the school has no information to the contrary, it can assume that both parents or guardians have parental rights. However, if the school is informed that there has been some modification of parental rights, then the noncustodial parent does not have the right to remove the child from school without permission of the custodial parent. Although it may cause some embarrassment or inconvenience, it is better to err on the side of protecting the child.

Because schools can be held legally responsible, school administrators should be concerned about releasing a child to any adult. Principals must be alert not only to the possibility of a stranger taking a child without permission but also to the possibility of a child being taken by a parent, contrary to a custody decree. When deciding whether or not to release a child from school, the first issue to be resolved is the question of who has parental rights. The legal parent is the person the legal system recognizes as having the legal rights of parenthood. Usually, both parents' rights are recognized. Therefore, either parent, acting alone, has the legal right to make decisions on behalf of the child.

Traditional notions about "family" and "marriage" don't reflect the reality of what demographics are present in schools today. The Uniform Parentage Act (UPA) originated in 1973 and was designed to remove the legal status of illegitimacy and provided presumptions used to determine a child's legal parentage. The UPA includes provisions related to surrogacy agreements, for example, as well as language written in non-gendered terms. Earlier authorizations of the UPA presumed couples as parents consisted of one man and one woman, but the 2017 reauthorization recognizes the parental rights of same sex couples (Uniform Parentage Act of 2017).

Modern adoption laws have created a new and exclusive parent–child relationship and have established parental rights and duties where they would not otherwise exist. When a court issues a decree of adoption, the natural parents no longer have a legal relationship to the child.

The bottom line for principals and school personnel is that although at times determining the parties who have parental rights can be an uncomfortable and emotional process, it is imperative to only allow authorized individuals to make contact with a child and even more importantly, to take the child from the school.

Health Considerations of Students

Students With a Communicable Disease

At one point in time, the schooling of students with HIV was a controversial and highly emotionally charged situation faced by principals. By the end of 2003, there were 8,549 reported AIDS cases among children under thirteen years of age in the United States. Of those cases reported between 1996 and 2003, 20 percent acquired AIDS by injection drug use and 42 percent acquired AIDS from heterosexual contact (Centers for Disease Control and Prevention, 2005).

Due to advances in both medicine and an understanding of HIV, such controversy is not common today. But the underlying concerns about students with communicable diseases exist. With the presence of COVID-19, the concerns are the same but with the focus on a different disease. With HIV and AIDS, the disease was determined to not be transmissible through airborne or casual contact, and within a school setting there was not a significant risk of spreading the virus. Prior to the introduction of treatments known as antiretroviral therapy, many children infected with the virus were very ill and were not able to function normally in school. Successful drug treatments have enabled more HIV-infected children to attend school, causing the American Academy of Pediatrics (AAP) to ask teachers and school administrators to provide students infected with HIV with the same education and services that they provide for those with other chronic illnesses.

Similar principles should apply to other communicable diseases, including COVID-19. State laws guarantee that a public education is the legal right of every child in this country. The difference between HIV and COVID-19 is that students continue to carry HIV even when never showing signs of illness, and those who have COVID-19 do not. The courts have recognized that children benefit from the socialization process in a class of their peers and that education has a great impact on their social and psychological well-being. As a result, children with HIV or AIDS have the legal right to a free public education with their peers.

A child with a long-term communicable disease such as HIV or AIDS clearly has a "physical impairment" and thus is considered handicapped within the meaning of the Rehabilitation Act. All students with AIDS are covered under Section 504 of the Rehabilitation Act. The U.S. Department of Justice believes that the disabling consequences of AIDS infection qualify as handicaps, but the mere presence of the HIV virus in the body does not. In other words, individuals experiencing the opportunistic infections of full-blown AIDS are protected as handicapped under the act, but those who are asymptomatic are not handicapped by the virtue of their communicability. This distinction would likely exist for COVID-19-affected students unless such students are designated as having "long hauler" effects of COVID-19.

Immunizations and Immunization Hesitancy

Although there continues to be some public resistance and legal challenges to mandatory vaccination, all states require some immunization for most children prior to the admission to public school to protect them from infectious diseases. The vaccines for COVID-19 are tangled with political considerations that will likely spill over into school settings in the coming months or years. It is likely that until COVID-19 vaccines are fully approved by the Food and Drug Administration (FDA), such vaccines will not be required for school admission. However, should the FDA fully approve vaccines for all school age groups, it is also likely that some states will move to require the COVID-19 vaccine. All states have statutes requiring vaccination for diphtheria, measles, rubella, and polio. There are state-by-state variations in the requirements for vaccines for tetanus, whooping cough (pertussis), and mumps. Parents who refuse permission for their child to be vaccinated and who do not qualify for some exemption may be fined or even imprisoned. Medical exemptions are permitted if a physician states that a specific child would be endangered by immunization. Several states provide exemptions for philosophical reasons, and religious exemptions are permitted in the majority of the states.

Most challenges arise where parents' religious beliefs do not allow them to have their children vaccinated. When groups have challenged legislation requiring all school children to be immunized, the courts have held that a person's religious freedom ceases when it overlaps and transgresses the rights of others. The courts have reasoned that other school children have a right to be free from mandatory association with persons not immunized against deadly diseases. This right is so compelling that it overrides religious freedom rights. *Maack v. School District of Lincoln* (1992) is one example of the many cases that affirm that the protection of public health permits the state to require the vaccination of all persons for the common good. In this case, the question was whether a school could exclude children from school who had not been immunized against a dangerous disease. In this case, the Supreme Court of Nebraska held that (a) the board of education was legally authorized to exclude the children under the circumstances; and (b) classification between unimmunized and insufficiently immunized students did not violate unimmunized students' equal protection rights.

The U.S. Supreme Court declined to hear a case from West Virginia that upheld the state mandatory immunization requirement, stating that the religious beliefs of the parent do not prevent enforcement of the immunization law (*Workman v. Mingo County Schools,* 2009).

Medical Marijuana in the Educational Space

An emerging issue for some school districts is the administration of medical marijuana in the school setting. There is an intersection between federal drug policies, school drug policies, and some state medical marijuana laws. This is another example where state laws will vary considerably, and principals must be aware of their own circumstances.

Some states allow the students with prescribed marijuana to consume it on school grounds, most often in nonsmokable forms. Others only allow parents to administer the products. Clearly principals face complicated management issues when a substance legal for possession and use by some students is illegal for other students. It also creates concern about school nurses who may be tasked to store or distribute medical marijuana, unless such issue is addressed in state law (which still may technically be in violation of federal law). As stated, this is an emerging issue in schools, and will continue to become a focus of education law as more states legalize both medical and recreational marijuana (Colwell, 2019).

Student and Family Privacy

Family Educational Rights and Privacy Act (FERPA), a.k.a. the Buckley Amendment

In 1974, the U.S. Congress enacted legislation in the form of the Buckley Amendment, which became known as the Family Educational Rights and Privacy Act (FERPA). This act set forth several guidelines related to the protection and sharing of student records. Prior to the passage of FERPA, educators maintained student records and shared the contents of those records at their own discretion, including the posting of student grades. As a result, it was possible for incorrect, misleading, embarrassing, or damaging information to be maintained and disclosed without the knowledge or consent of the parent or student. Furthermore, parents had no access to the records or any right to correct inaccurate information.

FERPA was enacted to correct some of the real or potential abuses in the access to and disclosure of education records. FERPA established students' right to privacy in their education records. For purposes of this legislation, the term *education records* means those records, files, documents, and other materials that

- Contain information directly related to a student

- Are maintained by an education agency or institution or by a person acting for such agency or institution

Education records do not include notes, memory aids, and other similar information that is maintained in the personal files kept by school officials and are not accessible or revealed to authorized school personnel or any third party. Such information can be shared with the student or parent, but if it is released to authorized school personnel or any third party, it becomes part of the student record subject to all the provisions of FERPA.

FERPA was written decades before the availability of the internet, and the electronic means and ease of sharing student data quickly open many areas educators must oversee.

FERPA requires that schools formulate a policy and procedures related to parental access to the education records of their children. This policy should provide parents with the right to

- Inspect and review the education records.

- Amend the education record.

- Limit the disclosures of personally identifiable information from education records.

Education records may not be destroyed when there is a current request by a parent or student to see them.

Family Educational Rights and Privacy Act Rights

Parents have certain rights with respect to their child's education records, and those rights transfer to the student at age eighteen. These rights include the right to inspect and review the education records maintained by the school; the right to request that a school correct records believed to be inaccurate or misleading; and when a disagreement exists, the parent has a right to a hearing and place a statement in the record regarding the contested information.

Family Educational Rights and Privacy Act Access

In general, schools must have written permission to release information in the education records. FERPA does allow schools to disclose records in certain conditions. Those include school officials with a legitimate educational interest; other schools to which a student may be transferring; appropriate parties in connection with financial aid; appropriate officials in cases of health and emergency; and in compliance with court orders or within state law to state or local authorities. State and local education authorities are now allowed to share data with other government agencies that are not under their direct control, as long as those other agencies are involved in federal- or state-supported education programs.

Data can also be shared with early childhood education programs, postsecondary education programs, special education programs, job training, career and technical education programs, and adult education programs. However, data for children older than seven cannot be shared with agencies with programs promoting social, emotional, and physical development (but can be shared for children under age seven for early childhood literacy and language programs).

FERPA and Directory Information

Directory information refers to information that is generally available through various sources and is often reported by the schools in student directories, athletic programs, and news releases. The law requires that public notice must be given by any school regarding the categories of directory information that it intends to make public. A reasonable period of time must be given after the notice so that a parent can inform the school of any material that cannot be released without the parent's prior consent. In other words, schools must give parents a reasonable opportunity to prevent the release of directory information. Directory information includes the following:

- Name, address, and telephone number
- Date and place of birth
- Major field of study
- Participation in officially recognized activities and sports
- Weight and height of members of athletic teams
- Dates of attendance
- Degrees and awards received
- Most recent previous school attended
- Other similar information

Family Educational Rights and Privacy Act and IDEA

When the Elementary and Secondary Education Act (ESEA) and the IDEA were reauthorized in 1997, IDEA incorporated FERPA language. However, specific details of IDEA provide additional protections related to age of consent procedures for students who receive special education and related services. For example, IDEA allows the disclosure of a student's special education records without parental consent

- When it affects law enforcement officials' ability to serve the student
- When necessary to protect the health or safety of the student or other persons
- To school-employed campus police solely for law enforcement purposes
- Under court order or subpoena

However, even in these cases, the school administrator must make a reasonable effort to notify the student or the student's parents.

Family Educational Rights and Privacy Act in the Classroom

In 2002, the U.S. Supreme Court, on an appeal of an earlier decision in the Tenth Circuit, *Falvo v. Owasso* (2000), rendered a decision interpreting the constitutional right of privacy as a result of a grading practice used by many teachers. The original case, *Owasso Independent School District v. Falvo* (2002), concerned the practice of students exchanging papers and grading each other's work as the teacher went over the answers. In this case, the teacher permitted students to announce aloud the grades on papers that they had graded. The Court ruled that student grading of assignments does not violate the provisions of FERPA. The Court offered five reasons for its decision: (1) the teacher does not maintain a grade until it is recorded; (2) by grading assignments, students do not constitute persons acting for an educational institution within FERPA; (3) peer-graded items do not constitute education records protected by FERPA until a teacher collects the students' papers or other items and records the grades in the teacher's grade book—in reaching its conclusion, the Court noted that peer-graded items were not maintained within the meaning of FERPA, as the student graders only handled the items for a few moments; (4) permitting parents to contest each student-graded work would bury the school in hearings; and (5) Congress did not mean to intervene in this drastic fashion with traditional state functions. This case is particularly important because it reinforces the long-standing tradition of the courts' reluctance to substitute their opinion for those of professional educators when it comes to issues of instruction. According to Mawdsley and Russo (2003), "[T]he Court refused to be drawn into classroom management of public schools. The Court made it clear that peer grading is a matter of pedagogy and not a proper matter within the expertise of courts."

ADDITIONAL CASES OF INTEREST TO EDUCATORS

SCHOOL ATTENDANCE; PARTICIPATION; GRADUATION

Serna v. Portales, 499 F.2d 1147 (10th Cir. 1974). Other contemporary court cases followed the same logic as the *Lau* court. In *Serna v. Portales* (1974), a federal court ruled that a city school district must implement a bilingual and bicultural curriculum, revise procedures for assessing achievement, and hire bilingual personnel to provide equal education opportunities for students whose home language and culture was Hispanic.

Cintron v. Brentwood Union Free Sch. Dist., 1455 F.Supp. 57 (E.D.N.Y. 1978). A federal court ordered a school district to retain its bilingual program rather than substitute a program that would segregate Spanish-speaking children from their English-speaking peers in certain classes.

Ríos v. Reed, 480 F.Supp. 14 (E.D.N.Y. 1978). A federal court ruled that a school district's transitional bilingual program was really an English immersion program that denied Spanish-speaking students equal education opportunity by not providing academic instruction in Spanish. The court further ruled that "a denial of educational opportunities to a child in the first years of schooling is not justified by demonstrating that the educational program employed will teach the child English sooner than a program comprised of more extensive Spanish instruction."

State v. M.M., 407 So.2d 987 (Fla. App. 1981). A case from Florida in 1981 held that parents could not simply declare their home a private school in order to avoid enrolling their children in a public school.

Gomez v. Illinois State Board of Education, 811 F.2d 1030 (7th Cir. 1987). SEAs are required under EEOA to ensure that language minority students' educational needs are met.

Shuman v. Cumberland Valley School District Board of Directors, 536 A.2d 490 (Pa. Commw. Ct. 1988). A high school student completed all requirements for graduation, including final exams, but was expelled for selling drugs before the graduation ceremony. The school district sought to deny his diploma, but the court ruled that since he had completed the graduation requirements, he was entitled to his diploma.

Lampkin v. District of Columbia, 27 F.3d 605 (D.C. 1994). The Circuit Court of the District of Columbia ruled that the McKinney-Vento Act permits homeless children to sue government officials to obtain the educational rights guaranteed by the act.

Swanson v. Guthrie Independent School District No. I-L., 135 F.3d 694 (10th Cir. 1998). A court held that a school board policy that prohibited part-time attendance was permissible because the school board had the right to control the use of its resources. For religious reasons the parents chose to homeschool but sued the school district to allow their child to enroll in selected classes at the school.

Herrman v. Board of Education of Unified School District No. 256, No. 01–4019-RDR, 2002 U.S. Dist. LEXIS 21700 (D. Kan. Oct. 16, 2002). A high school student was suspended and denied participation in her graduation ceremony for behavior during a senior class trip. The student intended to commit a prank against another student by defecating into a Pringles can, but the plan backfired when the can ended up in a shoe belonging to a different student. Although her parents agreed that she should be punished, they felt the denial of participation in graduation was too severe. The court upheld her suspension but granted an injunction to allow her to participate in the ceremony.

Jones v. West Virginia State Board of Education, 622 S.E.2d 289, 218 W. Va. 52 (2005). This case reversed a decision that sided with parents who claimed that a policy banning homeschooled students from participating in school-sponsored activities violated their constitutional rights. Schools in West Virginia were not required to allow such participation.

Menard v. La. High School Athletic Association, 30 S0.3d 79 (La. Ct. App. 2009). The court ruled that there was no procedural or substantive due process to participate in interscholastic sports. In addition, the possibility of a college athletic scholarship based on playing in high school is not a protected property interest, but instead a "speculative and uncertain expectation or opportunity."

CHILD ABUSE

Korunka v. Dept. of Children and Family Services, 259 Ill.App. 3d 527, 197 Ill. Dec. 537, 631 N.E. 2d 759 (4th Dist. 1994). While restraining a student, a teacher assistant fell to the floor with a ten-year-old student, which caused a bruise to the head of the student. An appellate court upheld an earlier court decision that reversed an administrative hearing against the teacher assistant, noting that an educator bruising a child does not automatically qualify as abuse of the child, and in this instance the injury was accidental.

PUBLIC SCHOOLS AND RELIGION

Illinois ex rel. McCollum v. Board of Ed. of Sch. Dist. No. 71, Champaign County, 333 U.S. 203 (1948). The U.S. Supreme Court held that it was a violation of the Establishment Clause for the public school district to conduct "release time" during the school day for religious instruction. The voluntary classes were conducted by private third parties. A parent filed suit because she felt her son was ostracized for not attending the classes. The Court reasoned that the system was a utilization of a tax-supported public school system to aid religious groups.

Meek v. Pittenger, 421 U.S. 349 (1975). The Supreme Court held that it was a violation of the Establishment Clause to authorize the use of state-purchased materials and equipment in nonpublic schools and providing services to children in those schools. The Court, however, held that loaning textbooks to the same students was not unconstitutional. Later rulings in *Agostini v. Felton* (1997) and *Mitchell v. Helms* (2000) modified the holding in the case.

Peloza v. Capistrano Unified School Dist., 37 F.3d 517 (9th Cir. 1994). When a teacher challenged that the teaching of evolution conflicted with his religious beliefs, the Ninth Circuit stated, "While at the high school, whether he is in the classroom or outside of it during contract time, [the teacher] is not just an ordinary citizen. He is a teacher. . . . [T]he likelihood of high school students equating his views with those of the school is substantial. To permit him to discuss his religious beliefs with students during school time on school grounds would violate the Establishment Clause of the First Amendment" (p. 522).

Coles Ex Rel. Coles v. Cleveland Bd. of Educ., 171 F.3d 369 (6th Cir. 1999). In 1999, in *Coles v. Cleveland Board of Education,* the court was asked to consider the issue of prayer at a school board meeting. A student appearing at a school board meeting to accept an award indicated that she was shocked and surprised when the board began the meeting by having a Baptist minister offer a prayer that she believed showed favor to Christians and was offensive to anyone of another religion attending the meeting. A teacher who was similarly offended by this practice joined in filing a suit alleging that the board's practice violated the Establishment Clause. The district court concluded that the board meeting was fundamentally an adult gathering to conduct the business of schools. The judge felt that prayer at a school board meeting should be treated in a similar manner to prayers that open legislative sessions. The Sixth Circuit rejected the board's contention that a school board meeting fell within the legislative exception found in *Marsh v. Chambers* (1983). The *Marsh* decision held that "paying a chaplain with public funds to offer an opening prayer for a Nebraska legislative session was not unconstitutional." The court followed the Supreme Court's lead in striking down any instance of government-sponsored religious expression or involvement in public education. In striking down the school board prayer as unconstitutional, the court asserted that the practice had the primary effect of endorsing religion and further reasoned that prayer at a board meeting was arguably more coercive than at a graduation.

Borden v. School Dist. of Tp. of East Brunswick, 523 F.3d 153 (3d Cir. 2008). The Third Circuit ruled against a coach who sued after the school district adopted a policy prohibiting faculty participation in student-initiated prayer. The coach had participated for over twenty years in a practice that took varying forms and times of prayer. By the time the practices had been reduced to a moment of silence, the court determined that after twenty-three years, any observer could conclude that the activity endorsed religion.

Parker v. Hurley, 514 F.3d 87 (1st Cir. 2008). A court held that parents have no constitutional right to prevent their children from being exposed to books they find religiously repugnant.

Busch v. Marple Newtown School Dist., 567 F.3d 89 (3d Cir. 2009). A court held that parents could not direct or lead Bible reading in classes. In this case, a parent filed suit after the district placed restrictions against her reading scripture aloud to her son's kindergarten class.

Doe v. Indian River School Dist., 653 F.3d 256 (3d Cir. 2011). A Third Circuit opinion determined that school board prayer is analogous to other school prayer cases when it comes to protecting students from the coercion of school-sponsored prayer.

CENSORSHIP

Presidents Council, District 25 v. Community School Board No. 25, 457 F.2d 289 (2nd Cir. 1972). A federal appeals court upheld the right of a school board to remove Piri Thomas's *Down These Mean Streets* from junior high school libraries because some patrons believed that some of the language and scenes in the book were "ugly and violent." The court found no violation of any basic constitutional right and concluded that any intrusion on any First Amendment right was only "minuscule."

Minarcini v. Strongville City School District, 541 F.2d 577 (6th Cir. 1976). A federal appeals court overruled a lower court and denied a school board's right to remove Joseph Heller's *Catch-22* and Kurt Vonnegut Jr.'s *Cat's Cradle* from a high school library. The court ruled that if a school board sets up a library, that library becomes a forum of silent speech protected by the First Amendment. Therefore, it is unconstitutional to place conditions on its use based solely on the social or political tastes of school board members.

Case v. Unified Sch. Dist. No. 233, 908 F. Supp. 864 (D. Kan. 1995). A court ruled in favor of plaintiffs who objected to the removal from libraries by school district officials of young adult novels that contained a fictional romantic relationship between two girls. After the books were originally donated to the school board, they declined the donation and removed existing copies from the shelves in school libraries. The court held that rights of the plaintiffs were violated, and the district failed to follow existing procedures for removing challenged books from its libraries.

Counts v. Cedarville School District, 295 F. Supp 2d 996 (W.D. Ark. 2003). Parents of a child attending the Cedarville School District became concerned when they learned that the *Harry Potter* books were in circulation in the district's school libraries. They contacted their child's school librarian and were told that, under the district policy, they would have to complete a "Reconsideration Request Form." The parents completed the form and requested that *Harry Potter and the Sorcerer's Stone* be withdrawn from circulation. The school's library committee considered the request and recommended, without reservations, that the board of education keep the book in circulation. The school board voted to restrict the circulation of all of the books in the *Harry Potter* series to only those students who provided a signed permission statement from their parent or guardian. The parents of Counts brought a suit alleging that her rights under the First and Fourteenth Amendment were being abridged. In ruling that Counts had sufficient injury to give her standing to pursue her claims, the court stated, "The right to read a book is an aspect of the right to receive information and ideas, an inherent corollary of the rights of freedom of speech and the press." The court found that the school district's policy of restricting access to the *Harry Potter* books infringed on Counts's First Amendment rights.

COMMUNICABLE DISEASE

Martinez v. School Board of Hillsborough County, 861 F.2d (11th Cir. 1988). The case involved the appropriate educational placement of a mentally disabled child infected with AIDS. At the time the action was filed, the child was seven years old and had an IQ of 41. The child was not toilet trained and suffered from thrush, a disease that can produce blood in the saliva. She sucked her thumb, resulting in saliva on her fingers. Section 504 of the Rehabilitation Act provides that no otherwise qualified individual with a disability shall, solely by reason of their disability, be excluded from participation in the benefits of school. The court was asked to balance the risks to the child versus the benefits from attendance at school. The court held that the remote theoretical possibility of transmission from saliva, tears, and urine did not support segregating the child from a regular trainable mentally handicapped classroom.

B.W.C. v. Williams, No. 20-1222 (8th Cir. 2021). The Eighth Circuit affirmed the U.S. district court's dismissal of plaintiffs' complaint challenging Missouri's form to claim a religious exemption from mandatory immunizations for school children, as violations of their First and Fourteenth Amendment rights. The court held that the form did not violate parental rights and communicates neutrally to anyone considering opting out on religious grounds that the government discourages it, but the ultimate decision belongs to the parents.

CHAPTER 10

Copyright Law

This chapter clarifies the components of copyright law and offers suggestions to help educators understand the law and decide whether particular situations involve a legitimate fair use of copyrighted works. Copyright law applies to teachers, support staff, and principals as well as students, and educators must be more vigilant than ever due to advances in technology.

CONSIDERATIONS RELATED TO COVID-19

Changes in instruction due to COVID-19 have implications related to copyright. Perhaps a majority of teachers have never taught in an online environment or posted a significant number of instructional materials in an online classroom management system. While COVID-19 itself does not present copyright concerns, additional attention to the basics of copyright law is warranted.

Copyright changes were included in the original CARES Act, which extended the timing of requirements under copyright law and in the case of a declared national emergency.

SUGGESTED GUIDELINES FOR PRACTICE

A separate chapter dedicated to copyright law may seem for some as placing too much emphasis on the topic, but copyright violations are easy to commit and, should they occur, can create potentially significant legal risks and career damage. In addition, the purpose of copyright is sometimes either misunderstood or even waived off and ignored, and principals and other educators should make themselves appreciate that copyright violations are a form of theft.

SUGGESTED GUIDELINES FOR PRINCIPALS

The following suggestions may reduce the risks associated with schools and copyright, especially in an increased online teaching environment.

Conduct professional development regarding copyright. Such professional development should be aimed at increasing the awareness of the purpose of copyright, the basics of what constitutes fair use, explanations of a copyright infringement, and securing understanding of the implications involved when employees sign on to school networks under their acceptable use policies. Although the vast majority of teachers would not think of stealing something, many educators routinely use copyrighted material *without* permission. Most teachers violate copyright law because they are uninformed or confused about what they may and may not legally copy.

Be mindful of the content posted and linked on school-created websites and other media, especially when posting links and advertising. These sites may contain copyrighted material, student work assignments, and artistic, musical, or dramatic productions. These sites also may link to other sites or import other material onto the district's site. School districts and individuals have been sued for tweets and retweets of copyrighted material, including copyrighted phrases. In addition, some posted links may themselves be in some type of violation or include bad information that may have expired.

Check the copyright guidelines posted within your classroom system. Blackboard, Canvas, Google Classroom, Khan Academy, and other platforms all have copyright policy and guidance. Such information would be good to share in professional development training.

Educators should exercise caution when tempted to circulate materials via social media. It is easy to circulate materials through social media but care must be taken when doing so. Sending links that others could access on their own is not a problem, but scanning images of articles and widely dispersing them to others, including students, would not be advised. Sending copies you accessed instead of providing a link for others to access could also be problematic.

Bear in mind that guidelines also apply to students. Schools are responsible to not only model appropriate behavior but also to teach that behavior. Experienced educators also recognize that in the mind of many students today, the definition of plagiarism, cheating, and copyright are not the same as their definition.

Trademark infringement also requires attention. Although not the focus of this chapter, trademark infringement is similar to copyright, and in a school could be an issue with school mascots, logos, and other similar images.

As always, keep in mind local board policy regarding the use of materials. What may be "allowable" in terms of digital media related to copyright law may still violate a board policy such as watching films during class time.

SECTION A. SOURCES OF COPYRIGHT LAW

Copyright Statutes

The source of copyright law is the copyright clause of the U.S. Constitution, which states, "To promote the Progress of Science and useful Arts, by securing for limited Times to Authors and Inventors the exclusive Right to their respective Writings and Discoveries" (Article I, Section 8, Clause 8).

The Copyright Act of 1976

The Copyright Act of 1976 (17 U.S. Code Title 17) extends protection to any original works of authorship in any tangible medium of expression. Section 106 of the act generally gives the owner of a copyright the exclusive right to reproduce the work and to authorize others to do so, prepare derivative works based on the work, distribute copies of the work, perform the work, or display the work. This protection is available to both published and unpublished works.

It is illegal for anyone to violate any of the rights provided by the copyright law to the owner of a copyright. These rights, however, are not unlimited in scope. The act establishes limitations on these rights. In some cases, these limitations are specified exemptions from copyright liability. One major limitation is the doctrine of "fair use." In other instances, the limitation takes the form of a "compulsory license," which permits certain limited uses of copyrighted works upon payment of specified royalties and compliance with statutory conditions.

Only the author or those deriving their rights through the author can rightfully claim a copyright. In the case of works made for hire, the employer and not the employee is considered to be the author.

The Sonny Bono Copyright Term Extension Act (CTEA) (1998)

The Copyright Term Extension Act (17 U.S.C. 108 *et seq*) was passed to extend the terms for copyright protection and to incentivize the digital archiving of materials. The act set the copyright term to life of the author plus seventy years, and copyright protection for works created before 1978 to a total of ninety-five years after their publication date. The extension may be even longer under other circumstances. Any work no longer protected by copyright is in the public domain and may be used by anyone without prior permission.

The Digital Millennium Copyright Act of 1998 (DMCA)

The Digital Millennium Copyright Act of 1998 (Pub. L.105-304) was enacted to align U.S. copyright law to international intellectual property treaties and amended the Copyright Act of 1976. The DMCA provided for criminal penalties for any circumvention of any measures to control copyrighted works, including digital works. The DMCA provided mechanisms for copyright owners to request through takedown orders that online providers remove infringing materials.

The Technology, Education, and Copyright Harmonization Act (TEACH Act) 2002

Because technology changed the definition of a classroom through the expanded use of distance education, the Technology, Education, and Copyright Harmonization Act (TEACH) in 2002 (Pub. L. 107-273) broadened what is permissible in educational activities in distance settings and online teaching. The purpose of the act is to make distance learning activities similar to those in face-to-face settings, and clarified permissible use in distance teaching.

SECTION B. COPYRIGHT PROTECTIONS

What Copyright Protects

Copyright protects "original works of authorship" that are fixed in a tangible form of expression. The Copyright Act of 1976 and later revisions protects such items of expression as literary, dramatic, and musical works; pantomimes and choreography; pictorial, graphic, and sculptural works; audiovisual works; sound recordings; and architectural works. As soon as an original expression is fixed in some tangible form, it is eligible for copyright protection. Consequently, even without applying for a copyright, almost any original expression is protected as soon as it is created. For example, a webpage would be protected as soon as the file is saved as an html file. Therefore, it is important for educators and students to understand that most of the items they access on the internet are most likely protected by a copyright.

Copyright protection generally covers such literary works as books, periodicals, manuscripts, sound recordings, computer programs, film, tapes, discs, and digital media. Copyright protection generally covers such musical and dramatic works as musical compositions, stage plays, screenplays, television plays, pantomimes and choreography, still or motion pictures, and other audiovisual media. The copyright law also protects such pictorial, graphic, and sculptural works as fine art, graphic art, applied art, photographs, prints and art reproductions, maps and globes, charts, technical drawings, diagrams, models, sculptures, statues, figures, and forms. Copyright protection also extends to sound recordings of music, the spoken word, and sound effects.

Copyright protection applies to trademarks and logos, but does not extend to names, short phrases, and slogans; familiar symbols or designs; mere variations of typographic ornamentation, lettering, or coloring; the mere listings of ingredients or contents; or works consisting entirely of information that is common property and containing no original authorship (e.g., standard calendars, height and weight charts). Ideas, procedures, methods, systems, processes, concepts, principles, discoveries, or devices are protected by patent.

The U.S. Copyright Office makes it clear that mere ownership of a book, manuscript, painting, or photograph, film or DVD, or sound recording (i.e., record, tape recording, CD) does not give the possessor the copyright. This is the critical point. It does not matter that you bought the greeting card; you do not have the right to make twenty copies of the cartoon image to decorate your classroom. It does not matter that your school purchased computer software; teachers may not copy it and install in their personal computers. Intellectual property is just like any other property; it is owned by someone. Using someone's intellectual property is analogous to stealing another's possession.

Clearly, technology has significantly affected the creation of works, the availability of such works, the need to apply copyright protections to those works, and the reality that digital mediums have made copyright nearly unenforceable in the same manner that existed before such technology existed.

The Differences Between Copyright and Plagiarism

There may be some confusion between copyright and plagiarism. Plagiarism is using someone else's work and passing it off as one's own. Plagiarism is not illegal, and is instead a moral issue rather than an illegal one. However, there may be serious negative consequences associated with plagiarism since most businesses and schools have policies regarding plagiarism, and people accused of or found to have committed plagiarism often lose jobs; are denied college admission; are failed in a class; or suffer other negative social consequences. Copyright infringement, on the other hand, is illegal when such infringement meets the parameters set out in the law. What might seem illogical is that the stigma associated with committing plagiarism may stick to a person longer than a "minor" copyright violation. One purpose of copyright protections is to encourage and promote creativity by protecting the creators of such works.

Educators are often at risk for both because it's very easy to find material written or created by others that is useful in the classroom. Teachers who now post material online in a classroom management system could unintentionally (or intentionally) make works they did not create appear as though they created themselves.

SECTION C. PUBLIC DOMAIN AND FAIR USE

Copyright Law Guidelines

Over the past several decades, copyright law has been significantly modified. Publication is no longer the key to obtaining a federal copyright, as it was under the Copyright Act of 1909. Since January 1, 1978, registration is also no longer necessary, although it is recommended by the Copyright Office. Consequently, a copyright is secured automatically when it is fixed in a copy for the first time. "Copies" are material objects from which a work can be read or visually perceived either directly or with the aid of a machine or device, such as books, manuscripts, sheet music, film, videotape, microfilm, cassette tapes, LPs, or digital forms (CDs, DVDs, etc.). By registering the work with the Copyright Office, the author has more legal remedies under the law against unlawful use than with an unregistered work. The copyright owner may also recover any actual damages, including any profits the infringer gained as a result of the infringement, an award of attorney's fees, injunctive relief against future infringement, and impoundment and destruction of infringing material. Additionally, registration is a deterrent to violators because most copy centers are reluctant to copy works when each item has the copyright mark.

A copyright notice contains the following three elements: the symbol © or word *Copyright*; the year of the first publication of the work with different requirements depending on the work; and the name of the individual owner of the copyright or with a recognizable abbreviation or alternative designation of the owner. The three elements of the notice should appear together on the copies or on the label and should be affixed to copies in such a way as to "give reasonable notice of the claim of copyright."

Public Domain

The public domain is that repository of all works that for whatever reason are not protected by copyright. As such, they are free for all to use without permission. Works in the public domain include the following classifications: originally noncopyrightable, lost copyright, expired copyright, and government documents. Facts, names, short phrases, ideas, and titles are noncopyrightable. Although it is difficult to lose copyright protection today, works published prior to January 1, 1978, that were not copyrighted may be considered in the public domain. If, for any reason, a copyright owner failed to renew their copyright, the material generally reverts to the public domain. Federal documents and publications are not copyrighted and therefore are considered to be in the public domain. Consequently, laws, statutes, agency circulars, federal reports, and any other documents published or generated by the federal government are not protected.

However, if the document was contracted by an individual for use by the federal government, the work is copyrighted.

Fair Use Doctrine

For educators, one of the most important limitations on the exclusive rights of copyright owners is the fair use doctrine.

Fair use is the legal principle that defines the limitations on the exclusive right of the copyright holder. Electronic publication and communication technologies have combined to significantly modify how information is published and disseminated. File sharing technologies that were popular in the late 1990s and early 2000s kept the courts, legislatures, and consumers in a constant state of flux dealing with the emerging technology. Two such cases ruled against free file sharing websites. In *A&M Records Inc. v. Napster* (2001), the court shut down the free Napster file sharing of music and film. *In re Aimster Copyright Litigation* (2003) held that Aimster had knowledge of infringement and that they had multiple opportunities to remove sharing from their site after many warnings.

Over the years, a substantial number of court decisions have sought to balance the rights of copyright owners to profit from their creativity and the legitimate interests of educators to use and disseminate copyrighted works. The primary impact of the fair use doctrine is the elimination of the need to obtain permission or pay royalties for purposes such as criticism, comment, news reporting, teaching (including multiple copies for classroom use), scholarship, and research. Unfortunately, the statute does not specifically delineate what a teacher may and may not do. Consequently, every decision must be made on a case-by-case basis according to the guidelines set forth in the statute.

The following four factors must be considered in determining whether the proposed use of copyrighted work constitutes fair use:

1. The *purpose* and character of the use, including whether the use is of a commercial nature or is for nonprofit educational purposes. (Nonprofit educational purposes seem to be less strictly controlled than commercial purposes.)

2. The *nature* of the copyrighted work. Newspaper articles and other material that are very timely or out of print are more likely to be considered fair use than books or video programs. However, more and more newspaper stories are carrying a copyright notice.

3. The *amount* and substantiality of the portion used in relation to the copyrighted work as a whole. This aspect may be the most difficult to understand. Even the Copyright Office holds that there is no specific number of words, lines, or notes that may be safely taken without permission. Excerpts are more likely to be permissible than are entire works. If large portions of the work, or that part of the work that is considered to be the core of the work, are copied, there is a higher likelihood of copyright infringement.

4. The *effect* of the use on the potential market for or value of the copyrighted work. Courts give this factor greater weight than the other three. If a

reasonable person would conclude that the work was copied to avoid purchasing the copyrighted work, or it is proven that the market for the work was damaged as a result of the copying, a court is likely to consider this to be a copyright infringement.

Each of these four factors must be considered when determining if the copying falls under fair use.

Fair use has been generally defined as the privilege of people other than the owner to use copyrighted material in a reasonable manner without consent (Henn, 1988, quoting *Rosemont Enters. v. Random House, Inc.,* 1966). School leaders face the challenge of encouraging teachers and students to discover and use the most current research while still complying with copyright law.

In school settings, timely access to tools and resources that enhance the teaching and learning process is of paramount importance.

Congress has developed guidelines to clarify the fair use doctrine. These guidelines establish minimum standards and have won acceptance by some courts. See, for example, *Marcus v. Rowley* (1983). They allow teachers to make single copies of a chapter from a book, an article from a periodical or newspaper, a short story, short essay, or short poem, or a chart, graph, diagram, or cartoon for research or teaching purposes. Teachers may make multiple copies for classroom use if the copying meets the test of brevity, spontaneity, and cumulative effect.

- Brevity is defined to mean 250 words of a poem or not more than two pages of poetry; a complete article, story, or essay of fewer than 2,500 words; an excerpt of 10 percent of a work or 1,000 words; or one graph or one cartoon.

- Copying is spontaneous when done at the inspiration of an individual teacher and when it occurs so close in time to the use of the work that it would be unreasonable to expect the teacher to obtain permission to copy.

- The cumulative effect limitation is violated if the copying is for more than one course in the school; more than one poem, story, or article or two excerpts are copied from the same author; more than three items are taken from a collective work or periodical volume during one class term; or a teacher uses multiple copies more than nine times in one course during one class term.

There are "Fair Use" worksheets available online that can be used as a guide to judge if what you are considering posting qualifies for fair use. In general, fair use is not exact but instead subject to variation and differences in situations. Therefore, it is wise to err on the side of caution if it's unclear that what is posted may be a copyright infringement. Teachers and school districts have faced severe criminal or civil penalties for copyright violations. The Houston Independent School District was ordered to pay over $9 million in damages to a company that created study guides that employees intentionally copied despite their acknowledgment that they knew the material was copyrighted. After a jury verdict the district settled for over $7 million in damages.

Considerations in the Expanded Virtual Teaching Environment

The movement toward the increased use of virtual learning, either by choice or by necessity, increases the need for school districts to be especially cognizant of copyright issues as well as the accessibility issues addressed in Chapter 8. To avoid problems, it may be best to focus on the issue as a whole rather than spend too much effort worrying about every single piece of work posted in a classroom management system. It's one thing to post a video you should not have and quite another to have a classroom set up for a semester with an entire library of hundreds of potential infringements.

It is unlikely that school districts will be held liable for student or employee internet copyright infringements, although they could, but the DMCA indicates that liability will occur only if a district received direct financial benefits and the ability to control the acts of the infringer, who in such cases would be employees in the district. School districts that provide internet service through district servers could be considered an ISP (Internet Service Provider), a fact that could open them to limited liability for copyright infringement.

Some of the scope of these issues are best directed to IT professionals and investigated how a school district manages their systems, such as the potential to be in violation by how information is stored, or if the district itself could be open to limited liability if they are considered to be an ISP itself. That focus is beyond the range of this book.

If the following requirements are met, the TEACH act permits the same activities in distance classrooms that would be allowable in regular classrooms. Performances or displays must be

- At the direction or supervision of an actual instructor
- Part of instructional activities of an accredited nonprofit educational institution
- Directly related to the teaching content
- Made solely for enrolled students
- Properly cited and copyright information provided to staff and students
- Made under conditions that limit the time the copyrighted material is available, and measures taken to prevent retention or further dissemination of copyrighted materials

There is still a gap between what is allowable in a face-to-face classroom and what may be posted online. What follows are some suggested guidelines for online instruction.

- It is allowable to post links to your classroom system but it is not allowable to copy content from a link/website and post.
- It is also permissible to link to articles and journals but not permissible to copy the articles/journals and post. You may scan and post a single article for a semester but should remove it upon conclusion, and should not scan multiple articles or repeatedly scan the same article over time.
- Video and audio clips have time and length limits and cannot be repeatedly used over semesters.
- Posting videos from sites such as YouTube should be linked from YouTube. Take precautions to avoid content that itself may be in violation of

YouTube—typically they remove such content but in some cases that may take time for them to do so.

- It is strongly suggested that direct links to services such as Netflix not be run through a classroom management system.

- Copyrighted web page images and scanned images are allowable as long as they are posted within classroom management guidelines and only posted for a semester and not repeatedly.

- Students may incorporate portions of lawfully acquired copyrighted works when producing their own educational multimedia programs for a specific course. They may also perform or display their own educational multimedia projects and may use them in portfolios for their own use.

- Educators must seek individual permissions for all copyrighted works incorporated in their educational multimedia projects for noneducational or commercial purposes, duplication beyond guidelines limitations, and distribution over an electronic network other than the remote instruction uses described previously.

SECTION D. MINIMIZING RISK

Suggested Risk Management Guidelines

Note: The suggested guidelines should be considered *guidelines* to assist educators in making educationally and legally sound decisions regarding the permissibility of quoting, photocopying, downloading, or making other uses of copyrighted materials. However, digital media may increase the need for obtaining permission. Although copyright owners are under no obligation to respond, most are cooperative. The person desiring permission must contact the author or publisher directly. Permission may be denied, granted with no fee, or granted on the condition of paying a fee. Oral permission granted over the telephone may be valid. However, it is a better practice to have written documentation of all permissions.

- In-service faculty and staff may believe that because they have purchased a book, CD, DVD, software program, or internet subscription, they have permission to make copies of these items. Ensure that all understand that these works are protected by copyright law, and that violation of the copyright law could result in a civil action.

- Staff and students must recognize that material in both hard copy and online is subject to copyright. All parties should be educated surrounding copyright violations and how to comply with the law.

Educational Uses of Music

It *is* permissible to

- Copy sheet music in an emergency situation (providing replacement copies are purchased) and excerpts of no more than 10 percent of the whole work, and to edit (as long as the fundamental character of the work is not distorted or lyrics altered or added).

- Make a single copy of a sound recording of a student performance for evaluation or rehearsal purposes, as long as it is only used for exercises or examinations.

It *is not* permissible to

- Create anthologies or compilations.
- Copy from "consumables" like workbooks.
- Copy to substitute for purchase of sheet music or recordings. (Emergency copying is the only allowable use of copying for performances, and all copies made must include the copyright notice and a citation.)

Off-Air Recording of Broadcast Programming for Educational Purposes

It *is* permissible to

- Make copies of educational programs. (Some offer commercial-free educational programming with copyright clearances.)
- Make off-air recordings to be held for a forty-five-calendar-day retention period. During the first ten consecutive school days, the tapes may be used once in teaching activities and repeated once for reinforcement. After the first ten days, the tapes may only be used for teacher evaluation purposes. At the end of the forty-five-day retention period, the tapes must be erased.

It *is not* permissible to

- Make copies of off-air programming at the request of individual teachers.
- Conduct advance taping in anticipation of possible teacher requests.
- Alter recorded programs or include them in anthologies or compilations.
- Omit copyright notice and a citation from any copy.

Face-to-Face Teaching Activities

It *is* permissible to perform copyrighted material, such as a videotape, without having to obtain a public performance license if certain conditions are met.

- A performance or display of a copyrighted work must take place in a classroom or similar place of instruction (such as a school library).
- The performance or display must be directly related to the curriculum and not connected with recreation or a reward. For example, treating a class to a movie (unrelated to course content) would require obtaining permission.

Transmission of a Performance

It *is* permissible to

- Transmit certain copyrighted works, including singing a song, reciting a poem, reading a short story aloud, or displaying paintings—provided the performance is a "regular part of systematic instructional activities" and "directly related and of material assistance to the teaching content." Also, such transmissions must be received in a classroom or similar place of instruction.

- Perform a copyrighted nondramatic literary or musical work if (1) the transmission is part of the activities of a governmental body or a nonprofit educational institution, (2) the performance or display is directly related and of material assistance to the teaching content of the transmission, (3) the transmission is made primarily for (i) reception in classrooms or similar places normally devoted to instruction, or (ii) reception by persons to whom the transmission is directed because their disabilities or other special circumstances prevent their attendance in classrooms or similar places normally devoted to instruction, or (iii) reception by officers or employees of government bodies as a part of their official duties or employment.

It *is not* permissible to transmit copyrighted plays, movies, and most audiovisual works.

Transmission of Live Performance

It *is* permissible to

- Transmit a nondramatic literary or musical work without having to obtain a public performance license if the performance is without commercial advantage and is nondramatic (e.g., a concert, choral work, or poetry reading).

- Transmit a performance of a nondramatic literary or musical work otherwise than in a transmission to the public, without any purpose of direct or indirect commercial advantage and without payment of any fee or other compensation for the performance to any of its performers, promoters, or organizers, if (1) there is no direct or indirect admission charge; or (2) the proceeds, after deducting the reasonable costs of producing the performance, are used exclusively for educational purposes, where the copyright owner has served notice of objection to the performance.

Multimedia

As more teachers are creating new learning environments in their classrooms and helping students develop educational multimedia projects, it is important to keep the fair use doctrine in mind. The following guidelines are adapted from material developed by Groton Public Schools Media Technology Services.

- Students may perform and display their own educational multimedia projects for the course for which they were created and may use them in their own portfolios as examples of academic work.

- Educators may perform and display their own education multimedia projects for face-to-face instruction, assigning to students for directed self-study, peer conferences, and evaluation.

Material Downloaded From the Internet and Internet Use by Students

Unfortunately, much of the material on internet websites has been posted without permission from the copyright holder. Because the internet is so readily accessible, it is easy to forget that digital material is often copyrighted.

- Alterations of copyrighted works must support specific instructional objectives.

- Fair use guidelines do not preempt or supersede license agreements and contractual obligations.

- Access to works on the internet does not automatically mean that these works can be reproduced and reused without permission or royalty.

It *is not* permissible

- To download copyrighted software of any kind via the internet. (This applies to pirated software, not software you have paid for.)

- To download material from an internet website and store it in an offline browser without obtaining permission from the site's webmaster.

- To paste materials from the internet onto a school webpage or incorporate such material into a multimedia project without obtaining permission.

Computer Software and Courseware

It *is* permissible

- For the owner of a computer program to make another copy or adaptation of the program for archival (backup) purposes

- For nonprofit libraries to lend computer programs, provided a warning of copyright is affixed to the program

You should always read the terms and conditions of license agreements, especially clauses relating to permitted uses, prohibited uses, restrictions, and copying limitations before you use a computer program.

School Library Copying

Note: The DMCA amends Section 108 subsection (a)(3) by adding requirements to the notice of copyright that must appear on a copy: The reproduction or distribution of the work includes a notice of copyright that appears on the copy or sound recording that is reproduced under the provisions of this section, or includes a legend stating that the work may be protected by copyright if no such notice can be found on the copy or sound recording that is reproduced under the provisions of this section. The DMCA also amends Section 108 subsections (b) and (c) by allowing libraries to make three copies (now including digital ones) from their collections for archival or replacement purposes. These exceptions to the single copy limit, still in force under subsection (a), apply only if certain conditions are met.

The library must prominently display a warning of copyright in accordance with regulations from the Register of Copyrights. This notice should be at the place where the copying requests are accepted and be included on its request form.

It *is* permissible for a library to

- Duplicate an unpublished work for purposes of preservation and security or for research use.

- Duplicate a published work for purposes of replacement if the work is damaged, deteriorating, lost, stolen, or in an obsolete format.

- Scan an article from a periodical issue, a chapter, or portions of other copyrighted works and provide an electronic copy to the user.

- Fax or otherwise transmit a copy to the user (however, the library must not retain the incidental copy made to facilitate transmission).

- Print a copy of an article, a chapter, or portions of other copyrighted works at the request of a user if the library interprets the purpose to be *fair use*.

- Download a copy of an article, a chapter, or portions of other copyrighted works to satisfy the request of a user and forward it electronically to the user.

- Make a single copy of a single article or a copy of a small part of a copyrighted work in the library's collections.

It *is not* permissible for a library to

- Systematically reproduce or distribute single or multiple copies to substitute for a subscription or purchase of a work.

- Distribute digital copies in digital format.

- Make copies available to the public in digital format outside the premises of the library.

Coin-Operated Copying Machines

- Libraries (media centers) must refuse to accept a copying order if the fulfillment of the order would violate copyright law.

- Libraries (media centers) must post a warning concerning copyright restrictions. The warning must be printed on heavy paper or other durable material, in type at least eighteen-point in size, and displayed prominently so as to be clearly visible, legible, and comprehensible to a casual observer within the immediate vicinity of the place where orders are accepted.

- A warning should be placed on all coin-operated copying machines in the school building. The warning should notify the user of potential liability for any copyright violation. The content of the proposed warning is as follows:

WARNING CONCERNING COPYRIGHT RESTRICTIONS

The copyright law of the United States (The Copyright Act of 1976, 17 U.S.C. 101) governs the making of photocopies or other reproductions of copyrighted material. Under certain conditions specified in the law, libraries and archives are authorized to furnish a photocopy or other reproduction. One of these specified conditions is that the photocopy or reproduction is not to be "used for any purpose other than private study, scholarship, or research." If a user makes a request for, or later uses, a photocopy or reproduction for purposes in excess of "fair use," that user may be liable for copyright infringement.

NOTICE

The copyright law of the United States (Title 17 U.S. Code) governs the making of photocopies or other reproductions of copyrighted material. The person using this equipment is liable for any infringement.

Please check our companion website for several resources that may provide up-to-date information for educators regarding copyright law and issues: http://resources.corwin.com/principalsquickreferenceguide4e.

ADDITIONAL CASES OF INTEREST TO EDUCATORS

Sony Corporation of America v. Universal City Studios, Inc., 464 U.S. 417 (1984). In a U.S. Supreme Court case, the court determined that selling recording equipment (in this case, the now obsolete Betamax) to the general public did not constitute contributory infringement of copyrighted public broadcasts.

Basic Books, Inc. v. Kinko's Graphics Corporation, 758 F.Supp. 1522 (S.D.N.Y. 1991). In a famous ruling, the copy company Kinko's was found in violation of copyright infringement for creating and selling course packets without seeking any permissions to do so.

Princeton University Press v. Michigan Document Services, 99 F.3d 1381 (6th Cir. 1996). The court held that it is not fair use for a commercial copy business to copy and distribute course packets for profit when a permissible fee market existed.

Universal Studios Inc. v. Corley, 273 F.3d 429 (2nd Cir. 2001). Group was prevented from posting on its website code that circumvented encryption code that allowed copying of DVDs.

DVD Copy Control Association v. Bunner, 10 Cal. Rptr. 3d 185 (Cal: Court of Appeal, 6th Appellate Dist. 2004). Prohibiting the distribution of codes that circumvent encryption is not a violation of speech rights.

Metro-Goldwin-Mayer Studios, Inc. v. Grokster, 545 U.S. 913 (2005). Software distributors could be liable for indirect copyright infringement when they had knowledge that the software could be used to infringe on protected works. The fact that evidence of knowledge or encouragement of possible infringement can lead to liability should be noted for educators and give reason to be vigilant with technology policies for employees and students.

Bosch v. Bell, WL 2548053 (C.D. Ill. 2006). In a higher education case, the court held that it was not fair use for an instructor to reuse the syllabi and course materials of a departing colleague, primarily holding against the defendant for failing to attribute the colleague.

Brooks-Ngwenya v. Indianapolis Public Schools, 564 F.3d 804 (7th Cir. 2009). A former school district employee alleged that the school district had infringed upon a copyrighted educational program that she had created while employed in the district. Affirming the district court's decision, the Seventh Circuit held that although her work was copyrightable, she mistakenly stated in her complaint that the district copied her ideas. Under federal copyright law, it was not the idea that was protected, but rather the original expression of the idea.

Authors Guild v. Google, Inc., 804 F. 3d 202—Court of Appeals, 2nd Cir. (2015). The Author's Guild sued Google for copyright infringement after Google archived millions of works, including those of the plaintiffs. The Court held that Google did not violate the copyright for several reasons, including the fact that Google used a snippet function that serves a different purpose than what the plaintiffs' markets provide. Google providing digital copies to libraries for noninfringing use does not make them a copyright infringer.

Dynastudy Inc. v. Houston Ind. Sch. Dist., 325 F.Supp.3d 767 (SD Tex. 2017). Dynastudy sued the Houston Independent School District after learning that teachers in the district made copies of their copyrighted materials for students. After a jury award of over $9 million was reached, a settlement agreement was made between the district and the company in excess of $7 million.

Bell v. Chicago Cubs Baseball Club, LLC, No. 19-cv-2386, 2020 U.S. Dist. LEXIS 17527 (N.D. Ill. 2020). An employee of the Chicago Cubs retweeted an exact copy of a phrase from a passage taken from a book without permission of the author of the book. The court allowed a direct copyright infringement claim to continue because there was an unresolved question about whether retweeting creates a new digital copy of copyrighted material. The court held for the defendant in a separate argument, stating that the plaintiff had not proven the Cubs had actual knowledge of the potentially infringing activity.

CHAPTER 11

Human Resources Management

Principals have major responsibilities in human resources management and are continuously involved with employee relations. Principals recommend teachers and support personnel for employment, evaluate personnel, and document cases for dismissal or nonrenewal. In this pursuit, principals operate in accordance with often-confusing federal and state constitutional provisions, statutes, regulations, and local school board policies.

CONSIDERATIONS RELATED TO COVID-19

COVID-19 has impacted the human resources functions of school districts and principals. The majority of these issues will relate to employment issues that will be addressed locally by state teacher contract policies, district collective bargaining agreements, and school board policy. Therefore, school districts and principals must be cognizant of their own policies related to sick leave; what qualifies as a workday if quarantined; what liquidated damages may exist related to when teachers resign/retire; what staffing and workload requirements may shift due to virtual learning; what staffing shortages will need to be addressed in the event of high numbers of absences; and a host of other human resource problems.

While these may seem like obvious areas of challenges, the point of emphasis is that how these are addressed fully depends on the state and school district where they occur. Even in cases where federal dollars or services may be provided that address COVID-19 problems, how they are allocated might look very different depending on the school district.

SUGGESTED GUIDELINES FOR PRACTICE

The human resources functions within a school district are often underappreciated. Employees at all levels don't simply appear and show up for work; they have been hired through the services provided

(Continued)

through a process at some level. Capable, ethical, and competent human resource efforts yield positive results for school districts.

Principals are essentially attempting to answer just three basic questions during any job search, regardless of the job description of the vacancy they are in need of filling. These questions are (1) Is this candidate qualified to do the job? (2) How well can the candidate do the job? (3) How will this person fit within our existing needs?

Human resource functions are highly regulated through federal and state laws, as well as guidance by local policy. Not only are there significant areas where principals could make mistakes in the hiring (or dismissing) process that create legal problems, but making the wrong choice in the selection process has negative effects on student learning, school culture, and school improvement efforts.

But for principals, the best way toward school improvement is to hire people who are better than the ones they replace, as well as improve the ones they already have.

SECTION A. HUMAN RESOURCE FUNCTIONS AND DEMANDS ON PRINCIPALS

Principals have key responsibilities related to human resource functions, with perhaps the most vital role being the selection of staff for their school. In some school districts, principals have a high degree of authority and make final hiring decisions, while in other districts the role of the principal is to make hiring recommendations.

Principals also have responsibilities such as the induction and orientation process for newly hired staff, professional development, performance reviews, yearly staffing, efforts to ensure teacher retention, and the approval of leaves. A significant responsibility for principals surrounds employee discipline. In larger school districts, other human resource functions such as those related to salary, benefits, payroll, contracts, and employee separation will be performed by a central office, but in smaller districts principals may oversee those functions as well.

In reality, the responsibilities related to human resources are in many ways the heart of the school district, because without a successful and functioning HR department, the overall district will suffer. To that point, a significant number of leadership standards such as the National Educational Leadership Preparation (NELP) for school leaders relate to human resource functions, including those related to ethics, inclusion, equity, operations and management, building professional capacity, and learning and instruction (NPBEA, 2018). And in another reality, it should be recognized by principals that those HR responsibilities are highly regulated and impacted by both federal and state law, as well as school board policies, negotiated agreements, employee handbooks, and even employee unions.

No matter who makes the final hiring decision, it should be remembered that school employees work for the school board, not the administrators.

Navigating through issues related to human resources is often difficult, with competing internal and external demands frequently complicating the decision-making process. Internal and competing demands could come from school boards, central office administrators, building administrators, as well as licensed and nonlicensed staff. Along with internal demands, external demands from parents, community groups, federal agencies, state agencies, and teacher unions can also impact HR functions and decisions.

The job of the principal is often placed squarely in the middle of those competing demands. However, the decisions made in hiring great teachers and staff are among the most critical a principal ever makes. This text is not intended to replace any book dedicated to educational human resource administration, but this chapter will highlight important considerations principals must keep in mind as they perform these functions.

SECTION B. IMPORTANT LAWS RELATED TO HUMAN RESOURCES

Failure to recognize and implement nondiscriminatory and appropriate procedures is one of the most common sources of liability in human resources management. In a litigious society, principals are wise to consider every employment situation as a source of potential litigation and to conduct personnel business in such a way that legal defense will not be needed.

School employment decisions are ultimately the responsibility of school boards who, by law, select and contract with all school district personnel. However, school principals must be aware of the legal constraints on employment practices because they are actively involved in recruiting, interviewing, and recommending teachers and support staff for employment.

The growing complexity of employment relationships can be traced primarily to the enactment of Title VII of the Civil Rights Act of 1964. Title VII established the fundamental concept of equal employment opportunity, which has become the guiding principle of employment practices in the United States today. Subsequent amendment of Title VII and the enactment of other federal laws governing employment practices have broadened the scope of protection for employees and restricted discriminatory employment practices by employers, including school boards and their administrative staffs.

Federal laws prohibiting discrimination in employment are based on both the Thirteenth and Fourteenth Amendments to the U.S. Constitution. These post-Civil War amendments served as the basis for the Civil Rights Acts of 1866, 1870, and 1871, which were enacted by Congress during the Reconstruction Period to define and protect the newly established rights of freedmen. These civil rights acts are identified as Sections 1981, 1982, and 1983 of Title 42 of the U.S. Code, commonly cited as 42 U.S.C. 1981.

The following brief descriptions of major federal laws that affect faculty and staff selection and management highlight areas in which principals need to exercise knowledge and caution.

Title VII of the Civil Rights Act of 1964

Title VII of the Civil Rights Act of 1964 prohibits discrimination in employment by employers or employment agencies, and in membership by unions, on the basis of race, color, religion, gender, or national origin. Probably the most pervasive federal legislation governing employment practices, this law was amended in 1972 to include state and local governments, government agencies, and political subdivisions including school districts. Not only does the law protect employees from discriminatory employment practices, it also makes it illegal to refuse to hire any individual on the basis of race, color, religion, gender, or national origin. Section 701 of the act was amended to require that women experiencing pregnancy, childbirth, or related medical conditions be treated, for all employment-related purposes including the receipt of benefits under fringe benefit programs, the same way as other persons not so affected but similar in their ability or inability to work.

A major civil rights victory for LGBTQ+ workers occurred in the summer of 2020 when the U.S. Supreme Court held in *Bostock v. Clayton County* that Title VII provides workplace protections against discrimination. Before the decision, it was legal in more than half the states to fire employees based on their sexual orientation, and in some cases, because the right to same-sex marriage was affirmed in 2015 in *Obergefell v. Hodges* five years earlier, it was theoretically possible for an employee to be legally married, yet legally fired based on that marriage even on the same day.

The Equal Pay Act of 1963

The Equal Pay Act of 1963 is an amendment to the Fair Labor Standards Act of 1938, which governs various labor practices including minimum wages and overtime pay. The Equal Pay Act prohibits wage discrimination on the basis of gender among employees who perform equal work in jobs that require equal skill, effort, and responsibility and that are performed under similar working conditions. Legitimate wage rate differences are permissible under certain circumstances, for example, a seniority system or a merit pay plan.

The Age Discrimination in Employment Act (ADEA)

The ADEA of 1967 prohibits employment discrimination against individuals aged forty or older. Employees as well as job applicants are protected under the terms of the act. The act was amended in 1974 to extend coverage to state and local governments, including school districts. The original law provided coverage up to age sixty-five, but an amendment in 1978 increased the age limit to seventy years, and in 1986, an additional amendment removed any upper age limit, with certain exceptions for collective bargaining agreements and higher education tenure policies.

Under ADEA, school districts may not establish any policies or practices that limit the employment opportunities of people aged forty and older, such as identifying a mandatory retirement age. It is also impermissible for a school district to adopt a policy or practice of hiring only beginning teachers, as opposed to those with experience, as part of an effort to control or reduce district expenses.

In *General Dynamics Land Systems, Inc. v. Cline* (2003), the U.S. Supreme Court resolved a split among the federal courts of appeals by deciding that ADEA does not prohibit an employer from favoring older employees over relatively younger employees. The Court found that to read ADEA as barring discrimination against younger workers in favor of older employees did "not square with the natural reading of ADEA."

In 2005, the U.S. Supreme Court struck a major blow for age equality in the workplace when it declared that a bulwark of civil rights laws against race and sex discrimination also protects employees who bring suits in federal court under ADEA. Under the Court's ruling in *Smith et al. v. City of Jackson Mississippi, et al.* (2005), plaintiffs can now bypass what was often the hardest-to-prove aspect of their cases—showing that their employers' discrimination was deliberate. Instead, plaintiffs need only show that they were victims of a policy that caused harm to older workers and went beyond "reasonable" business considerations. This decision elevated age discrimination legally closer to the level of race or gender bias. The scope of discrimination based on age will continue to be narrower because ADEA, although generally modeled on race and sex discrimination laws, allows employers to treat older workers differently as long as they do so based on "reasonable factors other than age." The *Smith* decision applies to all employers (private as well as local, state, and federal government) that have twenty or more employees and to labor unions that have twenty-five or more employees.

The Rehabilitation Act of 1973

The Rehabilitation Act of 1973 is a comprehensive statute designed to aid persons with disabilities in securing rehabilitation training and access to federally funded programs, public buildings, and employment. Section 504 of the act provides, in part, that no otherwise qualified individuals with a disability, solely by reason of their disability, may be excluded from participation in, denied the benefits of, or subjected to discrimination under any program or activity receiving federal financial assistance.

An employer cannot discriminate against individuals with disabilities who are "otherwise qualified" for the particular program or activity, that is, those who can perform the job requirements despite their disabling condition. Individuals with disabilities include "any person who has a physical or mental impairment which substantially limits one or more of such person's major life activities, has a record of such an impairment, or is regarded as having such an impairment." The U.S. Supreme Court ruled in 1984 that Section 504's ban on employment discrimination was applicable to any program receiving federal funds.

Section 504 covers a wide range of diseases as well as mental and physical conditions. The law protects employees who are active alcoholics or drug abusers only if (a) they are in active rehabilitation and (b) their employment would not constitute a direct threat to property or the safety of others.

Many states and Washington, DC, through legislative and administrative action, now specifically include HIV, AIDS, or AIDS-related complex (ARC), within the definition of a handicap or a disability in their human rights, civil rights, disability rights, or fair employment and housing statutes. Sections 503 and 504 of the act protect employees of government contractors who are "otherwise qualified" and who suffer from, are regarded as suffering from, or have a record of suffering from HIV, ARC, or AIDS.

The Selective Training and Service Act (1940)

The Selective Training and Service Act of 1940 (updated in 1994 by the enactment of the Uniformed Services Employment and Reemployment Rights Act) provides certain protections and benefits to veterans of military service. Individuals who have left employment to serve in the military are guaranteed certain reemployment rights. The law provides that veterans, if still qualified, must be restored to their former position or one of like seniority, status, and pay on their return from military service. If a returning veteran is no longer qualified for the former position by reason of a disability, then the veteran is entitled to an offer of reemployment in a position that will provide similar seniority, status, and pay. Employers are exempted from compliance with the law only when the employer's circumstances have so changed as to make it impossible or unreasonable to reemploy the veteran. The law covers private employers as well as federal and state governments, including school districts.

In 1974, the law was expanded to include Vietnam-era veterans. One provision of the amended law requires that contractors entering into contracts of $10,000 or more with the federal government are required to take affirmative action on behalf of Vietnam-era veterans.

A 1982 amendment to the law established that volunteers who serve as members of the National Guard and Reserve Force of the United States are entitled to various employment rights. Congress requested that employers abide by the provisions of the Veterans' Reemployment Rights law, grant a leave for military training (exclusive of earned vacation), and provide such employees the same consideration for job benefits and promotions as they would any other employees. More recently, under the same act, reservists called to duty in the Persian Gulf not only were entitled to reclaim their old jobs on return from active duty, but were also entitled to all the privileges and benefits that would have accrued had they not left.

The Americans with Disabilities Act of 1990 (ADA)

The ADA incorporates, expands, and intensifies the Rehabilitation Act of 1973. ADA extends comprehensive protection against discrimination in hiring, promotion, discharge, compensation, and training to individuals with disabilities as well as ensuring them access to public buildings, public transportation, and other public services. ADA permits employers to identify essential job responsibilities that are central to the job and need to be more than generally accommodated. If a candidate with a disability is not able to fulfill core essential job responsibilities, this core can be used to disqualify that person.

ADA is one of the most difficult acts for schools and other employers to address. Employers are required to make every "reasonable" accommodation that is not financially unreasonable to accommodate physical disabilities. In the area of mental disabilities, the district must evaluate and be prepared to defend any concerns that a mental disability presents (e.g., foreseeable imminent danger to students, school personnel, or the community).

The Immigration Reform and Control Act of 1986 (IRCA)

The IRCA of 1986 requires employers to verify the eligibility of every person to work in the United States. The act is designed to protect the employment rights of American citizens and legal immigrants (foreign nationals who are authorized to work in this country and possess a valid green card).

Documents that can verify citizenship include a U.S. passport, birth certificate, or driver's license (if a photograph is included). It is not recommended, however, that employers ask applicants to verify their citizenship or that they examine documents prior to hiring. Such documents can reveal information about an applicant that an employer has no right to examine under antidiscrimination laws (e.g., race, age, gender).

IRCA's antidiscrimination provisions make it an unfair employment practice for an employer to discriminate against any individual (other than an unauthorized immigrant) because of national origin or citizenship status.

Title IX of the Education Amendments of 1972

Title IX of the Education Amendments of 1972 provides that "no person in the United States shall, on the basis of sex, be excluded from participation in, denied the benefits of, or be subjected to discrimination under any education program or activity receiving federal financial assistance."

In 1975, the Department of Health, Education, and Welfare (HEW) issued regulations governing the operation of federally funded education programs. These regulations were based on HEW's interpretation that the term *person* in Title IX included employees as well as students. Consistent with that interpretation, the regulations included Subpart E covering employment practices.

Although the initial focus of compliance with Title IX was on student access to school activities on a gender-neutral basis, female employees soon began to challenge alleged discriminatory employment practices based on gender, opening a series of contradictory federal court rulings regarding the validity of HEW's regulations and the assurance that employees were, in fact, covered by Title IX.

It was not until 1982 that the U.S. Supreme Court clarified the issue. In *North Haven Board of Education v. Bell,* the Court held that the regulations promulgated by HEW, interpreting "persons" in Section 901(a) of Title IX to encompass employees, were a valid exercise of the department's regulatory authority. However, the Supreme Court also ruled that HEW's authority to make regulations and terminate federal funds was limited to the specific programs receiving the financial assistance. It is clear from the *North Haven* case that employees in federally funded education programs are protected from gender discrimination.

In *Grove City College v. Bell* (1984), the U.S. Supreme Court held that the receipt of federal financial assistance by some of the college's students did not trigger institution-wide coverage under Title IX but rather limited coverage to the specific program. Until then, the common interpretation had been that it applied to all the activities at a school that received federal aid for any reason. Congress restored the broader interpretation of Title IX when it passed the Civil Rights Restoration Act in 1988.

The final aspect of Title IX that has direct application to employment practices is the remedies for violation of an individual's rights under the law. The express remedy under Title IX for a violation of its provisions is the termination of federal funds to the specific program. In 1979, the U.S. Supreme Court held, in *Cannon v. University of Chicago,* that a private cause of action, although not explicitly provided in Title IX, was an implied remedy under the law.

The Family and Medical Leave Act (FMLA) of 1993

The FMLA of 1993 provides every covered employee with up to twelve work weeks of unpaid leave in any twelve-month period in four specific situations: (1) the birth of a child; (2) placement of a child for adoption or foster care; (3) care of a spouse, child, or parent who has a serious health condition; or (4) the serious health condition of the employee. A serious health condition is defined as inpatient care at a hospital, hospice, or residential medical care facility or continuing care of a doctor of medicine or osteopathy or other health care provider identified by the Secretary of Labor. To be eligible for this unpaid leave, the employee must have worked for the employer for at least twelve months prior to requesting the leave and have worked at least 1,250 hours during the past year. FMLA generally includes the following:

- An employee who takes leave under the law must be able to return to the same job or a job with equivalent status, pay, and benefits.

- The employer must continue the employee's health benefits during the period of leave as if the employee were still working. If the employee does not return to work, the employer may require the employee to repay the premium for the health care coverage.

- The employer may require a doctor's certification of the health condition.

- The employee may take the twelve weeks of leave in a block of time or, with the prior concurrence of the employer, intermittently (taking a day periodically or using the leave to reduce the hours worked in a week or a day).

- When spouses are employed by the same employer, the aggregate number of weeks of FMLA leave to which they are entitled in any twelve-month period is twelve weeks, except when the leave is for their own serious health condition.

- The employee may request or the employer may require that the employee use all accrued paid leave (sick leave, vacation leave, etc.) before taking the unpaid FMLA leave. In addition, prior to the employee's taking any unpaid leave under this act, the employer may require the employee to use up accrued paid leave first and count the paid leave taken toward the total twelve weeks leave mandated by this law.

- Special rules apply with regard to staff "employed principally in an instructional capacity" (Section 108[c][1]) in both public and private schools. First, if the instructional employee requests FMLA leave for a planned medical treatment and the leave would be for more than 20 percent of the total number of working days in the period during which the leave would extend, the school may require the employee to take leave for periods of a particular duration or to transfer temporarily to an available alternative position that better accommodates recurring periods of leave. Second, under certain specified conditions, if an instructional employee requests FMLA leave within five weeks of the conclusion of an academic term, the school may require that the leave extend to the end of the term.

- Employers are required to post conspicuous notice of employees' rights under FMLA in all work locations.

- FMLA does not diminish an employer's obligation under more generous state and local statutes, collective bargaining agreements, or employment policies.

Workers' Compensation

Workers' compensation provides benefits to employees who suffer injuries or ailments that arise out of and in the course of employment. Unlike the Americans with Disabilities Act and the FMLA, workers' compensation insurance is mandated by state statutes rather than federal law. Texas is the only state that makes workers' compensation insurance elective.

Because workers' compensation insurance derives from fifty-three different statutes (fifty states, the District of Columbia, U.S. Virgin Islands, and Puerto Rico), the specific provisions that apply can vary widely. However, the basic concepts on which all workers' compensation laws are founded include the following:

- Workers' compensation benefits for employees who suffer occupational injuries or other covered ailments include payment for medical treatment, vocational rehabilitation, time away from work (income protection), and death and burial costs.

- The employer's workers' compensation insurance is responsible for any injury or ailment that is directly related to employment, regardless of who actually caused the accident. However, that liability is limited to the benefits specified in the workers' compensation law.

- Workers' compensation benefits are provided on an exclusive-remedy basis. This means that an injured employee who receives benefits under the plan gives up the right to sue the employer for damages. The trade-off is between guaranteed and timely benefits and the possibility, but not assurance, of a larger settlement as the result of litigation at some uncertain future date.

- Depending on the state's statute, workers' compensation insurance may be provided by state funds or private insurance carriers or through self-insurance by the county or school district.

Principals, like other employers, have a dual interest in workers' compensation claims. The first is to limit the school district's liability for workers' compensation claims by anticipating and preventing situations that could cause employment-related injury. The second is to ensure that when an employee suffers an employment-related injury, the incident is reported and the determination regarding workers' compensation benefits is made as soon as possible. When the school district is liable, workers' compensation benefits are far less expensive than the potential cost of civil litigation and any resultant damage awards.

The primary tenet of workers' compensation is that an injury or illness is compensable when it arises both out of and in the course of employment. The term *arising out of* describes the accident and its origin, cause, and character; the term *in the course of* refers to the time, place, and circumstances surrounding the accident. A claimant must establish both. For example, a custodian who falls from a ladder while changing a light bulb in the boys' locker room and fractures his elbow will likely be eligible for benefits under workers' compensation. His job required him to use the ladder to complete an assigned task, and he was doing the assigned task when he fell. A corollary to this primary tenet is that coverage under workers' compensation does not begin until the employee arrives at work and ends when the employee leaves work; that is, injuries incurred during the normal commuting to and from work are generally not covered. (Your school district's attorney has additional information on the subject of commuting.)

The distinction between employment-related and nonemployment-related injuries is not always clear, and problems can arise when interpretation is needed to determine whether there is a direct causal relationship between an injury and the employment situation.

SECTION C. STAFF SELECTION

School districts throughout the United States have developed several methods of staff selection depending on the size and administrative structure of the particular district. The management style of the superintendent determines the degree to which principals are involved in the staffing process. For example, in highly centralized school districts, teachers and support personnel may be assigned to a building with little or no input from the building principal. However, in a decentralized or site-based school district or in a smaller district, the principal is often involved in all phases of teacher and support personnel selection, from recruitment to recommendation for employment. In many districts, the central office maintains a pool of applications and allows principals to review appropriate files and select and interview candidates prior to making a recommendation to the superintendent.

Discrimination in selection and hiring is a dangerous error for any school district, and when done intentionally it is illegal, as well as ethically and morally unacceptable. Principals need to be aware of their vulnerability to litigation when they act as agents of the board in any preemployment matters. This chapter examines the problems that school districts and principals must avoid in the recruitment, selection, hiring, and evaluation of qualified personnel. A wealth of resources exist related to the hiring of educational personnel that are designed to improve the hiring process, increasing the number of qualified applicants as well as increasing the likelihood of the selection of the best candidates. The purpose of this chapter is to provide awareness of potential legal pitfalls in that process.

Regardless of the method of staff selection used, it is imperative that school principals have a working knowledge of the legal aspects of employee selection. As indicated in the previous examination of legislation, a number of federal laws and court cases have instituted constraints on employment decisions in an effort to reduce discrimination in the workplace. Employment decisions must be based on nondiscriminatory factors or factors that can be justified as legitimate exemptions under the law. It is important to remember that equal employment opportunity laws apply to both employees and job applicants and that all selection criteria and employment decisions must be based on job-related standards. In other words, any criteria used, information required, or interview questions asked must be directly related to required job performance or be justified as a bona fide occupational qualification (BFOQ) for a particular job. Principals and other interviewers are faced with the three-pronged task of recommending the best qualified teacher or staff person (after a careful and deliberate process), complying with a multitude of employment laws (and school board policy), and protecting the rights of all the applicants for an open position.

No one expects to be sued for asking frank questions of a prospective employee. However, litigation in the area of personnel matters continues. This legal activity may be attributed to the public's willingness to go to court but, more likely, is based on an increased awareness of equal employment rights by prospective employees.

Before examining the various facets of the selection process, it is important to note that it is impossible to provide unambiguous guidance as to what inquiries or practices are permissible during the preemployment phase. There are few, if any, categorical rights and wrongs in selection, either legally or professionally. Every employment situation has to be evaluated individually to determine what selection standards are valid and legal. This ambiguity, however, does not relieve school officials of the responsibility for ensuring equal employment opportunities in the school system, while legally and ethically securing the services of the best qualified individuals for particular jobs. Equal employment laws have been, and continue to be, enacted specifically to expand employment opportunities for qualified minorities, females, and others in a protected classification who have been at a disadvantage in the labor market and workplace.

Employment Selection

Improving your school is dependent on great principals and great teachers. The quickest way toward school improvement is making great hires, by hiring better teachers than the ones they replaced, or improving the teachers that are already on staff. The improvement of teachers is not the focus of this text; however, the hiring of quality teachers in a deliberate, legal, and ethical process is the focus.

Keep in mind that when hiring for any position, the hiring team or individual is essentially attempting to answer just three basic questions during any job search, regardless of the job description of the vacancy they are in need of filling. These questions are (1) Is this candidate qualified to do the job? (2) How well can the candidate do the job? (3) How will this person fit within our existing needs?

Often determining if a candidate is qualified to perform the job is the easiest to determine, because some qualifications are mandated, such as required licensures or certifications. However, how well that otherwise qualified candidate can perform the job is more difficult to determine, and that is where past experiences and recommendations play a significant role. The final question of determining how the person fits into existing needs involves knowing your own school culture, how the candidate may fill gaps in current skillsets, and what additional roles the candidate could assume. But the question also frankly comes down to factors that are important yet could cloud the decision-making process and result in missing an otherwise quality candidate, such as simply whether you personally like the candidate. Extra caution needs to be considered with this final question, and proper interviewing and due diligence helps to minimize problems at this final stage.

Hiring presents a quandary at times, because any given candidate may be highly qualified and capable, but they may not necessarily be a great overall fit into the school needs or culture. Or the candidate may appear to be a great fit and someone you would like to hire, yet they don't fully meet the qualifications set forth for your open position.

The following information outlines the major steps in the selection process and suggests guidelines that can be used by district-level administrators and school principals to evaluate the process. The material presented has been adapted to fit the education enterprise and was drawn largely from the comprehensive work of Milner and Miner (1978) and Panaro (1990).

Position analysis: Once it has been determined that a position becomes available and is authorized to fill, a job analysis helps to determine the job description and the skills, knowledge, and abilities needed to perform the job. This additionally develops more valid and fair measurements of job performance in the future. You should be able to justify all standards as necessary for requirements for the job and ensure that there are no listed requirements that might disqualify a disproportionate number of members of a protected class. Some required qualifications are mandatory, but others may be those you have chosen. However, those must be legal to require, and should not be deviated from once you have posted the job opening.

Recruitment: It is essential that recruitment efforts reach the most diverse audience as possible. The more diversity that is already employed in a school or district allows for the inclusion of a greater number of people in the process, which is a part of the cycle to increase overall diversity. Records should be maintained that document these efforts.

Initial applications and screening: It is particularly at this step where implicit bias and discriminatory practices can occur. Steps can be taken to minimize these risks, including training and awareness of implicit bias, as well as overall training in human resource hiring practices to increase hiring skills. In addition, the following are important considerations:

- Do not ask preemployment questions that may lead to charges of discrimination.

- Ensure that all information required on the application form or asked in an initial interview is job related and designed to give information about the applicant's qualifications for a particular job.

- Ask all applicants the same questions.

- Do not use information volunteered by an applicant as a basis for rejecting the applicant if it would be illegal to ask for such information in an interview. Liability for discrimination exists on whether the information was solicited or volunteered.

- Investigate further to determine whether the applicant can be reasonably accommodated to perform the job if the applicant volunteers information that indicates a problem with the applicant's suitability for the position (e.g., a disability).

- Be sure that notes or summaries of interviews with job applicants

  - Refer only to job-related aspects of the position.
  - Use neutral, objective words and language.
  - Have no negative inferences. (The interviewer should be sensitive to the negative inferences that can be drawn from seemingly harmless written comments.)
  - Do not include coded information (e.g., colored-in circle to indicate Black applicant, clear circle to indicate white applicant).

Interviews: Those who are on interview teams should have some type of training, and at the very minimum must be cautioned about illegal questions. If those on a team are skilled at listening, you can have multiple people asking questions, but often even with a team, it may be better to have just one skilled person guide the process. Documentation of the interviews is an essential practice, including dates, times, locations, those involved, and the questions asked.

To gain the most from the interview process, all team members should know in advance what they are listening for, based on knowing the answers to their own questions. What teacher qualities are you listening for? What school culture factors are you listening for? In addition, it's imperative that you allow the person being interviewed do most of the talking. You will learn nothing from a candidate if you as the interviewer dominate the conversation.

Other things to listen for are patterns of success, increasing levels of responsibility, and their own personal educational and personal codes and beliefs. What questions candidates ask is critical, so make certain you provide candidates with the opportunity to do so.

Illegal questions: Case law has demonstrated that the most dangerous questions, from the perspective of legal liability, are questions that the interviewer regards as the most innocent—from icebreakers or small talk from even outside of the formal interview. Interview questions should be based on what was determined in your position analysis and based on your expectations, culture, and demands.

Ignorance regarding the asking of illegal questions is not a defense against claims that such questions occurred. This is a nonnegotiable element to the hiring process. Avoid questions that are not only clearly prohibited but also those you may suspect might be prohibited, because if you suspect the question may be illegal, there is likely no real justification for asking it. Only focus on questions that may relate to a BFOQ when in doubt. Examples of areas to avoid include, but are not limited to, the following:

- *In the area of health*: disability, mental illness, whether currently under a doctor's care

- *In the area of income*: Social Security income, garnishment or bankruptcy record, credit record, alimony or child support paid or received, charge accounts, own or rent home, furniture, car, method of transportation, lowest salary you will accept, spouse's occupation

- *In the areas of marital status or lifestyle*: married, intent to marry, engaged, LGBTQ+, living with someone, divorced, prior married name, maiden name, spouse's name

- *In the areas of race, religion, politics*: race, ancestral origin, nationality or national origin, place of birth, citizenship, parentage, native language, fluency in English, color of eyes, hair, religion, religious holidays observed, belief in the existence of a Supreme Being, available for Saturday or Sunday work, feelings about Equal Rights Amendment, National Organization of Women, various interest groups

- *In personal areas*: age, date of birth, height, weight, gender

- *In the area of issues not related to work*: leave job if spouse transferred, friends or relatives working for the district (lawful if pursuant to an antinepotism policy and there is no adverse impact)

- *In the area of children*: plans to have a family, children under eighteen, arrangements for care of minor children, intent to become pregnant, time off to have baby, resign or request leave, practice birth control, been pregnant or given birth, abortion, female problems, age (to determine whether of child-bearing age).

Reference checking: It cannot be more strongly emphasized that it is 100 percent totally inexcusable to not check references on any candidate under consideration for the final job offer. It is not only professional malpractice, but the failure to check references could lead to a hire that puts others in danger at worst, or potentially with an incompetent or otherwise unsuitable person in a position under your responsibility and supervision. That being said, to not check references puts your own employment in jeopardy and for good reason.

Although checking references cannot guarantee the candidate will end up being the employee you had hoped or expected to hire, having checked the references increases the odds that the candidate will be what you expected. Additionally, you cannot be totally certain as to the quality and honesty of the reference you have received. That problem can be minimized to a degree by checking multiple references. Being able to discern what the reference is saying is important as well. You could be intentionally deceived perhaps, which creates its own set of problems. But you must also be able to "read between lines" at times, knowing how to analyze a generic reference or one filled with ambiguous statements. To ignore or disregard negative references would also be difficult to justify.

Always comply with district policy regarding the authorization to release information by references, as well as other district policies. Finally, the checking of references should be conducted in the same manner for all candidates.

The hiring decision: Don't just look for those who can lead students, but also look for those who can be teacher leaders as well. And even though everyone can improve in their job performance, great talent is inherent and not learned. So can those you hire improve? Certainly. Is there a ceiling to their abilities? Probably.

It is wise to become familiar with hiring decision factors that make the difference in selecting the best candidates. There are factors that relate to such things as ability, motivation, and compatibility that increase the likelihood of success as a teacher. It is also better to avoid a single rating of candidates because the criteria are complex and a single rating risks over- or underrating. It is better to give a range on different measures.

The emphasis in terms of the legal aspects is to ensure that no decision is based on discriminatory elements such as age, gender, race, nationality, religion, or sexual orientation. And amplifying the importance of reference checking, you decrease the odds of a successful hire, and substantially increase the odds of a poor hire and potential legal implications if you do not prepare and do not do your homework in advance of the hiring process.

SECTION D. NEGLIGENT HIRING, DEFAMATION, AND REFERENCING

This section covers three extremely important areas that can easily expose a principal and school district to liability. First we focus on negligent hiring, which, simply defined, is an employer's failure to exercise reasonable care in the selection of applicants relative to the type of position being filled. The second section centers on defamation and referencing. A negative reference can harm a person's reputation and limit or preclude employment opportunities, and if a reference contains any allegations that are proven to be not true, a person's interest in their reputation is protected by laws concerning libel and slander, collectively called "defamation."

Negligent Hiring

Most of the litigation in negligent hiring is the result of an employer's failure to screen applicants, conduct thorough background checks, or discover criminal records. With a systematic mechanism in place for checking applicant backgrounds, school districts add three valuable components to the selection process: additional liability prevention, avoidance of the embarrassment of selecting an inappropriate applicant, and protection for students from preventable risk of harm.

Negligent hiring, retention, assignment, and training are all torts that are based on the premise that schools have a common law duty to protect their students. They are expected to use reasonable care to select employees who are competent to do the work assigned to them. Negligent hiring is a doctrine of primary liability, holding the employer liable for its acts, in contrast to the legal theory of *respondeat superior,* which holds the employer liable for acts of its employees.

Liability is generally determined by answering the "but for" causation-in-fact test. In other words, if the district owed a duty to hire a competent person, and if negligence is demonstrated, the next question is "Did the harm occur because of the negligence of the employer?" This is often referred to as "proximate cause." Was there a natural direct and continuous link between the negligent act and the plaintiff's injury? For example, if a school district hired a person who had been convicted of child molestation, placed a thirteen-year-old female in his band class, and the teacher molested the child, a case can be made for "but for" causation. On the other hand, if a school district conducts a thorough background check and the teacher rapes a youngster from another school in the parking lot of the mall, there is probably not a "but for" causation. The issue is whether the school should have been able to anticipate that an employee would cause harm.

Generally, negligent hiring or retention cases involve acts that occurred during working hours while the employee was doing their job. However, an employer may be found negligent if it can be shown that the plaintiff and the employee would not have come into contact if not for the employment relationship. For example, extracurricular activities, field trips, and sponsored trips could involve negligent hiring or retention. However, there comes a point when the event is so distant from the employment relationship in time and place that the responsibility for adequate supervision lies with the parents.

Background Checks

Schools, daycare centers, sports programs, and other organizations are increasingly using various services to check on the backgrounds of prospective employees in order to protect children. For example, the National Alliance for Youth Sports (NAYS) believes that background checks are "critical for ensuring well-being of youngsters participating in youth sports programs" (National Alliance for Youth Sports, n.d.).

A comprehensive system of background checking, consistently followed, not only provides increased protection for the students, but also bolsters the district's defense should it face a claim of negligent hiring. The theory of negligent hiring is based on the assumption that an employer whose employees are in contact with the public in the course of their employment must exercise reasonable care in the selection and retention of its employees. In 1982, the Supreme Court of New Jersey explained,

> A majority of jurisdictions that have addressed this issue have concluded that an employer who negligently either hires or retains in his employ an individual who is incompetent or unfit for the job, may be liable to a third party whose injury was proximately caused by the employer's negligence. (*DiCosala v. Kay*, 1982)

In order for a determination of negligent hiring to be made, it must first be determined that an employee was unfit and/or caused an injury to another in the course of their work. Second, it must be shown that the school was negligent in hiring that individual. Negligent retention is a cause of action related to negligent hiring. An allegation of negligent hiring argues that the employer knew or should have known the employee was unfit before they were employed, while an allegation of negligent retention argues that during the course of employment, the employer became aware that the employee was unfit. Courts also recognize negligent assignment and negligent training as related causes of action.

Background checks are one tool a school district can use to weed out individuals with backgrounds involving crimes against children. School officials should have a clear understanding of the information that will and will not be found when running a background check. For example, a criminal background check will not identify mental disorders.

Although background checks serve a purpose, they are only a supplement to a careful screening process that includes a careful evaluation of all other supporting documents. Each applicant should be asked to submit letters of reference. All work experience should be carefully verified. Every candidate should be specifically asked whether they have ever been charged with child molestation or whether they were under any type of investigation when they left any employment.

Screening programs should be integrated into a comprehensive preemployment process. School districts should develop a preemployment questionnaire that asks specific questions about the candidate's involvement in criminal activity. Abusers, like any other criminals, move to locations with the easiest targets. If they know a school district is doing background checks, it is less likely that they will apply.

Failure to Warn

Increasingly, plaintiffs are bringing suits against school districts alleging that the district that formerly employed the educator failed to warn the current employer about allegations of abuse. A California case illustrates the current judicial thinking on this matter. The case concerned letters of recommendation that school district officers allegedly wrote. Randi W. claimed that the school district unreservedly recommended an educator for employment without disclosing to prospective employers that they knew complaints of sexual misconduct had been leveled against him. The receiving school district argued that they were induced to hire the educator, who later sexually assaulted Randi W. The Supreme Court concluded that the defendants' letters of recommendation, containing unreserved and unconditional praise for the former employee despite the defendants' alleged knowledge of complaints of sexual misconduct with students, constituted misleading statements that could form the basis for tort liability for fraud or negligent misrepresentation. Ordinarily, a recommending employer is not held accountable to third persons for failing to disclose negative information regarding a former employee. Nonetheless, liability may be imposed if the recommendation letter amounts to an affirmative misrepresentation presenting a foreseeable and substantial risk of physical harm to a third person. The Supreme Court ruled that the defendants could foresee that, had they not unqualifiedly recommended the former employee, the receiving district would not have hired them. And finally, the defendants could foresee that the former employee might molest or injure a student such as plaintiff (*Randi W. v. Murdoc,* 1997).

Nondisclosure Provisions

It is all too common for a district to allow an employee who is under investigation or has been accused of sexual exploitation to resign and apply for a position in another district or state. In many of these cases, the sending district does not tell the receiving district about the suspicions or allegations. In fact, in some cases, there is a negotiated settlement that includes an agreement not to tell future employers about the accusations. This is a classic example of how a "mobile molester" gets passed from one district to another. This all-too-common situation is often referred to as "passing the trash." Generally, nondisclosure agreements contain a provision that allows the employee to resign and prevents the employer from disclosing negative information about the employee. Consequently, future employers considering hiring the former district's employee may be unable to obtain essential information about the employee's fitness to teach. Although these agreements may not always be illegal, they are always wrong. Such agreements conceal information from both the local community and prospective employers. Additionally, they often violate state child abuse reporting laws.

An Illinois case, *Doe-3 v. McLean County Unit District No. 5* (2012), found a school district liable when a former teacher in their district sexually abused students in his subsequent district. The Illinois Supreme Court held the district liable for falsely stating in a reference that the teacher had worked the entire previous year when he had not. Although the case included many technical arguments, one justice noted that the case did not necessarily arise from statutory authority but from the doctrine of negligence.

Especially difficult are situations in which the allegations are never proven. In *Dale v. Stephens* (2007), parents sued two school districts in Georgia, one that previously employed a teacher who was alleged to have committed misconduct in a classroom and another district that later hired the teacher. The previous school never determined any allegations at their school that could be verified and allowed the teacher to resign. Reference calls were elusive and never mentioned the allegations. After their daughters were molested by the teacher while employed in his new district, the parents alleged the previous school passed along a teacher they knew would abuse students. The Eleventh Circuit ruled that neither district was to blame for what happened, and the case was not accepted for review by the U.S. Supreme Court. The accused teacher committed suicide.

Defamation and Referencing

Principals are frequently asked to write letters of reference or to provide a telephone reference regarding a former employee's qualifications or performance. Whether done to support a staff member's application for transfer or promotion or for inclusion in a professional credential file, agreeing to provide a written or oral reference is not something that should be done lightly.

This area of tort liability is somewhat confusing because it often involves two competing rights: the referrer's right to freedom of expression and the candidate's right to the protection of reputation. When these two rights come into conflict, the courts are often asked to determine whose right is more compelling. Principals and others in a position to provide references or recommendations may open themselves to potential defamation litigation if they include statements that the candidate might consider damaging.

Defamation is generally defined as any language, spoken or written, that tends to lower an individual in the esteem of any substantial and respectable group. Written defamation is called *libel*; spoken defamation is *slander*. Although the elements that constitute actionable defamation may vary from state to state, the essential elements that apply in the employment context include the requirement that the communication must be defamatory. To understand what makes a communication defamatory, it is useful to keep three principles in mind:

1. No matter how damaging it may be, no statement of factual truth is defamatory.

2. A false statement is not defamatory unless it damages the reputation of the person about whom it is made.

3. A statement of pure opinion is never defamatory. Pure opinion, no matter how outrageous it may be, is neither true nor false.

   - The communication must be published, it must reach some third party or parties either by spoken or written word, and it must refer to the plaintiff.
   - The third party or parties must understand the communication to be unfavorable to the plaintiff.
   - The plaintiff must have been injured by the communication.

Letters of Reference

Writing a letter of reference sometimes places school administrators on the horns of a dilemma. On the one hand, they feel a professional responsibility to prevent incompetent or unfit educators from gaining future employment. On the other hand, they fear being sued for defamation by a former employee who does not get a job because of a negative letter of reference.

Former employees who bring defamation suits commonly argue that the negative reference contained false statements that injured the employee's reputation. These suits usually allege that the former employer impugned the former employee's ability or fitness to teach. Generally, in order to promote candid and open communication, employers are protected by a form of qualified or conditional privilege. This privilege does not protect the employer who provides information that is known to be false or who acts with reckless disregard for the truth or falsity of the information.

Because of the fear of being sued for defamation, some districts are refusing to provide any substantive information about former employees. Ironically, at the same time some school districts are refusing to provide candid information on employees departing their employ, they are seeking information about prospective employees. In an attempt to foster honest communication and discourage frivolous lawsuits, most states have enacted some form of reference immunity statute.

For a referrer's statement to be defamatory, it must be false and must have a tendency to harm the candidate's reputation. It is not necessary that the statement actually demeaned the plaintiff's reputation; it must simply be shown that if the statement were believed, it would have this effect. Courts usually hold that an untrue statement is defamatory if a significant and *respectable* minority of persons would draw an adverse opinion of the candidate after reading or hearing the statement. If the candidate can demonstrate *actual malice*—in that the referrer knew that the statement was false or that the statement was made with a reckless disregard of the truth—punitive damages would likely be awarded in a typical court action.

If you are asked to write a letter of reference by a candidate, it is a good practice to secure their prior consent to provide the reference in some type of writing, typically even in an e-mail. Such permission may serve as a defense against any malice claim should a future defamation claim be made against you. You should decline to provide a reference to anyone you feel you cannot provide with a positive reference. Additional caution should be taken if you are in a situation where you are the sole individual who can provide a reference, such as with an intern you are supervising. In such cases, make certain that the information you provide is objective, factual, and precise, and where appropriate, make the person fully aware of the contents of the recommendation you will provide.

Additionally, ensure that statements of fact are indeed true and you can provide evidence of your statements, whether they are positive or negative. Negative statements that are factual and that can be proven are not defamatory. Make certain that you also clearly note statements that are your personal opinion, and do not include information based on rumors or suspicion.

ADDITIONAL CASES OF INTEREST TO EDUCATORS

Aldridge v. School District of North Platte (Sup. Ct. of Neb., 1987. 225 Neb. 580, 407 N.W.2d 495). A former superintendent sued the school board for actions taken after he was convicted of third-degree sexual assault. He alleged that the school board took improper action when members met with the school attorney prior to their published board meeting. The court determined that it was not a violation and no decisions were made prior to the meeting when the attorney met with two board members at a time and not with the entire board present.

Fremont RE-1 School District v. Jacobs (Sup. Ct. of Colorado, 1987. 737 P.2d 816). The case involved whether, under existing state law, a school board could lawfully delegate to the superintendent, and through the superintendent delegate to another the power to terminate the employment of a school bus driver. The court held that the termination was lawful, and the court was reluctant to question the legislature and the school board.

Smith v. Dorsey (Sup. Ct. of Miss, 1988. 530 So.2d 5). Constitutional prohibition of nepotism is violated when school board enters into a teaching contract with spouse of board member. The case involved hiring of teachers who were spouses of school board members.

Williams v. Augusta County School Board (Sup. Ct. of Va., 1994. 445 S.E.2d 118). Conflict of interest statutes are designed to create confidence in public entities. The case involved the refusal to hire a teacher who once worked for the school district and after a number of years attempted to be reemployed by the district, but this time was the sister-in-law of the chair of the school board. Although there existed certain exemptions to the statute, the court held in favor of the school board.

Bauer v. Board of Education USD 452, 765 P.2d 1129 (KS. Supreme Ct. 1988). A teacher sued after being dismissed as a result of a reduction-in-force action, asserting that he was qualified to teach another subject even though he had not taught the subject for a number of years. The court determined that because he was certified to teach the subject, under state law he was therefore deemed qualified to teach it.

NEA-Goodland v. Board of Education USD 352, 775 P.2d 675 (KS. Ct. App. 1989). In Kansas, while lunchroom duty is considered a supplemental duty and can only be assigned voluntarily, noontime hallway supervision and noontime recess duty are considered primary duties that can be assigned as part of the primary contract.

CHAPTER 12

Teachers' Rights

School boards have the statutory authority to make employment decisions for the school system. Because principals often take an active part in the enforcement of contracts, they need to understand the various types of employment documents commonly used by school districts.

SUGGESTED GUIDELINES FOR PRACTICE

It is imperative that principals know the procedural due process requirements in their collective bargaining agreement as well as state law related to teacher contracts. Any deviations from mandatory procedures, dates, practices, and deadlines will not only reflect poorly on a principal, but also violate the rights of teachers in the case of employee discipline or dismissal.

Speech rights for teachers also apply to those of principals. Principals should become knowledgeable about the limitations of speech rights that are placed on public employees, especially the differences between speaking as a private citizen or as a public employee.

Develop procedures that will ensure sufficient documentation of evidence that might be used in a dismissal action. In a general sense, you can never have too much documentation, but you never want to have too little documentation.

Be aware of your own conduct and be a positive role model. Remind the faculty and staff that although we all have our own private lives, there are times when that life may be deemed to interfere with the ability to continue employment as an educator.

With any allegations against a teacher, always gather all available facts before making any decisions. You are obligated to ensure due process in order to ensure fairness. If you conduct a thorough investigation, follow the facts, and ensure due process, the likelihood of a correct outcome, no matter what that decision is, will increase.

It is important to note that any correspondence between the school district and a prospective employee may constitute an implied contract under law. The same is true of statements made on application forms and job descriptions or in job postings or advertisements. Even selected statements in personnel manuals have been found by the courts to constitute a contract. Section A looks at the issue of teacher licensure and the types of employment contracts most commonly found in the education enterprise.

Education is a state function, and the state has the power to enact statutes that regulate the operation of schools and the activities of school employees. However, these statutes must conform to the significant substantive rights guaranteed under the U.S. Constitution. These rights are absolute and cannot be obstructed by state constitutions or by state or federal statutes except in very limited circumstances. Section B examines teachers' constitutional rights—legitimate situations that often place principals in the difficult position of trying to balance teacher rights against the rights of students, parents, administrators, and school boards. Section C continues the examination of teachers' rights in light of their exemplar status.

During the past few decades, school districts have seen a significant increase in teacher activism. Teachers have continuously challenged the right of school boards to control their professional and private lives through contracts, bargaining agreements, evaluation, and monitoring. Many of these challenges have been debated in the courts and form the foundation for this chapter.

SECTION A. LICENSURE AND EMPLOYMENT CONTRACTS

Generally, state departments of education are responsible for issuing educator licenses, approving teacher education programs in their state, and accrediting the teacher education units at those institutions. Many states require acceptable postgraduation standardized test scores for teachers as a criterion for gaining a teaching license. Local school boards may add requirements to those of their state.

The term *contract* generally describes a document that has signatures, seals, and witnesses for official notarization. Any written document, however, may serve as a contract between individuals if it is sufficiently definite, extends an offer, solicits acceptance, and denotes consideration. *Consideration* is defined as something of value that is exchanged by the parties to the contract. In terms of employment contracts, consideration is the salary and other benefits that the school district is willing to pay in exchange for the teaching services of the professional employee. The terms of the consideration must be specific enough to enable each party to know and understand their obligations under the contract.

Teachers are generally employed under one of two types of contracts: a term/probationary contract or a continuing/tenure contract. Teachers may also hold a supplementary or an *addendum to* contract. Teacher contracts are governed by the laws of contracts, applicable state statutes, and local school board policies and typically include those elements necessary for an enforceable contract—an agreement including both offer and acceptance, consideration, a description of competent parties, and legal subject matter.

An agreement results from an offer and acceptance between the parties to a contract and refers to the mutual consent by the parties to be bound by the terms specified. When a school district makes an offer to a potential employee, the offer must be made with the intent to enter into a contract and communicated to the offeree in a form that is definite and certain and not presented as an invitation to negotiate.

The acceptance of an offer to contract can be made only by the person to whom the offer was made and must reflect some tangible evidence, either by word or deed, that the person intends to comply with the terms of the offer. The offer may be accepted anytime before it is withdrawn or expires according to its terms.

Teacher contracts are usually straightforward agreements drawn on standard forms that specify the basic elements of salary, position, and length of employment. In many states, these standard employment contracts are supplemented by a master contract developed through a collective bargaining process and ratified by the school board and teachers' union. Such contracts have different names but serve the same purpose. Negotiated agreements, collective bargaining agreements, and master agreements are essentially the same; however, there are differences between the states about how such contracts are agreed upon and enforced. In each case, if all the basic elements of the contract are present, then a valid contract exists. The teacher works in accordance with the contract until the contract expires or the school board terminates it for cause.

It is not necessary to specify in detail all expectations of employment within the contract document. State laws and regulations, school district policies, and general duties are assumed to be part of the contract. Teachers can be required to perform tasks and duties within their areas of competence and certification even if they are not delineated specifically in the employment contract. Although a teacher's legal rights of employment are derived from the contract, additional rights accrue from any collective bargaining agreement (master contract) in effect at the time of contract issuance.

Probationary Contracts, a.k.a. Term Contracts

A probationary or term contract is valid for a specified period of time after which the employee has no guarantee of reemployment. Both parties are released from the contract's obligations at the end of the term specified. Under such a contract, a probationary period is served during which school officials determine whether the teacher merits continuing/tenure status. The maximum length of the probationary period varies, although three years is most common. At the end of the probationary term, the school district must either terminate the teacher's employment or employ the teacher under a continuing/tenure contract.

Regulations concerning probationary contracts usually include statements that, at a minimum, specify that neither party is entitled to specify reasons for separation at the expiration of the contract, unless mandated by state statutes. A district is often only required to provide notice prior to the expiration date of the contract that the contract will not be renewed. Some state statutes or bargaining agreements require a specific date that notice must be given regarding the intent to not renew the contract. The difference for probationary teachers is that they are not entitled to be given any reasons for the nonrenewal of the contract.

Continuing Contracts

The award of a tenure or continuing contract (hereafter referred to as a "tenure contract") requires affirmative acts by both the school district and the teacher (offer and acceptance). Because tenure contracts involve statutory rights, specific procedures and protections vary from state to state. Most tenure statutes specify both the requirements and procedures for obtaining tenure and the causes and procedures for dismissal of tenured personnel.

Often the general public assumes that "tenure" for teachers either means a lifetime contract or that teachers who have attained tenure are somehow "fireproofed" from being disciplined or terminated from their position. Such misconceptions are false. For public educators, the awarding of tenure, or more specifically moved as an employee from probationary status to nonprobationary status, gives the employee due process protections that are not present for probationary employees. In most states, once a teacher attains tenure, it means that they can only be dismissed for causes specified in state statutes and can only be dismissed after some type of procedural due process takes place.

The vast majority of states have some form of teacher tenure. Historically such rights have been put in place to protect the teacher from termination due to noneducational reasons such as holding certain political or social beliefs or having a philosophical disagreement with a school board member. Some states have recently modified or eliminated teacher tenure altogether. In Kansas in 2014, despite the fact that most school districts did not lobby for the elimination of tenure, the state legislature eliminated due process hearings for teachers as part of a school finance bill. Teachers in Kansas had such rights since 1957, and after the move by the legislature, some school districts reinstituted due process in their own districts. The state statute was upheld by the Kansas Supreme Court in 2018.

In interpreting tenure laws, courts have attempted to protect teachers' rights while simultaneously maintaining flexibility for school officials in personnel management.

It is critical that principals understand and convey to teachers that in states with tenure laws, the authority to grant a tenure contract rests with the school board rather than the principal. Although tenure does provide a degree of job security, it does not guarantee employment or the right to teach in a particular school or specific grades and subjects. In many states, teacher tenure statutes do not apply to administrators, although in some states a teacher who was awarded tenure and then served as an administrator, only to later return to teaching, may retain the previously held tenure as a teacher. Tenure may also be school district specific, meaning a tenured teacher employed in a different district may again be considered a probationary employee. As with most educationally related issues, each state will have different laws and different ways those laws are executed in policy.

Supplemental Contracts; Addendums and Supplemental Duty

In addition to a term/probationary or continuing/tenure contract, a teacher may also hold an addendum to contract, more commonly called a "supplemental contract," for services such as coaching, supervising, sponsoring, directing, monitoring, or other similar activities. Generally, the law excludes supplemental contracts from the guarantees inherent in a continuing/tenure contract and from due process requirements.

There is considerable variation in the ways states address supplemental duties, and because courts are bound by the specific facts of the individual situation and their state statutes, there is wide variation in court decisions. Some states view supplemental duties as independent of teaching assignments, some issue a single contract that includes both teaching and supplemental duties, and some states use both single and separate contracts for supplemental duties. For these reasons, it is impossible to recommend or suggest guidelines that fit all jurisdictions. The question of additional pay for supplemental duties is a continuous point of contention between school boards and teacher associations. Typically, school boards want to retain the authority to assign teachers additional duties on an as-needed basis, whereas teachers' associations generally believe that

- Professional employees should have the right to accept or reject cocurricular or extracurricular assignments.

- Acceptance or rejection of supplemental assignments should in no way affect employees' teaching contracts.

- Professional services required outside of the students' school day should be compensated through supplemental salary or overtime pay.

When disagreements about these issues cannot be resolved at the local level, they frequently result in litigation. As courts have ruled on the issue of supplemental duties and supplemental contracts, three key precedents have emerged.

1. Coaching duties must be performed under supplemental contracts; teachers cannot be required to accept such duties as part of their primary contracts, and teachers can unilaterally terminate or not renew their supplemental contracts without affecting their primary contracts. Prior to 1984, it was generally assumed that primary contracts and supplementary contracts were indivisible and the elimination of one type of duty automatically eliminated the other. Teachers were expected to perform all supplemental duties as a part of their primary contract. This assumption was dispelled by the Kansas Court of Appeals in *Swager v. Board of Education, U.S.D. 412* (1984), a case in which the court ruled in favor of a teacher who claimed his teaching contract was unaffected by the termination of his coaching contract. In 1986, the Kansas Court of Appeals ruled that a negotiated contract does not require a teacher to accept supplemental duties (*Ct. App. Kansas, No. 58353*, 1986). In *Hachiya/Livingston v. U.S.D. 307* (1988), the Supreme Court of Kansas ruled that supplemental duties, even when conducted during the school day, are not part of a teacher's primary contract. It is important to understand that this contract law is specific to Kansas and based on the court interpretation of Kansas's statute, and other states' statutes may differ.

2. Teachers employed as coaches are not deprived of property rights when that employment is discontinued. For example, in *Smith v. Board of Education* (1983), the court reviewed a case in which a school board offered to continue two teachers' employment as physical education instructors after dismissing them from coaching responsibilities. The teachers argued that they had tenure in their coaching positions and should have been accorded a hearing before being dismissed. The court ruled that the Fourteenth Amendment Due

Process Clause does not guarantee a coach continued employment in that capacity.

3. Extracurricular duty assignments must be nondiscriminatory and related to a teacher's interest and expertise and must not require excessive hours beyond the contractual workday. An example is a West Virginia case, *State ex rel. Hawkins v. Board of Education* (1980), in which the court ruled that "the board of education's power to assign extracurricular duties to teachers is not unlimited and must be exercised in a reasonable manner."

Employment Requirements

School districts possess broad authority in the establishment of job requirements or conditions of employment for school personnel. Many school districts, for example, require teachers to meet continuing education requirements or have regular physical examinations. Some school districts require teachers and administrators to reside within the district, and others prohibit employees from taking other employment during the school year. Courts have generally upheld school districts' rights to establish and enforce such requirements as long as the requirements are reasonable, directly related to the school district's mission, and consistently applied.

The following is an overview of the authority that courts have generally allowed school boards regarding employment requirements:

Continuing Education Requirements

- Although states demand minimum certification requirements for professional educators, such requirements do not preclude individual school districts from requiring personnel to seek and acquire higher professional or academic standards, as long as the requirements are applied in a *uniform and nondiscriminatory* manner.

- The right of school districts to dismiss personnel for failing to satisfy continuing education requirements has been upheld by the courts.

Health and Physical Requirements

- School districts may adopt *reasonable* health and physical requirements for professional personnel. The courts have recognized that such requirements are necessary to protect the health and welfare of students and others.

- Such requirements *must not be applied in an arbitrary manner* and must not contravene any state or federal laws that protect the rights of individuals with disabilities.

Requirement That Teachers Reside Within the School District

- A school district can require and enforce residency for school district employees if state statutes do not prohibit such a requirement.

- The policy should be clearly intended to promote and support the school district's primary mission and should be uniformly enforced.

Prohibition of Outside Work During the School Term

- A school district may adopt a policy prohibiting outside work by school employees during a school term if the rule is *definite, communicated to the employees,* and *applied in a uniform and consistent manner* to all employees.

Nepotism and Conflict of Interest

- Board policies prohibiting conflict of interest and, as a separate issue, nepotism have been upheld by the courts.

- Nepotism policies prohibit employment of relatives and family members of employees.

- Conflict-of-interest policies prohibit employees from entering into a relationship with companies or organizations that conduct business with their school district either directly (direct sales) or indirectly (consulting or contracting for direct sales).

Requirement That Teachers Be U.S. Citizens

- A state may require an individual to be a citizen or be in the process of seeking citizenship before they can receive a teaching license.

- Immigrants who are eligible for U.S. citizenship but refuse to seek naturalization may be excluded from teaching.

Collective Bargaining and Contracts

Collective bargaining is a common practice in public school districts. Most states have laws that give teachers the right to join employee organizations, and the courts have held that teachers have a constitutional right to organize. Most state laws outline procedures for identifying which organization will have the right to bargain on behalf of teachers. The laws vary widely from state to state but generally require school boards to bargain with teacher organizations about wages, working hours, and other terms and conditions of employment. About half of the states prohibit strikes by teachers. When state law prohibits strikes or teachers fail to meet the specified conditions for a strike, courts have upheld a district's right to dismiss striking teachers. In addition, the courts have issued injunctions against teachers who strike and have upheld the board's authority to impose economic sanctions on striking teachers.

A recent trend has been for state efforts to pull back union and the collective bargaining rights of public employees, including those held by teachers. For example, Wisconsin restricts what can be negotiated and whether bargaining may take place at all.

In both collective bargaining states and "meet and confer" states, courts have generally held that

- Unless prohibited by statute or regulation, teachers have the right to organize for the purpose of negotiating the conditions of employment.

- There are no federal laws that regulate teachers' unions.

- Teachers have a constitutional right to organize, but there is no constitutional right to bargain collectively.

- State laws determine the procedure by which the exclusive bargaining representative is chosen; typically the representative is selected (elected) by a majority of the teachers.

- Teachers cannot be required to join the organization selected as the bargaining representative but, depending on state law, may be required to pay dues to that organization even if they don't wish to join as members.

- Teachers cannot be required to participate in or support union political activities.

SECTION B. TEACHERS' RIGHTS

Although the U.S. Supreme Court has repeatedly emphasized and affirmed the comprehensive authority of states and local school authorities to control the schools, this authority cannot infringe on the constitutional rights of teachers or students. Over the years, judicial interpretation of the U.S. Constitution has expanded individual rights and interests and dramatically reshaped the relationship between the principal and the teacher in employment matters.

The following is an overview of the major tenets of law regarding teachers' rights that are the most common and recurring in litigation:

- Employees have constitutionally protected rights that are not surrendered in public employment.

- A constitutionally protected right cannot be the substantial or motivating factor in a school board's decision to dismiss an employee.

- The exercise of a teacher's constitutional rights to free speech or expression can be balanced against the interests of the school district in the operation of an efficient system.

- Most courts recognize that teachers should not be penalized for their private behavior unless it has a clear impact on their effectiveness as educators.

- Comments made by a school district employee, as a citizen, on matters of public concern generally are constitutionally protected. Employee comments about the internal concerns of the school that undermine supervisors' authority are not protected. When public employees make statements pursuant to their official duties, they are not speaking as citizens for purposes of the First Amendment freedom of speech guarantee.

- Private comments made by a teacher to a superior are constitutionally protected but may be subject to reasonable time, place, and manner restrictions.

- In mixed motives dismissals, plaintiffs have the initial burden of demonstrating that their conduct was constitutionally protected and was a substantial or motivating factor in the decisions to dismiss. If plaintiffs meet this burden, courts will generally enter a judgment in their favor unless the defendant school board proves by a preponderance of evidence that the *same* decision to dismiss would have been reached in the absence of the protected conduct.

Given the legal environment, the principal stands as the primary arbiter in problems that require balancing the legal interests of the public school as an agency of the state and of teachers as individuals. It is important to keep this concept of balance in mind.

Public School Employee Speech Rights

Although teachers have free speech rights, they are limited speech rights. Teachers are considered government actors, and they must be careful about speech that creates the appearance that they are speaking for the school instead of as a private citizen.

When public employees make statements pursuant to their official duties, they are not speaking as citizens for First Amendment purposes. A public employee is not protected simply because it is speech as a citizen on a matter of public concern. The next test is whether there is adequate justification for treating the employee differently from any other member of the public based on the needs as an employer.

Teacher speech case analysis is based on multiple contexts. Key questions need to be addressed when determining if the speech of the teacher is protected:

- Was the employee speaking in the performance of their job duties? (If yes, it is not protected speech.)

- Was the employee speaking as a private citizen, meaning not in performance of their job duties—and was the speech a matter of public concern? (If yes, it might be protected speech.)

- Does the speech interfere with coworker relationships . . . or interfere with the performance of job duties? (The speech may not be protected.)

- Is the speech disruptive in terms of time, place, or manner? (Use your imagination about when and where some speech is made.)

Employees are likely not protected when making speeches about their employer, such as complaining about some job-related circumstance. For example, it's likely not a First Amendment protected right to have a social media message that complains that the principal is incompetent because of disapproval of the daily class schedule. Such a person would not only be speaking in the performance of their job duties but it could harm colleague working relationships. In addition, the class schedule would not be a matter of public concern. Private criticism may not be protected given certain circumstances. A court upheld the dismissal of a teacher who told her Black principal, "I hate all Black folks" (*Anderson v. Evans*, 1981).

As is always the case, there are multiple areas of ambiguity, and no two situations are exactly the same. What about a teacher who is an employee, lives in the school district, but also has a student attending school? When do they remove their employee hat, put on a taxpayer hat, or a parent hat? How can any speech by such a situated person be separated into each category?

Courts balance the rights of employees to speak on matters of public interest against the school's interest in efficiency. Courts have rationalized that First Amendment rights cannot be conditioned on whether the image of the school is adversely affected, in part because such a right would nearly always be denied since challenges to such speech are made when the speech is complimentary about the school or school officials. There are numerous circumstances where the interest of the school prevails, such as when a teacher was fired after publishing copyrighted standardized tests in order to start a debate about such tests (*Chicago School Reform Board of Trustees v. Substance, Inc.*, 2000).

The constitutionality of regulating public employee speech was set forth in *Pickering v. Board of Education* in 1968, when the Supreme Court held that the employment relationship creates different speech expectations. The interest of the state in regulating the speech of employees is significantly different from those related to regulating the speech of ordinary citizens.

Teacher speech issues are similar to student speech issues in many ways. However, employees are on the "other side of the fence" from students, and are agents of the school board and subject to closer regulation. Because they are adults, they hold a different level of expectation and a different level of accountability. Still, there are some elements from student speech that apply:

- Public educational employees have First Amendment rights.

- Such rights are not unlimited.

- The concepts from *Tinker* may apply—could the speech be disruptive or invade rights of others?

- The concepts from *Fraser* may apply—this should be obvious in a school setting.

- The guidelines of *Hazelwood* may apply—this is especially relevant. Speech and actions are frequently connected to the school or related to the educational program.

- Educators have a certain degree of academic freedom, but not unlimited freedoms.

- Circumstances could be different based on local community standards.

Speech that is related to matters of public concern (political, social, other community issues) is more protected. However, there may be local policy against political campaigning in classrooms and so forth.

- Courts will look at the entire record—context, content, manner of form—when determining if speech is a matter of public concern.

- Speech that is related to matters such as employee grievances are not considered a matter of public concern, and are less protected.

The courts will examine if the speech was made as a private citizen or as a public employee.

- When speaking on a matter of public concern, employees have more protection with their speech and are considered private citizens.

- When speaking on matters not of public concern, they enjoy fewer and limited protections and are considered employees.

These elements may become complicated when an issue may be both a matter of public concern *and* may be an employee grievance type of issue, such as alleging the misuse of public funds, or something that may not be a matter of public concern but runs contrary to community standards.

Pickering was the guiding standard until 2006, when it was significantly modified in *Garcetti v. Ceballos*. Although not a school case, the decision reshaped guidance and had far-reaching implications for public employees. *Garcetti* held that there is no First Amendment protection when a public employee's speech is made pursuant to their official duties. In such circumstances, there is no balancing that must occur and such speech may be regulated by the employer. Employers are considered to have heightened interest in regulating speech made in the professional capacity of the employee.

To some, this decision was interpreted to have the potential to have chilling effects on teachers in classrooms. However, others refer to what some have called the *Garcetti caveat*, which recognized that there may be protection for public employee speech related to "scholarship and teaching." Unfortunately for educators, since *Garcetti,* courts have not been consistent and some have been more restrictive of teacher speech. In some decisions, the guidance of *Pickering* has still applied, such as holding that academic writing and teaching performed pursuant to official duties was not governed by *Garcetti*. But other cases such as a special education teacher alleging incompliance with IDEA may be viewed through *Garcetti* as speaking pursuant to official duties.

The bottom line for principals is to be cautious in their own personal actions, but to additionally take caution when considering teacher discipline when there is any connection to speech rights. Educators outside of the classroom (school) have the right to express opinions about matters of public concern even if such opinions are controversial or unpopular. Statements made in private about responsibilities and duties are not matters of public concern. Teachers cannot be punished using a different reason as pretext, such as incompetence, when the real motive is retaliation against some protected speech expressed by a teacher. Whistle-blower laws exist in all 50 states, protecting employees who make good faith reports of violations of the law.

Teacher Employment and Sexual Orientation

Until the 2020 decision of the Supreme Court in *Bostock v. Clayton County, GA*, protections for LGBTQ+ educators were dependent on where a person lived. Although in *Obergefell v. Hodges* in 2015 the right for same-sex marriage was affirmed by the Court, in theory in some states a person could be legally married in the morning and then legally fired later in the day for their same-sex marriage. *Bostock* clarified what had previously been conflicting circuit court decisions and held that the language of sex discrimination in Title VII of the Civil Rights Act of 1964 applied to discrimination based on sexual orientation.

The decision stated, "An employer who fires an individual merely for being gay or transgender defies the law" (*Bostock v. Clayton County*, 590 U.S. ___ 2020). There are many implications for this decision, including, notably, the intentional inclusion of the term "transgender," a group who has been the focus of state statutes that are now working into the court system. The decision not only relates to the termination of employees, but puts LGBTQ+ individuals under Title VII protections entirely, meaning someone not hired or is fired or denied a promotion due to their sexual orientation may use the Equal Employment Opportunity Commission (EEOC) in their action against such discrimination.

One additional outcome could also change school culture as educators do not need to fear losing their jobs and increase their willingness to assist LGBTQ+ students as well as placing more affirmative steps in incorporating sexual orientation and gender identity into nondiscrimination district policies.

The decision in *Bostock* clarifies what previously was considered unsettled law. The privacy rights of teachers have been jeopardized when other factors such as community standards are given greater weight. Two school administrators lost their jobs in Wyoming when a "concerned parent" reported seeing the two women holding hands and entering a Victoria's Secret store in a nearby state. When confronted by their superintendent, they were told that upon investigation the superintendent learned from their previous district that they had been in a long-term intimate relationship. Later in the school year, the district staff was reorganized, and the two women lost their jobs. They were the only staff let go during the reorganization.

When the two women sued, a jury concluded that the school district had violated their Equal Protection Rights, but the Tenth Circuit reversed the decision and held that the school district and the superintendent could not be held liable because the law had not firmly established that firing gay school employees violated the Constitution (*Milligan-Hitt v. Board of Trustees of Sheridan County School District No. 2*, 2008).

Drug Testing of School Employees

A drug-free school environment must include teachers, administrators, bus drivers, coaches, custodial workers, secretaries, and food service workers in addition to students. Some schools have attempted to test all people who work in a school building (Demitchell & Carroll, 1997). There is a distinction between drug testing of students and of employees. Although the primary object of student search is to preserve safety in schools (*People v. Scott D.*, 1974), the testing of school employees is concerned with determining an individual's fitness for employment, and a causeless search may result in loss of employment, breach of contractual rights, and possible criminal charges. School districts have variously initiated policies for school employees that require (a) drug testing of all prospective employees, (b) drug testing of employees who exhibit some signs of drug use (reasonable-suspicion testing), (c) random drug testing of current employees, (d) random drug testing of current employees in safety-sensitive positions, (e) drug testing of employees who are involved in accidents, and (f) drug testing as part of an annual physical examination.

In 1987, the New York Court of Appeals dealt with the issue of drug testing of teachers in *Patchogue-Medford Congress of Teachers v. Board of Education*. The school district required that all teachers eligible for tenure submit to random drug testing. The court of appeals held that the policy was unconstitutional under the constitutions of both the United States and New York State. It then held that the particular testing involved was not reasonable. However, the court did indicate that "under certain special circumstances it may be reasonable to permit the government to search without a warrant on grounds not amounting to probable cause."

Some state and federal courts have used the U.S. Supreme Court's "special needs" doctrine to justify the testing of employees in safety-sensitive positions. For example, the Sixth Circuit's decision in *Knox County Education Association v. Knox County Board of Education* (1998) disagreed with the New York Court of Appeals decision in *Patchogue*, holding that teachers applying for promotion could be tested. In *Knox*, teachers were considered to be in safety-sensitive positions. The policy developed by the school board permitted suspicionless testing for people applying for safety-sensitive positions, including "principals, assistant principals, teachers, traveling teachers, teacher aides, substitute teachers, school secretaries, and school bus drivers." Potential candidates for employment or employees seeking a transfer or promotion were drug tested before the hiring or promotion. The policy did not, however, provide for random drug testing. The court said,

> We can imagine few governmental interests more important to a community than that of insuring the safety and security of its children while they are entrusted to the care of teachers and administrators. . . . [W]hile serving in their *in loco parentis* capacity, teachers are on the "front line" of school security, including drug interdiction.

The court concluded,

> On balance, the public interest in attempting to ensure that school teachers perform their jobs unimpaired is evident, considering their unique *in loco parentis* obligations and their immense influence over students. These public interests clearly outweigh the privacy interests of the teacher not to be tested because the drug-testing regime adopted by Knox County is circumscribed, narrowly tailored, and not overly intrusive, either in its monitoring procedures or in its disclosure requirements. This is particularly so because it is a one-time test, with advance notice and with no random testing component, and because the school system in which the employees work is heavily regulated, particularly as to drug usage.

Courts have consistently permitted drug testing based on *reasonable individualized suspicion*. Reasonable-suspicion drug testing means drug or alcohol testing because of a belief that an employee is using or has used drugs or alcohol in violation of the covered employer's policy, based on specific objective facts and reasonable inferences drawn from those facts, in light of experience.

It has been indicated that drug testing as part of a physical examination is less intrusive than other forms of drug testing. In *Allen v. Passaic County* (1986), the court said that "the requirement of physicals at the commencement of employment or regular annual physical checkups are common and normal employment practices and should not be deemed as rendered impermissible by this decision."

Other Public Educator Employee Rights

Academic Freedom

Teachers have academic freedoms and generally have the right to speak about their subject matter and raise questions relevant to their instruction. However, the school has authority to choose texts, materials, and curriculum, and methods of teaching. This is an area that will be tested in light of new legislation aimed at restricting the teaching of Critical Race Theory in schools.

Teachers are not protected by academic freedom for teaching methods that are not appropriate for the age of the students or when they are prohibited by school policy. In a 1993 case, a court held that schools may restrict teaching methods that are related to legitimate educational concerns, and the school had notified the teacher that the method was prohibited. However, the court did not require schools to expressly prohibit every imaginable inappropriate conduct (*Ward v. Hickey*, 1993).

Freedom of Association

Teachers have the right to be members of organizations as long as they do not participate in unlawful activities. Although this would apply to membership in controversial organizations, this may in some cases run afoul of role model and community standards concerns. While belonging to the Ku Klux Klan, for example, may in and of itself be permissible, it would be likely that a school board would deem such membership, if it became public, to be contrary to acceptable role model standards necessary for teaching children.

Exercise of Religion

With the dilemma of avoiding school violations of the Establishment Clause against violating the Free Exercise Clause, the issue of freedom of religion for employees is a frequent occurrence. Teachers have free exercise rights, but they themselves are also obligated to avoid violating the Establishment Clause when their actions may appear to endorse, promote, or even coerce students in areas of religion. When does the right to practice one's religion violate the obligation to not promote or endorse a particular religion?

Although further discussed in Chapter 9, it's important to note that reevaluating employee religious freedom appears to be headed for the agenda of the current Supreme Court, especially related to employees who may view expanded LGBTQ+ and transgender rights as clashing with their own personal religious beliefs.

Political Campaigning

Teachers can be prohibited by school policy from promoting political candidates during class although, unless specifically prohibited, they may wear political buttons or other items promoting a candidate as long as they do not attempt to indoctrinate or coerce students while doing so.

Holding Political Office

State laws differ whether public school teachers can at the same time hold political office. In Kansas, current employees may not be a member of the school board that employs them. Some courts have held that it is reasonable for teachers to resign before running for any office. Critics point that as long as running for or holding office while an employee does not interfere with the operation of the school, such restrictions deprive teachers of participation in governance.

Personal Appearance

Teachers generally do not have the right to dress as they wish as long as any policy is not otherwise discriminatory. Disciplinary action against a teacher for dress or grooming policy violations should include adequate notice that they are in violation of such policy.

Right to Privacy

Teachers have a constitutional right to privacy, and discipline or dismissal for personal conduct outside of the school and in their private life may encroach on that right. Because of the uncertainty concerning the definition and amplitude of privacy rights, as well as their inexplicit constitutional basis, court decisions provide an inconsistent pattern or basis on which to use privacy rights as a defense against violations of a teacher's right to employment. The courts have, however, tended to agree on several points of law. Courts have ruled that the conduct of an educator's private life must be just that: private. They hold that there exists not only an educator's right to privacy but also an educator's duty of privacy. As a result, it appears that the educator's duty to maintain privacy within the school environment is absolute. If school employees value their privacy and their positions as educators, allowing their private lives to become public is a choice that may bear consequences.

In addition, a nexus must be evident between educators' private acts and their work in the school in order for the private acts to have any bearing on their employment. If a nexus cannot be shown—that is, that something in the educator's private life has reduced the educator's ability to maintain discipline, present curriculum, or in some other way perform their professional duties—then actions in the educator's private life may not be usable in a disciplinary or termination proceeding.

Courts have also agreed that idle speculation is usually considered to be an infringement on one's private life. Although a school board can inquire into the character, integrity, and personal life of its employees, reprimands or dismissals must be based on supported facts that are neither arbitrary nor capricious.

Student Teachers, Interns, and Substitute Teachers

Generally, states permit local school districts to enter into student teacher contracts with colleges and universities for the practical training of prospective teachers. In some states, the state board of education issues student teaching certificates and permits student teachers to assume certain responsibilities as fully certificated teachers. Regardless of how student teachers or interns are assigned, principals need to understand that a potential for liability exists with student teachers just as it does with certificated teachers. Student teachers are ultimately the responsibility of the principal, acting in concert with the college or university and the assigned supervising teacher.

The legal problems involving student teachers are generally the same types of problems that affect certificated teachers. Among the most frequently reported are negligence that results in an injury to a student, hitting students or use of corporal punishment, and felony arrest or conviction. In addition, student teachers have been involved with the courts as a result of school district and college or university decisions involving grades in student teaching, discrimination against student teachers, and withdrawal of student teachers from assignments.

One area of continuous concern for principals is determining whether or not student teachers can be used as substitutes for their supervising teachers or other teachers in the school building. Local school district policies often do not address this issue. Principals should not use student teachers in this manner without consulting superiors and the student teacher's college or university supervisor. Principals should approach the use of student teachers as substitutes with caution and in accordance with local school district policies.

Generally, depending on individual state statutes, the courts have held that a student teacher may substitute under the following kinds of circumstances:

- A substitute teacher is not immediately available.

- The student teacher has been in that student-teaching assignment for a specified minimum number of school days.

- The supervising teacher, the principal of the school, and the university supervisor agree that the student teacher is capable of successfully handling the teaching responsibilities.

- A certificated classroom teacher in an adjacent room or a member of the same teaching team as the student teacher is aware of the absence and agrees to assist the student teacher if needed.

- The principal of the school or the principal's representative is readily available in the building.

- The student teacher is not paid for any substitute service. (This matter is negotiable in some jurisdictions.)

It is imperative that schools ensure that any person selected to do substitute work has had a background check. Substitute teachers should be contracted under the same preconditions as a full-time teacher. Substitute teachers are held to the same duty of care as full-time teachers and are liable for foreseeable injuries that are caused by their negligent acts.

Reduction in Force (RIF)

The courts have generally recognized the following as reasonable rationale for school districts to implement an RIF: enrollment decline; fiscal, economic, or budgetary basis; reorganization or consolidation of school districts; change in the number of teaching positions; curtailment of programs, courses, or services; or other good or just cause. Because staff salaries constitute the major portion of the operating budget, eliminating faculty and administrative positions through an RIF clearly results in reduced school district expenditures. However, RIF actions have also resulted in a proliferation of court actions. Most states have enacted legislation concerning staff reduction; however, the scope and specificity of RIF provisions vary from state to state. (*Note*: Although RIF is the standard term used for the public sector, some school districts use private-sector terms such as *downsize* or *right size*, and others use the term *de-staff*.)

SECTION C. TEACHER DISCIPLINE AND DISMISSAL

The legal doctrine that suggests that a teacher serves as an exemplar or role model for students rests in the belief that students, in part, acquire their social attitudes and other important behaviors by replicating those of their teachers. As early as 1885, courts accepted this assumption as "self-evident fact." If it is accepted that the examples set by teachers and others in the education enterprise affect students, then a determination must still be made concerning what personal conduct is permissible and what may not be permissible and warrants disciplinary or employment action. Standards of acceptable behavior vary widely from community to community and constantly change over time.

Although the U.S. Constitution does not specifically grant a person a right to employment, the courts have derived a right to work from the Fourteenth Amendment. As early as 1923, the Supreme Court declared that the concept of liberty includes the right of the individual "to engage in the common occupations of life" (*Meyer v. Nebraska,* 1923). If the state denies a person the right to work, due process must be provided.

It has been established that tenured teachers have both property and liberty interests in their employment contracts and must be afforded due process protection. Property interests are legitimate claims or entitlements to continued employment under contract. Term contract teachers have property interests during the specified period of their contract. The granting of tenure or a continuing contract expands this property interest to include a right to continued employment. In other words, once a teacher earns tenure or a continuing contract, the teacher may not be denied continued employment without due process.

What may be considered a liberty or property interest is particularly open to interpretation, allowing for a wide variety of protected conduct in areas considered to be fundamental rights, such as religion, speech, press, and right to work.

Some dismissal cases take on constitutional dimensions when teachers allege a violation of a protected right. In such cases, the court must balance the constitutional rights of the individual teacher with the needs and interests of school authorities to maintain employee discipline, order, and proper supervision of public schools.

In *Miles v. Denver Public Schools* (1991), a teacher was suspended and given a letter of reprimand for a comment made in a ninth-grade government class. When asked by a student why he thought the quality of the school had declined, he commented, "I don't think in 1967 you would have seen two students making out on the tennis court." The comment was related to rumors that were going around the school that two students had sex on the tennis court. The teacher sued on the basis of his speech rights and academic freedom, but the Tenth Circuit ruled, using a *Hazelwood* analysis, that his comments were school-sponsored expression and that the school had a legitimate pedagogical interest in controlling the speech. The court held that teachers should not make statements that embarrass students among their peers. Additionally, the court held that there is no constitutional right to academic freedom.

Extreme sarcasm is not protected speech. The termination of the contract was upheld in a case where a teacher had multiple incidents of making inappropriate sarcastic comments to students (*School District Board of Directors v. Lundblad*, 1995). In response to a student's oral presentation reviewing a film where the student stated he would rather be taken to the parking lot and beaten to death than have to watch the film again, the teacher wrote on his paper, "I'd be glad to take you out to the street and beat you to death. The way your face looks, I think someone already has." At the time, the student was suffering from a severe acne outbreak. In another incident he told a student that the student would go bankrupt if he ever tried to sell himself for sex, and that if he did his brother would be his first customer. The teacher admitted in a deposition that on a paper submitted by a student regarding teenage suicide, he wrote, "for extra credit why don't you try it?"

Teacher Discipline or Termination of Employment for Cause

Courts have consistently ruled that when educators subscribe to personal habits or behaviors that may be contrary to currently accepted norms, they can place their positions at risk. The courts have agreed that no amount of standardization of teaching materials or lesson plans can eliminate the personal qualities teachers bring to the learning environment. Furthermore, educators serve as role models for their students, exerting a subtle but important influence over students' perceptions and values. Through both the presentation of course materials and the examples they set, educators have the opportunity to influence the attitude of students toward government, the political process, and a citizen's social responsibilities. The courts are in agreement that this influence—this exemplar status—is critical to the continued good health of a democracy.

Because public schools are perceived as having the moral development of the child as one of their primary goals, society has historically seen teachers as guardians of community morals and expected them to conduct their personal lives accordingly. Society's desire to ensure the highest level of moral excellence often takes statutory or contractual form.

General cultural values are those commonly accepted by the majority of a society. Such values, often referred to as the "core value system," are generally well defined, traditional, and relatively stable. Society expects school districts to support and preserve the traditional values inherent in the core of the society. However, teachers may, just as other members of society, elect to adopt patterns, values, and ideals that are considered alternatives to the traditional or core values. In this event, when the issue of individual freedom versus institutional responsibility is in dispute, termination is often the result.

The vagueness doctrine is well defined in law, and the courts have generally held that when a rule, policy, or statute forbids or requires individuals to do something using terminology so vague that individuals of common intelligence must guess at its meaning and may differ as to its application, the rule violates due process of law. This doctrine is significant when school districts and principals develop policies, rules, and regulations for the district or individual schools.

Due process requires that the dismissal of a teacher or other limitation of property or liberty be justified by demonstration of a rational nexus between the proscribed activity and a serious disruption of the education process. A *nexus* is commonly defined in teacher employment issues as a connection or link between personal conduct and fitness to teach. Considerations in determining whether or not a nexus exists often include the following:

- The likelihood that the conduct has or may adversely affect students or fellow teachers

- The degree of such adversity now or anticipated

- The proximity or remoteness in time of the conduct

- Extenuating or aggravating circumstances, if any, surrounding the conduct

- The praiseworthiness or blameworthiness of the motives resulting in the conduct

- The extent to which disciplinary action may cause an adverse impact or "chilling effect" on the constitutional rights of the teacher

Principals must keep in mind that there are differences between the states as well as local school districts, and what may be an action of a teacher that requires discipline and/or dismissal in one school district may not be in another. For the purposes of this text, general examples rather than specific examples are highlighted.

Areas that most commonly require disciplinary action or termination fall under the following causes:

- *Incompetency.* Although *incompetency is not a disciplinary issue,* there may be cause for termination due to incompetency. This is also sometimes called inefficiency and could be due to a range of reasons—ineffectiveness, inability to teach or maintain order, unfitness to teach, and so forth.

- *Insubordination.* This is the willful disregard or refusal to obey reasonable directives. This area is very broad and includes dishonesty. Such acts are usually intentional, but could be inadvertent. Examples include not following school board policy, administrative directives or rules, or making false reports of sick leave, grading, or misuse of property and funds. A pattern may not be required for discipline or termination because sometimes one act is egregious enough in nature to require such action.

- *Immorality.* In many cases, the inappropriate behavior is obvious, such as sexual or other abuse of students, and at other times it may not be. As an example, smoking recreational marijuana is legal in some states, and remains illegal in others. This is an area where community standards may play a role. The question in that example is when is smoking marijuana serious enough to warrant termination, and when is it something that is completely ignored?

- *Poor role model.* This may be at times related to the immorality question, while other times it is not. Teachers have lost their jobs because of behavior outside of school that is deemed to be beyond what is acceptable behavior for the profession of teaching, such as being arrested, or for acts of public intoxication.

- *Incapacity.* This may also not be a disciplinary issue but still a reason for termination of contract. There may be an unfitness to teach concern due to addiction, an anger management issue, a mental health issue, and so forth. Such causes may at times edge against disability rights, so principals must be mindful and respectful of such rights of employees.

- *Unprofessional conduct.* This is a general term that could also relate to some of the above categories. Some state statutes provide for a general category of reasons for dismissal under the cover of *just or good cause* or *conduct unbecoming a teacher* (unprofessional conduct). This umbrella approach allows school boards to dismiss employees for a great variety of activities. Because it would be impossible for a state legislature to delineate all possible reasons to justify a dismissal, legislators in such states believe that it is necessary for school boards to have some flexibility in applying employment functions. Not all states allow the use of just cause because of its broad interpretation. Where applicable, just cause is generally defined as a cause that bears a reasonable relationship to a teacher's unfitness to discharge the duties assigned or is in a reasonable sense detrimental to the students being taught.

- *Teacher's misuse of social media.* While this also relates to the earlier listed categories, the potential for the need of disciplinary action or termination of contract is prevalent enough to be highlighted. Social media likely involves freedom of speech issues as well as potentially off-campus behavior, which may or may not complicate the decisions involved. Depending on the content, inappropriate social media messages could be categorized as unprofessional conduct; poor role model behavior; an act of immorality; or even an act of insubordination if the posting of the message was in violation of school policy.

Additional discussion of some of these areas is warranted.

Incompetence

Teachers who continue to perform poorly in the classroom or to demonstrate an inability to follow standard operating procedures after reasonable assistance has been given should be nonrenewed or terminated. However, *incompetence,* the general term used to cover a variety of performance problems, needs clarification before it can safely be used as grounds for dismissal. The courts alone decide what constitutes incompetence after considering all the particular facts of each case. Although the courts have given broad interpretation to the term, incompetence is generally defined as a lack of physical, intellectual, or moral ability; insufficiency; inadequacy; or specific lack of legal qualifications or fitness. School boards have offered a wide variety of reasons to substantiate charges of incompetence, and the courts have generally found that the following conduct is sufficient to sustain dismissals based on incompetence:

- Excessive tardiness and absence during the school year with no excuse

- Lack of classroom management, control, or discipline, including unreasonable discipline

- Failure to provide expected leadership as described in a job description

- Lack of knowledge necessary for competent instruction and inability to convey such knowledge effectively

- Refusal of a teacher to allow supervisory personnel to enter the teacher's classroom

- Willful neglect of duty

Some specific examples may help to clarify the concept of incompetence. In one instance, a school board cancelled the contract of a teacher with fourteen years of experience on the basis of incompetence and insubordination. Evidence presented at the hearing showed that the teacher willfully refused to follow reasonable rules and regulations, refused to follow grading procedures, engaged in several heated discussions with the supervisor, and blatantly refused to submit to the supervisor's authority. The court, in *Aaron v. Alabama State Tenure Commission* (1981), found the evidence sufficient to support the conclusion that the teacher was *both* incompetent and insubordinate. Among the reasons used by another school board to dismiss a teacher for incompetence were excessive lateness, negligent conduct that resulted in a minor classroom fire, and instructional deficiencies (*Levyn v. Amback,* 1981).

Some school boards have used the results of student grades or student scores on standardized achievement tests as a means to justify a charge of incompetence on the part of a teacher (*Scheelhasse v. Woodbury Central School District,* 1973). The Eighth Circuit Court of Appeals, in *Karstetter v. Evans* (1971), reversed a federal district court in Iowa and held that low student scores on standardized achievement tests were a lawful reason for a school board to consider in making a decision not to renew a teacher. In a similar case, a federal district court in Texas ruled that a teacher's procedural due process rights were not violated when the school board introduced the low achievement of the teacher's students as evidence. It is important to note that the courts have consistently held that a teacher's competence or incompetence must be measured by the same standards required of other teachers as demonstrated by yearly evaluations. In other words, a teacher's performance is not measured in a vacuum or against a standard of perfection but is measured against the *standard* required of others performing the same or similar duties.

Insubordination

Insubordination generally refers to the failure of an employee to submit to the reasonable and lawful authority of a superior or to an employee's willful disregard of express or implied directions of the employer and a refusal to obey reasonable orders. This is the most common and simplistic rationale advanced by school officials in dismissal cases based on insubordination. However, insubordination cannot be judged in the abstract. As with all other reasons for termination, specific evidence is necessary to substantiate a charge of insubordination. The courts have generally agreed that school employees are insubordinate when they *willfully refuse to obey a reasonable and lawful order given by a superior* or one who has the authority to give such orders.

Charges of insubordination are generally *not supportable* in court actions if

- The alleged conduct was not proved.
- The existence of a pertinent school rule or a supervisor's order was not proved.
- The pertinent rule or order was not violated.
- The teacher or employee tried, although unsuccessfully, to comply with the rule or order.
- The teacher's or employee's motive for violating the rule or order was admirable.
- No harm resulted from the violation.
- The rule or order was unreasonable.
- The rule or order was beyond the authority of its maker.
- The enforcement of the rule or order revealed possible bias or discrimination against the teacher or employee.
- The enforcement of the rule or order violated First Amendment or other constitutional rights.
- The rule or order was unlawful.

Immoral Conduct

Because it is generally believed that the character of the teacher is of fundamental importance in children's development, school boards feel that they can demand that teachers conform to the boards' interpretations of community values. Teachers who adopt values that conflict with the mores of their communities' school boards are likely to place their teaching positions at risk. The key question is not whether or not teacher actions are immoral but whether or not they negatively affect the education process in a particular school district in a particular location.

Immorality, moral turpitude, unfitness to teach, conduct unbecoming of a teacher, teacher misconduct, violation of a code of ethics, and subversive activity are common statutory grounds for the dismissal of a teacher when community values conflict with teacher values or lifestyles.

School districts that attempt to develop guidelines in this area quickly find that courts tend to leave it to communities to define "immorality," and the courts' decisions generally reflect core values. To make the development or recommendation of definitive guidelines even more difficult, the courts modify their definitions as societal values change. What was once cause for dismissal as an immoral act may later be seen as acceptable behavior. *Immorality* is a value-laden word that is defined in a subjective manner. Behavior that does not conform to the established norm is defined as deviant. Deviant behavior of school personnel inside or outside of the school may be cited as cause for dismissal.

The following is an overview of legal tenets generally followed by the courts with regard to questions of teacher immorality.

- The conduct of a teacher or any public employee outside the job may be examined, but disciplinary action against the employee based on that conduct is proper *only* when there is a proven rational nexus between the conduct and the duties to be performed.

- Courts have ruled that the conduct of a teacher's private life must be just that: private. They hold that not only do teachers have a right to privacy but they also have a duty to keep their private lives private.

- The conduct of a teacher or any other public employee ceases to be private in at least two circumstances: when the conduct directly affects the performance of the occupational responsibilities of the employee and when, without contribution on the part of the school officials, the conduct has become the subject of such notoriety as to significantly and reasonably impair the capability of the particular teacher or other employee to discharge the responsibilities of the teaching or other public position.

- The courts demand proof that a teacher's private, personal actions directly affected the teacher's classroom performance, relationship with students, and overall teaching effectiveness. Without such proof, a court would likely say that, at most, the evidence may raise a question regarding the teacher's good judgment in personal affairs.

- The courts have approved inquiries by boards of education into the personal associations of teachers, and school boards may legitimately scrutinize teachers as to any matters that might have an adverse effect on students as demonstrated by a direct nexus between the teacher's out-of-school behavior and the teacher's effectiveness in the classroom.

- Unconventional sexual behavior does not, according to judgments in a number of cases nationwide, indicate unfitness to teach, and a clear relationship must be shown between the conduct of a teacher and the teacher's job performance and effectiveness.

Immorality could apply even in cases where the conduct in question was not completely directly related to behavior of the teacher in question. In *Kari v. Jefferson County School District* (1993), a teacher was dismissed for "immorality" and "neglect of duty" after her house was raided by the police and evidence of marijuana growing and selling was uncovered. The teacher's husband grew and sold marijuana from their home for nearly two years, with the knowledge of the teacher. She urged her husband to seek counseling but never took other action to stop the operation because she did not want her family to break up.

Although she was acquitted of possessing and selling drugs, the school district felt she would no longer have credibility in her job as an antidrug counselor. Although she was ultimately reinstated, the issue became whether her failure to report the marijuana sales by her husband in their home constituted a "neglect of duty."

SECTION D. HEARINGS AND PROCEDURAL DUE PROCESS

With any consideration of discipline for teachers, appropriate steps must be taken throughout the process, and while it should go without saying that recognizing constitutional and statutory rights of teachers must be respected, adherence to collective bargaining agreement language and school board policy is essential and mandatory. Discipline procedures should be progressive, with policy in place that has steps for verbal and written warnings, sanctions and remediation, as well as the procedures required for dismissal. Some behaviors, as noted above, may be serious enough to move for immediate dismissal, but even under those circumstances, following all contractual and procedural steps is mandatory.

The Fifth and Fourteenth Amendments to the U.S. Constitution (the Fifth applying to activities of the federal government and the Fourteenth to those of the states) have been the sources of the greatest volume of constitutionally based education litigation. The Fourteenth Amendment states that no person shall be deprived of "life, liberty, or property, without due process of law." As courts have interpreted this amendment over time, they have added requirements that procedures must not be arbitrary, unreasonable, or discriminatory in policy or practice. Essentially, then, this amendment demands *fair* procedures.

Courts view due process in two ways: substantive due process and procedural due process. *Substantive due process* requires that the policies, rules, or regulations be fair in and of themselves. The basic attributes of substantive due process may be best understood by those features showing its absence. A rule, law, regulation, policy, or action violates substantive due process when it is overly broad or unnecessarily vague, is arbitrary or capricious, invades the protected zone of personal privacy, is unrelated to a valid education objective, or does not use reasonable means to achieve the objective.

Procedural due process means that the policies, rules, and regulations are applied in a fair manner. Procedural due process encompasses such basics as the right to timely, clear notification of charges and their basis and the right to an impartial hearing on the charges in which the accused is given an opportunity to defend against them. As the severity of the potential penalty increases, so does the extent of due process procedural protection.

In determining what process is due, courts apply a balancing-of-interest test that weighs the interests of society, as represented by the school, against the rights of the individual teacher. This test does not have complex technical rules; rather, it is an application of theory about what is fair and just that allows considerable latitude in judicial examination and judgment.

The basic elements of procedural due process are the notice of the charges and the hearing. The procedural aspects of a hearing generally are delineated in state statute or school board policy and typically include the following:

- A notice of charges

- Representation by counsel

- Protection against self-incrimination

- Cross-examination of witnesses

- Compulsory attendance of witnesses

- Access to records and reports in the school district's possession

- Record of the hearing

- The right to appeal

Aspects that often cause legal problems are the standard of proof, burden of proof, evidence, and the impartiality of the school board as the hearing body. *The burden of proof in establishing just and sufficient cause for nonrenewal rests with the school district.* If an aggrieved party is not satisfied with the results of a hearing and files a lawsuit, the court may reason that because the teaching contract was a property right requiring a due process hearing, the school board has the burden to establish the basis for its adverse decision. In the process of examining the school districts' procedures, courts will closely scrutinize any procedural oversight that had the effect of denying a dismissed employee a substantive right.

State statutes or local board policies generally establish professional employees' rights to a hearing and the requirements for notice of nonrenewal or termination, including deadlines for notification, form and content of the notice, and parties designated to issue the notice.

A common challenge from aggrieved employees is whether or not certain evidence used against a teacher by school officials is proper. Although the rules of evidence applicable in court proceedings do not apply in a *strict* sense to dismissal hearings, it is *imperative* that administrators understand that any evidence presented must be substantial, relevant to establish the alleged facts, developed in a constitutionally approved way, documented (which, in its simplest form, means recording time, date, and place, with witnesses listed, if any), and limited to the charges made.

In addition, aggrieved employees often charge that school boards serving as hearing bodies are biased and unfair in their actions. The courts have ruled that familiarity with the facts of a case gained by a school district board of education in the performance of its statutory role does not disqualify them as a decision-making body. A board member cannot be disqualified simply because the member has taken a position, even in public, on a policy issue related to the dispute. To deny a school board or a school board member the authority to conduct hearings concerning aggrieved teachers requires convincing proof that the board or member is so corrupt with prejudice and partiality that the board or member is incapable of rendering a fair determination on the evidence presented.

SECTION E. PERFORMANCE EVALUATION

Although the primary purpose of employee evaluations is to improve the quality of instruction, from a strictly legal point of view, the purpose of employee evaluations is to provide justification (due process) for any action the school district takes in regard to its employees.

Prior to the education reform movement in the 1980s, there was little legislation that directly focused on teacher evaluation. Although the stated purpose of every system of teacher evaluation is the improvement of instruction, every educator understands that the evaluation system is going to be used for teacher evaluation. This is appropriate, in that teacher evaluation is one of the primary means of enhancing education. Generally, developing and implementing teacher evaluations is the responsibility of the building administrator. However, this is easier said than done. There is a great degree of disparity in evaluation systems among states and within states.

According to Veir and Dagley (2002), "Presently there is no model statute from which a legally and legislatively sound evaluation system can be developed." They report, "These evaluation systems give the school a means for removing poor or problematic teachers. However, due to regular incongruities in the legislation—its language, structure, procedures, and requirements—the process often cannot be carried out" (p. 4). They conclude that "criteria used to measure teachers must be valid and observable and the behaviors must be linked to teacher performance" (p. 13).

If done accurately, thoroughly, truthfully, and in a timely manner, evaluations can be a valuable asset to the education profession and the population it serves as well as a definitive defensive instrument for employers in the event that their action regarding a particular employee is challenged. If an evaluation demonstrates contemporaneous and early documentation of deficiencies and misconduct, documents repeated instances or patterns of poor performance, and evidences warning or opportunities to improve, such evaluation can be used to refute allegations that the employer acted arbitrarily, inconsistently, or without warning or that the employer's stated reason for any action was a pretext for discrimination. Thus one important reason for a formal evaluation program is to avoid subjective or arbitrary employment decisions on the part of the school district.

Well-defined evaluation programs benefit employees by providing an opportunity for school district and primary evaluators to formally praise employees for work well done and justify monetary or position advances. At the same time, evaluations provide a warning system by which the employee can be legally advised of any deficiencies and afforded reasonable time and guidance to correct them.

To help ensure accountability and quality teaching, many states, by statute, require periodic appraisal of teaching and principal performance. In states or local districts in which formal evaluation is mandated, principals place their jobs in jeopardy if they fail to satisfactorily evaluate their personnel. Although most professional educators assert that the primary reason for evaluation is improvement or remediation based on a "developmental assessment," the results of evaluations are used in a variety of employment decisions including retention, tenure, promotion, salary, reassignment, RIF, or dismissal based on "personnel rating." When adverse personnel decisions are the result of evaluations, legal concerns often arise regarding issues of procedural fairness and due process. For example: Were established state or local procedures followed? Did school officials employ "equitable standards"? Was sufficient evidence collected to support the decision? Were evaluations conducted in a uniform and consistent manner?

Evaluation Linked to Student Achievement Scores

Recent education reforms have changed teacher and principal evaluation by linking principals' and teachers' effectiveness to student performance, including student performance on standardized tests. The term *value-added measurements* refers to controversial designs that use a model to assess teacher and principal effectiveness on student achievement and performance. Between 2009 and 2011, as many as thirty-four states made policy changes to teacher evaluation (Papay, 2012). The District of Columbia and nearly half of the states now evaluate teachers using some form of student standardized test data.

Evaluation Guidelines and Congruence

Courts are generally reluctant to enter into the teacher evaluation process. Judicial reviews are usually limited to procedural issues of fairness and reasonableness. Two overall objectives are intrinsic in conducting performance evaluations:

1. *Developmental assessment.* The evaluation program must be directed toward the improvement of instruction in the classroom. Developmental assessment is the evaluation of a teacher to help that individual grow professionally. The evaluator does not use distinct evaluative criteria or assign the teacher a formal score or rating. The process spotlights development and improvement. The process is often regarded as a form of clinical supervision.

2. *Personnel rating.* There must be clear strategies for documentation of effectiveness as well as deficiencies in performance that support recommendations for promotion, nonrenewal, or dismissal. A personnel rating is the evaluation of a teacher in order to make performance-based administrative decisions relative to overall accountability in granting or denying tenure or promotion, renewing contracts, or requesting resignations. This rating process allows for both formative and summative evaluations in helping determine the teacher's professional future. Principals need to distinguish between these two evaluation objectives and formulate standardized methods of observation, documentation, and conferencing.

Successful evaluation programs are clear about the purposes of evaluation and match process to purpose. Teacher evaluation programs must match the educational goals, management style, concept of teaching, and community values of the school district. Evaluation programs must solicit a strong commitment from district-level administrators, principals, and teachers. All participants must believe that the program is useful, valid, and cost effective.

Successful evaluation programs allow for adequate resources, with the two most critical ones being time to conduct evaluations and evaluator–evaluatee training. Principals often complain that time and training are the major obstacles in implementing successful evaluation programs. District-level administrators can assist principals by reducing other demands and helping principals manage their time more effectively. Principals need to be trained in the skills of formal evaluation: helping teachers set goals, making accurate observations, evaluating teachers' plans and tests, coaching teachers in specific skills, and conferencing.

School districts are using formal and informal walkthrough observations in increasing numbers. What is observed and documented for walkthrough classroom visits is determined by local policy.

Evaluation Instruments

Long gone are the days when an informal discussion between a teacher and the principal near the end of the school year often constituted a teacher's yearly performance evaluation. Usually, such discussions were subjective and focused on behaviors that often did not relate to teaching performance. Today, evaluation instruments are usually formal documents that have been developed through collaborative efforts from the school district, administrators, and teachers. Evaluation programs have greater impact on improved performance when teachers have had viable input into evaluation criteria. A clear mission coupled with goal-based results-oriented criteria that are fully understood by teachers is an invaluable factor in the success of the evaluation program. The ideal instrument provides the basis for the assessment of teachers' knowledge, skills, and attitudes and is related directly to effective teaching and professional growth. Such instruments should be periodically validated against actual job requirements and expectations, and personnel subject to formal evaluation should be familiar with the instruments used in the process.

Documentation

The evaluation of teachers must be a continuous process. For clearly effective teachers, formal evaluations may need only to be conducted the number of times required by state or local policy. However, for some teachers, whether they are new to the profession or experienced, more frequent evaluations may be necessary to help identify inadequate performance and provide a rational basis for any employment decision that might be reached concerning the teacher.

Three difficult areas of documentation are often challenged when questions arise about the kinds of documentation that can be used in the evaluation process. The courts in some jurisdictions have held that third-party documentation, shared with the principal, can be grounds for continuing employment decisions (*In re Feldman*, 1978; see also *Dore v. Dedminster Board of Education*, 1982). Some courts have also ruled that school districts have the right to base continuing employment decisions on matters outside of a teacher's evaluation. In one such case, the court noted that decisions made about the nonrenewal of a nontenured teacher can be made on a "broad basis of input received from a variety of people, including members of the public, parents of students, and a district member's own knowledge of a teacher even if that knowledge is acquired through having a child in the teacher's class" (*Derrickson v. Board of Education*, 1989).

Accurate documentation of evaluation findings is necessary for diagnosing strengths and weaknesses in teacher performance and for specifying any necessary remediation. Such documentation serves as a prerequisite for validating an adverse employment decision during due process proceedings or litigation. Several types of written memoranda, in addition to actual evaluation instruments, can be used to strengthen the documentation process. These might include the following:

- *Memoranda to the file* to record less significant infractions or deviations by an employee

- *Specific incident memoranda* to record conferences with an employee concerning a significant event

- *Summary memoranda* to record conferences with an employee in which several incidents, problems, or deficiencies are discussed

- *Visitation memoranda* to record observations made of an employee's on-the-job performance

The use of memoranda, if done appropriately, can provide comprehensive documentation of employee performance and evaluation. Teachers must be informed of the type of documentation that will be made by the principal as evaluator, how it will be used, and the teacher's right of access to the record.

Negative evaluations are never a pleasant experience, particularly when the results will be used to substantiate an adverse employment decision. However, documentation is critical in helping a teacher improve performance as well as in justifying a decision not to renew or to terminate a contract. When done right, memoranda can make the difference between win or lose in a civil action.

The Evaluation Conference

Evaluation conferences provide the opportunity for the teacher or staff member and the principal to meet professionally to discuss the evaluation. For many principals, this conference often proves to be the most difficult part of the evaluation process because of the direct, personal contact involved. The purposes of the conference are to review the evaluation findings, reward and reinforce demonstrated strengths and accomplishments, and discuss any recommendations. The teacher should be invited to review all the evaluation instruments and any memoranda or other notes made during the process. If deficiencies are noted, the evaluator should be prepared to offer both specific steps and a reasonable timeframe for improvement. When deficiencies are significant enough that they could lead to a decision to dismiss or non-renew, the teacher must be advised that failure to demonstrate a specified level of improvement could have such consequences. The teacher must be offered the opportunity to ask questions and seek clarification of all issues discussed during the conference and should be given the opportunity to sign the evaluation report. A signature simply attests to the fact that the teacher has been shown the materials and afforded the opportunity to review the contents of the report, not that the teacher agrees with the conclusions. If the teacher refuses to sign the materials, the evaluator should simply make a file memorandum to the effect that the opportunity was offered but declined by the teacher.

The tone of the conference is important, and the principal as evaluator should maintain a professional demeanor at all times. Demonstrations of anger, threats, or attempts to harass or intimidate the teacher have no place. Private remarks made by a teacher in a principal's office, even though made in a hostile manner, are protected by the First Amendment and cannot be a basis for an adverse employment decision.

An unusual case, *Maxey v. McDowell County Board of Education* (2002), illustrates what can happen when teachers are not afforded the necessary elements of a proper performance evaluation, including the opportunity to discuss the evaluation and correct deficiencies the evaluator observes. A West Virginia teacher had exemplary evaluations until a new principal observed teacher methods or behaviors he wanted corrected. For several months, the principal did not allow the teacher to explain or refute his observations. Eventually the teacher was required to meet with the principal and district administrators concerning her evaluation, and again she was not given a chance to explain her side of the issues. She was instead told to sign the evaluation or face discipline. The teacher responded by telling the principal that she should have just blown his head off with a shotgun, at which point the principal called 911. The teacher was subsequently terminated from her job.

The West Virginia Supreme Court of Appeals held that although she clearly demonstrated unprofessional conduct, she was never given proper opportunities at the time of her evaluation for remediation. The court felt that this was in part due to the fear of confrontation held by the principal. Her case was sent back to a lower court, with the likelihood that she would be reinstated in her job.

In the day-to-day proceedings of school operations and, particularly, during an evaluation conference between a teacher and a principal, it is likely that a variety of comments will be exchanged between the parties. Such private expressions can result in legal problems if they are used as a substantial basis for an adverse employment decision. The U.S. Supreme Court stated, in *Givhan v. Western Line Consolidated School District* (1979), that private expressions of a teacher's views to a principal are constitutionally protected. The Court noted, however, that a teacher's expression of disagreement with superiors may be subject to reasonable time, place, and manner restrictions to prevent the disruption of day-to-day school activities. In addition, a Court held, in *Eckerd v. Indian River School District* (1979), that speech, unless it can be documented as disruptive of day-to-day school activities, cannot be the substantial or motivating factor in a board's decision to terminate a teacher and that the teacher–principal relationship does not require maintenance of personal loyalty and confidence.

ADDITIONAL CASES OF INTEREST TO EDUCATORS

Baggett v. Bullitt, 377 U.S. 360 (1964). The Supreme Court overturned a lower court and held as unconstitutional state statutes in Washington that required teachers and all other employees to take a loyalty oath as a condition of employment. A 1931 oath required, among other things, teachers to swear to promote respect for the flag of the United States and Washington state, and reverence for law and order and undivided allegiance to the government of the United States. The 1955 oath for state employees required, among other things, a sworn statement that the employee was not a "subversive person."

Beilan v. Board of Education, 357 U.S. 299 (1958). The Court held that a Philadelphia schoolteacher could validly be dismissed on grounds of incompetence for the lack of candor shown by the refusal to answer questions concerning possible membership in the communist party.

Connell v. Higginbotham, 403 U.S. 207 (1971). The Supreme Court struck down as unconstitutional one of two oaths that Florida employees had been required to affirm. The Court held as permissible the requirement of a pledge to support the Constitution of the United States, but held that dismissal for refusing to sign the oath without a hearing violated the Due Process Clause of the Fourteenth Amendment.

Cramp v. Board of Public Instruction of Orange County, 368 U.S. 278 (1961). A Florida statute that required every employee of the state to swear in writing that he has never lent his "aid, support, advice, counsel or influence to the Communist Party" was deemed so vague and uncertain that the state could not force an employee to take such an oath.

Elfbrandt v. Russell, 384 U.S. 11 (1966). Like *Baggett,* the Court struck down an Arizona oath required of teachers. The statute subjected those who signed the oath to prosecution of perjury and discharge from office anyone who took the oath yet knowingly or willingly remained a member of the Communist Party or any subordinate organizations. The Court held there is a "hazard of being prosecuted for knowing but guiltless behavior."

Epperson v. Arkansas, 393 U.S. 97 (1968). A law forbidding the teaching of evolution was determined by the Court to violate the Establishment Clause because the law was expressly written based on the beliefs of fundamentalist Christians. Concurring opinions in the unanimous decision agreed with the result and added that the law also likely violated the Due Process Clause of the Fourteenth Amendment due to vagueness or violated the freedom of speech of the teacher who filed the suit.

Ambach v. Norwick, 441 U.S. 68 (1979). The Supreme Court held that a state had a rationale government interest requiring teachers to either be citizens or in the process of becoming citizens.

Cleveland Board of Education v. Loudermill, 470 U.S. 532 (1985). The Court held that most public employees have property interest in their jobs and are therefore allowed due process rights if they face termination. Such rights are known as

"Loudermill Rights" and give the employees a right to a pretermination hearing and the opportunity to present their side. The rights also include a written or verbal notice regarding the reasons for the termination and the specific evidence against them.

Monell v. Department of Social Services, 436 U.S. 658 (1978). A case where the Supreme Court held that local governmental units, such as school districts or police departments, are considered persons to which 42 U.S.C. Section 1983 applies. Plaintiffs alleging civil rights violations may make claims, known as *Monell claims,* but limit the scope of their liability only to those instances where rights were violated from a custom, policy, or practice. Local governments should be liable only for actions which it is directly responsible for, meaning that plaintiffs may sue employees in their personal and/or official capacity.

Mount Healthy City School District v. Doyle, 429 U.S. 274 (1977). The case involved a teacher who was fired after he had been involved in several disruptive incidents including allegedly making obscene gestures toward students. The teacher claimed he was fired because of statements he made during a local radio interview in protest of a new teacher dress code. The Supreme Court vacated lower court decisions that favored the teacher and sent the case back to be decided on a different standard. The Court held that his First and Fourteenth Amendment claims did not apply to his tenure denial, but he might nonetheless establish a claim if the decision to not rehire him was by due to his exercise of First Amendment freedoms. The Court held that the record was unclear as to whether the interview with the radio station was the reason for the denial of tenure. The case is important because it offered school districts the defense that they would make the same decision even in the absence of the First Amendment expressive conduct.

Givhan v. Western Line Consolidated School District, 439 U.S. 410 (1979). The case established the principle that public employees do not lose First Amendment protection simply because they speak on matters of public concern privately to a superior. In this case, a Black teacher complained to her principal that a school with more Black students was not adequately supplied compared to a school with more white students and was subsequently fired. In the appellate court, it was determined that the teacher had no First Amendment protection because she expressed her views in private. The Supreme Court reversed and sent the case back to the lower courts to determine if she would have been terminated even if she did not engage in the protected speech. She eventually was reinstated, after the lower court determined the reasons given by the school district for her termination were pretextual.

Perry Education Association v. Perry Local Educators' Association Relations Commission, 460 U.S. 37 (1983). The case centered on free speech rights on government property in a case involving the use of teacher mailboxes and the school delivery system. The Court upheld a policy that allowed the teacher union representing the teachers, but not other employee organizations, to use the district mail system. The decision analyzed three types of forums when speakers use government-owned property to convey a message. A public forum is a public space where speech restrictions must be content neutral. A designated public forum is public property the state has opened for use by the public for expression. Finally, a nonpublic forum is not open to the public for expressive purposes although speakers may gain access by invitation or permission. In this case, the mail system was determined to be a nonpublic forum.

North Haven Board of Education v. Bell, 456 U.S. 512 (1982). The Court determined that Title IX applies not only to students but to employees as well and that it is enforceable through the Office for Civil Rights (OCR).

Belcourt v. Fort Totten Public School District (454 NW 2d 703-ND, Supreme Court 1990). Teachers were nonrenewed for "incompetence" and "lack of funds." The school board questioned why students receiving As and Bs in math classes were functioning well below their grade level and below grade level on achievement tests.

Boring v. Buncombe County Board of Education (136 F.3d 364, 4th Cir. 1998). The development of curriculum is the right of public school officials rather than individual teachers. The court held the view that teachers would be accountable to courts rather than administrators if districts did not have the responsibility.

Bradley v. Pittsburgh Board of Education (910 F.2d 1172, 3d Cir. 1990). A school district could ban a teacher from using an instructional method she preferred and from advocating the method. Had she advocated for the methodology outside of school, her speech rights would be protected.

Sekor v. Board of Education, 240 Conn. 119 (Conn. Supreme Court 1997). A tenured business teacher earned additional certification to teach social studies and English due to low enrollment numbers in business classes. She was assigned to teach business and social studies classes but the school placed her on an assistance plan for the social studies classes due to difficulties in those classes. She was then assigned to business and English classes, but the administration determined she could not teach those classes satisfactorily. Her contract was terminated and she sued for unlawful termination. The question for the court was to determine if the law allowed for the termination for general incompetence despite the fact that the teacher was deemed competent in another subject area. The court concluded that it was allowable and that teachers had a right only to a generic position and not a specific position and that the school board had the authority over teacher assignment.

Altsheler v. Bd. of Educ. of the Great Neck Union Free Sch. Dist., 83 AD 2d 568 (NY App. Div. 2 1981). The termination of a contract of a tenured teacher was upheld in a case where a teacher was accused of providing inappropriate assistance to students on a standardized test. Students in her classroom scored significantly higher than students in other classes on the same test, and those students also had significantly higher scores than their previous year before entering her class. In addition, those student scores dropped the next year. The teacher denied the allegation that she provided words to the students that would appear on the test, and expert witnesses disagreed about the statistical probabilities of having 41 percent of the words that appeared on the test also appear on study cards for the test.

Keyishian v. Board of Regents, 385 U.S. 589 (1967). The case involved the concept of academic freedom, with the Court noting the value of such freedom as important to the nation, not just to teachers, and a specific concern of the First Amendment. The Court noted, however, that such freedom is not an "unlimited liberty" and must be viewed in the entire context and conduct of the school.

Cleveland Board of Education v. LaFleur, 414 U.S. 632 (1974). The Court held that school board regulations requiring pregnant teachers to stop working after the fifth month of pregnancy violated the Fourteenth Amendment. The school board argued that the rules were required because some pregnant teachers were incapable of teaching after the fifth month of pregnancy. The Court also struck down a requirement that teachers could not return to work until the newborn was three months old because the school board failed to show a reasonable justification for the policy.

Harrah Independent School District v. Martin, 440 U.S. 194 (1979). The Supreme Court held that it was not a denial of equal protection when a tenured teacher was fired after refusing to comply with the continuing education (CE) requirements of the district. The Court reasoned that the requirements were the same for all teachers, and her tenure was based on an agreement that she maintain her CE requirements.

Hortonville Joint School District No. 1 v. Hortonville Education Association, 426 U.S. 482 (1976). The Supreme Court held that school board members who had no personal or financial interest in negotiations have no conflict of interest. This decision allows school board members to serve on tribunals and other hearings and deemed impartial as they perform their statutory duties.

Wygant v. Jackson Board of Education, 476 U.S. 267 (1986). The Supreme Court held that a provision in the negotiated agreement violated the Equal Protection Clause because it was not sufficiently narrowly tailored and there were other means to achieve a similar purpose. The agreement allowed tenured nonminority teachers to be laid off before nontenured minority teachers in an attempt to alleviate racial tension in the district.

Lee v. York County School Division (418 F.Supp.2d 816, E.D. Va. 2006). Removal of bulletin board material by principal did not violate speech rights. The religious materials were curricular in nature and not a matter of public concern and therefore not subject to First Amendment protected speech.

O'Connor v. Ortega, 480 U.S. 709 (1987). The Court held that employees had constitutionally protected privacy interests in the work environment, but that the reasonableness of employees' expectation of privacy must be determined on a case-by-case analysis. The Court applied *T.L.O.* standards of reasonableness to employer intrusions on employee privacy for noninvestigatory work-related purposes as well as for investigations of work-related misconduct. Employees should have no expectation of privacy when material reviewed or downloaded was created on school time using school-owned equipment including school cable or phone lines.

Monroe v. Central Bucks School District, 805 F. 3d 454 (3rd Cir. 2015). Although a court assumed that a teacher blog post may have raised a public concern about students and coworkers, the court found against the teacher due to the school's interest in avoiding workplace disruptions. The teacher alleged her termination was in retaliation for comments she made on her personal blog, which was limited in subscribers, but somehow reached the press and ultimately students and teachers. The majority of her posts surrounded things like recipes and family vacations, but some were highly critical of her students and coworkers. She stated she wished she could tell the truth on report cards and described some as "rat-like," "frightfully dim," or "rude, belligerent, argumentative f*cks" and described one student as dressed like a streetwalker. She also described a coworker as a "douche."

Matter of Rubino v. City of New York, 106 AD 3d 439 (NY App Div. 1., 2013). A teacher who had been fired for online statements won her case on appeal when the court held that her positive employment record as well as a lack of evidence that her postings negatively affected her teaching made her termination disproportionate and unfair. After what she described as a long and tiring day, she vented on Facebook in response to a story about the drowning of a NYC public school student. In her post she said, "After today, I am thinking the beach sound like a wonderful idea for my 5th graders? I HATE THEIR GUTS! They are the devils [*sic*] spawn!"

Mayer v. Monroe County Community School Corporation, 474 F.3d 477 (7th Cir. 2007). The appellate court noted that a school system does not "regulate" teacher speech as much as it hires the speech. That rationale was used to hold against a teacher, noting that the First Amendment does not entitle teachers to cover topics or advocate viewpoints that depart from the curriculum or policies of the school district. The case was brought by a teacher who was nonrenewed after the school alleged that she took a political stance in her classroom, which upset some parents, who complained that she was taking sides during classes in a political controversy. The teacher noted during a current events session in class that she had passed a demonstration against military operations in Iraq and saw a sign that stated "Honk for Peace," and when asked if she would ever take part in a peace march, she said, "I honk for peace."

Webster v. New Lenox School District No. 122, 197 F.2d 1004 (7th Cir. 1990). The Circuit court held against a teacher who wanted to teach his class that the world was much younger than the 4-billion-year age stated in the textbook used by the district, and propose to students to consider the possibility of a divine creation as an alternative to scientific understanding. The court held that teachers do not have a right to introduce their own views on the subject but must stick to the prescribed curriculum—not only on the prescribed subject matter, but also on the perspective of the subject matter. Teachers must use the approach prescribed by the school district.

Spanierman v. Hughes, 576 F. Supp.2d 292 (D.C. Conn. 2008). The dismissal of a teacher for "exercising poor judgment" was upheld by the courts. The male teacher created a MySpace page to communicate with students, but included pictures of naked men along with other inappropriate comments. A concerned colleague convinced him to remove the page, but he later created another with similar content. When the colleague learned of the new page, she alerted the school administration. A court rejected his claims of due process violations as well as free speech claims, noting it was not unreasonable to find his behavior as being disruptive to the school.

Snyder v. Millersville University. Civil Action. No. 07-1660 (E.D. Pa. Dec. 3, 2008). An aspiring teacher in training was denied a teaching degree after school officials discovered an image on her MySpace page showing her in a pirate hat drinking alcohol. Although there was no contact with students, and no evidence that students ever even saw the image, the teaching district also contended her conduct as a student teacher was unprofessional. Subsequent legal action went against the plaintiff. The case did raise a significant question. For First Amendment purposes, is a student teacher a student, a public employee, and an apprentice in relation to both the placement school and the school to which she is enrolled? The question was not answered because the defendants argued they would have taken the same steps against her without the posting of the image.

Mailloux v. Kiley, 323 F. Supp. 1387 (D. Mass. 1971). A judge sided with a fired teacher, noting that his use of the word "fuck" written on a blackboard was relevant to the discussion of taboo words in society in the eleventh-grade class. The court held that the teaching method did not disturb the students, and there was disagreement among educational experts whether it was appropriate to use the word in class.

Blanchet v. Vermilion Parish Sch. Bd., 220 So.2d 534 (La. 1969). A court determined that a rule requiring male teachers to wear ties was to enhance the professional image of teachers and therefore was not arbitrary or unreasonable.

Lucia v. Duggan, 303 F. Supp. 112 (D. Mass. 1969). A teacher was suspended for insubordination after he grew a beard, which at the time was only an unwritten policy. He was not invited to the hearing held to dismiss him. A court determined that his due process rights were violated because there was no prior notice given that the beard violated any policy, and that he was not notified that growing a beard would result in his dismissal.

Morrison v. State Board of Education, 461 P.2d (Cal. 1969). The California Supreme Court spelled out factors widely used to determine unfitness to teach, often referred to as *Morrison* factors. Those include (1) the likelihood that the conduct may adversely affect students or fellow teachers [and] the degree of such adversity anticipated; (2) the proximately or remoteness of the time of the conduct; (3) the type of teaching certificate held by the party involved; (4) any extenuating or aggravating circumstances involved; (5) the praiseworthiness or blameworthiness of the motivations involved; (6) the likelihood of recurrence; and (7) the extent to which disciplinary action may have an adverse impact or chilling effect upon constitutional rights of the teacher involved or other teachers.

Gabbard v. Madison Local School Dist. Bd. of Educ., Slip Opinion No. 2021-Ohio-2067. The Ohio Supreme Court held that the Madison Local School District Board of Education's policy that authorized school district employees to carry deadly weapons at work was in violation of a state law that required 728 hours of training or twenty years of experience to legally carry such weapons. The district policy did not require weapon-carrying employees to have the training or experience, and the Court ruled that the law did not exempt school employees from the requirements.

Ison v. Madison Local Sch. Dist. Bd. of Educ., No. 20-4108 (6th Cir. 2021). The Sixth Circuit case centered on the constitutionality of alleged restrictions on parents' ability to comment at school board meetings. The Court found that restricting antagonistic, abusive, or personally directed speech was impermissible viewpoint discrimination in violation of the First Amendment since it "prohibit[ed] speech purely because it disparages or offends" or opposes the board. The content-neutral requirement to register in person at least two days prior was supported by a satisfactory board interest.

CHAPTER 13

Education Law 101 for Teachers

Priorities for Professional Development

Principal preparation programs typically require an education law class as part of the curriculum for licensure, although what form that takes varies widely. Preservice leadership licensure exams require the application of education law knowledge to scenarios principals may face in their schools. Of course, on-the-job training and facing new and unique dilemmas are always present in any job, and everyone should improve their skills through experience.

Unfortunately for teachers, such a focus on education law is at best a minimal part of their preparation programs and at worst never taught at all. That may be understandable when considering all that is required of a teacher preparation program in a limited amount of time, but many teachers and principals express wishes to have more exposure to education law topics.

Such preparation should in theory, at least, help teachers avoid potential legal entanglements, which also benefits students, parents, and the school culture. Ongoing staff development is critical but limited in time and requires prioritization, and ultimately not every important training can be covered. What follows, however, is a basic blueprint that could be used to touch on important highlights that could be presented in different ways—through short sessions; book or article studies; a focus for PLCs; or in whatever manner that works for a school. What principals may discover is that teachers are generally highly interested in learning more to increase their foundational knowledge of education law.

SECTION A. CODE OF ETHICS FOR EDUCATORS

A great place to start would be to discuss local, state, or national teacher code of ethics, a discussion which then extends directly into education law-related topics. Just as with other professions, the teaching profession has basic codes that are common throughout the various state codes or with those from professional organizations such as the National Education Association and the National Federation of Teachers. The National Association of State Directors of Teacher Education and Certification (NASDTEC) provides a great model code of ethic for educators.

These organizations and their codes typically have some language related to professional responsibilities to the profession of teaching; to their students; to the school community; to the use of technology; to professional colleagues; or similar groups. What these codes do is to help emphasize what is important to create positive learning environments for students and to perform their jobs in the highest professional manner.

In staff development, a principal should use not only any local code that is available, but also state or national models. Getting into more details of the codes reaches into areas of school law such as rights of students, privacy rights, professional behavior, and other education law-related topics. One enriching activity is to have teachers write their own personal and professional codes. On the surface, this seems like an easy task, but in practice it's not. Although most people have strongly held beliefs and favorite practices, seldom are we asked to write out and reflect on our beliefs.

SECTION B. TEACHERS AND STUDENTS

In any abbreviated staff development, it would be necessary to narrow the focus to the most important topics, and that may perhaps be the most difficult task. Principals should include those topics they feel are the most important to their current school environment as well as what they would be most comfortable leading. A good practice could be to survey the staff to focus on what they would like the focus to be, since each school has its own needs and current "hot topics" that require additional study. The following might serve to prompt some of the most important ideas and concepts to prioritize.

Rights of Students

Students do not shed their constitutional rights while at school. Teachers should have a basic understanding that student speech is protected while at school, with the limitations outlined in the prongs of *Tinker,* and the guidelines of *Hazelwood, Fraser, Morse,* and now *B.L.* The concepts of "imminent or substantial disruption" should be a feature in any discussion.

Teachers should understand the basics of student search guidelines, whether or not they conduct student searches. Understanding how to determine "justified at inception" and "reasonable in scope" when a search is considered are the two most basic elements all teachers should know. They must also understand that only in extreme circumstances when there is a danger to a student or others should any strip searching ever take place. Finally, they should avoid the temptation to search the contents of a student-owned device such as a cell phone, and that the scope of such search could be called into question.

Teachers should understand that Fourth Amendment rights are not just about search, but include seizure as well. Detaining, restraining, or placing students in isolation needs to be understood in terms of how they are impacted by any Fourth Amendment protections. While not prohibited per se, in what manner such practices occur could be called into question.

The due process rights of students should be understood by all teachers. They should know the basics of student due process rights and appreciate the concept that the greater the discipline consequence under consideration, the greater the level of due process must be in place.

Student Privacy and Release of Students

Teachers should be aware of student privacy rights related to FERPA. It is very easy to make a careless mistake and innocently provide protected information of students to parties that do not have the right to see the information. Staff development noting the differences between directory information and protected information would not take long and could prevent disclosures that could cause negative consequences.

Teachers should understand the critical importance of protecting students from being released to unauthorized parties. This should be an emphasis at all times, but unfortunately it isn't always as easy to adhere to in practice as it would seem. Custody agreements change frequently, and adults are not always honest about their identity or relationship to students. This area, however, should be a priority for every adult in order to protect all students.

Child Abuse and Mandatory Reporting

Teachers should be able to recognize signs of child abuse and understand their obligations as mandatory reporters. State laws differ, as do local policies, but all contain elements of mandatory reporting requirements. Teachers should understand that the obligation to report falls upon them, as it isn't enough to report suspected abuse to their superior. Their obligation is to notify the appropriate child protection agency.

Bullying and Harassment

Although some guidelines have changed, teachers have a moral and legal obligation to prevent bullying and harassment, as well as take action when bullying and harassment are witnessed or reported. All school employees are now required to report such incidents. Teachers should know who to report such incidents to as well as the required procedures necessary in the process.

Respecting Diversity, Equity, and Student Opportunity for All

Respecting and appreciating the dignity of all students, regardless of their background, is an essential practice. This is especially important in schools today, as societal challenges and tensions spill over into our schools. Although difficult at times, teachers and principals must also understand the relationship between performing their job as a public school educator and their own personal viewpoints. Awareness is the first step in what should be a life-long journey in this endeavor.

Special Education as a Right; IDEA and Section 504

Teachers should know that special education for qualified students is a right for both the student and parents. The basic core of FAPE should be well understood and should identify how schools can avoid taking actions that become any type of denial of FAPE.

Although most if not all teachers are aware of additional due process rights for students with IEPs related to discipline, the topic should be emphasized. Sometimes it is misunderstood that "there is nothing that can happen" to students with IEPs in terms of discipline, and such misunderstanding should be dispelled. This also helps protect students from types of bias that either increase referrals or cause some behaviors to be ignored.

The issue of disproportionality in special education as well as student discipline should be raised in awareness and practice. Such discussion should go deeper than merely saying it's a problem, in part because such acknowledgment doesn't change practices. This is another area where increasing knowledge of the problem and the origins of the problem are essential. It fits fully into education law due to the serious implications for students.

Section 504 is based on a civil rights law and is enforced by the OCR. Any student at some point may have a condition that qualifies them for a Section 504 plan. A student may qualify for a 504 plan even temporarily, such as after they are injured in an accident.

SECTION C. RELATIONSHIP WITH ADMINISTRATORS

Hierarchy of Laws and Authorities

Teachers should be exposed to the hierarchy of the authority of laws related to education in order to help them see a more balcony view of how the entire legal system fits into their practice. While some may not appreciate the civics lesson, knowing the relationship between their own classroom rules, school board policies, and their own negotiated agreement allows for more systems thinking, which in theory should help avoid potential disputes, disagreements, or misunderstandings.

Dilemmas for Principals

All staff can benefit from understanding the ethical dilemmas regularly faced in the classroom and the principal's office. What Kidder (2009) describes as *right vs. right* dilemmas we see nearly every day in schools. A right vs. right dilemma is one in which a decision must be made and the choices of action to take may be opposite of each other and yet both could be right choices. For example, when considering a discipline consequence for a student, it could be *right* in some cases to suspend the student, yet at the same time it could be *right* to consider an alternative to suspending the student. Both could be right, but are clearly different from each other.

Right vs. right dilemmas sometimes provide no choices that are desirable, yet one option must be chosen. Kidder notes four common paradigms including justice vs. mercy; truth vs. loyalty; short-term gain vs. long-term gain; and individual vs. community. These paradigms are present in many situations faced by both teachers and administrators when they are required to make decisions about students. Understanding these concepts can help with practice and also improve understanding of how principals arrive at the decisions they make.

SECTION D. TEACHER PROTECTION IN PRACTICE

Licensure and Contracts

Teachers would benefit from knowing the requirements related to their licensure as well as the basics of their own contracts. Seldom is professional development dedicated to the topic, but frequently problems occur related to license renewals, deadlines, release time, leave time, and other daily practices.

Essential Documents—Negotiated Agreement; Crisis Plans; Suicide Prevention

Teachers should have at their immediate disposal essential documents that affect their practice. Too often there is just a handful of teachers who know about the contents of the negotiated (collective bargaining) agreement. But that is just one document all teachers should be made aware of. While staff development going over the agreement may not appear to be too "exciting," the avoidance of potential misunderstandings and possible grievance procedures is even less so.

Some documents are mandatory and come with some required staff development but too many times are put into a drawer and forgotten. Documents such as the school crisis plan, a suicide prevention plan, or a student resources guide are important and should never be made a "one time per year" item of discussion.

Duty

A discussion of duty, breach of duty, foreseeability, and negligence would elevate school safety awareness and decrease the likelihood of student or staff injury. The Gauging Risk activity in the book would also be a valuable exercise and could help identify problematic areas of risk in the school. Taking the time to emphasize these areas helps to refocus and break from daily routine practices that can lead to complacency and potential injury.

Distinguishing between discretionary and ministerial duty would also help remind everyone regarding their obligations to keep students safe, as well as protect teachers from making decisions that could negatively impact their careers. Teachers make hundreds of decisions each day, with most of those decisions having no negative results. Unfortunately, one bad decision can become devastating to a student, a family, and the teacher. Spending time to detail what is required of teachers by policy is time very well spent toward prevention.

- Adhere to applicable federal, state, and local laws and regulations; adhere to and enforce established school policies, procedures, and rules in the performance of assigned duties and responsibilities.

- Develop and present instructional activities that are appropriate to, and consistent with, the approved education program and specifically designed to increase students' knowledge; facilitate the development of learning skills, life skills, and appropriate social behavior; and prepare students to interact effectively in general society.

- Provide effective supervision of students participating in instructional activities that are within the scope of assigned responsibility to ensure students' safety and general well-being.

- Facilitate effective, two-way communication about school-related issues (including student progress) in programs within the scope of assigned responsibility, between administrators and parents, administrators and teachers, administrators and students, teachers and parents, and teachers and students.

Title IX

Although Title IX is by no means new, the landscape is changing, and how Title IX applies and what is required has changed as well. Teachers' awareness of LGBTQ+ student needs is the first step toward a more safe and inclusive school for all students. Teachers should also become aware of how Title IX and Title VII apply to their own workplace in relation to adult behaviors.

Social Media and Speech

Surprising as it may be, there are many school districts that do not have explicit social media policies for teachers. This may be one area which places the most teachers "at risk" because their social media presence and one ill-advised posting can derail and end a teaching career. Regardless of what policies may be in place, appropriate staff development directed to prevent social media disasters is more important than ever.

Teachers should be aware of their own speech rights as a public employee. Teachers should also understand that "freedom of speech" may not be what some think it is. It is essential that teachers understand the limitations of their speech by knowing when they may be speaking as a private citizen and when they are not; knowing what may be a matter of public concern and when such a concern is not; and understanding the different forums where their speech is more protected.

SUMMARY

This chapter is designed to provide a small blueprint of potential topics that could be used for basics of education law for teachers and is acknowledged to have left out topics others may deem more important. As is nearly always the case, there is precious little staff development time, especially with increased demands from other areas. However, if doing such professional development has the potential to keep students and staff safer or avoids any protracted and expensive legal proceedings, that time will be well worth taking.

This book ends with two expressions to consider. When it comes to any lawsuit, you don't want to be on the wrong side of the "v"—meaning as a defendant. And related to that, it is much better to work with everyone collaboratively to avoid injuries to any party, since it's much better to call someone your partner than your codefendant.

Table of Cases

Board of Education of the Hendrick Hudson Central School District v. Rowley, 457 U.S. 176 (1982).

Board of Education of Westside Community Schools v. Mergens, 496 U.S. 226 (1990).

Board of Education, Island Trees Union School District No. 26 v. Pico, 457 U.S. 853 (1982).

Board of Regents of State Colleges v. Roth, 408 U.S. 564 (1972).

Boatright v. Copeland, 783 S.E.2d 695 (Ga. Ct. App. 2016).

Bolling v. Sharp, 347 U.S. 497 (1954).

Borden v. School Dist. of Tp. of East Brunswick, 523 F.3d 153 (3d Cir. 2008).

Boring v. Buncombe County Board of Education. (136 F.3d 364, 4th Cir. 1998).

Boroff v. Van Wert City Board of Education, 220 F.3d 465 (6th Cir. 2000).

Bosch v. Bell, WL 2548053 (C.D. Ill. 2006).

Bostock v. Clayton County, 590 U.S. 207 (2020).

Boyd County High School Gay Straight Alliance v. Board of Education, 258 F. Supp. 667 (E.D. Ky. 2003), p. 690.

Bradley v. Pittsburgh Board of Education. (910 F.2d 1172, 3d Cir. 1990).

Bradstreet v. Sobol, 630 N.Y.S.2d (Supp. Ct. 1996).

Brannum v. Overton County School Board, 516 F. 3d 489 (6th Cir. 2008).

Brevard County v. Jacks, 238 So.2d 156 (Fla. Dist. Ct. App. 1970).

Brooks-Ngwenya v. Indianapolis Public Schools, 564 F.3d 804 (7th Cir. 2009).

Brown v. Board of Education of Topeka (Brown II), 349 U.S. 294 (1955).

Brown v. Board of Education of Topeka, 347 U.S. 483 (1954).

Brown v. Tesack, 566 So.2d 955, (La. Sup. Ct. 1990).

Brownell v. Los Angeles Unified School District, 4 Cal. App. 4th 787, 5 Cal. Rptr. 2d 756 (1992).

Burge ex rel. Burge v. Colton School Dist. 53, 100 F. Supp.3d 1057 (D. Oregon 2015).

Burlington School Community v. Department of Education, 471 U.S. 359 (1985).

Burlison v. Springfield Public Schools, 708 F.3d 1034. (8th Cir. 2013).

Burnside v. Byars, 363 F.2d 744 (5th Cir. 1966).

Busch v. Marple Newtown School Dist, 567 F.3d 89 (3d Cir. 2009).

BWA v. Farmington R-7 School District, (554 F.3d 734, 8th Cir. 2009).

Bystrom v. Fridley High School Independent School District No. 14, (822 F.2d 747, 8th Cir. 1987).

C.C. v. Harrison Cnty. Bd. of Educ, No. 20-0171 (W.Va Sup. Ct. App. 2021).

C.C. v. Hurst-Euless-Bedford Independent School District, 641 Fed. App'x 423 (5th Cir. 2016) *cert denied.*

Campbell v. BOE of New Milford, 475 A.2d 289 (Conn. 1984).

Campbell v. State of Hawaii Dept. of Educ. 892 F.3d 1005 (9th Cir. 2018).

Camreta v. Greene, 131 S.Ct. 2020 (2011).

Canady v. Bossier Parish Sch. Bd, 240 F.3d 437 (5th Cir. 2001).

Cannon v. University of Chicago, 99 S.Ct. 1946 (1979).

Carter v. Pointe Coupee Par. Sch. Bd, 268 Sl. 3d 1064 (La. App. 1 Cir. 2018).

Case v. Unified Sch. Dist. No. 233, 908 F. Supp. 864 (D. Kan. 1995).

Cash v. Lee County, Civil Action No. 1: 11-CV-00154-SA-DAS (N.D. Miss. Dec. 28, 2012).

Cass v. Town of Wayland, 383 F. Supp.3d 66 (D. Mass. 2019).

Castalado v. Stone, 192 F. Supp.2d 1124 (D. Colo. 2001).

Castañeda v. Pickard, 648 F.2d 989 (5th Cir. 1981).

Cedar Rapids Community School District v. Garret F, 526 U.S. 66 (1999).

Chandler v. James, 180 F.3d 1254 (11th Cir. 1997).

Chandler v. McMinnville School District, (U.S. Ct. of App, 9th Cir. 1992, 978 F.2d 524).

Chicago School Reform Board of Trustees v. Substance, Inc, 79 F.Supp.2d 919 (N.D. Ill. 2000).

Cintron v. Brentwood, 455 F. Supp. 57 (1978).

Clements v. Board of Trustees of Sheridan County School Dist. No. 2, 585 P.2d 19 (Wyo. 1978). See also 53 A.L.R.3d 1124, 68 Am. Jur.2d, Schools §§ 256 and 266.

Clements v. Board of Trustees of Sheridan County School District No. 2 (585 P.2d 197 Wyo. 1978).

Cleveland Board of Education v. LaFleur, 414 U.S. 632 (1974).

Cleveland Board of Education v. Loudermill, 470 U.S. 532 (1985).

Clinton Municipal Separate School District v. Byrd. (477 So.2d 237, Miss. 1985).

Cole v. Newton Special Municipal Separate School District, 853 F. 2d 924 (5th Cir. 1988).

Coles v. Cleveland Board of Education, 171 F.3d 369 (1999).

Connell v. Higginbotham, 403 U.S. 207 (1971).

Connick v. Myers., 461 U.S. 183 (1983).

Cook v. Raimondo, Case 1:18-cv-00645-WES-PAS (Dist. Ct. RI 2020).

Cooper v. Aaron, 358 U.S. 1 (1958).

Cornfield v. Consolidated High School District No. 230, 991 F.2d 1316 (7th Cir. 1993).

Counts v. Cedarville School District, 295 F. Supp. 2d 996 (2003).

Coy v. Board of Education of the North Canton City Schools, 205 F. Supp.2d 791 (N.D. Ohio 2002).

Cramp v. Board of Public Instruction of Orange County, 368 U.S. 278 (1961).

Crosby v. Holsinger, 852 F.2d 801 (4th Cir. 1988).

D.J.M. v. Hannibal Public School District, 647 F.3d 754 (8th Cir. 2011).

D.L. v. Baltimore City Board of School Commissioners, 706 F.3d 256, 264 (4th Cir. 2013).

Dale v Stephens County, United States Court of Appeals for the Eleventh Circuit 237 Fed. Appx. 603; 2007 U.S. App. LEXIS 15457 (unpublished).

Davis v. Monroe County Board of Education, 119 S. Ct. 1661, 1673 (1999).

Defoe ex rel. Defoe v. Spiva, (625 F.3d 324, 6th Cir. 2010).

Deminski v. State Board of Education, No. 60A20 (N.C. Sup. Ct. 2021).

Derrickson v. Board of Education, 537 F. Supp. (E.D. Mo. 1989. Opinion written after trial, March 31, 1982).

Deshaney v. Winnebago County Department of Social Services, 489 U.S 189 (1989).

DesRoches v. Caprio and School Board of Norfolk, 156 F.3d 571, 129 Educ. L. Rep. 628 (4th Cir.1998).

Dextraze v. Bernard, No. 2020-48-Appeal (R.I. June 28, 2021).

DiCosala v. Kay, 450 A.2d 508 (1982).

District of Columbia v. Royal, 465 A.2d (D.C. 1983).

Dixon v. Alabama State Board of Education, 186 F. Supp. 945, rev'd 294 F.2d 15, cert. denied, 368 U.S. 930, 825 (Ct. 368 1961).

Doe v. Berkeley County School District, 189 F.Supp.3d 573 (D.S.C. 2016).

Doe v. Fairfax Cnty. Sch. Bd, No. 19-2203 (2021).

Doe v. Indian River School Dist, 653 F.3d 256 (3d Cir. 2011).

Doe v. Pulaski County Special School District, 306 F.3d 616 (8th Cir. 2002).

Doe v. Renfrow, 475 F. Supp. 1012 (N.D. Ind. 1979).

Doe v. Tangipahoa Parish School Board et al., 631 F.Supp.2d 823 (E.D. La 2009).

Doe v. Taylor Indep. Sch. Dist, 15 F.3d 443 (5th Cir. 1994), cert denied.

Doe v. Wright, 82 F.3d 265, 268 (8th Cir. 1996).

Doe-3 v. McLean County Unit District. No. 5, Nos. 112479/112501 (Ill. Aug. 9, 2012).

Does v. Southeast Delco Sch. Dist, 272 F. Supp 3d. 656 (Dist. ED Penn. 2017).

Doninger v. Niehoff, 527 F.3d 41 (2d Cir. 2008).

Doninger v. Niehoff, 594 F. Supp. 2nd (D Conn. 2009).

Dore v. Dedminster Board of Education, 449 A.2d 547 (N.J. Super. Ct. App. Div. 1982).

Duffy v. Long Beach City Sch. Dist, 22 N.Y.S. 3d 88 (N.Y. App. Div. 2015).

Dunn v. Fairfield Community High Sch. Dist. No. 225, 158 F.3d 962 (7th Cir. 1998).

DVD Copy Control Association v. Bunner, 10 Cal. Rptr. 3d 185 (Cal: Court of Appeal, 6th Appellate Dist. 2004).

Dynastudy Inc. v. Houston Ind. Sch. Dist., 325 F.Supp.3d 767 (SD Tex. 2017).

E.C. v. County of Suffolk, No. 12–1733-cv (2013).

E.W. ex rel T.W. v. Dolgos, (884 F.3d 172 188 4th Cir. 2018).

Ebonie S. v. Pueblo School District 60, 695 F. 3d 1051 (10th Cir. 2012) cert. denied.

Eckerd v. Indian River School District, 475 F. Supp 13500 (D. Del. 1979).

Edwards v. Aguillard, 482 U.S. 578 (1987).

Ehlinger v. Board of Education of New Hartford Cent. School District, 465 N.Y.S.2d 378 (App. Div. 1983).

Eisel v. Board of Education of Montgomery County, 597 A.2d 447 (Md. 1991).

Elfbrandt v. Russell, 384 U.S. 11 (1966).

Elk Grove Unified School District v. Newdow, 542 U.S. 1 (2004).

Ella T. v. California, Case No. BC685730 (Superior Court CA 2017).

Emmett v. Kent, 92 F. Supp 2d 1088 (Dist. Court, WD Washington, 2000).

Endrew F. v. Douglas County School District, 580 U.S. ___ (2017); 137 S. Ct. 988 (2017).

Engel v. Vitale, 370 U.S. 421 (1962).

Epperson v. Arkansas, 393 U.S. 97 (1968).

Espinoza v. Montana, 591 U.S. ___ (2020).

Estate of Olsen v. Fairfield City Sch. Dist. Bd. of Educ. 341 F.Supp.3d 793 (S.D. Ohio. 2018).

Evans v. Bayer, 684 F. Supp 2d 1365 (S.D. Fla.2010).

Everson v. Board of Education, 330 U.S. 1 (1946).

Fallon v. Indiana Trail School, 148 Ill.App.3d 931, 102 Ill. Dec. 479, 500 (N.E.2d 101 1986).

Falvo v. Owasso Independent School District No. 1-011 et al. 146 F.Supp.2d 1137 (N.D. Okla. 2009).

Fenton v. Stear, 423 F. Supp. 767 (W.D. Pa. 1976).

Fitzgerald v. Barnstable School Committee, 504 F.3d 165 (1st Cir. 2007).

Fitzgerald v. Camdenton R-III School District, 439 F. 3d 773 (8th Cir. 2006).

Flaherty v. Keystone Oaks Sch. Dist, 247 F.Supp.2d 698 (WD Penn. 2003).

Flores v. Morgan Hill Unified School District, 324 F.3d 1130 (2003).

Florida v. Jarines, U.S. 2542 (2013).

Forrest Grove v. T.A., 129 S. Ct. 2484 (2009).

Foster v. Houston General Insurance Company, 401 S0.2d 759, 763 (La. App. 1981).

Franklin v. Gwinnett County Public Schools, 503 U.S. 60 (1992).

Freeman v. Pitts, 503 U.S. 467 (1992).

Freiler v. Tangipahoa Parish Board of Education, 185 F.3d 337 (5th Cir. 1999).

Fremont RE-1 School District v. Jacobs. (Sup. Ct. of Colorado, 1987. 737 P.2d 816).

Fry v. Napoleon Cmty. Schools, 137 S. Ct. 743 (2017).

G.C. v. Owensboro Public Schools, 711 F.3d 623 (6th Cir. 2013).

G.D.M. v. Board of Education Ramapo Indian Hills Regional High School District, 48 A.3d 378 (N.J. Super 2012).

Gabbard v. Madison Local School Dist. Bd. of Educ, Slip Opinion No. 2021-Ohio-2067 (2021).

Gallimore v. Henrico County Sch. Bd, 38 F. Supp. 3d 721 (E.D. Va. 2014).

Garcetti v. Ceballos, 547 U.S. 410, 126 S. Ct. 1951, 164 L. Ed. 2d 689 (2006).

Gary B. v. Snyder, 329 F. Supp.3d 344 (Dist. Court. E.D. Mich. 2018).

Gebser v. Lago Vista Independent School District, 524 U.S. 274; 118 S.Ct. 1989 (1998).

General Dynamics Land Systems, Inc. v. Cline, 296 F. 3d 466 (2003).

GG ex rel. Grimm v. Gloucester County School Bd., 822 F.3d 709 (4th Cir. 2016); 132 F. Supp.3d 736 (ED Va. 2015).

Gitlow v. New York, 268 U.S. 652 (1925).

Givens v. Orleans Parish School Board, 391 S0.2d 976 (La. Ct. App. 1980).

Givhan v. Western Line Consolidated School District, 439 U.S. 410 (1979).

Gomez v. Illinois State Board of Education, 811 F.2d 1030 (7th Cir 1987).

Gong Lum v. Rice, 275 U.S. 78 (1927).

Gonzalez v. Ysleta Indep. Sch. Dist, 996 F.2d 745 (5th Cir. 1993).

Goss v. Lopez, 419 U.S. 565; 955 S.Ct. 729; 42 L.Ed. 2d 725 (1975).

Govel v. Board of Education in the City of Albany, 235 N.Y.S.2d 300 (N.Y. Sup. Ct. 1962).

Graham v. Knutzen, 362 F. Supp. 881 (D. Neb. 1973).

Grajko v. City of N.Y, 57 N.Y.S. 3d 11 (N.Y. App. Div. 2017).

Gratz v. Bollinger, 539 U.S. 244 (2003).

Green v. County School Board of New Kent County, Virginia, 391 U.S. 430 (1968).

Griffin v. County School Board of Prince Edward County, 377 U.S. 218 (1964).

Grimm v. Gloucester Cty. Sch. Bd, 580 U.S. ___ (2017) See also: 302 F. Supp 3d 730 (ED Va. 2018); 972 F.3d 586 (4th Cir. 2020); 400 F.Supp.3d 444 (ED Va. 2019); 869 F.3d 286 (4th Cir. 2017); 976 F.Supp.3d 399 (4th Cir. 2020).

Grove City College v. Bell, U.S.L.W. 4283 (1984), 465 U.S. 555 (1984).

Grutter v. Bollinger, 539 U.S. 306 (2003).

Guerriero v. Sewanhaka Central Sch. Dist, 150 AD 3d 831 (NY App. Div. 2, 2017).

Gusick v. Drebus, 431 F.2d 594 (6th Cir. 1971).

Guttenberg et al. v. The Broward County School Board, 303 So.3d 518 (S. Ct. Fla 2020).

H.W. v. State, 79 So. 3d 143 (Fla. Dist. Ct. App. 2012).

Hachiya/Livingston v. U.S.D. 307, Kans. S.Ct. No. 59594, Syllabus by the Court, February 19, 1988.

Hammond v. Board of Education of Carroll County, 100 Md.App. 60, 639 A.2d 223 (1994).

Hardwick ex rel. Hardwick v. Heyward, 711 F.3d 426 (4th Cir. 2013).

Harper v. Poway Unified School District, 445 F.3d 1052 (9th Cir. 2006).

Harrah Independent School District v. Martin, 440 U.S. 194 (1979).

Harris v. Forklift Systems, 114 S.Ct. 367 (1993). See also Meritor Savings Bank v. Vinson, 477 U.S. 57 (1986).

Hayden v. Greensburg Community School Corporation, 743 F.3d 569 (7th Cir 2014).

Hayes v. Faulkner County, Ark., 2004 WL 2414160 (8th Cir. 2004).

Hazelwood School District v. Kuhlmeier, 484 U. S. 260, 108 S. Ct. 562, 98 L.Ed. 2nd 592, 43 Ed. Law 515 (1988).

Hearring v. Sliwowski, 2012 U.S. Dist. LEXIS 9758 (M.D. Tenn. 2012).

Hebert v. Ventetuolo., 638 F.2d 5 (1st Cir. 1981).

Hedges v. Wauconda Community Unit Sch. Dist. No. 18, 1991 U.S.Dist. LEXIS 14873 (N.D. Ill. 1991).

Hernandez v. Grisham, No. CIV 20-0942 JB/GBW, WL 6063799 (D.N.M. Oct. 14, 2020).

Herrera v. Santa Fe Public Schools, 2013 U.S. Dist. LEXIS 96171 (D. N.M. June 28, 2013).

Herrman v. Board of Education of Unified School District No. 256, No. 01–4019-RDR, 2002 U.S. Dist. LEXIS 21700 (D. Kan. Oct. 16, 2002).

Hill v. Madison County School Board, No. 14-12481 (11th Cir. N.D. Al. 2015).

Hines v. Caston Sch. Corp, 651 N.E.2d 330 (Ind. App. 1995).

Hinterlong v. Arlington Independent School District, 2010 Tex. App. LEXIS 1010 (Tex. App. Feb. 11, 2010).

Hogenson v. Williams, 542 S.W. 2d 456, 459 (Tex. Civ. App. Texarkana 1976).

Honig v. Doe, 484 U.S. 305 (1988).

Hooks v. Clark County School District, 228 F. 3d 1036 (9th Cir. 2000).

Horton v. Goose Creek, 690 F.2d. 470 (5th Cir. 1982).

Hortonville Joint School District No. 1 v. Hortonville Education Association, 426 U.S. 482 (1976).

Hough v. Shakopee Public Schools, 608 F. Supp. 2d 1087 (D. Minn. 2009).

Howard v. Colonial School District, 621 A. 2d 362 (Del. Super. Ct. 1992).

Lampkin v. District of Columbia, 27 F.3d 605 (D.C. Cir. 1994).

Latour v. Riverside Beaver Sch. Dist, No. Civ. A, 2005 W.L. 2106562 (2005).

Lau v. Nichols, 414 U.S. 563 (1974).

Laveck v. City of Janesville, 204 N.W.2d 6 (Wis. Sup. Ct. 1973).

Layshock v. Hermitage School District, 2010 U.S. App. LEXIS 2384 (3rd Cir. February 4, 2010). See also Layshock ex rel. Layshock v. Hermitage School District, 593 F. 3d 249 (3d Cir. 2010) and 650 F. 3d 205 (3d Cir. 2011).

Lee v. Weisman, 505 U.S. 577 (1992).

Lee v. York County School Division. (418 F.Supp.2d 816, E.D. Va. 2006).

Lemon v. Kurtzman, 403 U.S. 602 (1971).

Levyn v. Amback, 445 N.Y.S.2d 303 (N.Y. App. Div. 1981).

Lewis v. Town of Newtown, 214 A.3d 405 (Conn. App. Ct. 2019).

Lillard v. Shelby County Bd. of Educ, 76 F.3d 716, 725 (6th Cir. 1996).

Littell v. Houston Independent Sch. Dist, 894 F.3d 616 (5th Cir. 2018).

Littlefield v. Forney Independent Sch. Dist, 268 F.3d 275 (5th Cir. 2001).

Longoria v. San Benito Ind. Sch. Dist., 942 F.3d 258 (5th Cir. 2019).

Love v. Penn-Harris-Madison Sch. Corp, Cause No. 3: 14-CV-2039 (N.D. Ind. 2016)

Lowery v. Euverard, 497 F.3d 584, 591–92, 596 (6th Cir. 2007).

Luce v. Board of Education, 157 N.Y.S.2d 123 (N.Y. App. Div. 1956).

Lucia v. Duggan, 303 F. Supp. 112 (D. Mass. 1969).

Lynch v. Donnelly, 465 U.S. 668 (1984).

M.C. v. Antelope Valley Union School District, 858 F.3d 1189 (9th Cir. 2017).

M.R. v. Ridley School District, 744 F.3d 112 (3rd Cir. 2014).

Maack v. School District of Lincoln, 241 Neb. 847 (1992).

Mahaffey ex rel. Mahaffey v. Aldrich, 236 F.Supp.3d 779 (ED Mich. 2002).

Mahanoy Area School District v. B.L. (594 U.S. ____ 2021).

Mailloux v. Kiley, 323 F. Supp. 1387 (D. Mass. 1971).

Mapp v. Ohio, 367 U.S. 643 (1961).

Marbury v. Madison, 5 U.S. 137 (1803).

Marcus v. Rowley, 695 F.2d 1171 (9th Cir. 1983).

Mark v. Borough of Hatboro, 51 EM 1137 (3rd Cir. 1995).

Marsh v. Chambers, 463 U.S. 783 (1983).

Martinez v. Bynum, 461 U.S. 321, 103 S. Ct. 1838 (1983).

Martinez v. School Board of Hillsborough County, 861 F.2d 1502 (1988).

Matter of Rubino v. City of New York, 106 AD 3d 439 (NY App Div. 1. 2013).

Maxey v. McDowell County Board of Education, 212 W. Va. 668, 575 S.E.2d 278 (2002).

Mayer v. Monroe County Community School Corporation., 474 F.3d 477 (7th Cir. 2007).

McClain v. Lafayette County Board of Education. (U.S. Ct. of App. 5th Cir. 1982, 673 F.2d 106).

Meek v. Pittenger, 421 U.S. 349 (1975).

Meltzer v. Board of Public Instruction of Orange County, 548 F.2d 559 (5th Cir. 1977).

Menard v. La. High School Athletic Association, 30 S0.3d 79 (La. Ct. App. 2009).

Mendoza v. Klein, No. H-09-3895, slip op. at 2 (S.D. Tex. Mar. 15, 2011).

Meredith v. Jefferson County Board of Education et al, 551 U.S. 701 (2007).

Mergens v. Board of Education of Westside Community Schools, 867 F.2d 1076 (8th Cir. 1989).

Meritor Savings Bank v. Vinson, 477 U.S. 57 (1986).

Metro-Goldwin-Mayer Studios, Inc. v. Grokster, 545 U.S. 913 (2005).

Metzger By and Through Metzger v. Osbeck, 841 F.2d 518 (3rd Cir. 1988).

Meyer v. Nebraska, 262 U.S. 390, 399 (1923).

Meyers v. Ferndale Sch. Dist, No. 98280-5 (Wash. Sup. Ct. 2021).

Miles v. Denver Public Schools, 944 F.2d 773 (10th Cir. 1991).

Miller v. Monroe School District, 159 F. Supp. 3d 1238 (W.D. Wash. 2016).

Miller v. Skumanick, 605 F. Supp. 2d 634, 637–39 (M.D. Pa. 2009). See also Miller v. Mitchell, 598 F. 3d 139 (3rd Cir. 2010).

Milligan-Hitt v. Board of Trustees of Sheridan County School District No. 2, 523 F.3d 1219 (10th Cir. 2008).

Milliken v. Bradley (Milliken II), 433 U.S. 267 (1977).

Milliken v. Bradley, 418 U.S. 717 (1974).

Mills v. Board of Education of the District of Columbia, 348 F. Supp 866 (D.C. 1972).

Minarcini v. Strongville City School District, 541 F.2d 577 (6th Cir. 1976).

Minersville School District v. Gobitis, 310 U.S. 586 (1940).

Mirich v. State ex rel, Board of Trustees of Laramie County School District Two, No. 20-1034 (Wyo. 2021).

Missouri v. Jenkins, 495 U.S. 33 (1990).

Missouri v. Jenkins, 515 U.S. 70 (1995).

Mitchell v. Helms, (98–1648) 530 US 793, 151 F.3d 347 (2000).

Monell v. Department of Social Services, 436 U.S. 658 (1978).

Monroe v. Central Bucks School District, 805 F. 3d 454 (3rd Cir. 2015).

Moore v. Tyson, No. 1190547 (Ala. 2021).

Richards v. Thurston, 424 F.2d. 1281 (1st Cir. 1970).

Riehm v. Engelking, 538 F.3d 952 (8th Cir. August 15, 2007).

Riley v. California, 573 U.S. 373 (2014).

Ríos v. Reed, 480 F. Sup. 14 (E.D.N.Y. 1978).

Rivera v. East Otero School District R-1, (721 F.Supp 1189, D.Colo. 1998).

Robbins v. Lower Merion Sch. Dist, Civil Action No. 10-665 (E.D. Pa. 2010).

Roberts v. Robertson County Board of Education, 692 S.W.2d 863 (Tenn. App. 1985).

Robertson v. Anderson Mill Elementary School., No. 19-2157 (4th Cir. 2021).

Rogers v. Christina School District, No. 45, A.3d 1 73 (Del. 2013).

Rosemont Enters. v. Random House, Inc, 366 F.2d 303, 306 (2d Cir. 1966).

Ruiz De Gutierrez v. Albuquerque Public Schools, 2019 U.S. Dist. LEXIS 7871 (D.N.M. 2019).

S.G. v. Sayreville Board of Education, 333F.3d. 417 (3rd. Cir. 2003).

S.J.W. v. Lee's Summit R-7 School District, 696 F.3d 771 (8th Cir. 2012).

S.R. v. Kenton County, 302 F.Supp.3d 821 (E.D. Ky. 2017).

Safford Unified School District No. 1 v. Redding, 129 S. Ct. 2633 (2009).

Safon v. Bellmore-Merrick Central High School District, 22 N.Y.S. 3d 233 (N.Y. App. Div. 2015).

Sagehorn v. Indep. Sch. Dist. No. 728, 122 F.Supp.3d 842 (D. Minn. 2015).

San Antonio Independent School District v. Rodriguez, 411 U.S. 1 (1973).

San Antonio Independent School District v. Rodriguez, 411 U.S. 907 (1997).

San Diego Community Against Registration and the Draft v. Governing Board of Grossmont Union High School District, 790 F.2d 1471 (9th Cir. 1986).

Sanches v. Carrollton Farmers Branch Ind. Sch. Dist, 647 F.3d 156 (5th Cir. 2011).

Santa Fe Independent School District v. Doe, 530 U.S. 290 (2000).

Schaffer v. Weast, 546 U.S. 49 (2005).

Scheelhasse v. Woodbury Central School District, 488 F.2d 237 (8th Cir. 1973).

School Dist. Bd. of Dir. v. Lundblad, 528 N.W.2d 593 (Iowa 1995).

School Dist. of Abington Township v. Schempp, 374 U.S. 203 (1963).

School Dist. of the City of Grand Rapids et al. v. Ball, 473 U.S. 373 (1985).

Scopes v. State of Tennessee, 154 Tenn. 105, 289, S.W. 363 (1927).

Scott v. City of Albuquerque, No. 15-2154 (10th Cir. 2017).

Scott v. County of San Bernardino, 903 F. 3d 943 (9th Cir. 2018).

Scott v. School Board of Alachua County, 324 F.3d 1246, 11th Cir. 2003).

Seal v. Morgan, 229 F.3d 567 (6th Cir. 2000).

Seamons v. Snow, 84 F.3d 1226 (10th Cir. 1996).

Sekor v. Board of Education, 240 Conn. 119 (Conn. Supreme Court 1997).

Serna v. Portales, F.2d 1147 (10th Cir. May 1974).

Sharp v. Fairbanks North Star Borough, 569 P.2d 178 (Alaska 1977).

Shuman v. Cumberland Valley School District Board of Directors, 536 A.2d 490 (Pa. Commw. Ct. 1988).

Simmons v. Beauregard Parish School Board, 315 S0.2d 883 (La. App. 3rd Cir. 1975).

Simonetti v. School District of Philadelphia, 308 Pa.Super. 555, 454 A.2d 1038 (1982).

Slane v. City of Hilliard, 59 N.E.3d 545 (Ohio Ct. App. 2016).

Smith et al. v. City of Jackson, Mississippi et al, 125 S. Ct. 1536 (2005).

Smith v. Board of Education, 708 F.2d 258 (7th Cir. 1983).

Smith v. Dorsey. (Sup. Ct. of Miss., 1988. 530 So.2d 5).

Smith v. School City of Hobart, 811 F. Supp 391 (N.D. Ind. 1993).

Smith v. Tammany Parish School Board, 448 F.2d 414 (5th Cir. 1971).

Snyder v. Millersville University. Civil Action. No. 07-1660 (E.D. Pa. Dec. 3, 2008).

Sony Corporation of America v. Universal City Studios, Inc. 464 U.S. 417 (1984).

South Gibson School Board v. Sollman, 768 NE 2d (S.C. Ind. 2002).

Spanierman v. Hughes, 576 F. Supp.2d 292 (D.C. Conn. 2008).

Spears v. Jefferson Parish School Board, 646 S0.2d 1104 (La.App.1994).

Sperry v. Fremont County Sch. Dist. No. 6, 84 F. Supp. 3d 1277 (D. Wyo. 2015).

State ex rel. Hawkins v. Board of Education, 275 S.E.2d 908 (W. Va. 1980).

State of Louisiana in the interest of K.L, 217 S.3d 628 (La. Ct. App. 2017).

State v. M.M. 407 So.2d 987 (Fla. App. 1981).

State v. Polk, 78 N.E.3d 834 (Ohio 2017).

State v. Riddle, 285 S.E.2d 359 (1981).

State v. Williams, 521 S.W.3d 689 (Mo. Ct. App. 2017).

Steirer v. Bethlehem Area School District, 987 F.2d 989 (3rd Cir. 1993).

Stephenson v. Davenport Community School District, 110 F.3d 1303 (8th Cir. 1997).

References and Resources

ACLU. (2017). *Bullies in blue: The origins and consequences of school policing.* [White Paper]. ACLU Foundation. https://www.aclu.org/report/bullies-blue-origins-and-consequences-school-policing

ACLU. (2019). Shawnee Mission School District settles ACLU of Kansas lawsuit; agrees to staff training, policy changes and plaintiff damages of $1. ALCU of Kansas. https://www.aclukansas.org/en/press-releases/shawnee-mission-school-district-settles-aclu-kansas-lawsuit-agrees-staff-training

Advancement Project. (2010). *Test, punish, and push out: How zero tolerance and high-stakes testing funnel youth into the school-to-prison pipeline.* Retrieved February 22, 2010, from http://www.advancementproject.org/digital-library/publications/test-punish-and-push-out-how-zero-tolerance-and-high-stakes-testing-fu.

Advancement Project. (2014). *Restorative practices: Fostering healthy relationships & promoting positive discipline in schools. A guide for educators.* http://schottfoundation.org/sites/default/files/restorative-practices-guide.pdf

Age Discrimination in Employment Act of 1967, 29 U.S.C. § 621 (§ 623).

Alexander, K., & Alexander, M. (1998). *American public school law* (4th ed.). West/Thompson.

American Academy of Pediatrics. (1995). *Some more things you should know about physical and emotional child abuse (adapted from Caring for your school-age child: Ages 5 to 12).* Bantam. Retrieved February 13, 2001, from www.aap.org/advocacy/childhealthmonth/ABUSE2.HTM

American Academy of Pediatrics. (2001). Retrieved February 13, 2001, from www.aap.org/advocacy/archives/janhiv.htm

American Association of University Women. (1993). *Hostile hallways: The AAUW survey on sexual harassment in America's schools.* Author.

American Law Institute. (1965). *The restatement of torts* (2nd ed., Section 21). Author.

American Library Association (ALA). https://www.ala.org/

American Library Association. (2005). *Challenged and banned books.* Retrieved May 30, 2005, from http://www.ala.org

American Library Association. (n.d.). *Censorship and challenges.* Retrieved May 30, 2005, from http//:www.ala.org

American Library Association. (n.d.). *Support for dealing with or reporting challenges to library materials.* Retrieved May 30, 2005, from http://www.ala.org

American Psychological Association. (2005). *Summary of the APA resolution recommending retirement of American Indian Mascots.* http://www.apa.org/pi/oema/resources/indian-mascots.aspx

American Psychological Association Zero Tolerance Task Force. (2006). *Are zero-tolerance policies effective in the schools? An evidentiary review and recommendations.* American Psychological Association.

Americans with Disabilities Act of 1990, 42 U.S.C. § 12101 et seq.

Americans with Disabilities Act, Pub. L. No. 101–336, 42 U.S.C. §§ 12101–12213.

Association of the Bar of the City of New York. (1926). *Lectures on legal topics.* Association of the Bar of the City of New York.

Bagby, R., Bailey, G., Bodensteiner, D., & Lumley, D. (2000). *Plans and policies for technology in education: A compendium* (2nd ed.). National School Boards Association.

Belluck, P. (1999). *Kansas votes to delete evolution from state's science curriculum.* Retrieved March 6, 2001, from www.nytimes.com/library/national/081299kan-evolution-edu.html

Black's Law Dictionary. (1979). West.

Board of Education of School District 228, Cook County, Illinois. (1984). *Prohibiting gangs and gang activities.* Policy adopted April 24, 1984.

Borsuk, A. J., & Murphy, M. B. (1999). Idle or otherwise, threats bring severe discipline; Where area students once faced a principal, now they face the police. *Milwaukee Journal Sentinel*, p. 8.

Brown v. Board of Education of Topeka (Brown I), 347 U.S. 453 (1954).

Buck, G. H., Polloway, E. A., Smith-Thomas, A., & Cook, K. W. (2003). Prereferral intervention processes: A survey of state practices. *Exceptional Children, 69,* 349–360.

CDC (2021). *LGBT Youth | Lesbian, Gay, Bisexual, and Transgender Health | CDC.* Cdc.gov. (2021). Retrieved August 20, 2021, from https://www.cdc.gov/lgbthealth/youth.htm

Cable in the Classroom. (n.d.). Retrieved from http://www.ciconline.com

California Assembly Bill 1266 for Transgender Student Rights (2013).

Calvert, C. (2001). Off-campus speech, on-campus punishment: Censorship of the emerging Internet underground. *Boston University Journal of Science & Technology Law, 7,* 243–271.

Calvert, C. (2009). *Sex, cell phones, privacy, and the First Amendment: When children become child pornographers and the Lolita effect undermines the law. Comm Law Conspectus, 18*(1). Retrieved from https://scholarship.law.edu/commlaw/vol18/iss1/3

Canicosa, J. C. (2020). *Bill addressing discipline in virtual classrooms is changed to cover only students who've been recommended for expulsion.* Retrieved November 5, 2021, from https://lailluminator.com/2020/10/19/bill-addressing-discipline-in-virtual-classrooms-is-changed-to-cover-only-students-whove-been-recommended-for-expulsion

Centers for Disease Control and Prevention. (2005). *Fact sheet—HIV/AIDS among youth.* Retrieved June 1, 2005, from http://www.cdc.gov/hiv/pubs/facts/youth.htm

Centers for Disease Control and Prevention. (2013). *Get a heads up on concussion in sports policies.* Retrieved August 31, 2013, from http://www.cdc.gov/concussion/pdf/HeadsUpOnConcussion InSportsPolicies-a.pdf

Chase, A. (2001). Violent reaction: What do teen killers have in common? *In These Times, 25*(16), 1627. Retrieved November 1, 2005, from www.zumba.org/pbedu/backtoschool/bullyingGayYouth.cfm

Child Abuse Prevention and Treatment Act Amendments of 1996 Pub. L. No. 104–235, Section 111; 42 U.S.C. 5106 g.

Child Abuse Prevention and Treatment Act of 1974 (CAPTA) Pub. L. No. 93–247.

Children's Online Privacy Act of 1998, 15 U.S.C. 6501–6506 (1999).

Civil Rights Act of 1871, 42 U.S.C. § 1983.

Civil Rights Act of 1964 § 7, 42 U.S.C. § 2000e et seq (1964).

Clery Act (20 U.S.C. §1092(f) (2018)).

Cohen, R. (1986). Drug use testing: Costly and corruptible. *New York Times,* p. A23.

Columbia Deaf, Dumb, and Blind Institution Incorporated. (1857). Pub. L. No. 34–5, 11 Stat. 161.

Colwell, W. (2019). In Education Law Association Annual Conference, Norfolk, VA.

Commonwealth Fund. (1999). *Improving the health of adolescent girls: Policy report of Commonwealth Fund Commission on Women's Health.* Author.

Communications Decency Act of 1996, 47 U.S.C. 230(c) (1999).

Conn, K., & Zirkel, P. (2000). Legal aspects of Internet accessibility and use in K–12 public schools: What do school districts need to know? *Education Law Report, 146,* 56–61.

Copyright Act of 1976. Pub. L. 105–304 112 Stat. 2860; 17 U.S.C. 101.

Copyright Term Extension Act (CTEA) 17 U.S.C. §§ 301–304.

Cordes, H. J., & Ferak, J. (2011). Millard South shooting: Suspension ignited fury. *Omaha.com.* Retrieved September 29, 2013, from http://www.omaha.com/article/20110105/NEWS97/110109863.

Courthouse News Service. (2011). *Family claims H.S. principal went ballistic.* Retrieved September 9, 2013, from http://courthousenews.com/2011/05/10/36439.htm

Demitchell, T. A., & Carroll, T. (1997). Mandatory drug testing of student athletes: A policy response to Vernonia School District, 47J v. Acton. *Journal of School Leadership, 7*(1), 50–68. https://doi.org/10.1177/105268469700700103

Dieterich, D., & Greschler, G. (2018). *After months of criticism and bad press, Texas high school reverses prior review policy, allows editorials.* Student Press Law Center. Retrieved August 17, 2021, from https://splc.org/2018/05/0522prosper-2/

Digital Millennium Copyright Act of 1998. Pub. L. 105–304 112 Stat. 2860; 17 U.S.C. 101.

Dunklee, D. R., & Shoop, R. J. (1993). *A primer for school risk management: Creating and maintaining district and site-based liability prevention programs.* Allyn & Bacon.

Eckes, S. (2017). Homophobic expression in K-12 public schools: Legal and policy considerations involving speech that denigrates others. *Berkeley Review of Education, 7*(1). https://doi.org/10.5070/b87129436

Education for All Handicapped Children Act of 1975, 20 U.S.C. § 1400 et seq.

Education of the Blind Acts of 1879, Pub. L. No. 45–186, 20 Stat. 467.

Education of the Handicapped Act Amendments of 1986, 20 U.S.C. § 1400 et seq.

Education of the Handicapped Act of 1970, Pub. L. No. 91–230, 84 Stat. 175, Part B.

Education Week. (1998). *A trust betrayed*. Retrieved from http://www.edweek.org/ew/collections/trust_betrayed/

EFF. (2020). *Schools are spying on students—but students can fight back*. Retrieved January 4, 2022, from https://www.eff.org/press/releases/schools-are-spying-students-students-can-fight-back

Elementary and Secondary Education Act Amendments of 1966, Pub. L. No. 89–750, § 161, 80 Stat. 328.

Elementary and Secondary Education Act of 1965, Pub. L. No. 89–10, 79 Stat. 27.

Eltagouri, M. (2018). A Santa Fe shooting survivor's reaction has shaken people around the country. *The Washington Post*. Retrieved November 5, 2021, from https://www.washingtonpost.com/news/post-nation/wp/2018/05/18/i-always-felt-it-would-eventually-happen-here-a-santa-fe-high-school-survivors-reaction-to-the-shooting/

Equal Access Act, P.L. 98–377 § 802 (1984).

Equal Educational Opportunities Act Section 1703, 20 U.S.C. § 1703.

Equal Pay Act of 1963. Pub. L. 88–38, 1963, 77 Stat. 56; 29 U.S.C. 201.

Establishment of Religion Clause of the First Amendment, 736 F. Supp. 1247, 1253 (1990).

Every Student Succeeds Act (ESSA) 20 U.S.C. § 6301 (2015).

Fair Labor Standards Act of 1938, 52 Stat. 1060; 29 U.S.C. 201.

Family and Medical Leave Act of 1993, Pub. L. No. 103–3, 29 CFR § 825.

Family Educational Rights and Privacy Act, 20 USCS § 1232g (2002).

Family Educational Rights and Privacy Act of 1974, 20 U.S.C. § 1232G.

Federal Register. (2005). 34 C.F.R. Parts 300, 301, and 304. Assistance to States for the education of children with disabilities; Preschool grants for children with disabilities; and service obligations under special education—personnel development to improve services and results for children with disabilities; Proposed rule. U.S. Department of Education, 35782–35892.

Fields, C. L. (2005). *Good news? Advancing religion through litigation against the public schools*. Paper presented July 14, 2005, at the Oxford Roundtable: Education Law and Public Policy. Oxford University, Oxford, England.

First, P., & Cooper, G. (1989). Access to education by homeless children. *Education Law Report, 53*(757), 759.

Foodallergy.org. (2013). *School guidelines for managing students with food allergies*. Retrieved September 3, 2013, from http://www.foodallergy.org/document.doc?id=135

Freiler v. Tangipahoa Parish Board of Education, 975 F. Supp. 819 (1997). See also Freiler v. Tangipahoa Parish Board of Education, 201 F.3d 602 (2000); Tangipahoa Parish Board of Education v. Herb Freiler 120 S.Ct. 2706 (2000).

Friedlander, M. (1991). The newcomer program: Helping immigrant students succeed in U.S. schools. *Program Information Guide 8*. Washington, DC: National Clearing House for Bilingual Education.

Gay, Lesbian, & Straight Education Network. (2003). *National school climate survey*. Retrieved from http://www.glsen.org

Gillis, J. (1995). 15-member Colorado association staff serves 285 schools across state. *National Federation News, 12*(5), 23–25.

Graca, T., & Stader, D. (2007). Student speech and the Internet: A legal analysis. *NASSP Bulletin, 91*(2), 121–129.

Grindal, T., Schifter, L., Schwartz, G., & Hehir, T. (2019). Racial differences in special education identification and placement: Evidence across three states. *Harvard Education Review, 89*(4), 525–553.

Hachiya, R. (2010). *Balancing student rights and the need for safe schools*. Retrieved from http://hdl.handle.net/1808/6476

Heaviside, S., Rowand, C., Williams, C., & Farris, E. (1998). *Violence and discipline problems in U.S. public Schools: 1996–1997*. (NCES 98–030). U.S. Department of Education, National Center for Education Statistics.

Hendrie, C. (2003). States target sexual abuse by educators. *Education Week*. Retrieved from http://www.edweek.org

Henn, H. G. (1988). *Copyright law: A practitioner's guide* (2nd ed.). Practicing Law Institute.

Hickman, D. (2000). Athletic associations and disabled student-athletes in the 1990s. *Education Law Report, 143*, 12–13.

Hofheimer, A. *Saved by the bell? Is online, off-campus student speech protected by the First Amendment?*, 40 Fla. St. U. L. Rev. (2013). https://ir.law.fsu.edu/lr/vol40/iss4/5

Hudson, D. Jr. (2005). Adam Porter's case: Epitome of overreaction in Columbine age. *First Amendment Center*. Retrieved February 22, 2010, from http://www.firstamendmentcenter.org/analysis.aspx?id=15062

Huefner, D. S. (2000). *Getting comfortable with special education law: A framework for working with children with disabilities*. Christopher-Gordon.

Imber, M., & Van Geel, T. (1993). *Education law*. McGraw-Hill College.

Immigration Reform and Control Act of 1986. Pub. L. 99–603. 100 Stat. 3359; 8 U.S.C. 101.

Individuals with Disabilities Education Act (IDEA), 20 USCS § 1415 (2002).

Individuals with Disabilities Education Act Amendments of 1997, Pub. L. No. 105–17. 20 U.S.C. § 1400 et seq.

Individuals with Disabilities Education Act of 1990, 20 U.S.C. § 1400 et seq.

Individuals with Disabilities Education Improvement Act of 2004, Pub. L. No. 108–446, 118 Stat. 2651.

International Child Abduction Remedies Act, 42 USCS § 11601, et seq. (1988).

Kaiser Family Foundation. (2000). *National survey of teens on HIV/AIDS.* Retrieved June 1, 2005, from http://kff.org/hivaids/issue-brief/national-survey-of-teens-on-hivaids/

KANAE (2021). Kansas Association for Native American Education. Kansas State University. https://coe.ksu.edu/collaborations/partnerships/kanae/

Katsiyannis, A., Yell, M. L., & Bradley, R. (2001). Reflections on the 25th anniversary of the Individuals with Disabilities Education Act. *Remedial and Special Education, 22,* 324–334.

Katz, H. (2007). *Can the "heckler's veto" trump Tinker-protected student speech?* National School Boards Association.

Kidder, R. (2009). *How good people make tough choices: Resolving the dilemmas of ethical living.* Harper Collins.

Kim-Prieto, C., Goldstein, L. A., Okazaki, S., & Kirschner, B. (2010). Effect of exposure to an American Indian mascot on the tendency to stereotype a different minority group. *Journal of Applied Social Psychology, 40*(3), 534–553. https://doi.org/10.1111/j.1559-1816.2010.00586.x

Kosciw, J. G. (2004). *The 2003 national school climate study: The school-related experiences of our nation's lesbian, gay, bisexual and transgender youth.* GLSEN.

LawAtlas. (2012). *Youth sports TBI laws map.* Retrieved August 31, 2013, from http://www.lawatlas.org/preview?dataset=sc-reboot

Levin, M. L. (2000). It's the law. *PSBA Bulletin,* 33–40.

Lieb, D. A. (2011). Missouri repeals law restricting teacher-student internet and Facebook interaction. *Huffington Post.* Retrieved October 4, 2013, from http://www.huffingtonpost.com/2011/10/21/missouri-repeals-law-rest_n_1025761.html

Lipinski, T. A. (1999). Designing and using web-based materials in education: A webpage legal audit. *Education Law Report, 137,* 6–9.

Llewellyn, K. N., Gewirtz, P., & Ansaldi, M. (1988). The case law system in America. *Columbia Law Review, 88*(5), 989–1020. https://doi.org/10.2307/1122696

Lorang, M. R., McNiel, D. E., & Binder R. L. (2016). Minors and sexting: Legal implications. *The Journal of the American Academy of Psychiatry and the Law 44,* no. 1, 73-81.

Martin, E. W., Martin, R., & Terman, D. L. (1996). The legislative and litigation history of special education. *The Future of Children, 6,* 25–39.

Martin, M. (2009). *Asst. principal vindicated of 'sexting' charges.* NPR Tell Me More. Retrieved August 17, 2021, from https://www.npr.org/templates/story/story.php?storyId=103562915

Massachusetts Governor's Commission of Gay and Lesbian Youth. (1993). *Making schools safe for gay and lesbian youth.* Author.

Mawdsley, R. D., & Russo, C. J. (2003). FERPA, student privacy and the classroom: What can be learned from Owasso School District v. Falvo? *Education Law Report, 171,* 23–27.

McGinely, C. (2010). *Statement released on Lower Merion Township School District website.* Retrieved February 28, 2010, from http://www.lmsd.org

McKinney-Vento Homeless Assistance Act, P.L. 100-77, 101 Stat. 482 (1987).

Megan's Law, 42 U.S.C. 14071(e) (2000).

Merkwae, A. (2015). *Schooling the police: Race, disability, and the conduct of school resource officers,* 21 Mich. J. Race & L. 147, 158 (2015) (quoting The Nat'l Ass'n of Sch. Res. Officers, https://nasro.org/ (last visited August 25, 2017)).

Migrant Education Program (MEP), Sections 1301, 1302, 1303, 1304, 1305, 1306(a) of Title I, Part C; Section 9302 of Title IX; Section 421(b) of GEPA.

Mills v. Board of Education of the District of Columbia, 348 F. Supp. 866 (D.D.C. 1972).

Milner, M. G., & Miner, J. B. (1978). *Employee selection within the law.* Bureau of National Affairs.

Minow, M. (1990). *Making all the difference: Inclusion, exclusion, and American law.* Cornell University Press. Available at http://www.jstor.org/stable/10.7591/j.ctt1tm7j8t

Molsbee, S. (2008). Zeroing out zero tolerance: Eliminating zero-tolerance policies in Texas schools. *Texas Tech Law Review, 40,* 325–363.

Mulvey, E., & Cauffman, E. (2001). The inherent limits of predicting school violence. *American Psychologist, 56,* 797–802.

National Alliance for Youth Sports. (n.d.). *Background screening in youth sports.* Retrieved December 20, 2003, from http://www.nays.org/fullstory.cfm?articleid=225

National Alliance on Mental Illness-NAMI (2021). *COVID-19 information and resources | NAMI: National Alliance on Mental Illness.* Nami.org. (2021). Retrieved August 20, 2021, from https://www.nami.org/Support-Education/NAMI-HelpLine/COVID-19-Information-and-Resources

National Center for Education Statistics. (2003). *1.1 million homeschooled students in the United States in 2003.* Retrieved June 1, 2005, from http://nces.ed.gov/nhes/homeschool

National Center for Learning Disabilities (NCLD). (2020). *Significant disproportionality in special education: Current trends and actions for impact.* Retrieved from https://www.ncld.org/sigdispro.

National Center for Missing and Exploited Children. (1999). *1998 missing children statistics fact sheet.* Author.

National Clearinghouse for Bilingual Education. (n.d.). Retrieved March 1, 2001, from http://www.ncbe.gwu.edu

National Council of Teachers of English. (2014). *Position statement guidelines for selection of materials in English language arts programs.* Retrieved from https://ncte.org/statement/material-selection-ela/

National Council of Teachers of English. (n.d.). Retrieved February 13, 2001, from http://www.ncte.org/resolutions/textbook891989.html

National School Boards Association. (2004). *Dealing with legal matters surrounding students' sexual orientation and gender identity.* Author.

National School Boards Association. (2011). *Legal clips: California district hires company to monitor students' online activity.* Retrieved September 9, 2013, from http://legalclips.nsba.org/? p=22959. Also, *Legal clips: California school district suspends student for insulting teacher on Facebook.* Retrieved September 9, 2013, from http://legalclips.nsba.org/?p=4559 and *Legal clips: Student paralyzed by beating sues bully's parent and school officials.* Retrieved September 10, 2013, from http://legalclips.nsba.org/?p=9267

National School Safety Center. (1998). *Checklist of characteristics of youth who have caused school-associated violent deaths.* Retrieved December 11, 2013, from http://www.schoolsafety.us/news/freearchiveof-schoolsafetynewsjournals

NCES. (2021). *Homeschooling.* National Center for Education Statistics. (2021). Retrieved August 20, 2021, from https://nces.ed.gov/fastfacts/display.asp?id=91.

NCLD. (2020). *Significant disproportionality in special education: Current trends and actions for impact.* National Center for Learning Disabilities. Retrieved from https://www.ncld.org/sigdispro/

NEA. (2020). Truth in labeling. (2007). In *Significant disproportionality in special education: Current trends and actions for impact.* National Center for Learning Disabilities. Washington, D.C. Retrieved from https://www.ncld.org/sigdispro/

Newman, D. (2005). Breakthrough: A landmark Supreme Court decision is being hailed as "the Emancipation Proclamation for older workers." *AARP Bulletin, 46*(5).

NFL Evolution.com. (2013). *Health & safety.* Retrieved August 31, 2013, from http://www.nflevolution.com

No Child Left Behind Act of 2001, Pub L. No. 107–110, H. R. No. 108–446, 118 Stat. 2651 (2002).

Noel, A., Stark, P., & Redford, J. (2013). *Parent and family involvement in education.* National Household Education Surveys Program of 2012 (NCES 2013–028). National Center for Education Statistics, Institute of Education Sciences, U.S. Department of Education. Retrieved September 13, 2013, from http://nces.ed.gov/pubsearch

Nolet, V., & McLaughlin, M. J. (2000). *Accessing the general curriculum: Including students with disabilities in standards-based reform.* Corwin.

N.M. Stat. Ann. § 30-20-13(D)).

NPBEA. (2018). *National Educational Leadership Preparation (NELP) Program Standards—building level.* Retrieved from www.npbea.org

OCR Policy Guidance Portal. https://www2.ed.gov/about/offices/list/ocr/frontpage/faq/rr/policyguidance/index.html

Office for Civil Rights, Department of Education. (2000). Revised sexual harassment guidance: Harassment of students by school employees, other students or third parties. *Federal Register, 65,* 66091–66114.

Osborne, A. G., & Russo, C. J. (2007). *Special education and the law.* Corwin.

Osborne, A. G., & Russo, C. J. (2009). *Discipline in special education.* Corwin.

Panaro, G. P. (1990). *Employment law manual.* Warren, Gorham, & Lamont.

Papay, J. P. (2012). Refocusing the debate: Assessing the purposes and tools for teacher evaluation. *Harvard Education Review, 82*(1), 123–141.

Parental Kidnapping Prevention Act (PKPA), 28 U.S.C.A. 1738(a) (1994).

Pauken, P. D. (2005). *Religion in public school curricula in the United States and Ireland: The legal balance between educational authority and individual rights.* Paper presented July 12, 2005, at Oxford Round Table: Education Law and Public Policy, Oxford University, Oxford, England.

Pennsylvania Association for Retarded Citizens (PARC) v. Commonwealth of Pennsylvania, 343 F. Supp. 279 (E.D. Pa. 1972).

People for the American Way. (1999). *E-mail newsletter, 3*(1). Retrieved February 13, 2001, from http://www.pfaw.org

Pew Research Center. (2005). *Religion and public life project.* Retrieved May 6, 2005 from http://pewforum.org

Potts, K., Njie, B., Detch, E., & Walton, J. (2003). *Zero-tolerance in Tennessee: An update.* Nashville: Tennessee Comptroller of the Treasury, Office of Research and Educational Accountability.

Protection of Pupil Rights Amendment, 20 U.S.C. § 1232h; 34 CFR Part 98 (1978).

Protection of Pupil Rights Amendment, 20 U.S.C. § 1232h (2004).

Protectkids.com. (2001). *Downloading.* Retrieved February 13, 2001, from http://www.protectkids.com/index.html

Proctor, D., Foskett, J., & Yoder, L. (2016). *Civil rights liability in the public schools—A 19th century law wrestles with 21st century problems.* Presentation, School Law Seminar, Boston MA.

Reason, J. (1990). The contribution of latent human failures to the breakdown of complex systems. *Philosophical Transactions of the Royal Society of London, Series B, Biological Sciences.* 327 (1241).

RedCorn, S. (2017). *Set the prairie on fire: an autoethnographic confrontation of colonial entanglements* (Ed.). Kansas State University. Available at https://krex.k-state.edu/dspace/handle/2097/36214

RedCorn, S. (August 4, 2021). *Indian mascots and school bullying policies* [Interview].

Rehabilitation Act of 1973, § 504, 29 U.S.C. § 794.

Religious Freedom Restoration Act, P.L. 103–141 (November 16, 1993).

Riley, R. (1999). *The American high school in the 21st century* [Speech]. Retrieved December 12, 2013, from http://listserv.ed.gov/archives/edinfo/archived/msg00040.html

Rivera-Calderon, N. (2019). Arrested at the schoolhouse gate. *National Lawyers Guild Review,* 76(1), 1–32. Retrieved August 19, 2021, from https://www.nlg.org/nlg-review/article/arrested-at-the-schoolhouse-gate-criminal-school-disturbance-laws-and-childrens-rights-in-schools/

Robbins, B. (2010). *Statement of claim in Robbins v. Lower Merion Township School District.* Retrieved February 28, 2010, from http://safekids.com/robbins17.pdf

Rowling, J. K. (1990). *Harry Potter and the prisoner of Azkaban.* Scholastic Press.

Russo, C. J., & Osborne, A. G. (2008). *Essential concepts and school-based cases in special education law.* Corwin.

Russo, C. J., & Osborne, A. G. (2008). *Section 504 and the ADA.* Corwin.

Schatz, A. (2021). *Nebraska high school journalist refuses to back down, publishes her censored article on Confederate flags and racism in local paper.* Student Press Law Center. Retrieved August 17, 2021, from https://splc.org/2021/03/nebraska-high-school-journalist-publishes-her-censored-article-on-confederate-flags/

Schimmel, D. (2000). When schools are liable for peer harassment: An analysis of Davis v. Monroe. *Education Law Report, 141,* 437.

Schneider, R. (2014). *Serving Students with Disabilities.* School Law Institute: Columbia University

Schoonover, B. (2007). *Zero-tolerance policies in Florida school districts* [Dissertation]. University of Florida.

Section 504 of The Rehabilitation Act of 1973 (Rehab Act) 29 U.S.C. § 794 (§ 504).

Selective Training and Service Act of 1940. 54 Stat. 885.

Shaffer v. Weast (U.S. 546, November 14, 2005). On Writ of Certiorari to the United States Court of Appeals for the Fourth Circuit Court (377 F. 2d 449).

Shakeshaft, C. (2013). Know the warning signs of educator sexual misconduct. *Phi Delta Kappan, 94*(5), 8–13.

Shoop, R. J. (1999). Sexual abuse of children by teachers. *The High School Magazine,* 13–14.

Shoop, R. J. (2004). *Sexual exploitation in schools: How to spot it and stop it.* Corwin.

Shoop, R. J., & Dunklee, D. R. (1992). *School law for the principal: A handbook for practitioners.* Allyn & Bacon.

Shoop, R. J., & Dunklee, D. R. (1992). *School law for the principal: A handbook for practitioners.* Allyn & Bacon.

Silverstein, R. (2005). *A user's guide to the 2004 IDEA reauthorization (P.L. 108–446 and the conference report).* Center for the Study and Advancement of Disability Policy, from www.c-c-d.org/IdeaUserGuide.pdf

Skiba, R. (2000). *Zero tolerance, zero evidence: An analysis of school disciplinary practice.* Policy Research Report. Indiana Education Policy Center. Retrieved February 22, 2010, from http://www.indiana.edu/~safeschl/ztze.pdf.

Stenger, R. (1986, Winter). The school counselor and the law. *Journal of Law & Education, 1*(15), 12–17.

Sugarman, S. D. (2004). *The promise of school choice for improving the education of low-income minority children.* Paper presented at the symposium Rekindling the Spirit of Brown v. Board of Education, Berkeley, CA.

Susswein, R. (2000). The New Jersey school search policy manual: Striking the balance of students' rights of privacy and security after the Columbine tragedy. *The New England Law Review, 34*(3), 527–564.

Swanson v. Guthrie Independent School District, 135 F.3d 694 (1998).

Technology, Education and Copyright Harmonization Act (TEACH), 17 U.S.C. § 110.

Teitelbaum, H., & Hiller, R. (1977). *The legal perspective in bilingual education: Current perspectives* (Vol. 3). Arlington VA: Center for Applied Linguistics.

Thompson, D. C., & Wood, R. (2005). *Money and schools* (3rd ed.). Eye on Education.

Title I of the Electronic Communications Privacy Act (ECPA), 18 U.S. § 2511(1)(a).

Title II of the Digital Millennium Copyright Act (DMCA), P.L. 105–304.

Title IX and Sex Discrimination. (2022). Retrieved January 4, 2022, from https://www2.ed.gov/about/offices/list/ocr/docs/tix_dis.html

Title IX of Education Amendments of 1972, 20 U.S.C.S. § 1681–1688.

Title IX of the Education Amendments of 1972 34 C.F.R. § 106–1 *et seq*

Title VI Language Discrimination Guidelines, 45 Fed. Reg. 152, 52056 (1980).

Title VII of the Civil Rights Act of 1964, 42 U.S.C. § 2000e-2(a).

Title VII-B of the McKinney-Vento Homeless Assistance Act, 42 USC 11431 et seq. The program was originally authorized in 1987 and, most recently, reauthorized by the No Child Left Behind Act of 2001.

Torbet, P., Gable, R., Hurst, H., Montgomery, I., Szymanski, L., & Thomas, D. (1996). *State responses to serious and violent juvenile crime*. Office of Juvenile Justice and Delinquency Prevention.

Trump, K. (2018). In Education Law Association Annual Conference, Cleveland, OH.

Turnbull, H. R., III, & Turnbull, A. P. (2000). *Free appropriate public education: The law and children with disabilities*. Love.

Uggen, C. (2004). Males and adolescents are increasingly victims of sexual harassment. *American Sociological Review, 1*.

Uniform Parentage Act, 9A U.L.A. 579 (1983).

Uniform Parentage Act. (2017). National Conference of Commissioners on Uniform State Laws. In *Annual Conference Meeting in its One Hundred Twenty Sixth Year*. San Diego, CA.

Uniformed Services Employment and Reemployment Rights Act. Pub. L. 103–353, 1994, 108 Stat. 3149; 38 U.S.C. 101.

U.S. Constitution, Article I, Section 8, Clause 8.

U.S. Department of Education, Office for Civil Rights. (2010). *Dear colleague letter*. Retrieved September 10, 2013, from http://www2.ed.gov/about/offices/list/ocr/letters/colleague-201010.pdf

U.S. Department of Education. (2001). *Twenty-fourth annual report to Congress on the implementation of the Individuals with Disabilities Education Act*. Author.

U.S. Department of Education. (2005a). *New flexibility for states raising achievement for students with disabilities fact sheet*. Retrieved July 27, 2005, from www.ed.gov/policy/elsec/guid/raising/disab-fact-sheet.doc

U.S. Department of Education. (2005b). *Spellings announces new special education guidelines, details workable, "common-sense" policy to help states implement No Child Left Behind*. Retrieved August 1, 2005, from www.ed.gov/news/pressreleases/2005/05/05102005.html

U.S. Department of Education. (2020). *Guidance on constitutionally protected prayer and religious expression in public elementary and secondary schools*. Retrieved January 4, 2022, from https://www2.ed.gov/policy/gen/guid/religionandschools/prayer_guidance.html

U.S. Department of Education. (2021a). *Federal register notice of interpretation: Enforcement of Title IX of the education amendments of 1972 with respect to discrimination based on sexual orientation and gender identity in light of Bostock v. Clayton County*. Retrieved from https://www2.ed.gov/about/offices/list/ocr/docs/202106-titleix-noi.pdf

U.S. Department of Education. (2021b). *U.S. Department of Education confirms Title IX protects students from discrimination based on sexual orientation and gender identity*. Retrieved August 20, 2021, from https://www.ed.gov/news/press-releases/us-department-education-confirms-title-ix-protects-students-discrimination-based-sexual-orientation-and-gender-identity

U.S. Department of Education. (n.d.). *Department of Education religious expression guidelines*. Retrieved February 13, 2001, from http://www2.ed.gov/policy/gen/guid/religionandschools/index.html. See also The Freedom Forum. (n.d.). *A teacher's guide to religion in the public schools*. Retrieved February 13, 2001, from http://www.freedomforum.org/templates/document.asp?documentID=3964; and The National PTA. (n.d.). *A parent's guide to religion in the public schools*. Retrieved February 13, 2001, from http://www.freedomforum.org/publications/first/religioninpublicschools/parentsguidereligion.pdf

U.S. Department of Health and Human Services, Children's Bureau. (1991). *Child maltreatment 1997: Reports from the states to the national child abuse and neglect data system*. Author.

U.S. Departments of Education and Justice. (2003). *Indicators of school crime and safety: 2002*. NCES 2003–009/NCJ 196753. Author.

Veir, C. C., & Dagley, D. L. (2002). Legal issues in teacher evaluation legislation: A study of state statutory provisions. *BYU Education & Law Journal, 1*, 1–16.

Viadero, D. (1990). 350,000 abductions by family members documented. *Education Week*, 21–22.

Violence Against Women Act of 1994 (Pub. L. 103-322).

Vodak, K. R. (1999). A plainly obvious need for new-fashioned municipal liability. *DePaul Law Review, 48*, 785, 790.

Vossekuil, B., Fein, R., Reddy, M., Borum, R., & Modzeleski, W. (2002). *Final report and findings of the safe school initiative: Implications for the prevention of* school attacks in the United States. U.S. Department of Education, Office of Elementary and Secondary Education, Safe and Drug-Free Schools Program and U.S. Secret Service, National Threat Assessment Center.

Walker, T. (2002, Spring). School's out. *Teaching Tolerance, 21*. Retrieved from http://www.toler ance.org/magazine/number-21-spring-2002/feature/schools-out

Weiler, S. C., & Westbrook, P. (2020). Administering medical marijuana at school in Colorado: A legal analysis. *BYU Education & Law Journal, 1*(2). Retrieved from https://scholarsarchive.byu.edu/byu_elj/vol2020/iss1/2

West Virginia Code, 18-2-5 (1984).

Workman, E. (2011). *State collective bargaining policies for teachers* [e-book]. Education Commission of the States. Retrieved October 4, 2013, from http://www.ecs.org

Wormeli, R. (2006). *Fair isn't always equal.* Stenhouse/National Middle School Association.

YouTube. (2013). *YouTube Copyright Center.* Retrieved September 16, 2013, from http://www.youtube.com/yt/copyright/#yt-copyright-support.

Zirkel, P. A. (2013). *A national update of case law 1998 to the present under the IDEA and section 504/A.D.A.* Association of State Directors of Special Education, Inc. (www.nasdse.org).

Index

THE PRINCIPAL'S QUICK-REFERENCE GUIDE TO SCHOOL LAW

Leadership That Makes an Impact

PETER M. DeWITT

This step-by-step how-to guide presents the six driving forces of instructional leadership within a multistage model for implementation, delivering lasting improvement through small collaborative changes.

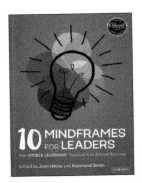

JOHN HATTIE & RAYMOND L. SMITH

Based on the most current Visible Learning® research with contributions from education thought leaders around the world, this book includes practical ideas for leaders to implement high-impact strategies to strengthen entire school cultures and advocate for all students.

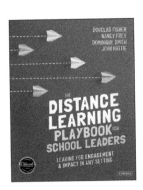

DOUGLAS FISHER, NANCY FREY, DOMINIQUE SMITH, & JOHN HATTIE

This essential hands-on resource offers guidance on leading school and school systems from a distance and delivering on the promise of equitable, quality learning experiences for students.

STEVEN M. CONSTANTINO

Explore the how-to's of establishing family empowerment through building trust, and reflect on implicit bias, equitable learning outcomes, and the role family engagement plays.

MICHAEL FULLAN, JOANNE QUINN, & JOANNE MCEACHEN

The comprehensive strategy of deep learning incorporates practical tools and processes to engage educational stakeholders in new partnerships, mobilize whole-system change, and transform learning for all students.

JOANNE QUINN, JOANNE MCEACHEN, MICHAEL FULLAN, MAG GARDNER, & MAX DRUMMY

Dive into deep learning with this hands-on guide to creating learning experiences that give purpose, unleash student potential, and transform not only learning, but life itself.

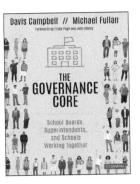

DAVIS CAMPBELL & MICHAEL FULLAN

The model outlined in this book develops a systems approach to governing local schools collaboratively to become exemplars of highly effective decision making, leadership, and action.

DAVIS CAMPBELL, MICHAEL FULLAN, BABS KAVANAUGH, & ELEANOR ADAM

As a supplement to the best-selling *The Governance Core*, this guide will help trustees and superintendents adopt a governance mindset and cohesive partnership.

To order your copies, visit **corwin.com/leadership**

**SIMON BREAKSPEAR &
BRONWYN RYRIE JONES**

Realistic in demand and innovative in approach, this practical and powerful improvement process is designed to help all teachers get going, and keep going, with incremental professional improvement in schools.

**JAMES BAILEY &
RANDY WEINER**

The thought-provoking daily reflections in this guided journal are designed to strengthen the social and emotional skills of leaders and create a strong social-emotional environment for leaders, teachers, and students.

**MARK WHITE &
DWIGHT L. CARTER**

Through understanding the past and envisioning the future, the authors use practical exercises and real-life examples to draw the blueprint for adapting schools to the age of hyper-change.

**ALLAN G. OSBORNE, JR.
& CHARLES J. RUSSO**

With its user-friendly format, this resource will help educators understand the law so they can focus on providing exemplary education to students.

**MICHAEL FULLAN &
MARY JEAN GALLAGHER**

With the goal of transforming the culture of learning to develop greater equity, excellence, and student well-being, this book will help you liberate the system and maintain focus.

**TOM VANDER ARK
& EMILY LIEBTAG**

Diverse case studies and a framework based on timely issues help educators focus students' talents and interests on developing an entrepreneurial mindset and leadership skills.

THOMAS HATCH

By highlighting what works and demonstrating what can be accomplished if we redefine conventional schools, we can have more efficient, more effective, and more equitable schools and create powerful opportunities to support all aspects of students' development.

LYN SHARRATT

Explore 14 essential parameters to guide system and school leaders toward building powerful collaborative learning cultures.

CORWIN

A SAGE Publishing Company

Helping educators make the greatest impact

CORWIN HAS ONE MISSION: to enhance education through intentional professional learning.

We build long-term relationships with our authors, educators, clients, and associations who partner with us to develop and continuously improve the best evidence-based practices that establish and support lifelong learning.